FOR REFERENCE

Do Not Take From This Room

Instruments of War

Instruments of War

*Weapons and Technologies
That Have Changed History*

Spencer C. Tucker

ABC-CLIO™

An Imprint of ABC-CLIO, LLC
Santa Barbara, California • Denver, Colorado

Library of Congress Cataloging-in-Publication Data

Tucker, Spencer, 1937–
 Instruments of war : weapons and technologies that have changed history / Spencer C. Tucker.
 pages cm
 Includes bibliographical references and index.
 ISBN 978-1-4408-3654-1 (alk. paper) — ISBN 978-1-4408-3655-8 (ebook)
 1. Military weapons—History. 2. Military art and science—History. I. Title.
 U800.T77 2015
 623.03—dc23   2014049928

ISBN: 978-1-4408-3654-1
EISBN: 978-1-4408-3655-8

19 18 17 16 15   1 2 3 4 5

This book is also available on the World Wide Web as an eBook.
Visit www.abc-clio.com for details.

ABC-CLIO, LLC
130 Cremona Drive, P.O. Box 1911
Santa Barbara, California 93116-1911

This book is printed on acid-free paper ∞
Manufactured in the United States of America

This work is dedicated to distinguished military historian
Colonel Jerry Morelock, U.S. Army (Rtd) and PhD.
I am grateful for the numerous instances of his assistance,
always graciously rendered.

Contents

Chronological List of Entries

Note: Influential weapons systems and advances in military technology, and notable individual examples of both, may be placed at locations other than indicated.

Alphabetical List of Entries

Introduction

Weapons both fascinate and repel. We marvel at the ingenuity and sheer genius in their creation but often abhor the results they bring. They are used to kill and maim individuals and to destroy states and societies and occasionally whole civilizations in addition to many of the greatest of man's cultural and artistic accomplishments. Throughout history tools of war have been the instruments of conquest, invasion, and enslavement, but they have also been used to check evil and, as deterrents, to serve the cause of peace.

Weapons have evolved over time to become both more lethal and more complex. For the greater part of man's existence, combat was fought at the length of an arm or at such short range as to represent no real difference; battle was fought within line of sight and seldom lasted more than the hours of daylight of a single day. Thus, individual weapons that began with the rock and the club proceeded through the sling and the boomerang, the bow and arrow, and the sword and ax to gunpowder weapons of the rifle and machine gun of the late 19th century. Study of the evolution of these weapons tells us much about human ingenuity, the technology of the time, and the societies that produced them. The greater part of technological development of weaponry has taken part in the last two centuries, especially the 20th century. In this process, plowshares have been beaten into swords; the tank, for example, evolved from the agricultural caterpillar tractor. Occasionally the process is reversed, and military technology has impacted society in a positive way. Thus, modern medicine has greatly benefitted from advances to save soldiers' lives, and weapons technology has impacted such areas as improvements in transportation and atomic power.

Weapons can have a profound impact on society. Gunpowder weapons, for example, were an important factor in ending the era of the armed knight and the Feudal Age. They installed a kind of rough democracy on the battlefield, making "all men alike tall." We now must grapple with the effects of weapons of mass destruction (WMDs) in our own time and civilization, especially in the hands of terrorist organizations with no regard for human life or civilization.

Often the effects of weapons have been minimized, with tactics lagging far behind. Thus, the generals seem not to have appreciated the changes wrought on the battlefield by the rifled musket and the minié ball in far longer effective range and greater volume of fire, and they sent men into battle in closely packed formations, bringing the horrific slaughter of the American Civil War. In similar fashion, the generals in World War I did not seem to appreciate the significance of the machine gun, despite its demonstrated success as early as the Battle of Omdurman in 1898 and the battles of the Russo-Japanese War of 1904–1905.

Sometimes the impact of new weapons has been overblown. Thus, there was a near universal belief in the 1930s that "the bomber will always get through." Numerous airpower prophets claimed that it alone would decide the outcome of the war, while British authorities morbidly predicted in early 1939 that 600,000 British civilians would be killed by bombs in the first two months of a war. Respected British military analyst General J. F. C. Fuller also predicted the collapse of civilian morale and riots in the cities. In all, 60,000 British civilians were killed by bombs and the V-1s and V-2s in five years of war. Certainly Allied fears of the possible destruction of London or Paris in a German air attack was a factor in the decision of the Western leaders to give way to Adolf Hitler's demands regarding Czechoslovakia at Munich in 1938.

Superior weapons do not always ensure victory in battle, of course. The training of the men utilizing the weapons is very important, as is how the weapons are employed. One such example will suffice. Contrary to the legends that arose after the defeat of France in 1940, the Allies actually outnumbered the Germans in tanks (3,383 to 2,445), and most of them were more heavily armored and heavily gunned than their German counterparts although somewhat slower and of shorter operating range.

The mainstay of the German panzer divisions was the Mark II with a 20mm gun. There were fewer than 350 Mark IIIs with a 37mm gun and fewer than 300 Mark IVs mounting a low-velocity 75mm gun. Of the Allied tanks, 310 were British: 210 light and 100 heavy (including 23 new Matildas). The British Matilda and Mark I and the French Char B all were a match for the best German tanks. The heavy Char B was probably the best tank in any army in 1940. Heavily armored, it had a 47mm gun in a revolving turret, but its primary armament, a 75mm gun, was mounted in the hull, while the primary German tank guns were in turrets. Thus, the crew of the Char B had to turn the whole tank to aim and fire the main gun. The French Somua tank also mounted the high-velocity 47mm gun, which had excellent penetrating power.

Despite French production delays, there were some 800 Char Bs and Somuas, or more than the German Marks III and IV. Also, few of the French vehicles had radios, forcing most crews to communicate by flags. The German tanks were equipped with radio receivers, although only the command tanks had transmitters as well.

The major Allied problem was, however, in tactical employment. French tank tactics were a war behind. The French saw the tank primarily in an infantry support role. The first three French tank divisions did not assemble for training until January 1940, and each had half as many tanks as the panzer divisions they would have to face. The majority of the French tanks along the country's eastern frontier were split into packets of up to 10 tanks apiece. The Germans massed their tanks to achieve sledgehammer-like breakthroughs. There are many other such examples in history. This lag in the introduction of new weapons and the proper tactics for their employment has been called the "tech-tac disjoint."

Civilian inventions are often adopted for military use. This is the case for the tank, the inspiration for which were the agricultural equipment Holt gasoline engine-powered caterpillar tractors pressed into service to reposition battlefield artillery in World War I. Bicycles, cars, trucks, railroads, planes, barbed wire, the telegraph, and the telephone were all first developed for civilian use. On occasion the reverse is true and weapons give rise to civilian applications, as in the atomic bomb and nuclear power.

This work traces the evolution of 270 key weapons systems and new technologies benefitting the world's militaries. There are also 25 sidebars that illustrate their employment and impact on tactics. I have deliberately avoided including entries on tactical changes. I also do not address inventions or processes that have directly impacted weapons development, such as improved metallurgical techniques, interchangeable parts, the Industrial Revolution, the steam engine, and the modern computer. All of these had major impacts, of course.

I am indebted to fellow military historians Jerry Morelock and David Zabecki. Jerry Morelock, PhD, is editor in chief of *Armchair General* magazine and a retired U.S. Army colonel whose 36-year career included a combat tour in Vietnam, two Pentagon assignments, and serving as head of the History Department of the Army's Command and General Staff College. Morelock was formerly the executive director of the Winston Churchill Memorial and Library and has published extensively on military matters. Major General David Zabecki, Army of the United States retired, also a PhD, served in Vietnam and is the author of numerous books of military history. He is editor emeritus of *Vietnam Magazine* and is an honorary senior research fellow in war studies at the University of Birmingham in England. Both of these individuals suggested changes to my initial entry list, and Morelock graciously read much of the manuscript and suggested helpful revisions. I take full responsibility for any shortcomings in the final work, however.

Instruments of War

Club and Mace

The club was man's first purpose-built weapon. It had its origins in the wooden sticks, bones, and stones used by primitive man to defend himself, to kill game, and to attack his enemies. A wooden stick or bone might have had a knot or joint at the end or might have been fashioned so that it had a larger blunt end. Such simple clubs are all of the same material, usually wood or bone. The Irish shillelagh, made of blackthorn wood, is one such example.

Combining the stick and the stone, however, produced a much more effective weapon. In composite clubs, two or more materials are combined in one weapon. Most often a heavier material is wedded to a wooden shaft. For example, a stone end might be drilled out to receive the stick or could simply be bound in place with sinew.

The morning star (*goedendag* or holy water sprinkler) came into use in the 14th century. It was a club with a ball at the top that had one or more spikes in it, combining blunt-force and puncture attack to kill or wound. The spikes distinguished the morning star from the mace, which at most had flanges or small knobs. The morning star was employed by both infantry and cavalry, with the cavalry version having a shorter handle. The mace ultimately became an all-metal weapon, the head of which had various forms.

Another category of club uses flexibility to achieve greater force in the delivered blow. Such articulated clubs usually connect a stick and a heavy object by means of a chain. These weapons are usually known as flails. A spiked ball on a chain might be employed against a person in body armor.

The mace typically consisted of a strong, heavy wooden or metal shaft, often reinforced with metal, with a head of stone, copper, bronze, iron, or steel. The head might have flanges or knobs

Detail showing Egyptian Pharaoh Narmer, founder of the First Dynasty, subjugating a priest with a mace. From a facsimile of the Palette of Narmer, Hierakonpolis, Egypt, ca. 3000 BCE. (The Art Archive/Corbis)

3

to allow greater penetration of plate armor. Maces for infantry varied in length from two to three feet for infantry but were longer for cavalrymen.

In many medieval armies the mace became a symbol of authority, a badge of rank. It was carried by the hetman (head man), or supreme commander. In the pre–World War II Polish Army, crossed maces were the rank insignia of marshals. In many West European armies the ceremonial mace was replaced by the marshal's baton. Crossed batons were the rank insignia for field marshals in both the German and British Armies of World War II.

Clubs continue in use today. The modern wooden baton or police night stick, used for riot control, is but one example.

Further Reading

The Diagram Group. *Weapons: An International Encyclopedia from 5000 BC to 2000 AD.* New York: St. Martin's, 1990.

Tunis, Edwin. *Weapons: A Pictorial History.* New York: World Publishing, 1954.

Ax

Worked stone axes date from the Old Stone Age, when they were employed both as tools to cut wood and as weapons. The addition of a wooden haft enhanced the value of the ax as a weapon. The haft might be split at one end and then wrapped around a groove in the stone head. Beginning in the Bronze Age, ax heads were cast of copper, then hardened by the addition of tin to form bronze. An ax head might be secured to its handle by being cast with a pointed end that was driven through a hole at the end of the haft. More often the head was cast with a hole into which the end of the haft was forced. Some primitive axes have heads of wood or of bone.

Frankish warriors of the sixth century CE employed a short-handled throwing ax with a curved head. The Vikings, Danes, and Norsemen used a large double-headed battle-ax. In the later Middle Ages, longer poleaxes appeared. The Anglo-Saxon broadax had a long handle and was swung as a battle-ax, but a shorter-handle taper ax was developed for throwing.

Axes remained in use as weapons until modern times. One of the most famous of ax weapons was the North American Indian tomahawk (from the Algonquian word *tamahak* or *tamahakan,* which designates a type of cutting tool). Europeans made a number of these and then used them with the natives as trading items. Some were cast with a head that combined a pipe and a tomahawk. This gave rise to the expression "burying the hatchet," since if the blade was driven into the earth only the pipe was exposed, symbolizing friendship rather war. Boarding axes formed part of the normal array of small arms aboard ships in the age of fighting sail. Even the modern era has seen the use of tomahawks in combat, as the U.S. Army issued them to some infantrymen during the Vietnam War.

Further Reading

The Diagram Group. *Weapons: An International Encyclopedia from 5000 BC to 2000 AD.* New York: St. Martin's, 1990.

Stone, G. C. *A Glossary of the Construction, Decoration and Use of Arms and Armor.* New York: Southworth, 1934.

Sling

The earliest standoff weapons were rocks or stones hurled by an individual against a foe. In propelling these at greater force, gravity provided an advantage, as in hurling rocks or large objects down on a foe from a cliff or wall.

Slings were the simplest method to increase the range at which a rock or other small projectile might be hurled. Slings used a leather pouch and cord and operated on centrifugal force. Slings are known to have been used in the Stone Age, and they continued to be employed through the Middle Ages. The light troops employing these weapons were known as slingers.

A throwing stick or launching stick could also be utilized to hurl stones. Peruvians used these against the Spanish conquistadores, as did Australian bushmen. Another variation was the *fustibal,* which had a rigid handle. Force in all these was achieved by pulling the stick or handle forward and then abruptly halting this motion, releasing the object. The best-known story of the sling in combat is the biblical account of David and Goliath.

Further Reading

Harding, David, ed. *Weapons: An International Encyclopedia from 5000 B.C. to 2000 A.D.* New York: St. Martin's, 1990.

Runis, Edwin. *Weapons: A Pictorial History.* New York: World Publishing, 1954.

Spears and Other Pole Arms

Spears are pole thrusting weapons; they appear universally in all cultures. The addition of a long haft to a cutting weapon provided a standoff capability. Such a weapon allowed infantry to attack cavalry without having to close with the horse and rider and even to hold off horsemen entirely. As a category of weapon, spears usually include most pole arms, including the lance, as well as throwing pole arms such as the javelin.

The fire-hardened points of the wooden spear of the Old Stone Age soon received spearheads of bone and stone. Shorter spears were developed for throwing. Their effective range was increased by leather slings or throwing sticks that enhanced their velocity.

The spear really came into its own as an infantry weapon in the classical era. In ancient Greece the throwing spear gave way to the *sarisa,* a long thrusting spear carried by the hoplites from the seventh century BCE and deployed in the closely packed infantry phalanx formation. By 400 BCE such spears were up to 23 feet in length. The Romans utilized several types of spears, or *pilum*. The *pilum muralis* was of wood and was used as an additional defense to encampments.

The basic parts of the spear were the butt (end); the shaft or haft; langets, cheeks, or straps (reinforcements running on each side of the haft); and the head (the socket that fitted over the end of the pole and the blade).

The introduction of the stirrup led to a new type of spear for use by cavalry and known as the lance. Stirrups enabled the rider to better withstand the shock of the lance striking an object. Lances were a key element in the ascendency of cavalry over infantry in medieval Europe.

By the 15th century another type of spear, known as the pike, had appeared. Issued to infantry, pikes were defensive weapons intended to protect infantry, and later musketeers, against cavalry attack. The end of the pike could be braced against the ground and pointed outward to defend against a cavalry charge. Pikes remained on the battlefield until the appearance of the bayonet, fitted to the end of the musket, that allowed each musketeer to become his own pikeman. Although pikes went largely out of use by the end of the 17th century, some were actually issued to members of the British Home Guard early in World War II against a threatened German invasion.

Other types of pole arms were the trident, the parisan (with a broad spear point and a widely flaring base), the poleax (with an ax head at the top of the pole), and the glaive (a pole with a long pointed cutting blade at the end, sharped on one side only). Among the most versatile of pole arms was the halberd of the 15th and 16th centuries. It combined a hatchet, a point, and a beak all in one weapon.

Spears designed to be thrown were shorter than those for thrusting. The long shaft helped ensure stability in flight, and its additional weight helped increase kinetic energy behind it. The disadvantage of the throwing spear was that once it was hurled at an enemy, it was lost to the thrower and might even be thrown back against him. In Roman times such spears often were given soft metal tips that bent on impact, making them difficult to retrieve and hurl back. In any case, throwing spears were only thrown in the last seconds before the collision of the opposing infantry. Most throwing spears were longer than the thrower, but shorter throwing spears existed in the form of the javelin; the shortest were known as darts.

Further Reading

Bull, Stephen. *Encyclopedia of Military Technology and Innovation.* Westport, CT: Greenwood, 2004.

Connolly, Peter. *Greece and Rome at War.* Englewood Cliffs, NJ: Prentice Hall, 1981.

The Diagram Group. *Weapons: An International Encyclopedia from 5000 BC to 2000 AD.* New York: St. Martin's, 1990.

Gonen, Rivka. *Weapons of the Ancient World.* London: Cassell, 1975.

Pilum

The Roman *pilum* (pl. *pila*), later known as the *spicumum,* is perhaps the most famous of javelins in the Ancient World. Javelins are spears developed specifically to be thrown. They are both lighter and shorter than regular spears. Prehistoric javelins might have simply a sharpened wood tip, while Stone Age javelins utilized flint. Javelin tips of the ancient world might be of copper, bronze, or iron.

The *pilum* was about 6 feet long, culminating in an iron pyramidal shaped head representing up to 1 foot of the length and secured to a wooden shaft. Overall weight of the *pilum* was between 4 and 9 pounds. Maximum throwing range was about 100 feet with an effective range of 50–70 feet.

Legionnaires of the late republic and early empire often carried two *pila,* sometimes one heavier with a shaft 5.5 feet in length surmounted by a triangular 9-inch iron head and another with a 3.5-foot shaft with a 5-inch head (the smaller javelin being known as *verriculum* and then *verutum*).

Tactical doctrine called for the *pila* to be thrown before engaging in hand-to-hand combat. If thrown with force by a skilled user, *pila* could penetrate shields and cuirassed armor. Once thrown, of course, the javelin was lost to the user, who needed other weapons such as a sword with which he might subsequently engage an enemy.

Later *pila* were constructed so that the iron shank would bend on impact. This would render it difficult to remove once it had penetrated through a shield, forcing the enemy to discard the shield altogether in the little time before actual hand-to-hand combat. This also had the advantage of disabling the *pilum,* preventing an opponent from throwing it back.

Very small javelins of about a foot in length are known as darts. A throwing stick, such as that employed by Australian bushmen, increased the range of small javelins. It consisted of a stick with a socket at the tip into which the base of the javelin was inserted. The stick acted as a lever, providing additional momentum. Forward movement of the arm powered the javelin, which was then released when the movement halted.

Further Reading

Connolly, Peter. *Greece and Rome at War.* Englewood Cliffs, NJ: Prentice Hall, 1981.
The Diagram Group. *Weapons: An International Encyclopedia from 5000 BC to 2000 AD.* New York: St. Martin's, 1990.

Throwing Sticks or Throwing Clubs

Most clubs can be thrown, but some clubs were developed specifically for that purpose. The addition of a handle to the club increases the momentum at which it can be thrown. Throwing sticks for hunting birds and small game and clubs for warfare have been known since ancient times and continued in use into modern times by primitive peoples in Africa, Asia, and Australia. Most throwing sticks were curved or bent in shape.

The most famous of the throwing sticks, the boomerang, appeared only in Australia. It was a flattened bent piece of wood, usually decorated, of precise shape and balance. Grasped at one end and thrown by a skilled user, the boomerang spun through the air on a curved path and, failing to hit its target, returned to the user, who nonetheless had to be highly skilled to catch it.

Larger nonreturning-type boomerangs were used for hunting larger animals and for war. These traveled end over end yet flew straight to the target. Injuries were inflicted either by cutting from a sharpened edge or by the blunt force of impact.

Further Reading

The Diagram Group. *Weapons: An International Encyclopedia from 5000 BC to 2000 AD.* New York: St. Martin's, 1990.

Ruhe, Benjamin, and Eric Darnell. *Boomerang: How to Throw, Catch, and Make It.* New York: Workman Publishing, 1985.

Picks and War Hammers

Picks are piercing weapons that have a pointed, daggerlike head fixed at a right angle to the haft. The related war hammer has a head with a hammer on one side combined with a pick on the other. The thin blade could easily penetrate mail and even plate armor, while the hammer was used to attack and stun a helmeted enemy or even to crush bones through armor.

Picks might be entirely of wood but more usually had a wooden haft and metal head or were entirely of metal, even steel. The East Indian or Persian fighting pick had a head that looked like the bill of a bird, leading to its name of crowbill.

Further Reading

The Diagram Group. *Weapons: An International Encyclopedia from 5000 BC to 2000 AD.* New York: St. Martin's, 1990.

Stone, G. C. *A Glossary of the Construction, Decoration and Use of Arms and Armor.* New York: Southworth, 1934.

Dagger (Knife)

The short-bladed knife, known as the dagger, dates from the New Stone Age. Daggers have existed throughout military history and are found in every part of the world fulfilling a wide variety of roles, including ceremonial. Daggers are edged weapons that generally range from as little as 6 inches to as much as 20 inches in length (the latter being in effect the short sword). During the Bronze Age, short daggers of metal appeared. Bronze and then iron daggers became major weapons in the close confines of early warfare, while the development of body armor led to the manufacture of long, thrusting narrow daggers.

The dagger was ubiquitous in the Middle Ages and was used for self-defense, eating, and ceremonial wear. Knights employed the dagger as a fallback weapon to the sword. In sword fights if an individual was right-handed, he might carry a long dagger, often referred to as a short sword, in his left hand as a parrying weapon. Thin stilettos also were favorite weapons in the early modern period.

Use of the dagger declined with the development of firearms that allowed stand-off warfare and with the advent of the bayonet, a long daggerlike device that could be attached to the end of a musket but also used in the hand if need be. Distinctive types of daggers and knives nonetheless remained, such as the Afghan Khyber knife, the Malay kris, the Scottish dirk, and the American Bowie knife.

Daggers enjoyed something of a comeback during World War I, when they became a favored weapon for stealthy trench raids. During World War II, U.S. marines were issued a multipurpose fighting knife called the K-bar. Special forces favored a knuckle dagger, which combined a blade with a brass knuckle device. Long machete knives proved effective in slashing through jungle foliage. Aircrews were also furnished knives as a part of survival gear, while the German Nazi regime issued vast numbers of ceremonial daggers. A large variety of specialized knives continue in use with the world's military establishments today, the most famous of which is the kukri of the Gurkha regiments.

Further Reading

Bull, Stephen. *Military Technology and Innovation.* Westport, CT: Greenwood, 2004.

Hughes, Gordon, and Barry Jenkins. *A Primer of Military Knives: European & American Combat, Trench & Utility Knives.* Brighton, UK: Military Press, 1973.

Stephens, Frederick J. *Fighting Knives.* London: Arms and Armour, 1980.

Sword

Swords are long metal flat-bladed, handheld weapons. Most are sharpened on each edge and usually at the tip. Swords were far more versatile than the ax. Because swords were not easily concealed like the dagger, most cultures regarded them as honorable weapons.

In sword nomenclature there are two principal parts: the hilt and the blade. The hilt is divided into the pommel (the wider, often ball-shaped end), the grip, and the guard. Blades came in a variety of types, including curved and straight. Long straight blades were the best for thrusting, while a backward curved blade proved highly effective in a slicing cut, and a forward curved blade was best for a chopping cut.

There are a great variety of sword types. The first swords appeared in the Bronze Age and were of copper. They were found to be too malleable and, on the discovery of the harder bronze (copper with the addition of some tin), were replaced with those of that metal. The next advance was in swords of iron, with continuing improvements in forging, hammering, and tempering.

The Greeks favored the short sword. Swords of the ancient Roman period included the short-bladed *gladius* carried by infantry, the long-bladed cavalry *spatha*, and the curved single-edged Spanish *falcata*. The favored sword of the Middle Ages was a straight-bladed long sword with cross hilt. Swords were a status symbol, associated with knights and the age of chivalry. In Japan they were also essential in the cult of the samurai. The two *daisho* ("large-small") curved Japanese swords carried by samurai were long and short types, renowned for their high quality and style.

In the Renaissance two-handed swords gained in popularity, while at the same time single-handed swords underwent considerable change, with the appearance of more elaborate guards to protect the hand and with long, thinner blades. By the 16th century the most favored sword was the long thin-bladed, thrusting rapier, well suited to the swordplay then in favor. Another new type, the short sword or long dagger, appeared, to be used in a swordsman's other hand to parry an opponent's thrusts. Other types continued in existence, including curved hangers and double-handed broad swords, of which the most famous may be the claymore of Scotland and Ireland.

By the 16th century, military establishments regulated sword types to ensure quality, uniform appearance, and ease of supply. The short hangers served as backup infantry weapons for pikes and muskets, while swords remained a principal weapon for cavalry. Into the 19th century, curved cutting sabers were a favored weapon for light cavalry, whereas the heavy cavalry carried longer straight swords. Swords continued to be carried by cavalry into World War I, but the development of the carbine and especially the revolver in effect ended their practical usefulness. Today swords and sabers are still worn on ceremonial occasions as a sign of office.

Further Reading

Coe, Michael D., et al. *Swords and Hilt Weapons.* New York: Barnes and Noble, 1996.

Connolly, Peter. *Greece and Rome at War.* Englewood Cliffs, NJ: Prentice Hall, 1981.

The Diagram Group. *Weapons: An International Encyclopedia from 5000 BC to 2000 AD.* New York: St. Martin's, 1990.

Oakeshott, R. Ewartt. *The Sword in the Age of Chivalry.* New York: Praeger, 1965.

Lance

The lance was a long pole arm cavalry weapon. It is most identified in the popular mind with medieval Europe. Dating from ancient times and ranging in length from 9 to 14 feet, the lance was the cavalry version of the pole arm spear or pike carried by the infantry. Next to the sword, the lance was the most important cavalry weapon. Lances were of wood, usually ash, and had a small metal tip to penetrate armor. The advent of the stirrup greatly facilitated its use. A horseman held the lance pointing forward under his arm but stationary in the charge, utilizing the momentum of the horse for shock power. Most often, lances were used to unseat other knights. Lances often bore a small triangular pennon with the knight's colors, while a banner lord, commanding several dozen other knights, might have a rectangular banner.

Lances continued in use even into the 20th century. They are especially identified in the popular mind with the jousting of medieval Europe, but all the major continental powers of the Napoleonic era had lance-equipped units, and Napoleon Bonaparte adopted the lance for selected cavalry units of his Grande Armée. Lances were also adopted by the Native Americans of the Great Plains after the arrival of the horse. The lance continued in service for such a long time because of the difficulty of reloading early firearms while on horseback.

Further Reading

Davenant, Charles. *An Essay upon Ways and Means of Supplying the War.* London: Printed for Jacob Tonson, 1695.

Starkey, Armstrong. *European and Native American Warfare, 1675–1815.* Norman: University of Oklahoma Press, 1998.

Bow and Arrow

Dating to the Mesolithic period some 12,000 years ago, the bow is one of mankind's oldest weapons. Cave paintings depict bows in use for hunting. The bow was one of the most widely used weapons in history, appearing worldwide in virtually every military force from antiquity through at least the end of the 16th century. Silent, accurate, and deadly, bows have also been employed by resistance groups and special forces in modern times.

The bow was actually an improvement on the throwing stick, used to hurl a small javelin, known as an arrow, often with great power. The bow was a wooden stave the ends of which were connected by a cord or bowstring under tension. Grasping the grip in the center of the bow with one hand, the archer used the other hand, most usually two or three fingers, to draw back the bowstring with the notched arrow. When the archer let go of the string, it released the energy in the bow, driving the arrow toward the target. Even primitive bows were quite powerful, and their arrows could easily penetrate metal armor.

Materials available determined bow construction. For example, American Indian bows were made of Osage orange, hickory, or ash. Bowstrings might be formed of rawhide, animal tendons, flax, hemp, silk, or sinew. Arrows were of straight or straightened strong and light wood. Their heads were usually of flint or stone. The arrow was notched, and the tip was inserted and lashed in place. Stability in flight was provided by two or three feather strips (or "flights" in the case of another material) at the opposite (nock) end of the arrow, running parallel to the shaft and lashed or glued in place.

Bows took a variety of forms. The earliest were the simple bow or self-bow, consisting of one piece of the same type of wood or metal. Backed bows received additional material, usually animal sinew, to provide strengthening. Laminated bows consisted of three or more layers of the same type of material, usually wood, while composite bows were made of three or more different types of wood and other materials for greater flexibility. Composite bows include the Japanese *yumi*, constructed of strips of bamboo in various states of seasoning. "Compound bow" is a term that is also used to describe both laminated and composite bows. The Turkish bow was a short reflex bow, that is, with strong curvature in the opposite direction. The most important of all European bows was the English longbow, of great military importance during the 14th and 15th centuries.

Photograph of a Nuu-chah-nulth hunter with a bow and arrow. The Nuu-chah-nulth Indians live on the west coast of Vancouver Island in British Columbia. The photograph is from Volume 9 of *The North American Indian* by Edward S. Curtis, published in 1916. (Edward S. Curtis/Historical/Corbis)

Among accessories for the archers were bracers to protect the arm from the bowstring and quivers to hold the arrows.

Further Reading

Bradbury, Jim. *The Medieval Archer.* New York: Barnes and Noble, 2000.

Webb, Alf. *Archaeology of Archery.* Tolworth, UK: Glade, 1991.

Blowgun

The blowgun is a long wooden tube. Darts are propelled against a target by means of a person blowing into the tube. Blowguns are used primarily for hunting but are also used in war by aboriginal peoples in Asia and Latin America.

The long tube of reed, bamboo, or wood is usually sufficiently light that it can be gripped near the mouthpiece. A tuft of cotton serves as wadding behind the long dart, made from the spine of a leaf with a soft plug to fit the bore. The tip of the dart might be poisoned.

Further Reading

The Diagram Group. *Weapons: An International Encyclopedia from 5000 BC to 2000 AD.* New York: St. Martin's, 1990.

Shields

The term "shield" can be applied to a wide range of protective devices, including plates mounted on guns on land and on ships in order to provide some defense for their crews against small-arms fire and shrapnel. Here the term is used solely to describe a protective device carried into battle by individual soldiers or cavalrymen to defend against sword and lance thrusts and missiles. Shields were made of a wide variety of materials, including wood (to include plywood), leather, and metals such as bronze, iron, and steel. Shields were of almost every shape, from round to kite-shaped, oblong, hexagonal, and rectangular. Size varied widely, from the small to large types that would protect virtually the entire body.

Shields were in widespread use in ancient times and were widely employed in Sumer and Egypt. In the classical period, Greek soldiers carried a large, heavy round shield, known as the *argive.* This evolved from a central handgrip type but was more convex and had a reinforced rim. The *argive* had a central armband, with the left forearm thrust through it so that in effect the shield was fastened to the forearm. A handgrip near the rim prevented the shield from slipping on the user's arm. The shield was sufficiently large to protect its user from chin to knee. A good bit of the shield protruded past the soldier, providing protection to the hoplite to his immediate left. The shield helped make possible the rigid phalanx formation, in which however there was a tendency to shift to the right. The Spartan mother's farewell to her soldier son was "Return with your shield or on it." Flight with the heavy shield was very difficult.

The Romans developed a long oblong or rectangular convex-shaped shield, known as the *scutum.* These could be held by legionnaires in formation order to form a solid defensive barrier known as a *testudo* (tortoise), providing all-around protection against missile attack, such as from arrows.

Shields remained in use into the medieval period. Firearms led to the demise of the shield, which had largely disappeared in Europe by the 16th century. Primitive societies retained the shield, such as in Africa. The plains Indians employed small leather shields on horseback. Today, troops and police employ lightweight 4-pound transparent shields of polycarbonate in riot control.

Further Reading

Connolly, Peter. *Greece and Rome at War.* Englewood Cliffs, NJ: Prentice Hall, 1981.

Stone, G. C. *A Glossary of the Construction, Decoration and Use of Arms and Armor.* New York: Southworth, 1934.

Helmet

The helmet is body armor designed specifically to protect the head. Even in prehistory, men employed helmets to protect themselves from blows by swords or missiles.

During the classical period, Greek infantry (hoplites) wore elaborate full-faced helmets of bronze. Greek helmets were largely cone shaped, open at the front for the eyes and often with a piece that extended downward to protect the nose. Because the helmets completely covered the ears, they made hearing all but impossible. Finally, this area was cut away.

Roman soldiers wore a variety of different helmets of steel, iron, and leather. Typically they were not as full as those of the Greeks. Perhaps the best known, the Montefortino type, had hinged cheek guards that left the ears exposed but protected the face from blows from that direction.

By the 10th century, helmets were of steel. Helmets of the Middle Ages, especially for cavalry, were among the most elaborate ever produced. The advent of gunpowder weapons helped bring the use of helmets to a close. While some cavalry units retained them, helmets for the infantry largely went out of use by the late 17th century.

The advent of modern artillery and explosive shell in the form of airbursts led to the universal reintroduction of the helmet in World War I. Typical of World War I helmets was that worn by British soldiers. Designed by John L. Brodie, it was of shallow soup dish shape with a brim. Designed largely to protect the wearer from shell fragments from above, it offered little protection from the side. U.S. forces adopted this type and used it into the beginning of World War II. The German

A Greek Corinthian bronze helmet, ca. 500 BCE. (Christie's Images/Corbis)

Stahlhelm (steel helmet), widely called the coal scuttle because of its distinctive shape, was much more effective in protecting the side of the face. Helmet covers also appeared. These allowed the attachment of camouflage. Helmet liners provide a better fit for the steel helmet to the head and made its wearing more comfortable.

Helmets of World War II built on the designs of World War I, most especially the German helmet of 1935. The U.S. M1 helmet was more pot-shaped and provided far better protection than its World War I predecessor. Used by American forces from World War II through the Vietnam War, the M1 helmet was affectionately called the "Steel Pot." Its lightweight helmet liner could be worn separately. World War II tankers wore special padded headgear.

Helmets continued in widespread use during the Cold War, but new materials were introduced, including Kevlar and lightweight plastics. These were lighter and yet allowed more effective protection. The United States developed a helmet that somewhat resembled the German type of World War II. Protecting against head wounds remains a priority in the development of new body armor.

Further Reading

Connolly, Peter. *Greece and Rome at War.* Englewood Cliffs, NJ: Prentice Hall, 1981.

Curtis, Howard M. *2,500 Years of European Helmets: 800 B.C.–1700 A.D.* North Hollywood, CA: Beinfield Publishing, 1978.

Dean, Bashford. *Helmets and Body Armor in Modern Warfare.* New Haven, CT: Yale University Press, 1920.

Haselgrove, Michael J. *Helmets of the First World War: Germany, Britain, and Their Allies.* Atglen, PA: Schiffer, 2000.

Reynosa, Mark A. *Post World War II M-1 Helmets: An Illustrated Study.* Atglen, PA: Schiffer, 1999.

Body Armor

This entry discusses body armor in general but concentrates on upper-body, torso protection (helmets are discussed separately, and this entry also ignores metal arm and full-length lower-leg guards, known as greaves, that were widely used in the ancient world to protect these limbs against sword cuts).

Soldiers have employed body armor almost from the beginning of warfare. The earliest body armor was fashioned from bark, horn, bone, and leather. Padded jackets came into widespread use by ancient armies. These provided some protection against sword thrusts and continued in use into modern times. Metal armor appeared beginning in the Bronze Age. Usually this torso protection was supported by shoulder straps. The Romans widely used a metal breastplate, known as the cuirass for its initial hardened-leather composition.

Metal scales were also fastened to leather. Known in ancient China, this type of body armor saw service into the early modern period. It is commonly known today as chain mail but is also known as *maille* (French) or chain *maille,* although a more proper description would be ring mail. It probably dates from the fifth century BCE and was both lighter and allowed greater freedom of movement than the old plate armor. Utilized both as coats and shirts, it was also suspended from helmets to protect the neck of the wearer. Mail consists of many small metal rings linked together to form a mesh.

Mail seems to have been developed independently in both Asia (especially in Japan) and in Europe. The earliest European mail was worn by the Celts and may be 2,500 years old. The Romans first encountered it while fighting the Gauls and soon adopted it for their own use. Its greatest use was probably in the 13th century, when it appeared as full suits of body armor. In the 14th century plate armor began to supplant mail for personal protection, although mail continued in wide use thereafter. The common European mail pattern was one in which a single ring was linked to four others. Until the 14th century, mail consisted of alternate rows of solid rings that were riveted shut.

During World War I the British experimented with mail hung down from a helmet. Despite its proven effectiveness as a defense against shrapnel, it was unpopular with the soldiers and was soon discarded. Today mail clothing is often used as specialist protective clothing; for example, British police employ mail gloves in dealing with knife-wielding assailants.

Plate armor continued to evolve and reached its most sophisticated form in the 15th century. Knights were clad in metal armor from head to foot that varied in thickness depending on the area protected and had specialized pieces protecting particular parts of the body. Although arrows from longbows could pierce some plate armor, it was gunpowder weapons that really brought its use to an end. By 1600 body armor was known as half armor, with full suits giving way to the helmet and to back and breast protection, if that. During 1700–1914 body armor went out of widespread use, particularly for infantrymen.

This changed in World War I with the danger from artillery airbursts to individual soldiers in trench warfare. In addition to metal helmets, the major warring powers experimented with shields and lightweight body armor. Aside from the near universal adoption of helmets, relatively few troops received body armor, however.

World War II also saw little use of body armor. The most important body armor of the war was that developed to protect aviators from shrapnel airbursts. The U.S. Army Air Forces fielded the M1 armored front and back vest for bomber crews, followed by the M3 and M4 apron. Such vests employed steel plates sewn on the inside and were thus too heavy for ground troops.

The discovery of new materials during the war ushered in a new era in body protection. In 1943 the Dow Company produced Doron, a material made of glass fiber bonded with an ethyl cellulose resin. These so-called flak vests saw service at the end of World War II. During the Korean War the U.S. Army issued the M-1952 body armor. Although uncomfortable to wear and hot, it was the most widely issued flak jacket of the Vietnam War and became one of the conflict's ubiquitous symbols.

Beginning in 1969, U.S. troops received new vests of Doron and ballistic nylon. The vest had a collar to protect the wearer's neck as well as additional panels, although the high collar often interfered with the helmet. The new vest did away with the shoulder straps of the M-1952. The new Fragmentation Protective Body Armor M-1969 vest weighed 8.5 pounds. Not bulletproof, the vests were designed to protect against shrapnel and to slow down and minimize the effects of bullets and also sometimes stop bullets fired from long range.

The search for an effective vest able to stop bullets continued. In 2003 the U.S. Marine Corps adopted the Interceptor System. It was capable of protecting vital body areas from improvised explosive device (IED) fragments as well as shrapnel and even small-arms rounds. The vest held a number of special small-arms protective inserts (SAPI) plates. The success of the system is shown in that during the Vietnam War 70 percent of U.S. casualties with penetrating chest wounds and a third of those with abdominal wounds died. During the 2003–2011 Iraq War, however, only 5 percent of those with torso wounds died. The new vests as well as more rapidly available medical care counted for this sharp reduction in fatalities. Research continues into more effective armor able to protect more of the human body.

Further Reading

Ashdown, Charles H. *European Arms and Armor.* New York: Barnes and Noble, 1995.

Bull, Stephen. *Encyclopedia of Military Technology and Innovation.* Westport, CT: Greenwood, 2004.

Connolly, Peter. *Greece and Rome at War.* Englewood Cliffs, NJ: Prentice Hall, 1981.

Dunstan, S. *Flak Jackets.* London: Osprey, 1984.

Granesay, S. V. *Arms and Armour.* London: Hamlyn, 1964.

Robinson, J. Russell. *Oriental Armour.* New York: Waler, 1967.

Chariot

Chariots derived from heavy carts with solid wheels pulled by draft animals beginning about 3500 BCE in Mesopotamia. The chariots that we would recognize today were apparently introduced in Sumer around 2500 BCE and were pulled by horses, with the period of their greatest use being about 1700–1200 BCE.

The chariot was a short-ranged fighting vehicle designed for very smooth terrain and apparently transported to the place of battle in a cart. Some chariots, especially those of Egypt, weighed as little as 75 pounds, made possible by the introduction of spoked wheels around 1900 BCE. Egyptian chariots were two-wheeled vehicles with a platform for archers. Some chariots were considerably heavier and employed armor, while others had blades projecting from the axles of the wheels so that they acted like great scythes, to mow down opposing infantry like so much wheat.

Most Egyptian chariots were pulled by two horses and were quite fast: 25–30 miles per hour. The Hittites or Hyksos also employed chariots, but they might carry three men and were used primarily for spearmen. The Assyrians became the greatest practitioners of chariot warfare in Western Asia, with combinations of light chariots for archers and heavier chariots for as many as four spearmen. The Chinese also made extensive use of war chariots.

Charioteers usually fought from the vehicle, but on occasion they dismounted to fight. The preferred weapons were spears and the light composite bow.

Armies of the ancient Near East often deployed very large numbers of chariots. We are told that the Egyptians had 2,500 of them in the Battle of Kadesh (1274 BCE); their opponents probably had comparable numbers of chariots. By the time of Alexander the Great in the fourth century BCE, more maneuverable cavalry formations had largely replaced chariots in warfare.

Further Reading

Cotterell, Arthur. *Chariot: From Chariot to Tank, the Astounding Rise and Fall of the World's First War Machine.* Woodstock, NY: Overlook, 2004.

Galley

The galley was a long, narrow wooden warship with a shallow beam and low freeboard. It was propelled by rows of oars and almost always sails on one or two masts. In the early days galleys carried a square sail on a single mast, but in later years lateen sails on two masts were more common. Galleys varied widely, although this ship type was the predominant warship of the ancient Mediterranean world and thrived for almost 5,000 years. Galleys were in use on the Nile and in the Mediterranean as early as 3,000 BCE. The Phoenicians borrowed the design, which was then further refined by Greek naval architects. Originally galleys had a single bank of oars, and the ship was used both for transport and war. Homer makes reference to galleys in *The Iliad.*

The war galley was effective because it could move quickly to an enemy vessel for boarding. In the eighth or ninth century BCE the ram—a massive pointed bronze projection set at the waterline—was introduced in war galleys. The ram could punch a hole in an opposing ship, sinking it.

War galleys evolved throughout the centuries. The single row of oarsmen soon gave way to two banks of oarsmen. This was known as a bireme. The change to three superimposed banks produced the trireme. Originally each oar was pulled by one man, but later several men were put to each oar. Some galleys had four or five superimposed banks of oars; the latter were known as quinquiremes and carried crews of up to 500 men. By the first century CE, however, the Romans had returned to the trireme as their main battle ship.

During the 16th and 17th centuries Genoa, Venice, and France maintained fleets powered by 25 three-man oars to a side and later five-man oars. The usual

Undated engraving of a galley. This ship type, especially employed in the Mediterranean, could be propelled by either oar or sail. (Bettmann/Corbis)

practice until about 1450 had been to employ volunteers or hired mercenaries, but captives and convicts then came to row the ships. The 15th-century galley had a displacement of about 200 tons and was approximately 164 feet in length and 20 feet in beam.

Following the introduction of cannon at sea, heavy guns were mounted on a platform at the bow—usually one large gun and one or two smaller ones to each side of it. The guns were fixed in traverse and were aimed by turning the vessel.

Galleys were swift (up to 10 knots for short periods) and maneuverable. They were also not dependent on the wind, which was ideal in the Mediterranean, but they were vulnerable to adverse weather and unable to stay at sea for long periods because of their scant cargo capacity.

The galley had a considerable impact on the naval history of the Mediterranean. Eventually it gave way to the galleass, which combined the freedom of movement of the galley with the seaworthiness and fighting power of the sailing warship. The galleass combined a single bank of rowers on each side with a three-masted lateen sail rig. Above the rowers, the galleass had a gun deck that allowed broadside fire by cannon. The Battle of Lepanto of October 7, 1571, established its importance as a warship. The last use of galleys in Mediterranean fighting occurred in the Battle of Matapan in 1717. They were present in the 1718 Battle of

Cape Passero but took no part in the action. Galleys also appeared in the Baltic during the 17th and 18th centuries, and they were in use there as late as the Russo-Swedish War of 1809. A Russian galley built in 1791 carried sails on three masts, including a square-rigged main, and mounted 22 cannon.

Further Reading

Anderson, Roger Charles. *Oared Fighting Ships.* London: Percival Marshall, 1962.

Bamford, Paul. *Fighting Ships and Prisons.* Minneapolis: University of Minnesota Press, 1973.

Guilmartin, John Francis, Jr. *Gunpowder and Galleys: Changing Technology and Mediterranean Warfare at Sea in the Sixteenth Century.* New York: Cambridge University Press, 1974.

Guilmartin, John Francis, Jr. *Naval Warfare under Oars: 4th to 16th Centuries.* Annapolis, MD: Naval Institute Press, 1940.

Trireme

Triremes were long, low, and narrow galley warships. The name "trireme" is derived from the fact that its oars were ranged in three banks on each side of the vessel with the rowers, one man to an oar, pulling up to 200 oars. Seaworthiness, comfort, cargo capacity, and range were deliberately sacrificed to achieve speed,

---

The Battle of Salamis

No doubt the most famous naval engagement involving triremes is the Battle of Salamis in 480 BCE during the Persian Wars (499–479 BCE). Following the Persian land victory at Thermopylae, Greek fleet commander Themistocles sailed his triremes southward to Athens. Persian king Xerxes and his army soon took the city, its population fleeing to the island of Salamis, where they were protected by Themistocles' 310 triremes.

The Persian fleet of around 500 ships now arrived. It was important for Xerxes to destroy the Greek fleet before he could invade the Peloponnese and end his Greek campaign, but he was wary of engaging the Greeks in the narrow Salamis Channel.

With indications increasing that many of his captains would depart to assist the land forces defending the Peloponnese, Themistocles resorted to one of the most famous stratagems in military history. He sent a trusted slave with a letter for Xerxes that informed him that Themistocles was changing sides, that the Greeks were badly divided and would offer little resistance, and that elements of the fleet were intending to depart at night.

Xerxes immediately ordered his captains to block all possible escape routes, and early the next morning (possibly September 20) the entire Persian fleet attacked. Superior Greek tactics and seamanship prevailed. The Persians may have lost some 200 ships, the Greeks only 40. That night the remaining Persian ships departed, and Xerxes and much of the land force soon followed.

A replica of an ancient Athenian trireme off the Greek Island of Poros in 1987. Note the ram at the ship's bow. (Time & Life Pictures/Getty Images)

power, and maneuverability. In addition to its oars, the trireme carried sails on its two masts as a means of auxiliary power.

Little is known about Athenian triremes, but they were said to be sturdy in battle and very fast. Although thousands of triremes were sunk in antiquity, no wreck has been identified. What we know of the trireme comes from paintings or contemporary descriptions, none of these detailed. Although modern experts have built a full-scale copy of a trireme, they failed to discover how it could move so fast. We know even less about its Persian counterpart.

The Athenian trireme was approximately 100–120 feet in length and normally had a crew of 200, of whom 170 were rowers. Oarsmen were drawn from the poorer classes but were not slaves. At the Battle of Salamis (480 BCE) each trireme had 10 marines and 4 archers. The crew also included a flutist who piped time for the rowers. This left 15 deckhands.

The chief weapon of the trireme was its bronze ram at the bow. The captain of the trireme would attempt to place his own vessel perpendicular to an enemy ship, then, using his oarsmen, drive his own ship into the opposing vessel at high speed, sinking it. The Athenians also successfully used naval bowmen during the Peloponnesian War. Although far less frequent, crewmen might also take an opposing vessel by storm with swords, axes, and other small arms.

Such ships, with relatively large crews for their size, could not remain at sea for extended periods and were in fact usually employed in coastal operations. Operations over considerable distances were only possible if the warships were

accompanied by supply vessels. Indeed, commanders would often beach their
ships for the night, throwing up fortifications to protect against land attack.

Further Reading

Haws, Duncan, and Alex A. Hurst. *The Maritime History of the World,* Vol. 1. Brighton,
 UK: Teredo Books, 1985.

Kemp, Peter, ed. *The Oxford Companion to Ships and the Sea.* Oxford: Oxford University
 Press, 1988.

Morrison, John S., John F. Coats, and N. Boris Rankov. *The Athenian Trireme: The History
 and Reconstruction of an Ancient Greek Warship.* 2nd ed. Cambridge: Cambridge University Press, 2000.

Corvus

Taking its name from the Latin for "raven," the corvus was a boarding bridge that
gave the Romans a series of naval victories in the First Punic War (264–241 BCE).
The device was used for a few years only and is known primarily from a description by the Roman historian Polybius.

 The corvus consisted of a stationary pole, 24 feet high, on the prow of a quin-
quereme, with a pulley at the top and a movable gangway, 36 feet long and 4 wide,

Print showing a corvus in the bow of a Roman galley. The engraving is by Jacques
Grasset de Saint-Sauveur and L. F. Labrousse, 1796. (Stapleton Collection/Corbis)

with railings on either side as high as a man's knee. The pole went through an oblong hole 12 feet from the lower end of the gangway, which allowed the boarding bridge to be swung in different directions in battle and to be raised up at other times. The name "raven" came from the pestle-like iron beak at the far end of the bridge, having a pointed end so that it would hold fast the enemy ship. The gangway was raised and lowered by means of a rope that went through the pulley and attached to a ring at the top end of the iron spike. If the two ships met prow to prow, the Roman marines used the gangway to cross to the enemy ship; if the ships were side by side, the "raven" held them fast, but the Romans could climb directly onto the enemy ship without the gangway.

The gangway was raised and lowered as a unit; there was no hinge, and it could not be raised to a full 90 degrees. The gangway is estimated to have weighed about one ton.

The Romans first used the corvus at the 260 BCE Battle of Mylae. It figures also in Polybius's account of the Battle of Ecnomus (256 BCE) and may have played a role in other Roman victories at sea. At least by 242 BCE, when the Romans had built a new fleet of quinqueremes on a lighter model, their ships no longer had the boarding bridge. Grapnels or grappling irons (so-called iron hands) were employed by the Greeks as early as 425 BCE, and the Romans used them after they abandoned the boarding bridge.

Further Reading

Lazenby, J. F. *The First Punic War: A Military History.* Stanford, CA: Stanford University Press, 1996.

Thiel, J. H. *A History of Roman Sea-Power before the Second Punic War.* Amsterdam: North-Holland Publishing, 1954.

Wallinga, H. T. *The Boarding-Bridge of the Romans.* Groningen: J. B. Wolters, 1956.

Greek Fire

Greek fire was an inflammable composition employed at sea to attack enemy ships. It took fire spontaneously when wetted. Utilized effectively by the Byzantine Empire and also known as liquid or maritime fire, it was an important element in the defeat of the Muslim fleets during the great siege of Constantinople (717–718). Reputedly Callinicus, a native of Heliopolis in Syria, deserted from the service of the caliph to that of the Byzantine emperor and brought the secret of its composition with him.

Greek fire remains one of the unlocked secrets of history, but the most educated guesses suggest that its principal ingredient was naphtha, or liquid bitumen, a light inflammable oil that catches fire on contact with air. This was mixed with sulfur and pitch from pine trees. The resulting mixture produced a thick smoke and a fierce flame that was difficult to extinguish. It could not be put out by water, which only intensified the burning.

Greek fire was employed in warfare on both land and sea. On land it might be poured by defenders from the city walls or launched by catapults. It could even be sent against an enemy in the form of an impregnated material attached to javelins or arrows. At sea it was projected against an enemy vessel by means of long, thin copper tubes planted in the bow of a galley. The ends of the tubes were often formed in fanciful shapes of sea monsters, the flame seen to belch from their mouths. According to Edward Gibbon, the Byzantines managed to preserve the secret of its composition for more than 400 years until the Muslims managed to discover it and use it against the Christian forces during the Crusades. Greek fire continued in use until the middle of the 14th century, when a new mixture of salt-peter, sulfur, and charcoal led to a revolution in warfare.

Further Reading

Gibbon, Edward. *The History of the Decline and Fall of the Roman Empire,* Vol. 6. Edited by J. B. Bury. London: Methuen, 1912.

Mayor, Adrienne. *Greek Fire, Poison Arrows, and Scorpion Bombs: Biological and Chemical Warfare in the Ancient World.* New York: Overlook Duckworth, 2003.

Mechanical Artillery

The term "artillery" dates from the Middle Ages and comes from the French *attilier,* meaning "to arrange," and *attillement,* meaning "equipment." Initially applied to all military equipment, artillery is generally used to describe larger weapons designed to hurl missiles.

Before the advent of gunpowder as a propellant, artillery relied on nonexplosive principles. Thus, pregunpowder artillery is generally referred to as mechanical artillery and can be classified in three general types based on the propelling force utilized: springs, torsion, and counterweights.

Mechanical artillery probably appeared first in early Mesopotamia. Classical Greece and Rome developed large, highly sophisticated mechanical artillery. Medieval siege engines were also highly developed. No ancient siege weapons survive intact, so our knowledge of them is derived entirely from written contemporary sources. Since the second half of the 19th century, scholars and engineers have reconstructed models and in some cases full-scale replicas. Tests with these provide a reasonably accurate sense of their capabilities.

The nomenclature for early artillery, both pregunpowder and gunpowder, is problematic, for terms were often used interchangeably. Spring-powered weapons employed a single leaf spring or a double one, as in a large bow. Typical of these was the *gastraphetes* of ancient Greece. Torsion-powered weapons include the catapult, the larger examples of which might be able to hurl a 50-pound object some 400 yards. Whereas the catapult was powered by a single skein, ballista relied on a double skein. The larger examples of these might hurl a 10-pound arrow some 400 yards. The trebuchet is perhaps the best known of counterweight weapons. Large trebuchets could throw a 300-pound projectile some 300 yards.

Ancient artillery was employed primarily in sieges to hurl large missiles against walls in an effort to batter them down and to throw missiles, including incendiaries and human or animal carcasses to spread disease over a defender's walls and parapets. The Romans developed some lighter fieldpieces, but most ancient and medieval artillery pieces were quite large and were used in the prolonged siege operations that characterized much of the warfare of these periods.

Further Reading

The Diagram Group. *Weapons: An International Encyclopedia from 5000 BC to 2000 AD.* New York: St. Martin's, 1990.

Kinard, Jeff. *Artillery: An Illustrated History of Its Impact.* Santa Barbara, CA: ABC-CLIO, 2007.

Rihll, Tracey. *The Catapult: A History.* Yardley, PA: Westholme, 2007.

Spring-Powered Artillery Engines

One of the three types of pregunpowder mechanical artillery, along with torsion and counterweight-powered engines, spring- or tension-powered engines relied on a single or double spring (as in a bow) to project either a large arrow or a stone toward its target. In what may have been history's first ordnance research facility, in 399 BCE Dionysius I, tyrant of Syracuse in Sicily, assembled teams of experts to develop a whole series of new weapons to use against other city-states on the island. Two years later he employed his new weapons to besiege Motya.

The first mechanical artillery piece was probably the *gastraphetes,* or "belly bow." In essence a large crossbow, it projected a large arrow or stone. During his siege of Motya, Dionysius deployed numbers of the *gastraphetes.* Possibly derived from the Assyrians and fired by one man, they got their name from the fact that the user pushed down with his stomach against the concave butt of the weapon in order to cock the bowstring. Its compound bow consisted of a wood core sandwiched between layers of horn and flexible animal sinew. It fired a large arrow, also known as a bolt or dart, from a groove in the slider.

The *gastraphetes* proved to be an important factor in Dionysius's victory over Motya. With an effective range of some 250 yards, it exceeded that of conventional bows by some 50 yards, helped clear the defenders from the city's walls, and enabled Dionysius to advance six-story siege towers into position.

A much larger tension-powered *gastraphetes* appeared in about 375 BCE. This was the *oxybeles,* or "bolt-shooter," although variants could fire stone shot. Mounted on a wooden stand, it utilized a winch and lever arrangement to draw its powerful bow and fire larger projectiles farther and more accurately than its predecessor. The most powerful of these weapons was known as the *katapeltes,* or "shield piercer," for it fired bolts that could penetrate shields and armor at up to 400 yards.

One type of *oxybeles,* probably dating from about 330 BCE, had a 9-foot bow that fired two heavy 6-foot-long bolts from its double-slotted slider. The largest such weapons had bows approaching 15 feet in size and could hurl stone shot weighing 40 pounds about 300 yards. Both the *gastraphetes* and *oxybeles* were direct-fire weapons that hurled their projectiles in a relatively flat trajectory.

Archimedes probably employed similar spring-powered engines in the unsuccessful defense of Syracuse against the Romans in 211 BCE. In the Middle Ages, large springs of laminated wood positioned in a wooden frame were used to project spears. Leonardo Da Vinci designed a spring-powered engine to hurl two stones. The wooden arm was drawn back by means of a windlass. One stone was placed on the end of the arm, while the second was held in a sling at the end of the arm. Releasing the wooden arm hurled both projectiles.

Spring-powered devices again appeared during World War I, when both sides used them to hurl grenades into opposing trenches. The French grasshopper was a crossbow-like device capable of throwing a grenade 100 yards. The British West Spring Gun of 1915 employed metal springs to jerk the throwing arm.

Further Reading

The Diagram Group. *Weapons: An International Encyclopedia from 5000 BC to 2000 AD.* New York: St. Martin's, 1990.

Kinard, Jeff. *Artillery: An Illustrated History of Its Impact.* Santa Barbara, CA: ABC-CLIO, 2007.

Marsden, E. W. *Greek and Roman Artillery, Historical Development.* Oxford, UK: Sandpiper, 1999.

Nicolle, David. *Medieval Siege Weapons,* Vol. 1, *Western Europe, AD 585–1385.* Illustrated by Sam Thompson. London: Osprey, 2002.

Torsion-Powered Artillery Engines

Torsion-powered engines were, along with spring-powered and counterweight-powered engines, one of the three basic types of pregunpowder artillery. The first mechanical artillery was spring-powered, but steady increases in size of siege engines made its limitations all too apparent.

Sometime before 340 BCE, a form of the spring-powered *oxybeles* appeared, utilizing the torsion principle of elasticity of a tightly wound skein of hair or cord wrapped many times around two wood axles. The base of the wooden throwing arm, approximately two to three feet in length, was placed in the center of the skein. Winches and ratchets were then used to twist the ends of the skein. When released, the arm sprang forward and launched the projectile.

Torsion-powered engines could fire projectiles with higher velocity and greater range and accuracy than any other mechanical system and soon rendered spring- or

---

Archimedes and the Siege of Syracuse

During the Roman siege of Syracuse (213–212 BCE), the Syracusans had a formidable asset in celebrated geometrician Archimedes. Then in his 70s, he developed a number of innovative military devices. To attack the Roman ships, he arranged catapults and ballistae in batteries according to required range. Archimedes also developed a crane that extended over the walls and made use of a grapple, known as a claw, to hook onto a ship. A counterbalance enabled the crane to lift up the ship. Letting it go dashed the vessel to pieces. Another technique was to drop heavy stones on ships to crash through their hulls and sink them. These boulders, one of which was said to weigh 10 talents (670 pounds), were dropped on the Roman ships, destroying them. Archimedes also used smaller shorter-range catapults, known as scorpions, to hurl boulders and stones at the attackers. The most controversial story of the siege concerns Archimedes' supposed invention of so-called burning mirrors, whereby the sun's rays were reflected to set fire to the Roman ships.

---

tension-powered engines obsolete. They did, however, require heavy frames to withstand the stresses from the greater energy released.

Two early types of torsion weapons were the Greek *euthytone* and *palintone*. They derived their names from comparisons to hand bows. *Euthytone* means "straight spring" (as in a straight bow), while *palintone* means "V spring" (for the curved composite bow). The *palintone* appeared later and was the more powerful. It was used to hurl heavy stone shot, while the *euthytone* usually fired bolts against personnel.

In order to knock down a wall, artillerists would have to score a number of hits in the same spot. Optimum accuracy required standardized projectiles. Masons therefore shaped stone into equal-sized round shot, the shape of which enhanced its flight characteristics.

The Romans acquired significant quantities of artillery in their defeat of the Greeks, and Roman artillery was simply a refinement of earlier Greek forms. Thus, the Greek *euthytone* became the *catapulta,* and the *palintone* became the ballista. The ballista was a two-armed torsion machine used as an antipersonnel weapon in sieges and operated by a two-man firing crew. Julius Caesar equipped each of his legions with 30 ballistae. For portability, many ballistae were relatively small. Arm lengths varied from 2 to 4 feet. The larger stone-throwing weapons could hurl projectiles weighing up to 60 pounds as far as 550 yards. Bolt-firing ballistae could hurl 26-inch- to 3-foot-long projectiles 300 yards.

The onager (meaning "wild ass") was perhaps the best known of late Roman torsion-powered engines. It was also the simplest of Roman siege engines. Its name came from the powerful kick upon discharge when the arm reached the end of its travel against padded boards at its front. The onager was in common use in the fourth century CE. It had a leather sling attached to the opposite end of the arm to accept projectiles. Once it was loaded and ready to fire, a mallet was used to strike the retaining pin and release its projectile. The onager could be manned by a crew of five to six men, although a larger number improved efficiency. The largest onagers could hurl stone shot of up to 180 pounds. At a weight of as heavy as 6 tons apiece, however, these engines were difficult to transport even disassembled. In consequence, they were most often a defensive, garrison weapon.

The scorpio ("scorpion") was a relatively lightweight and mobile torsion-powered engine. Appearing in the mid-first century BCE, it had curved, tapered arms as with a recurved bow to increase its strength. It utilized metal on surfaces subject to wear. The scorpio could hurl a 7- to 10-pound shot 300 yards, while the bolt-firing scorpio usually fired a 27-inch arrow with a pyramidal iron head and three wood fletches.

The most sophisticated Roman two-armed torsion engine was the *cheiroballis-tra*. Appearing in the late first century CE, its torsion springs were supported by all-metal frames. It had two front-mounted wheels for rapid deployment. A well-trained 10-man crew, the majority of whom were ammunition handlers, could fire it three or four times a minute.

Further Reading

The Diagram Group. *Weapons: An International Encyclopedia from 5000 BC to 2000 AD.* New York: St. Martin's, 1990.

Kinard, Jeff. *Artillery: An Illustrated History of Its Impact.* Santa Barbara, CA: ABC-CLIO, 2007.

Marsden, E. W. *Greek and Roman Artillery: Historical Development.* Oxford, UK: Sandpiper, 1999.

Counterweight-Powered Artillery Engines

Counterweight-powered engines formed, along with spring- and torsion-powered engines, the three basic types of pregunpowder artillery. While spring- and torsion-powered engines were widely used in the ancient world, the simple system of counterweight artillery was not in general use until the mid-13th century. While the counterweight engines fired heavier projectiles than the other two systems, their range and accuracy were inferior to torsion-powered engines.

Counterweight-powered engines probably originated in China and arrived in Europe by way of the Muslim world. They required a large arm, massive counterweight (also known as a counterpoise), and a large frame. Because of their size, they were entirely siege weapons. They consisted of two large wood A-frames mounted on a wooden base and connected at the top by a freely rotating wooden axle. The throwing beam or arm passed through the center of the axle, with one-quarter of its length facing the target. The heavy counterweight (or counterpoise) was attached to the short end. The remaining three-quarters of the arm extended rearward. A rope at the rearward end connected to a leather sling, which held the projectile.

Exact timing of release of the projectile was essential. To achieve that, a stay rope ran from the sling to farther down the throwing arm. When the weapon was fired and the stay rope became taut, it spilled open the pouch and released the projectile. In an alternate release method, a horn at the end of the arm held one end of the rope, which slipped off when the sling was at the proper point in the throwing arc. Other ropes attached to the arm allowed the crew, no doubt assisted by onlookers, to set the engine again in the firing position by means of a system of windlasses and pulleys.

The earliest counterweight was most probably the small *pierrière* ("stone thrower," also called *petraria*). Undoubtedly the Arabs introduced it to the West as they employed an identical weapon, known as the *lu'ab*. The *pierrière* operated entirely by human traction power. The operator pulled on a rope attached to the small end of the throwing arm. Both sides during the Crusades employed such weapons. The *bricole* (also called a *biffa*) was a somewhat larger *pierrière* in which a counterweight rather than rope was its energy source. Both of these weapons could be fired quite rapidly. During the siege of Lisbon in 1147, two such English weapons manned in shifts reportedly fired 5,000 projectiles during only 10 hours.

The most famous of counterweight engines, however, was the trebuchet, the primary heavy siege weapon of the Middle Ages. Trebuchets could be very large; some had throwing arms of up to 50 feet in length and could hurl stone shot 300

A modern replica of a medieval trebuchet, a counterweight-powered siege engine. (iStockPhoto)

yards. Repeated hits in the same area could breach even the stoutest fortifications. The counterweights consisted of large wooden hoppers up to 9 feet across and 12 feet deep holding as much as 10 tons of stone, lead, earth, or sand. Because of their size, trebuchets were usually constructed on-site with local materials. Metal fittings and rope were hauled in by wagons. Large trebuchets required crews of 50 or more men. Often they operated in batteries in order to be able to concentrate fire on a particular point in an enemy fortification.

Although it certainly appeared some years earlier, the first reliable documentary evidence of a trebuchet was in 1199 during the siege of Castelnuovo, Italy. The trebuchet dominated medieval siege warfare through the early 14th century. It was employed in a variety of roles and hurled incendiary and biological projectiles. Incendiary projectiles included Greek fire and would be used to set fire to the roofs of buildings. Biological warfare consisted of hurling into a city animal carcasses and the corpses of plague victims in order to spread disease and weaken resistance. On occasion trebuchets were employed to launch the severed heads of captured enemies or even living prisoners in a form of psychological warfare.

Although gunpowder artillery appeared in the 14th century, it did not immediately supplant mechanical artillery. The trebuchets were more powerful and accurate and were far safer to use for their crews than early gunpowder artillery. Thus, for some time the two systems existed side by side.

Further Reading

The Diagram Group. *Weapons: An International Encyclopedia from 5000 BC to 2000 AD.* New York: St. Martin's, 1990.

Kinard, Jeff. *Artillery: An Illustrated History of Its Impact.* Santa Barbara, CA: ABC-CLIO, 2007.

Nicolle, David. *Medieval Siege Weapons,* Vol. 1, *Western Europe, AD 585–1385.* Illustrated by Sam Thompson. London: Osprey, 2002.

Saddle

The saddle is a girthed, usually padded and leather-covered seat for the rider of an animal such as a horse. In ancient times, riders went bareback or utilized only a blanket. Dating from the third century CE and usually attributed to the Sarmatians, nomads who lived in southern Russia along the Black Sea, the saddle was of immense importance in the development of cavalry. Camel and elephant saddles were developed about the same time in the Middle East and in Asia.

Since the medieval period, the saddle consisted of a wooden frame with padding and covered by leather. It was secured to the mount by means of a leather girth passing under the belly of the animal. Stirrups to hold the feet of the rider were suspended on either side.

The knightly or war saddle had a high raised rear part or cantle in order to hold the rider in place, especially with the shock from jousting or swordplay. The cantle was reduced in size considerably in later military models, which added leather holders for assorted weapons. Two types of modern saddles predominated: the Western/Moorish saddle, with a high horn on the pommel in front of the rider, and the lighter, flatter, and more padded English/Hungarian saddle.

Pack saddles were developed for horses and mules in order to carry weapons, military equipment, and supplies. These included disassembled machine guns and even the components of light artillery, such as mountain howitzers. The McClellan Saddle was the standard U.S. cavalry saddle from the American Civil War on.

Further Reading

Bull, Stephen. *Encyclopedia of Military Technology and Innovation.* Westport, CT: Greenwood, 2004.

Tylden, Geoffrey. *Horses and Saddlery: An Account of the Animals Used by the British and Commonwealth Armies from the Seventeenth Century to the Present Day, with a Description of Their Equipment.* London: J. A. Allen, 1965.

Stirrup

Stirrups are supports suspended on either side of a horse's saddle to take the rider's feet and help him or her maintain position and balance. The stirrup seems to have originated in Arabia in about 650 CE and was widely used in Western Europe by the 8th century. Metal stirrups were in general use in Europe by the 10th century.

The stirrup was an immensely important innovation in the development of horse cavalry, for it greatly eased the process of mounting the horse and also made the use of weapons from horseback much easier. In effect, it transformed the horse from a launching platform for weapons into an actual shock weapon of horse and rider. The rider used both the saddle and the stirrups to maintain stability on the horse when he was using a sword, and he could now for the first time employ a lance with full force from a gallop without himself being driven from the saddle by the impact. The Franks in particular used the stirrup with great effectiveness in their heavy cavalry. The stirrup and the iron horseshoe, developed in the ninth century, enabled horses to traverse more difficult terrain and revolutionized mounted warfare. Introduction of the stirrup meant the domination of heavy cavalry on the European battlefield for seven centuries.

Further Reading

Grbasic, Zvonimir, and Velimir Vuksic. *The History of Cavalry.* New York: Facts on File, 1989.

Vuksic, Velimir, and Zvonimir Grbasic. *Cavalry: The History of a Fighting Elite, 650 B.C.– A.D. 1914.* Herndon, VA: Cassell, 1993.

Viking Longboat

The Viking longboat or longship was employed throughout Scandinavia. The long-boat was, as the name implies, a long, narrow vessel. It was propelled at first by oars alone and then also by sail. Clinker-built of sturdy oak, with a strong keel and raised bow and stern, the longboat was directed by a steering oar at the starboard side of the stern. A deck ran between the beams and had a raised platform at bow and stern. Although there were smaller and larger longboats, the usual warship size seems to have been one pierced for 40 oars (20 per side), a vessel about 120 feet in length and 20 feet in beam and with a draft of 3.5 feet. The crew complement would have been about 50 men. A single centrally located mast, which could be dismounted, rested directly on the keel. Its sole yardarm supported a cloth square sail—often colored or embroidered—that was strengthened by a crossing pattern of linen or leather.

Surviving examples of the longboats do not have thwarts or benches for the row-ers. The men would either have rowed standing (the holes in the side of the vessel for the oars are set low) or while sitting on a chest containing their possessions or on a removable bench (none of which survive). The holes for the oars could be covered with wooden disks to keep the sea from coming in when the vessel was under sail. The ships were decorated at bow and stern, usually with a dragon head at the bow, which was, however, removed while the boat was in home waters.

The longboat was so important to the Norsemen that many prominent individu-als were buried in them. In consequence, several have been discovered in archaeo-logical digs. Two well-preserved examples of the longboat were found in Oseberg and Gokstad. The Oseberg ship was discovered near Tønsberg in Norway in 1904 and dates from the ninth century. It is 70 feet long and nearly 17 feet in beam. Clinker-built with overlapping planks, it has 12 planks to a side and is pierced for 15 oars on each side.

The Gokstad ship dates from the 10th century and was discovered in 1880. It contained the body of its owner and many of his animals as well as personal pos-sessions and weapons. It had been covered with clay that preserved it in excellent condition. The Gokstad boat has a length of 75 feet 6 inches and a width of 16 feet 5 inches and is 6 feet 7 inches from the bottom of the keel to the gunwale. Clinker-built largely of oak, it weighed about 7 tons unloaded and has a central mast of pine. Its sides are pierced for 32 oars (16 to a side). The oars are of spruce and are of different lengths to compensate for the profile of the vessel. The Gokstad boat contained 64 circular shields, indicating that there were two men per oar if neces-sary. More likely, the men rowed in shifts.

The Norsemen used such vessels to carry out pillaging expeditions against iso-lated towns and settlements in England, Ireland, and France in the 9th and 10th centuries. They reached into the Mediterranean in the 11th century. The shallow draft of the longboats allowed them easy river access. That such ships probably

The *Islendingur* in New York Harbor, October 5, 2000. A crew of nine Icelandic sailors sailed this replica 75-foot Viking longship from Iceland to Canada and then to New York. (AP Photo/Suzanne Plunkett)

reached North America was demonstrated in 1893 when a reconstructed Gokstad ship made the voyage from Norway to America in 28 days.

The longboat was superseded by faster sailing vessels that could carry larger payloads farther with smaller crews. Rowed galleys figured prominently in Scandinavian navies into the early 19th century, however.

Further Reading

Gibbons, Tony, ed. *The Encyclopedia of Ships.* London: Amber Books, 2001.

Landström, Björn. *The Ship: An Illustrated History.* Garden City, NY: Doubleday, n.d.

Caltrop

The caltrop (caltrap, calthrop) or *triboli* (*tribulus*) is an antipersonnel weapon employed on land and at sea from ancient times and used ever since. They were of iron with four or more points, so arranged that one of the spikes was always pointing upward. They might be hurled onto the deck of an opposing ship or strewn on the ground in front of a position in order to severely wound anyone stepping or falling on them. Caltrops were employed in World War I and World War II. Offspring have been employed to destroy tires on vehicles. The punji stake of the Vietnam War is one such modern version.

Further Reading

Bull, Stephen. *Encyclopedia of Military Technology and Innovation.* Westport, CT: Greenwood, 2004.

Tucker, Spencer C. *Arming the Fleet: U.S. Navy Ordnance in the Muzzle-Loading Era.* Annapolis, MD: Naval Institute Press, 1989.

Gunpowder

The introduction of gunpowder into Europe in the first half of the 13th century produced a military revolution. Various incendiary weapons, such as Greek fire, had existed since classical times, but gunpowder as an explosive propellant made firearms possible. Gunpowder consisted of three principal ingredients: potassium nitrate (saltpeter, roughly 75 percent), which provided oxygen for burning; sulfur (some 10 percent), which lowered the temperature at which ignition of the powder occurred; and charcoal (about 15 percent), which added bulk to the entire mixture while simultaneously acting as a burning agent.

Gunpowder when ignited generates great heat, releasing energy in the form of powerfully expanding gases. Properly channeled, these gases could be utilized to propel a projectile from a barrel at some velocity and distance. Originating in China perhaps as early as 850 CE, gunpowder was first employed as an ignition device and then used in fireworks, bombs, and mines. Gunpowder probably came to Europe from the Arab world via Spain, but the gun was a Western invention. Popular tradition from at least the beginning of the 15th century credits Black Berthhold (Berthold Schwartz, Bertholdus Niger), a monk in Freiburg, Germany. Gunpowder helped bring an end to the characteristic forms of warfare in the Middle Ages, as large projectiles could batter down castle walls, while the smallest projectiles could penetrate metal body armor worn by knights.

The first gunpowder was known as meal powder or serpentine powder. Quite literally a powder, it was relatively slow burning. The introduction of corned powder, probably in the second quarter of the 15th century, was an important step forward. In this process, the fine powder was compacted into cakes and then pushed through a mesh with holes of the desired size. When the corned powder was loaded into the weapon, the air spaces between the grains produced much more rapid burning and thus greater buildup of gases behind the projectile. Corned powder was employed in smaller sizes in individual firearms and in larger sizes for artillery. Gunpowder tended to deteriorate over time, especially in damp conditions, losing some of its propellant force. By the mid-19th century aboard ships it was stored in watertight sealed containers.

Gunpowder changed little over the years, and black powder remained the principal propellant for firearms until the end of the 19th century. Black powder burned imperfectly, leaving behind a considerable residue in the bore of the weapon. This fouling built up with successive firings, necessitating a fairly substantial difference between the diameter of the projectile and the bore of the weapon, known as windage.

The chief drawback of black powder on the battlefield, however, was the cloud of dense smoke it produced on ignition. This immediately revealed the weapon's location and also served to obscure the target. The situation only changed with the introduction of smokeless gunpowder at the end of the 19th century.

The most important innovation in gunpowder as an artillery propellant came with the development of prismatic powder by U.S. Army captain Thomas J. Rodman in the late 1850s. Rodman was the first to realize that the physical configuration of propellant powder should be designed specifically for the gun in which it would be used. He determined that the rate at which a propellant burned was directly proportional to its surface area. With the conventional grain powder of the period, the greatest surface area existed at the moment of ignition and then shrank as the powder grain burned. Hence the rate of burning slowed, and the subsequently generated power decreased. As the projectile moved farther down the cannon's bore, the chamber volume behind the round increased. This, combined with the decreasing rate of powder burn, reduced the pressure behind the projectile as it traveled down the bore of the gun.

Rodman reasoned that the optimum artillery propellant would burn at a progressively faster rate, thereby creating more pressure to offset the increasing volume in the chamber as the projectile moved down the bore. His solution was to press powder into hexagonal cakes, which then were perforated with longitudinal holes. This configuration caused a cake of propellant to burn from the inside out as well as from the outside in. As the propellant material around the holes burned away, the holes got larger, thereby increasing the exposed surface area and the rate of burning.

Prismatic powder did not increase the chamber pressure in the gun as the projectile moved forward and instead maintained the pressure at a constant level. The result was an increase in muzzle velocity without an increase in strain on the tube. Increased muzzle velocity brought with it increased range and accuracy. Rodman's discovery forms the basis of all modern artillery propellants.

Further Reading

Blair, Claude, ed. *Pollard's History of Firearms.* New York: Macmillan, 1983.

Cocroft, Wayne. *Dangerous Energy: The Archaeology of Gunpowder.* London: English Heritage Publications, 2000.

Hall, Bert S. *Weapons and Warfare in Renaissance Europe: Gunpowder, Technology, and Tactics.* Baltimore: Johns Hopkins University Press, 1997.

Kelly, Jack. *Gunpowder: Alchemy, Bombards, and Pyrotechnics: The History of the Explosive That Changed the World.* New York: Basic Books, 2004.

Partington, James Riddick. *A History of Greek Fire and Gunpowder.* Baltimore: Johns Hopkins University Press, 1998.

Temple, Robert. *The Genius of China: 3000 Years of Science, Discovery, and Invention.* New York: Simon and Schuster, 1986.

Land Mines and Mining

Mining, in the sense of digging a tunnel under an enemy fortification in order to collapse it, is as old as siege warfare itself, while the use of gunpowder in the mine chambers dates from the second half of the 15th century. The notion of using explosive devices as smaller antipersonnel and later antivehicular weapons dates from the 19th century. Mines may be used offensively, as in attacks on vehicle convoys or infantry patrols, or defensively to protect one's own position against enemy attack.

The world's navies had employed naval mines, known as "torpedoes," since the American Revolutionary War (1775–1783), but "land torpedoes" first appeared during the American Civil War (1861–1865). During his defense of Yorktown in the 1862 Peninsular Campaign, Confederate brigadier general Gabriel James Rains ordered 24-pounder artillery shells equipped with percussion fuzes and buried several inches belowground so that they would explode when stepped on. At the time, many on both sides of the war condemned the practice as barbarous and outside civilized warfare. But as the war increased in severity, such moral prohibitions were largely ignored.

Mines are both random and controlled. Random mines detonate when they are triggered. The four basic types of triggering devices are pressure, pressure-release, pull, and pull-release. Controlled mines are command-detonated, usually electronically.

Mines were employed in World War I but became a defensive mainstay in World War II, especially in North Africa and in some of the great Eastern Front battles. The Germans laid large numbers of mines as part of their defensive scheme known as the Atlantic Wall against an Allied invasion of France. Mines are laid both in large groups, known as minefields, and individually.

One of the best known of World War II mines was the German Shrapnellmine 35, known to U.S. soldiers as the "Bouncing Betty." Set off either by pull wire or by direct pressure, a propellant charge ejected the mine from the ground. An anchor wire triggered the mine at waist height, and a single pound of explosive hurled 350 ball bearings in every direction. This mine was widely copied, the U.S. counterpart being the M-16.

Typical of antitank mines was the German Tellermine 35. Made of steel, it was round in shape, 12.5 inches across and 3.2 inches thick. It had a handle mounted on the side for ease in carrying. Weighing 20 pounds, it contained an explosive charge of 12 pounds of TNT. Its pressure plate would detonate the mine only with 250 pounds of pressure. It could also be fitted with an antilifting device so that once it was set in place, it would detonate if lifted.

In the post–World War II period new types of mines appeared, such as those of plastic that could not be located by metal detectors. The plastic U.S. M14

A Canadian soldier disabling a land mine in February 1943. Such work is extraordinarily dangerous. In France, mines dating back to World War I continue to be unearthed by tractors and cause deaths and damage. (Hulton-Deutsch Collection/Corbis)

antipersonnel mine of the 1950s was designed to explode if stepped on. Antitank mines also became more sophisticated and employed shaped charges. Particularly effective was the new command-detonated, direction-type antipersonnel M-18A1 claymore mine employed by U.S. forces in Vietnam.

Mines continue to be employed in a wide variety of guises. They include the improvised explosive devices that often consist of rigged artillery shells such as those employed by the insurgents in the Iraq War (2003–2011). It is not essential that antipersonnel mines kill their victims. Indeed, serious wounding is often more desirable; this imposes logistical problems on the enemy force and immobilizes soldiers who go to the aid of the victim.

Mines can be laid by hand or by plow behind a vehicle, projected by launch tubes from vehicles, dropped by aircraft, or deployed from special artillery projectiles. Mine detection and clearance is a very difficult and dangerous enterprise. It may be accomplished by hand (the mine probe or stick) and special metal detectors. A path through a minefield might be cleared and the mines set off by means of a flail of heavy chains, rollers, a plow in front of a tank, or an explosive line charge. Shortly after the end of World War II, Soviet marshal Georgi Zhukov told a shocked U.S. general Dwight Eisenhower that the quickest means to clear a minefield was to march penal unit troops across it.

The millions of land mines laid during wars in several dozen countries around the world continue to claim thousands of innocent victims every year, and there is a worldwide effort to ban their use entirely. Following an effort led by Princess Diana of Wales and various human rights groups, representatives of 118 nations met in Ottawa, Canada, in December 1997 and there signed a treaty to ban land mines. As of 2014, 162 nations had ratified the treaty. Thirty-five states, including the major military powers of Great Britain, the People's Republic of China, Russia, and the United States, have refused to do so.

Further Reading

Croll, Mike. *The History of Land Mines.* Barnsley, UK: Leo Cooper, 1998.

Monin, L., and A. Gallimore. *The Devil's Gardens: A History of Land Mines.* London: Pimlico, 2002.

Sloan, C. E. E. *Mine Warfare on Land.* London: Brassey's, 1986.

Longbow

The longbow originated in Wales and was introduced in England in the 12th century. King Edward I (1272–1307) made it the standard weapon of his yeoman infantry, employing it with success in warfare against both the Welsh and the

---

Battle of Crécy

English longbowmen proved their worth in the battles of the Hundred Years' War (1337–1453). The Battle of Crécy, fought on August 26, 1346, was especially important. Pursued by King Philippe and some 30,000–60,000 Frenchmen, English king Edward III decided to stand and fight near the village of Crécy-en-Ponthieu.

Edward had only 11,000 men but selected an excellent defensive position on high ground overlooking a gentle slope. He placed archers between two large bodies of his dismounted men-at-arms and on the flanks, echeloning them forward in V formations to deliver enfilading fire.

Philippe attacked without reconnoitering. He first sent 6,000 Genoese crossbowmen against the English. The Genoese could fire their crossbows about one to two times a minute, while the English longbowmen could get off an arrow every five seconds. The storm of English arrows prevented the Genoese from closing to a range where their crossbows might have been effective.

Some 12,000 French knights then rode forward, only to encounter the same swarms of arrows. The French horsemen did reach the English line but were driven back by the English cavalry. The French repeatedly re-formed and attacked but each time encountered the arrows of the longbowmen. The battle ended that night.

The French suffered some 1,500 knights and men-at-arms and 10,000–20,000 crossbowmen and infantrymen killed, in addition to thousands of horses. Philippe VI was among the many wounded. English losses were only about 200 dead or wounded.

English longbowmen depicted during the Battle of Agincourt on October 25, 1415, during the Hundred Years' War. The illustration is from a French 15th century manuscript. (Stapleton Collection/Corbis)

Scots. The longbow dominated the battlefields of the Hundred Years' War at least through the Battle of Agincourt in 1415. The French so feared this weapon that orders were issued to cut off three fingers of the right hand of captured English bowmen. The bow itself was made of a 6-foot length of yew and fired a 3-foot-long arrow. The longbow was much more powerful than the shorter Norman bow and was far easier for a trained archer to use. It was also lighter, more adaptable, and had a greater rate of fire than the crossbow. The longbow was also extraordinarily powerful. Its arrows could penetrate two layers of chain mail armor and a 1-inch board.

The maximum range of the longbow was about 400 yards, twice that of the crossbow, with an effective range of about 150–250 yards. At about 60 yards the longbow arrow could even pierce plate armor. In the hands of a well-trained archer, the longbow was actually more accurate than the crossbow and had comparable penetrating power.

From the reign of Edward I, all English villages were required to contribute to a national pool of trained archers, who were required by law to practice each Sunday. Each archer carried as many as two dozen arrows, which could also be recovered and reused during battle. Additional supplies were transported by cart. A trained bowman could fire off 10–12 aimed arrows per minute. English longbowmen were also armed for hand-to-hand combat with either a sword, an ax, or a leaden mallet with a five-foot-long handle.

English longbowmen played the decisive role in the Battles of Crécy, Poitiers, and Agincourt during the Hundred Years' War, and the English longbow was certainly the most effective individual weapon introduced to that point in history.

Further Reading

Bradbury, Jim. *The Medieval Archer.* New York: Barnes and Noble, 2000.

Hardy, Robert. *Longbow: A Social and Military History.* Cambridge, UK: Patrick Stephens, 1978.

Crossbow

Crossbows existed from ancient times. They are known to have been used in China during the Han dynasty around the first century CE. Crossbows were also employed by the Romans but came into their greatest use in the Middle Ages.

The crossbow consisted of a small, very stiff bow (later of composite construction) perhaps 26 inches long and mounted crosswise at the end of a 3-foot short stock, or tiller, with a groove for the projectile. The crossbow had a metal stirrup on the front of the stock. To set the weapon, the archer placed one foot in the stirrup and then grasped the bowstring to pull it back and hook it over a small spool-like notched catch known as the nut. The crossbowman sighted the weapon on the target by looking down the stock directly over the bolt. Pulling the trigger on the crossbow rotated the catch and released the bowstring.

The crossbow fired short arrows about 15 inches long known as bolts. Later, they were called quarrels because they had square heads made of iron. Their shafts were made of wood, and they had "feathers" of either leather or paper. Quarrels for war had only two vanes so they would lie flat in the groove of the stock (actually one vane set in a saw cut in the back of the quarrel that was then lashed tight).

An improvement came in the form of a belt claw, so-named because it hung from the archer's belt when not in use. Hooked in the bowstring, it was used to draw it back to the nut. Later a short piece of rope set on a pulley eased the loading.

The crossbow was both heavy and slow to load. Archers with the longbow could outshoot it at a rate of perhaps 6:1. The great advantage of the crossbow was that it could be drawn ahead of time and then held in position to be fired whenever desired. Also, it could be fired with considerable accuracy and, unlike the longbow, did not require great training. Crossbows continued in widespread use throughout the Middle Ages. In recent years, small crossbows have been employed by special forces to dispatch both sentries and guard dogs.

Further Reading

Hall, Bert S. *Weapons and Warfare in Renaissance Europe: Gunpowder, Technology, and Tactics.* Baltimore: Johns Hopkins University Press, 1997.

Payne-Gallway, Ralph. *The Book of the Crossbow.* New York: Dover, 1995.

Payne-Gallwey, Ralph. *Crossbow: Medieval and Modern, Military and Sporting; Its Construction, History and Management.* New York: Bramhall House, 1958.

Harquebus

Late-16th-century term for any type of long individual firearm. In the late 14th and early 15th centuries a wide variety of individual hand "gonnes" appeared. The first primitive types consisted of a tapered wooden pole that was partially hollowed out at its larger end to hold a small, short metal barrel, which was secured to its gun stock by metal bands. Behind the barrel, a vertical metal spike running through the pole could be hooked over a portable rest in order to absorb recoil.

The earliest individual firearms were both unwieldy and heavy. Until about 1660, heavy so-called Spanish-style muskets were fired from a simple forked rest. Even the later lighter firearm models were cumbersome and difficult to load.

To fire the gun, the soldier would pour a set amount of gunpowder down the muzzle, then ram a round ball (usually of lead) after the powder to seat the ball against the powder charge at the bottom of the bore. The ball was wrapped in a cloth wad to ensure a tight fit between ball and barrel in order to hold the ball in place next to the powder. The charge was ignited by means of a slow-burning match applied to the small hole (touchhole) in the top of the breech end of the barrel.

Until the mid-19th century and the introduction of a new cylindro-conoidal bullet in a rifled barrel, all individual firearms were basically the same type: smooth-bore muzzle-loaders that differed only in their ignition mechanisms. Improvements in the firing process came steadily after the first appearance. The hand gonne, culverin, or culiver (there are a bewildering number of names for early firearms) gave way to the harquebus (arquebus). Shoulder stocks appeared around 1470. By the early 1500s, handheld firearms with new ignition mechanisms had arrived on the battlefield to stay.

Although early gunpowder weapons were difficult to handle and wildly inaccurate, infantrymen with them could kill or maim knights on horseback. Such weapons in the hands of well-trained individual infantrymen eventually ended the primacy of horse cavalry and knights on the battlefields of Europe.

Further Reading

Blair, Claude, ed. *Pollard's History of Firearms.* New York: Macmillan, 1983.

Lenk, Torsten. *The Flintlock: Its Origin and Development.* New York: Bramhall House, 1965.

Peterson, Harold L. *Arms and Armor in Colonial America, 1526–1783.* New York: Bramhall House, 1956.

Matchlock

The matchlock was the successor to the primitive early individual gun known as the harquebus (arquebus). The first illustration of a matchlock mechanism dates to 1475, and matchlocks were in general use in Europe by the 1500s. The Portuguese transported the technology to India, China, and Japan. As with most individual firearms through at least the mid-19th century, the matchlock had a long wooden stock. One end of the stock fitted against the individual's shoulder, while the stock itself held the long cast-iron barrel and firing mechanism. Unlike the primitive "hand gonne," the matchlock had a trigger mechanism. On the trigger being pulled, its mechanism plunged the glowing tip of the match (really a very slow-burning fuse) into priming powder in a pan, which then ignited the main charge in the barrel. There were a great many matchlock varieties, but in most cases the priming pan had to be opened by hand before the trigger was pulled.

Matchlocks did not immediately supplant bows or crossbows. Indeed, they had many limitations. The match proved susceptible to rain and wind, and it could reveal troop positions at night, compromising ambushes and surprise attacks. Matchlocks initially had great psychological impact against native peoples unfamiliar with firearms. The natives soon overcame their fear of the great smoke, noise, and flame from the matchlocks, and before long they were trading for or capturing these weapons for themselves. The matchlock was also far slower to load and fire than the longbow and the crossbow and could also not compete with them in terms of accuracy. There was also the concern of an accidental discharge. The matchlock's successors were the wheel lock and the far more reliable flintlock.

Further Reading

Blair, Claude, ed. *Pollard's History of Firearms.* New York: Macmillan, 1983.

Brown, M. L. *Firearms in Colonial America: The Impact on History and Technology, 1492–1792.* Washington, DC: Smithsonian Institution Press, 1980.

Lenk, Torsten. *The Flintlock: Its Origin and Development.* New York: Bramhall House, 1965.

Peterson, Harold L. *Arms and Armor in Colonial America, 1526–1783.* New York: Bramhall House, 1956.

Wheel Lock

The wheel lock was an improvement on the matchlock individual firearm. The sole difference was in the firing mechanism. The wheel lock may have been invented by Leonardo De Vinci around 1500. Drawings by him dating to about that time are its first known representation.

The lock ignited the charge by means of sparks from a piece of iron pyrite against a rotating wheel, very much as with a modern cigarette lighter. This new firing mechanism utilized a powerful spring. The gun fitted with a wheel lock was loaded in the usual manner, and the lock was spanned. The individual then placed a small amount of fine gunpowder (priming powder) in the priming pan. The pan cover was then closed either manually or by means of pressing a release button. The cock (an arm also known as the "dog-head") was then moved down so that the pyrites it held rested on the pan cover.

Pressing the trigger released the wheel, causing it to revolve. At the same time a cam on its spindle struck a lever attached to the pan cover, forcing it to slide forward. Also, the iron pyrites brushed against the rough-edged wheel as it turned. This action created a shower of sparks that ignited the exposed priming powder, which in turn touched off the main charge at the base of the bore, propelling the ball out of the barrel.

The great advantage of the wheel lock was that it did not have to rely on the slow match for ignition. The great expense of its mechanism meant, however, that it never completely supplanted the matchlock for military use.

Further Reading

Blair, Claude, ed. *Pollard's History of Firearms.* New York: Macmillan, 1983.

Brown, M. L. *Firearms in Colonial America: The Impact on History and Technology, 1492–1792.* Washington, DC: Smithsonian Institution Press, 1980.

Lenk, Torsten. *The Flintlock: Its Origin and Development.* New York: Bramhall House, 1965.

Peterson, Harold L. *Arms and Armor in Colonial America, 1526–1783.* New York: Bramhall House, 1956.

Snaplock (Snaphance)

Introduced in the mid-16th century, the snaplock (snaphance) was an important step forward in the development of individual firearms. The name was derived from the Dutch word *snaphaan* ("snapping hen").

The snaplock was a considerable improvement over the wheel lock and employed flint and steel for the first time. The snaplock consisted of a cock attached to a V-shaped mainspring, and a flat piece of steel (known as the frissen) pivoted vertically over the pan holding the priming powder. The cock was equipped with jaws to grip a piece of shaped pyrites or more often flint and was pulled back against a spring until held by a sear.

The snaplock was loaded in the same fashion as with the wheel lock. Pulling the trigger opened the pan cover, while at the same time the cock swung forward, scraping the flint against the face of the upright steel, pushing it forward and causing sparks to fall in the exposed pan below. This system, more reliable than the wheel lock, was the predecessor to the flintlock.

Further Reading

Blair, Claude, ed. *Pollard's History of Firearms.* New York: Macmillan, 1983.

Lenk, Torsten. *The Flintlock: Its Origin and Development.* New York: Bramhall House, 1965.

Pistols, Early Types

As a consequence of the introduction of gunpowder into Europe, in the late 14th and early 15th centuries a wide variety of individual hand "gonnes" appeared. Most were larger and evolved into the musket, but some were small enough to be classified as pistols. The true pistol came about with the introduction of the wheel lock, which made possible firing the weapon with one hand. The name, which was in common use in England in the 1540s, may have evolved from the term *pistolese,* a dagger made in Pistola in northern Italy that in France and England was known as a *pistolet.*

Pistols employing the wheel lock firing mechanism were certainly in use by the 1540s, and the snaplock appeared in English pistols by 1580. The final step in the evolution of early pistols was the flintlock (see separate entries on firing processes). All employed the same loading process as their counterpart longer firearms.

The first pistols were used by the military and civilians for personal defense, for hunting from horseback, and above all as a cavalry weapon. The Thirty Years' War (1618–1648) in Europe saw a great increase in pistol production. Pistols were especially favored for the close-in fighting at which cavalry actions occurred and in which accuracy was not an overriding factor. Pistols were also far easier to withdraw from saddle holsters and fire than were muskets. Often cavalrymen carried the pistols in pairs.

Pistols were also popular aboard ship for boarding an enemy vessel or to repel boarders from one's own vessel. Pistols intended for naval use often were designed with a belt hook, an iron clip on the left-hand side of the stock.

Pistols came to be the favored individual firearm for officers and also were often used in duels, commonplace to settle "affairs of honor" among gentlemen of the time. The second half of the 18th century saw the production in England of precisely manufactured dueling pistols.

Pistols appeared in a bewildering array of sizes and styles. They generally ranged in bore size of from .45 caliber to .62 caliber. Some early pistols were as much as .80 caliber. Barrel length, at first as long as 20–25 inches, was reduced in the course of the 17th century to 15–18 inches. It continued to decrease in the 18th century. Those pistols with the shortest barrels were known as pocket pistols. They had barrel lengths of up to 5 inches and an overall length of only 7–9 inches. The English light dragoons pistol that appeared around 1759 had a 9-inch barrel, while that of the heavy dragoons pistol was 12 inches. Most pistols were single-shot firing, but multiple-shot pistols were also manufactured. Coachmen utilized blunderbuss pistols with large bores and flared muzzles for close-in defensive work.

Most pistols were muzzle-loaders, but their small size made breechloaders possible, and from circa 1640 to 1850 there were turn-off pistols in which the barrel simply screwed off. The pistol was then loaded and the barrel screwed back in place.

Further Reading

Blair, Claude, ed. *Pollard's History of Firearms.* New York: Macmillan, 1985.

Kinard, Jeff. *Pistols: An Illustrated History of Their Impact.* Santa Barbara, CA: ABC-CLIO, 2003.

Land Artillery, Early Gunpowder Types

The term "artillery" first applied to military stores. Over time it came to denote larger weapons of war, such as catapults and siege engines, and then evolved to cover the largest crew-served weapons on the battlefield. Today, artillery includes large guns, mortars, howitzers, and certain types of unguided rockets and guided missiles. The term "gun" defines a strongly constructed metal tube used to project destructive projectiles by means of the increasing pressure of gases from fired gunpowder or other propellant. The word "cannon" dates to the 13th century and is derived from the Latin *canna* (meaning "reed" or "tube").

Modern artillery sprang from the introduction into Europe of gunpowder. Although it had been used as an explosive propellant in China since the 11th century, gunpowder did not arrive in Europe until the first half of the 13th century. The earliest known documentary evidence of gunpowder artillery appears in illustrations in two manuscripts written by Walter de Milimete dating from 1326 that show a soldier extending a heated metal rod to the touchhole of a large vase-shaped artillery piece that has an arrow projectile extending from its muzzle. The artillery piece itself was positioned on a fixed wooden support.

The first guns were probably employed against castles and other fixed fortifications. Part of the effectiveness of these early "thunder boxes" was in the fearsome noise they made when fired. The first use of cannon in European warfare cannot be dated with certainty, but they may have been used by the English against the Scots in 1327 and in the Battle of Crécy against the French in 1346. The English certainly employed them in their siege of Calais the next year.

Increased caliber and length of the early cannon led to them being made in the fashion of wooden barrels, with iron bars forged together to make a tube, the whole strengthened by metal hoops (hence the origin of the term of "gun barrel"). Such early guns tended to be breechloaders, with a separate powder chamber loaded with gunpowder wedged or screwed in place. Imperfect sealing, given the state of metallurgy of the day, made the early guns very dangerous to those employing

Mons Meg, a large bombard cannon presented to King James II in 1457 and today housed at Edinburgh castle. Mons Meg is 15 feet in length and weighs more than 15,000 pounds. It has a 20-inch bore and fired shot weighing some 400 pounds. (iStockPhoto)

them, and the breechloaders soon gave way to muzzle-loaders, the standard for gunpowder artillery until the late 19th century.

Cast guns also replaced those of wrought iron. The two favored metals were bronze and iron. Bronze, a mixture of copper and a little tin, had the chief advantage of greater tensile strength. Far less likely to crack or burst than the less flexible iron, it was also lighter than iron and thus easier to transport, a major factor in land combat. Through the period of the muzzle-loader, bronze was the favored material for field guns.

Perhaps the earliest known example of a gunpowder weapon is in the military museum in Stockholm. This "gunpowder bottle" dates from the 14th century and is 12 inches long and of 1.5-inch caliber (bore diameter). Among famous larger early artillery pieces are one of 35-inch caliber dating from about 1430 in the War Museum in Vienna; a cannon known as *Dulle Griet,* 16 feet in length and of 25-inch caliber bore and dating from 1414, at Ghent; and the so-called *Mons Meg,* reportedly made in Mons during the period 1461–1483 and located at Edinburgh Castle, Scotland. Fifteen feet long, *Mons Meg* fired a 330-pound stone shot and was reportedly charged with 105 pounds of powder.

Projectiles also evolved, from arrows to hand-hewn round stone balls and then balls cast of lead and finally of iron. Solid projectiles remained the rule, although explosive shell—always a danger to the crews firing it in the early period—was projected from mortars. The great variety of types and calibers of the early guns made it virtually impossible to maintain a rational system of ammunition, which had to be prepared for each gun individually. Beginning in the 16th century, artillery came to be standardized by caliber, and the many names gave way to denomination by weight of shot fired. Thus, a 24-pounder fired a ball weighing 24 pounds. Artillery was also divided into two main types: field and siege. The lighter of the two, field guns were utilized by armies in open warfare, while the heavier and less mobile siege guns were used to reduce fortresses.

Further Reading

Hogg, Ivan V. *A History of Artillery.* Astronaut House, Feltham, Middlesex, UK: Hamlyn Publishing Group, 1974.

Jobé, Joseph. *Guns: An Illustrated History of Artillery.* New York: Crescent Books, 1971.

Leather Gun

The leather gun was an important but short-lived artillery innovation. While cannon soon became essential on the battlefield, the weight of the individual guns was often so great that they were limited largely to siege operations. The great military reformer and artillerist Swedish king Gustav II Adolf (r. 1611–1632), known as Gustavus Adolphus, standardized the sizes of cannon and shot in his army. He also produced the first lightweight artillery, the leather gun of 1626.

The leather gun, which proved highly important in Gustavus's Polish campaign of 1628–1629, was invented by Colonel Melchior Wurmbrandt. This regimental gun was not of leather but consisted of a copper tube that was tightly wound with wire or cord, the whole then wrapped in leather. This reduced the total weight of the 3-pounder gun itself to only about 90 pounds. With its carriage, the leather gun was highly mobile and could easily accompany infantry in the field. It played an important role in the Swedish victories in the Thirty Years' War (1618–1648).

The Scots also employed leather guns to good effect against the English in 1640. Lighter guns sacrificed safety, however, and this soon led to their abandonment in favor of heavier, but safer, artillery pieces.

Further Reading

Downey, Fairfax. *Cannonade: Great Artillery Actions of History; The Famous Cannons and the Master Gunners.* New York: Doubleday, 1966.

Peterson, Harold L. *Round Shot and Rammers.* Harrisburg, PA: Stackpole, 1969.

Rogers, H. C. B. *A History of Artillery.* Secaucus, NJ: Citadel Press, 1975.

Fuzes

The fuze is the means by which military explosive ordnance such as artillery shells, hand grenades, bombs, and mines are detonated. The earliest fuzes consisted of trains of combustible material to ignite the main charge, while modern fuzes detonate on contact, trigger at a set time, or are triggered by an internal sensor, such as radar or infrared.

The first fuzes, employed in petards and hand grenades and later in mortars and artillery shells, consisted of a train of fine gunpowder. Early fuzes were quite unreliable, however, leading to an understandable reluctance on the part of artillerymen to fire explosive shell. Initially, the fuze had to be lit while the projectile was still in the bore. Then the weapon was fired. This was a dangerous process called firing with two strokes in which timing was absolutely critical to avoid a bore detonation. Gunners eventually discovered that if they did not light the fuze before firing the projectile, the hot gases in the bore would ignite the fuze anyway. This much safer and more reliable procedure was called firing with one stroke. The powder train fuze reached a certain peak of efficiency in the Bormann fuze, widely employed by the Union Army in the American Civil War.

At the same time, percussion fuzes came into use. These exploded on impact, perhaps utilizing the shock of the projectile striking an object to unite a heat source with the shell's main charge.

World War I requirements for different types of fuzes for aircraft bombs, hand grenades, and artillery shells of different types led to further developmental efforts. Small spinning vanes or propellers served to fuze bombs as they dropped through the air; others operated on striking the target. These remained in widespread use through World War II. Percussion fuzes came to be known during World War II as point detonating (PD) fuzes. Some PD fuzes could be set so as to explode the charge on a slight delay in order to allow the shell or bomb to penetrate and produce a subsurface burst. Mechanical time fuzes were used to produce an airburst in order to scatter fragments against a ground target below, especially troops in the open or, according to tables, against aircraft at set altitude above Earth. The time fuze was particularly difficult, as much depended on the skill of the forward observer and the ability to gauge the proper height of burst over the ground target. In 1943 the United States introduced the proximity or variable time fuze, which utilized a small radar transmitter and receiver unit to set off the shell.

Most modern fuzes fall into four basic categories. Point detonating fuzes detonate on impact or after a preset delay. Time fuzes detonate (or inactivate) at a set time, using either mechanical or electronic timers. Proximity fuzes are set to detonate at a given distance from the target, using various combinations of sensors, including radar, active sonar, passive acoustic, infrared, magnetic, photoelectric, seismic, or television cameras. Barometric fuzes detonate at a preset altitude above sea level or depth below sea level.

Further Reading

Bull, Stephen. *Encyclopedia of Military Technology and Innovation.* Westport, CT: Greenwood, 2004.

Hogg, Ivan V. *A History of Artillery.* Astronaut House, Feltham, Middlesex, UK: Hamlyn Publishing Group, 1974.

Tucker, Spencer C. *Arming the Fleet: U.S. Navy Ordnance in the Muzzle-Loading Era.* Annapolis, MD: Naval Institute Press, 1989.

Petard

The forerunner of today's satchel charge, a petard was an explosive device, generally employed to blast a hole in a gate or fortification. In use by the 16th century, it was originally a pot-shaped container that held perhaps five to six pounds of gunpowder. The petard had a fuze that would be lit by a sapper or military engineer. The term "petard" probably originated from the French verb *péter* (meaning "to break wind").

It required great personal bravery for engineers, often under enemy fire, to run to the location with a petard, fix it in place, light the fuze, and retreat. Often, engineers died from their own explosive devices. The expression "hoisted by one's own petard" comes from William Shakespeare's play "Hamlet" and referred to an engineer (sapper) blown up by his own bomb. The expression means a designed plan has backfired on its maker.

Further Reading

Peterson, Harold L. *Round Shot and Rammers.* Harrisburg, PA: Stackpole, 1969.

Wagner, E. *European Weapons and Warfare, 1618–1648.* London: Octopus, 1979.

Pike

The pike, a poled weapon, was the longest pole arm and was widely employed in the late Middle Ages and the early modern period, especially the 17th century when massed pikemen protected musketeers against cavalry attack while the musketeers were reloading. The standard length for the spear-shaped pike was 16 feet, which is as long as the *sarissa* employed in the Macedonian phalanx during the 4th century BCE. Some pikes were as long as 22 feet, and others were shorter, cut down by the soldiers who wielded them to make them easier to carry. The head of the pike was of iron, but owing to the great length, its shaft was of a strong wood, often ash, reinforced with two steel strips down the sides.

Pikes were inexpensive to make, and soldiers required little training in their use. The great length of the pike made it unwieldy for close combat, however. As a consequence, pikemen often carried swords to use if their ranks were broken. Pikes were employed en masse, in large hedgehog phalanx formations, the pikes projecting in the direction of an anticipated cavalry attack. Cavalry was the offensive arm, while pikemen were the primary means of defending against it. The pike reached its greatest effectiveness in the Spanish *tercio* formation, which employed pikemen in the center and harquebusiers on the flanks.

The pike proved unwieldy and ineffective in the woodlands of North America and was soon largely discarded there, but it remained in service in Europe until the advent of the bayonet and the improving effectiveness of the musket. A bayonet attached to the muzzle end of a musket made every musketeer his own pikeman. Pikes survived only as symbols of authority and were often used to carry regimental colors.

Further Reading

Blackmore, D. *Arms & Armour of the English Civil War.* London: Royal Armouries, 1990.

Foulkes, C., and E. C. Hopkinson. *Sword, Lance and Bayonet.* London: Arms and Armour, 1967.

Carrack

Type of sailing ship. By the end of the 12th century, twin-masted (mainmast and foremast) lateen-rigged ships were common in the Mediterranean. In Northern Europe, twin-masted ships also appeared in the early 15th century but with the addition of a third, after or mizzen, mast. This ship type was known in England as a carrack, in France as the *caraque,* in the Netherlands as the *kraeck.* The term is believed to have derived from Arabic.

Mary Rose

The *Mary Rose* was an English carrack. Constructed at Portsmouth in 1509 and named for King Henry VIII's sister Mary and the Tudor rose, it weighed some 700 tons, was 147 feet in overall length by 38 feet 3 inches in beam, and mounted 81 guns.

The *Mary Rose* served as the English flagship in Henry VIII's wars against the French in 1522 and 1536. In the course of the third war in 1545, the French sent a large number of ships to Portsmouth. Preparing to meet the French on July 19, the *Mary Rose* took aboard a large number of soldiers. The ship's normal crew was 415 men, but there may have been 700 men on board that day, many in armor and most of them on the main and castle decks. This extra weight high in the ship, combined with the ship's high bow and after-castle and weighty cannon there, made the *Mary Rose* unstable. Sailing out with other English ships against the French, the *Mary Rose* caught a light wind and suddenly heeled over. Water then rushed in through the ship's open gun ports, and it went down.

The wreck in the Solent was rediscovered in 1968, and what remained was raised in 1982. The ship and its artifacts have proved to be incredible sources of information about the Tudor period. For instance, 137 longbows and 3,500 arrows were recovered, the only ones to survive from that period. The ship and its contents are today displayed in a special museum at the Portsmouth Naval Base.

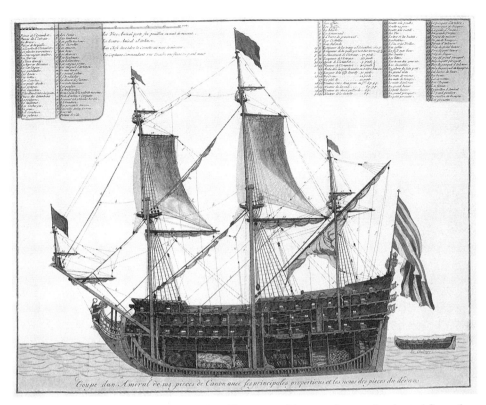

Woodcut of an armed Genoese carrack, a European ship type that predominated from the fourteenth to the seventeenth centuries. (Historical Picture Archive/Corbis)

The carrack predominated in Europe from the 14th to 17th centuries. The earliest types had a rounded stern in a carvel-built hull (planks flush rather than overlapping). The ships were rigged with square sails on the fore and mainmast and a lateen sail on the mizzen. A centerline ladder led to the round top of the mainmast. By the 16th century, the carrack had become a larger vessel of up to 125 feet in overall length by about 34 feet in beam. It also gained a fourth mast aft: an extra mizzen, known as the bonaventure mizzen or bonaventure for short.

Traditionally, in time of war merchant ships were simply fitted out to carry weaponry. With the introduction of gunpowder weapons at sea in the 14th century, the carrack's armament might range from as few as 18 small guns to as many as 56, some of them placed in the tops of the masts (the "fighting tops" as they became known). The carrack had considerable advantage as a gunship over the rowed galley, which mounted only a few guns forward. Because fighting at sea was very much like that at land, the higher structures fore and aft, which might actually be built up in time of war to gain height advantage, were known as the castles: the forecastle and aftercastle.

Further Reading

Howard, Frank. *Sailing Ships of War, 1400–1860.* New York: Mayflower Books, 1979.

Kihlberg, Bengt, ed. *The Lore of Ships.* New York: Crescent Books, 1986.

Landström, Björn. *The Ship: An Illustrated History.* Garden City, NY: Doubleday, 1961.

Galleon

A revolutionary 16th-century vessel, the galleon was a large sailing ship that offered great improvements over the earlier carrack and was widely adopted by the navies of Western Europe. The term "galleon" itself has become virtually synonymous with any vessel of the late medieval/early modern period, even though it was a Spanish term for a particular type of ship. The word "galleon" comes from the Latin *galea* (galley) through the Old French *galion*.

Despite the Spanish name, galleons were developed and first constructed in England during the later 16th century based on experiments by Sir John Hawkins. While the English did not call these ships galleons, they did develop the ship's layout. The hull featured a high, squared stern and a low forecastle set back from the stem with a prominent beakhead just above the waterline, which gave the vessel its characteristic shape and facilitated ramming. The hull was both long and

The *Golden Hinde* under sail. The ship is a reproduction of the galleon employed by Sir Francis Drake to circumnavigate the globe during 1577-1580. (Joel W. Rogers/Corbis)

slender and carried multiple masts. It sat higher above the water and was faster and easier to navigate than earlier vessels designed for the same purpose.

Galleons could be heavily armed. Rows of gun ports were cut into each side of the galleon's hull. It had been discovered much earlier in the 16th century that by cutting out ports and placing guns beneath the main deck, a ship could carry many more guns of a greater weight without destabilizing the vessel. Guns were also placed in positions that enabled them to fire directly ahead or astern the galleon. The typical Elizabethan galleon carried some 50 guns of various sizes and had a crew of some 250 men. It was approximately 135 feet in length (keel of 100 feet) and 38 feet in width. An example of the galleon is the English *Revenge* of 1577.

The galleon design proved superior to previous ships, and its use spread throughout Western Europe. Spain also built 20 galleons to participate in the armada sent against England in 1588. The galleon continued to be a mainstay in Western navies for years thereafter and established the basic design for the great ships of the line that would follow it.

Further Reading

Cipolla, Carlo M. *Guns, Sails, and Empires.* New York: Pantheon Books, 1965.

Kemp, Peter, ed. *The Oxford Companion to Ships and the Sea.* Oxford: Oxford University Press, 1988.

Rodger, N. A. M. *The Safeguard of the Sea: A Naval History of Britain,* Vol. 1, *660–1649.* London: HarperCollins, 1997.

Naval Artillery, Early Types

For 2,000 years until the appearance of cannon in the 14th century, the principal object at sea was to close with an opposing vessel and destroy it by ramming or take it by storm. The introduction of gunpowder artillery changed that.

Early naval cannon were small, averaging 20–40 pounds in weight, and were essentially man killers, part of an antipersonnel arsenal that included bows, crossbows, swords, pikes, cutlasses, and spears. They probably resembled the bombards used ashore—short weapons with wide bell mouths—and were probably positioned in a ship's rails. Later guns were made longer and heavier. The advent of heavy guns aboard ship meant that it was possible to stand off and engage an enemy vessel without actually having to close with it. Soon cannon became a warship's raison d'être, exercising tremendous influence on ship design.

The first use of guns at sea is unknown, although there may have been a few in the Battle of Sluys on June 24, 1340, during the Hundred Years' War between France and England (1337–1453). They were definitely employed on warships in 1376 when the Venetians bombarded the ports of Zara and Cattaro.

The earliest naval guns were breechloaders. They did not have to be hauled back into battery after firing and could thus be reloaded more quickly than muzzle-loaders. They could also be worked with fewer men. The basic problem with early breechloaders was the lack of adequate sealing of gases at the breech and the danger this posed to crews during firing. Improvements in gunpowder also hastened the change to muzzle-loaders, which could withstand heavier charges.

Muzzle-loaders were cast in both bronze and iron. Bronze was favored because it stood the shock of discharge better than iron. If defective, bronze was more likely to bulge than burst, and it was easier to cast. Bronze guns could also be easily re-cast when worn. Iron was heavier—not the factor at sea as on land with field artillery—but was far cheaper by a factor of as much as 4:1, and cost won out. By the end of the 17th century, iron guns predominated in European navies.

Late-16th-century muzzle-loaders were of three basic types: culverin, cannon, and perier (petrero, pedrero, or cannon pedro). Culverins were the biggest and heaviest and could project shot the farthest. They were some 30 calibers (bore diameters) in length. Because of its bore-to-length ratio, the culverin was the predecessor of the modern naval gun. Cannon were perhaps 15–20 calibers in length. Periers (or "stone throwers") were 16 to 8 or less calibers in length. These included petards, mortars, and howitzers. It is, however, quite impossible to categorize early guns. One source identified some 40 different types in 1588, and his is not an exhaustive list.

Guns were positioned in their carriage by means of lugs, known as trunnions, cast on the sides of the gun. The common ship carriage had four wooden wheels, or trucks. It was secured in place and moved about by stout rope breeching and tackle. The truck carriage remained little changed from the 16th to the 19th centuries.

Further Reading

Hogg, Ivan, and John Batchelor. *Naval Gun.* Poole, Dorset, UK: Blandford, 1978.

Padfield, Peter. *Guns at Sea.* New York: St. Martin's, 1974.

Robertson, Frederick L. *The Evolution of Naval Armament.* London: Harold T. Storey, 1968.

Tucker, Spencer C. *Arming the Fleet: U.S. Navy Ordnance in the Muzzle-Loading Era.* Annapolis, MD: Naval Institute Press, 1989.

Gunner's Quadrant

Early cannon were hardly accurate. Gunners might sight along the barrel, but doing so gave a slight elevation because of the greater diameter of the gun at breech than the muzzle. Raised sights at the muzzle end helped compensate for this.

In the 16th century, however, the gunner's quadrant appeared. Employed on land and sea, it enabled the guns of a battery to be laid all at the same elevation. Made of wood or brass and essentially a level, the quadrant was a long L in shape with a quarter circle marked in 10ths of degrees at the base of the L. The long arm of the quadrant was placed in the barrel, and a weighed plumb bob from the juncture of the L then provided a reading of the elevation by noting where the plumb line crossed the marks on the arc. At sea where a reading in degrees less than horizontal might be required, the quadrant might take the form of a full half circle at the end of the arm.

Although firing tables were soon developed that provided estimates of range depending on charge and elevation, firing was very inexact, and gunners preferred to operate at very close or point-blank range. Distant firing was very inexact, and the longer the range, the greater the possibility of error. Cannon powder could vary in power as much as 20 percent. The great windage (the difference between the diameter of the projectile and the diameter of the bore) of early guns also meant that the projectile bounced down the bore (known as balloting) and might leave the gun at any direction, determined by the last bounce before departing the muzzle. Projectiles also drifted in flight, depending on the wind and atmospheric conditions. It is little wonder, then, that firing at long range was referred to as "at random."

With the advent of rifled breech-loading cannon and uniform production methods for projectiles and propellant, long-range indirect fire became more effective, which required very precise measurements of the tube's angle of elevation. The modern gunner's quadrant remains to this day an essential piece of fire-control equipment on the artillery pieces of most nations. The modern gunner's quadrant is an adjustable clinometer that is placed on precision-machined pads on the breech of the gun and set to the desired angle. As the gun is elevated, the proper angle of elevation is indicated by the gunner quadrant's leveling bubble. Modern gunner's quadrants are calibrated in mils, with 17.777 mils to the degree.

Further Reading

Peterson, Harold L. *Round Shot and Rammers.* Harrisburg, PA: Stackpole, 1969.

Tucker, Spencer C. *Arming the Fleet: U.S. Navy Ordnance in the Muzzle-Loading Era.* Annapolis, MD: Naval Institute Press, 1989.

Turtle Ships

The *kobukson* (turtle) ships were the world's first armored warships. Ordered constructed in 1591 by Korean admiral Yi Sun Sin to meet a Japanese threat from the sea, the first of these vessels was launched just days before the Japanese invasion of Korea in April 1592. Yi then trained his men in the new warships, which then played a leading role in the Japanese-Korean War of 1592–1598.

Sufficiently detailed descriptions of the vessels survive to provide a fairly complete picture of their appearance. They were about 116 feet in length and 28 feet in beam. They had a raft-like rectangular-shaped hull, a transom bow and stern, and a superstructure supporting two masts, each with a square rectangular mat sail. A carved wooden dragon head was set at the bow.

The ships were powered by both sail and oar, with openings for 8–10 oars on each side of the superstructure. The oars provided additional speed and maneuverability. The superstructure was protected by a curved iron-plated top that gave the vessel a turtle shell–like appearance. The iron plating had spikes set in it to prevent an enemy crew from boarding. The ships also mounted a number of cannon, six on each side and several at the bow and stern. The *kobukson* proved highly effective in combat with the Japanese.

Further Reading

Galuppini, Gino. *Warships of the World: An Illustrated Encyclopedia.* New York: Military Press, 1989.

Turnbull, Stephen R. *Fighting Ships of the Far East (2): Japan and Korea, 612–1639.* Buffalo, MN: Osprey, 2003.

A model of American David Bushnell's submarine, the *Turtle*, employed against British in New York Harbor on the night of September 6-7, 1776. The model is at the Science Museum, London. (SSPL/Getty Images)

Frigate

Frigates were important warships in the age of sail. Of obscure Italian origin, the term "frigate" was apparently first attached to certain small, fast British ships of the 1640s modeled on Dunkerque privateers. By the 18th century, the term "frigate" had come to mean a square-rigged medium-sized warship with broadside artillery on one full gun deck and lighter pieces on the forecastle and spar deck.

Frigates proved useful for a wide array of missions, including scouting, screening, raiding, and escorting merchantmen. In the Royal Navy of the era, frigates carried from 22 to 38 guns, generally 18-pounders. Early frigates usually displaced from 500 to 1,000 tons, were constructed of weaker hull scantlings than were ships of the line, and were manned by smaller crews (generally of 200 to 400 men). Hence, frigates were much cheaper to build and operate, although they were too weak to stand in the line of battle.

During the French Revolutionary and Napoleonic Wars (1792–1815), British frigates often cruised on detached duty looking for enemy shipping. British

The U.S. Navy frigate *Constitution* depicted saluting George Washington's birthday during a port call at Malta in 1837. The *Constitution*, easily the most famous ship of the U.S. Navy, remains in commission at Boston and is the world's oldest warship still afloat. (United States Navy)

frigates compiled an enviable record against their foreign counterparts, taking or destroying 235 enemy ships from 1793 to 1812 while losing only 6 of their own to hostile action. The successes of the large U.S. superfrigates, such as the 44-gun *Constitution,* proved especially shocking and led the Royal Navy to develop larger frigates of its own mounting 24-pounder guns.

With the introduction of steam propulsion in the mid-19th century, a number of navies built steam frigates, some large and powerful. For example, vessels of the U.S. Merrimack class displaced 4,650 tons and were armed with 40 8- and 9-inch shell guns.

Shortly after the American Civil War, the term "frigate" fell into disuse. With the introduction of armor plate, the successor to the frigate was dubbed the cruiser, a designation in common usage by the 1880s. Then in World War II, the classification "frigate" was resurrected for a quite different type of warship: the oceangoing antisubmarine escort. The first of these were the 27 ships of the River class (2,000 tons and 20 knots). Although they carried an armament (two 4-inch guns and 150 depth charges) quite similar to that of the new destroyer escort type, frigates were designed to the lesser mercantile standards. By the end of the war, British and Commonwealth yards finished another 157 ships of the Loch and Bay classes. The

U.S. Navy constructed 98 similar vessels of the Ashville and Tacoma types (officially rated as patrol frigates).

Following World War II the term "frigate" mutated once again, with most navies
continuing to use the classification for oceangoing escorts smaller than a destroyer.
These could be sizable ships; some Soviet and British examples were as big as
World War II large destroyers.

Beginning in 1955, the U.S. Navy reclassified its large destroyers (or destroyer
leaders) as frigates, thereby commemorating the proud role that these warships had
played in the early American sailing navy. The principal mission of these Cold War
frigates was to escort fast carriers, and for that duty they carried extensive radar
suites and antiaircraft missile batteries. Some of these ships were big, such as the
7,900-ton Belknap class or, at the extreme, the nuclear-powered California class of
over 10,000 tons. In 1975, the U.S. Navy conformed to the more usual practice by
reclassifying its frigates as cruisers and its oceangoing escorts (such as the Perry
class of 3,500 tons) as frigates.

Further Reading

Gardiner, Robert. *Frigates of the Napoleonic Wars.* Annapolis, MD: Naval Institute Press,
2000.

Lavery, Brian. *Nelson's Navy: The Ships, Men and Organisation, 1793–1815.* Annapolis,
MD: Naval Institute Press, 1989.

Muir, Malcolm, Jr. *Black Shoes and Blue Water: Surface Warfare in the United States Navy,
1945–1975.* Washington, DC: Naval Historical Center, 1996.

Tucker, Spencer C. *Handbook of 19th Century Naval Warfare.* Stroud, UK: Sutton, 2000.

Ship of the Line

Ships of the line also known as liners, battleships of the line, or line of battleships,
were the largest and most powerful warships of the age of fighting sail. Such vessels were heavily armed, expensive, and complex and carried the greatest national
prestige. They were so-named because, with up to 30 inches of wooden planking
protection against enemy cannon fire, they were capable of standing in the main
battle line that characterized fleet engagements of the time. Ships of the line were
three-masted, square-rigged vessels of two to four gun decks. More than 200 feet
in length and 50 feet in beam, they carried crews of 600–800 men. By way of illustration, HMS *Victory* is 227 feet overall (186 feet on the gun deck) and 52 feet
in beam and displaces 3,500 tons. In 1805 it mounted 104 guns (30 32-pounders,
28 24-pounders, 44 12-pounders, and 2 68-pounder carronades).

The bigger the ship, the more expensive it was to build, and thus in 1789 a British 100-gun ship cost £24.10.0 per ton, a 74-gun ship cost £20.4.0, a 36-gun ship
cost £14.7.0, and a sloop only £12.3.0. Conversely, larger warships were less expensive to maintain per gun than smaller vessels.

The *Victory*

The Royal Navy ship of the line *Victory* of 1778 is the oldest warship in the world still in commission and one of the most famous museum ships. The first-rate three-deck *Victory* was laid down in 1759. Launched at Chatham in 1765, it was commissioned in 1778. Displacing approximately 4,000 tons fully loaded, it measures 328 feet overall, with a beam of 52 feet. Its mainmast is 203 feet tall. The *Victory*'s crew complement at the Battle of Trafalgar in October 1805 was 850 officers and men. Armament consisted of 30 32-pounders, 28 24-pounders, 30 12-pounders, 12 quarterdeck 12-pounders, and 2 68-pounder carronades.

The *Victory* participated in fighting against France and Spain in the American Revolutionary War and the French Revolutionary and Napoleonic Wars. After two years as a hospital ship and two years of refit, it was recommissioned in 1801. The *Victory*'s most famous action was undoubtedly as Vice Admiral Horatio Nelson's flagship in the Battle of Trafalgar in October 1805. In 1922 the *Victory* was moved to Portsmouth Naval Shipyard, where it was dry-docked and then restored as a museum ship to its Trafalgar appearance. The *Victory* is still manned by an active-duty Royal Navy crew and flies the White Ensign of a commissioned Royal Navy ship.

By the time of the French Revolution the smallest ships of the line carried 64 guns, although there were those who believed the smallest that could effectively stand in the line of battle was one rated at 74 guns. The largest first-rate ships of the line mounted 120 guns, although a few could carry more. But the workhorse ship of the line at the end of the century was the 74. On the eve of the wars of the French Revolution three-quarters of French Navy ships of the line were 74s, with the remainder being those rated at 80 guns and the three-deckers.

At the turn of the century there was a trend toward larger ships of the line. The world's only four-decker, the Spanish *Santísima Trinidad,* carried 136 guns. The largest ship in the Royal Navy at the end of 1793 was the French-built *Commerce de Marseilles,* a 120-gun behemoth taken during the British capture of Toulon in 1793.

Most navies possessed ships of the line, but the U.S. Navy had none in active service until after the War of 1812. The *Independence,* launched in 1814, was the first American ship of the line apart from the *America,* which was given to France upon its completion in 1782 and thus technically was never in U.S. service. The *Pennsylvania,* laid down in 1822 and completed in 1837, was the largest U.S. Navy sailing vessel and for a time the largest in the world. Originally designed for 136 guns, its initial armament was 16 8-inch shell guns and 104 32-pounders.

Although obsolete by the second half of the 19th century, the wooden battle ship of the line evolved into and gave its name to the steam-propelled steel-armored battleship.

The first-rate British ship of the line *Victory*, launched in 1765. The oldest warship still in commission, it may be seen at the Portsmouth Navy Yard in England. (Hulton-Deutsch Collection/Corbis)

Further Reading

Howard, Frank. *Sailing Ships of War, 1400–1860*. London: Conway Maritime, 1979.

Lambert, Andrew. *The Last Sailing Battlefleet: Maintaining Naval Mastery, 1815–1850*. London: Conway Maritime, 1991.

Lavery, Brian. *The Ship of the Line: Design, Construction, and Fittings*. 2 vols. London: Conway Maritime, 1983.

Lavery, Brian, ed. *The Line of Battle: The Sailing Warship, 1650–1840*. London: Conway Maritime, 1992.

Mortars, Early

Mortars are high-angle–fire muzzle-loading weapons designed for plunging fire to surmount obstacles such as fortress walls. Mortars utilize explosive shell. Along with guns and howitzers, mortars form the triad of artillery types. The first mortars were short, only two to four times the diameter of the bore. Most were of bronze, although some were cast in iron. Mortars had powder chambers at the base of the bore for their powder charge. Cast with trunnions (pivot) at the base, mortars were usually fixed to fire at a 45-degree angle, with range determined by the amount of the powder charge. The charge was considerably less than that for long guns, as was the windage (the difference between the diameters of the bore and the projectile). Range was adjusted by varying the amount of the powder charge.

To fire the mortar, a set amount of loose powder was measured into it and positioned in the powder chamber at the base of the bore. A shell was then loaded into the mortar. The larger heavy-round projectiles might have a ring to facilitate their loading. The shell was positioned so that the fuze faced the top of the bore. Placing the fuze against the powder chamber might cause its malfunctioning on firing. If the fuze was toward the muzzle, it was lit by means of linstock or port-fire, just before the main charge was lit and the shell lofted into the air. Ultimately gunners learned that windage allowed some of the charge to escape around the shell and ignite the fuze. This greatly reduced the hazard for the gunners.

Mortars varied greatly in size. In the 18th-century British Army they ranged from the small 4.5-inch coehorn mortar that could be transported by two men in 5.8-, 8-, 10-, and 13-inch models for siege work.

The coehorn was named for its inventor, Dutch captain and later general Menno van Coehoorn (1641–1704). It was first employed in the siege of Grave in 1674. The mortar was subsequently widely used by the English, who called it the coehorn. Designed to direct plunging shell fire into an enemy works, it was set in a fixed wooden mount at 45 degrees elevation, with range adjusted by varying the amount of the powder charge. The British coehorn mortar of the late 18th and early 19th centuries was a 4.5-inch–caliber weapon, 13 inches in overall length. It weighed 86 pounds and could be transported by two men by means of carrying handles on each side of the wooden mount.

The British also apparently employed very small 2.25- and 3.5-inch mortars for projecting hand grenades, although these were not listed in official armament. The largest British mortar ever was a 36-inch built-up model intended for the siege of Sebastopol in the Crimean War (1854–1856), but it was completed too late for the war and remains at Woolwich Arsenal.

Mortars were also employed aboard ship for shore bombardment. They were carried aboard special vessels known as bomb ketches (or bombs). Sea mortars, even heavier than those commonly employed on land, were mounted on strong wooden beds and usually fixed at a 45-degree elevation. Commonly the beds turned on vertical pivots. Some mortars were fixed in place; these were turned by moving the ship, usually by springs attached to the anchor cables. Since most mortars were fixed in elevation, range was adjusted by altering the charge.

The most common sea mortars in the 18th- and early-19th-century Royal Navy and U.S. Navy were of 10- and 13-inch bore size. The 13-inch mortar was a formidable weapon; weighing 5 tons, with its maximum powder charge of 20 pounds it could throw its 196-pound shell as far as 4,200 yards in 31 seconds. During the American Civil War (1861–1865) the U.S. Navy employed this same size mortar, although of newer model, against Confederate land forts, especially along the Mississippi River, although with mixed result.

Further Reading

Caruana, Adrian B. *The History of English Sea Ordnance,* Vols. 1 and 2. Ashley Lodge, Rotherfield, East Sussex, UK: Jean Boudriot Publications, 1994, 1997.

Hogg, Ivan V. *A History of Artillery.* Astronaut House, Feltham, Middlesex, UK: Hamlyn Publishing Group, 1974.

Peterson, Harold L. *Round Shot and Rammers.* Harrisburg, PA: Stackpole, 1969.

Tucker, Spencer C. *Arming the Fleet: U.S. Navy Ordnance in the Muzzle-Loading Era.* Annapolis, MD: Naval Institute Press, 1989.

Bomb Vessels

Bomb vessels were early shore bombardment vessels. The first bomb vessel may have been the French *galiote à bombe.* Based on the Dutch *galeote* or *galliot,* it was short in length and broad in beam and was an ideal gun platform. The French employed five of them to shell Algiers in 1682. These specially designed vessels were known in England as bomb ketches, bomb brigs, bombards, or bombs. In both the Royal Navy and the U.S. Navy, they were given names of volcanoes (such as *Aetna* and *Hecla*) or names that were expressive of their might (such as *Thunder* and *Spitfire*).

The ketch was a two-masted square-rigged vessel. Its mainmast was nearly amidships and had a course and square topsail and topgallant as well as a gaff sail. The mizzenmast carried the square sails of the ship and also a spanker. In appearance the ketch looked like a ship that was missing the foremast. This left the forward portion essentially clear for the mortar(s).

Bomb ketches were strongly built and fitted with more riders than any other vessel, a reinforcement needed to sustain the shock from the discharge of the heavy mortars they carried. Originally about 100 tons and 60–70 feet in length of deck, they were shallow-draft vessels requiring only about 8–10 feet of water, which allowed them to maneuver close to shore. Early-19th-century bomb ketches were larger—about 300 tons, 92 feet in length of deck, 27.5 feet in breadth, and 12 feet in depth of hold. When loaded, they drew about 12 feet of water.

The danger of explosions aboard bomb vessels led to special precautions in their construction. These included bulkheads of planks between mortars and magazines. During firing, square wooden screens were hoisted on a boom over each mortar to screen the flash, and wetted tarpaulins were lashed over the hatchways to the magazines.

Eighteenth-century Royal Navy bomb vessels were armed with one 13-inch and one 10-inch sea mortar. They also mounted eight 6-pounder long guns and assorted swivel guns in their rails for their own defense. By 1810, bombs in the Royal Navy carried two 10-inch mortars and four 68-pounder carronades. Later the 13-inch mortar came back into use, and the carronades were removed.

Bomb vessels were intended for shore bombardment only, not to fight other ships. The U.S. Navy employed them in fighting against Tripoli beginning in 1804 and during the Mexican-American War (when four bomb vessels each mounted a 10-inch columbiad). During the American Civil War, the U.S. Navy employed 13-inch iron mortars on schooners and small mortar boats.

Further Reading

Tucker, Spencer C. "The Navy Discovers Shore Bombardment." *Naval History* 8(5) (October 1994): 30–35.

Ware, Chris. *The Bomb Vessel: Shore Bombardment Ships of the Age of Sail.* Annapolis, MD: Naval Institute Press, 1994.

Howitzer

The howitzer is the third member of the artillery family. The last of the three to appear, it is a medium-trajectory weapon between the flat-trajectory cannon and the high-angle–fire mortar. The term "howitzer" is derived from the Dutch word *houwitser* and the German word *haubitze*. Descended from the *perrier* (stone thrower), the howitzer provided a bridge between the cannon and mortar. It is a comparatively short-barreled, relatively low-velocity weapon. As with the mortar, early muzzle-loading howitzers had a chamber smaller than the bore in order to hold the powder charge. Like the gun, the muzzle-loading howitzer had lugs (trunnions) cast on its sides near the balance point. Both the howitzer and the mortar were usually cast of bronze. The howitzer provided higher-angle fire than the flat-trajectory gun and was thus useful in reaching over terrain obstacles. It was also designed to fire explosive shell. Howitzers were also considerably lighter than long guns of comparable caliber.

Howitzers were first introduced in the late 16th century. Although in general use during the Napoleonic Wars, when they typically made up one-quarter or one-third of the tubes in each field battery, howitzers were especially favored by Frederick II (Frederick the Great) of Prussia (r. 1740–1786). Eighteenth-century British howitzers appeared in 8- and 10-inch bore sizes. Dahlgren boat howitzers in 12-pounder and 24-pounder sizes provided excellent service during the American Civil War.

At the beginning of World War I, the Germans fielded the mammoth Krupp 420mm (16.38-inch) siege howitzer, known as the "Big Bertha." The British introduced a slightly smaller 15-inch howitzer in 1915. Perhaps the most famous modern howitzer was the U.S. 105mm of World War II, the Korean War, and the Vietnam War, which alongside the French 75mm gun of World War I was probably the most successful modern artillery piece. It was not withdrawn from service until the late 1980s. The M102 howitzer was a 105mm of completely different design, which served alongside the M-101A1 but never completely replaced it. Currently both the M-101A1 and the M-102 have been replaced in U.S. service by the British Royal Ordnance M-119 105mm gun.

Further Reading

Hogg, Ivan V. *A History of Artillery.* Astronaut House, Feltham, Middlesex, UK: Hamlyn Publishing Group, 1974.

Zabecki, David T., ed. *World War II in Europe: An Encyclopedia,* Vol. 2. New York: Garland, 1999.

Shell

The term "shell" is derived from the outer covering of shellfish and dates from at least the eighth century. The term came to be used for any carcass (hollow artillery round) filled with explosive powder and set off by a fuze. Shells may have been employed for the first time in warfare in 1588 when they were used by Spanish troops in the siege of Bergen-op-Zoom in the Netherlands. Shells were particularly effective against enemy troop concentrations and were also used in mortars with high-angle fire to bombard fixed fortifications. As early as 1644 in England there is reference to grenades as "small shells" filled with fine gunpowder.

The first shells were very dangerous to the artillerymen firing them. Because they were unreliable and often exploded prematurely, for the most part they were not used in long guns but only in very short weapons known as mortars that were only about twice as long as their bore diameter. Here the round shell could be inserted fuze up and then lit before firing. If inserted fuze down, the force of the main charge invariably drove the fuze into the shell, causing a failure to detonate or, worse, a premature detonation in the tube.

The excessive windage in early muzzle-loading cannon, however, allowed the fire from the main charge to ignite the fuze even when the shell was loaded with the fuze facing toward the muzzle. This was discovered, reportedly during the siege of Limerick in 1689, when an English mortar was fired accidently without the fuze having first been lit, and yet the shell exploded anyway. Shells were then fired from long guns by being secured to wooden bases, known as sabots, that automatically positioned the fuze toward the muzzle. Fuzes also evolved.

Shells underwent great change in the late 19th century with the development of breech-loading guns, steel projectiles, and new high-explosive fillers. In modern parlance, the term "shell" has come to mean any artillery round. Shells come in a wide variety of types including, but not limited to, high-explosive, high-explosive antitank, armor-piercing discarding sabot, incendiary, smoke, illumination, chemical, and nuclear (which were removed from the U.S. arsenal in the 1990s). Fuzes have also become much more sophisticated and reliable and include mechanical time, point-detonating, delay, and proximity types.

Further Reading

Hogg, Ivan V. *A History of Artillery.* New York: Hamlyn Publishing Group, 1974.

Hogg, Ivan V. *The Illustrated Encyclopedia of Ammunition.* London: New Burlington, 1985.

Shrapnel (Spherical Case Shot)

The artillery projectile known as shrapnel or spherical case shot was invented in 1784 by Lieutenant (later lieutenant general) Henry Shrapnel (1761–1842) of the British Royal Artillery. Shrapnel came up with the idea in order to extend the range of highly effective case or canister shot against enemy troops.

During the Spanish siege of Gibraltar (1779–1783), the British successfully fired 5.5-inch mortar shells from their 24-pounder long guns, but in 1784 Shrapnel improved on this by inventing what he called "spherical case shot." The new artillery ammunition was later known simply by its designer's name. It consisted of a thin-walled hollow round shell filled with a small bursting charge and small iron or lead shot. A time fuze set off the charge in the air, scattering the shot and pieces of the shell casing among opposing troops. The bursting charge was only a small one, allowing the scattered balls and burst casing to continue on the same trajectory as before the explosion (a greater charge would increase the velocity but scattered the balls more widely and reduced their effectiveness). Explosive shell had for some time been utilized in high-trajectory fire mortars but had not before been widely projected in horizontal fire by guns.

Shrapnel shells had thinner walls than other shells and had to be carefully cast. Their weight empty was about half of that for solid shot of the same caliber, but their loaded weight was comparable to solid shot.

The British first fired shrapnel during the Napoleonic Wars in 1804 in the siege of Surinam and continued to use it thereafter. Early shrapnel had a wooden plug and a paper fuze but in the 1850s incorporated the more precise Bormann fuze. Shrapnel was widely used in the American Civil War both on land and in naval actions, most often in the 12-pounder Napoleon and Dahlgren boat howitzers. Shrapnel soon became a staple round in the world's artillery establishments. Britain alone produced 72 million shrapnel shells during World War I.

By the end of the 19th century, shrapnel rounds had evolved to a similar size and shape as the other cylindro-conoidal shells fired by breech-loading artillery. The operating principle was still similar to the original spherical case. The thin-walled projectile was packed with small steel or lead balls and an expelling charge. The expelling charge, however, did not rupture the projectile. Rather, it blew the fuze off the front end and expelled the shrapnel balls forward. Thus, the shrapnel round was something like a huge flying shotgun shell. Because of the imprecise burning times of the black powder time fuzes of the era, the adjustment of the proper height of burst was very difficult. Also, shrapnel was only effective against troops in the open. As trench warfare set in during World War I and field fortifications became more robust, shrapnel became virtually worthless. Meanwhile, advances in both explosives and metallurgy during World War I finally produced high-explosive shells that had both significant blast and fragmentation effects. After World War I shrapnel completely disappeared, replaced entirely by high-explosive (HE). Today, the fragmentation produced by the detonation of an HE round is popularly but incorrectly called "shrapnel."

Further Reading

Bull, Stephen. *Encyclopedia of Military Technology and Innovation.* Westport, CT: Greenwood, 2004.

Ripley, Warren. *Artillery and Ammunition of the Civil War.* New York: Van Nostrand Reinhold, 1970.

Tucker, Spencer C. *Arming the Fleet: U.S. Navy Ordnance in the Muzzle-Loading Era.* Annapolis, MD: Naval Institute Press, 1989.

Carcass

A carcass is an incendiary shell fired from a cannon. Beginning in the second half of the 17th century, carcasses were fired from smoothbore cannon, howitzers, or mortars on land to set fire to buildings and at sea against wooden ships. The carcass was a shell with three additional equally spaced vents. The shell was then packed with an incendiary mix that would be difficult to extinguish. One Royal Navy composition consisted of two parts pitch, four parts of saltpeter, one part of sulfur, and three parts of corned gunpowder. By the 19th century, the U.S. Navy employed a mixture of white turpentine, spirits of white turpentine, and portfire composition. The exact composition of the incendiary mix varied widely. Other ingredients employed included rosin, sulfide of antimony, tallow, and turpentine.

A wooden stick was used to poke holes from the vents through the composition to the center of the shell. Three strands of quick match were then inserted in the holes. These were long enough to be folded over the edge of the hole. Dry portfire was then pressed into the vents to keep the quick match in place.

The flame from the burning carcass might extend out three feet. Carcass shells burned for 8 to 10 minutes and were difficult to extinguish. Modern counterparts to the carcass are found in incendiary shells and bullets.

Further Reading

Tucker, Spencer C. *Arming the Fleet: U.S. Navy Ordnance in the Muzzle-Loading Era.* Annapolis, MD: Naval Institute Press, 1989.

Case Shot (Canister or Canister Shot)

Case or canister shot is an artillery round intended for extremely short-range actions against personnel. Known to have been in use in the 17th century, it took its name from a container with many smaller projectiles that was fired from an artillery piece. In its earliest form, the case was made of wood or canvas, which was then filled with many pieces of small trash, metal, musket balls, or even stones. Later case shot was made up of a cylindrical tin case containing iron balls packed in wooden shavings or sawdust. The iron balls weighed from as little as two ounces each to as much as one pound in the case of a 32-pounder gun. When fired, the thin case split in the bore of the gun and then broke open entirely on clearing the muzzle, producing an effect much like a shotgun.

Case shot was employed in artillery both on land and at sea. On land it was primarily used against enemy troops in the open but not at ranges beyond 500 yards. At sea, case shot could be used against light boats but was used primarily to clear the decks of an enemy vessel. Case shot found modern expression in the antipersonnel (APERS) artillery rounds used in the Vietnam War. Also called "Beehive," the APERS round also was fired directly at enemy troops at close ranges. Each round contained thousands of tiny finned flechettes, each no larger than a small nail.

Case shot is not to be confused with grapeshot, which employed larger-size balls packed around a central sabot and held in place in the bore by canvas and cord. Grapeshot was more effective at longer ranges than canister shot and was especially effective at breaking up cavalry charges.

Further Reading
Hogg, Ivan, and John Batchelor. *Naval Gun.* Poole, Dorset, UK: Blandford, 1978.

Peterson, Harold L. *Round Shot and Rammers.* Harrisburg, PA: Stackpole, 1969.

Tucker, Spencer C. *Arming the Fleet: U.S. Naval Ordnance in the Muzzle-Loading Era.* Annapolis, MD: Naval Institute Press, 1989.

Grapeshot

Grapeshot, a type of artillery round employed on land and at sea, appeared as early as the 14th century. At first it was merely a canvas cartridge, sack, or net containing small balls. Later it consisted of balls grouped around a wooden spindle on a wooden base (later an iron plate with an iron spindle that passed through its center, the whole being known as a stool). By the mid-19th century it was enclosed in a canvas bag, secured by a strong line. Such rounds were also known as quilted shot. Later grapeshot was formed on three individual tiers, each with three smaller round shot, the whole known as tier shot.

Individual grapeshot varied according to the size of the gun and might weigh up to three to four pounds each. The whole, however, weighed about the same as one large solid shot for the gun. The name "grapeshot" is derived from the fact that the finished article looked very much like a bunch of grapes. It differed from case or canister in that the individual balls were significantly larger.

When grapeshot was fired, the shock of the discharge broke the cloth, and the balls scattered on exiting the muzzle. Grapeshot was used on land against concentrated formations of enemy troops and especially in the defense against cavalry charges. It was not used much at sea except against boats or to sweep exposed decks of an enemy ship or a beach, but it could be effective against rigging. Although it carried farther than canister, grapeshot was employed only at short ranges, usually not more than 500 yards.

Further Reading

Hogg, Ivan, and John Batchelor. *Naval Gun*. Poole, Dorset, UK: Blandford, 1978.

Peterson, Harold L. *Round Shot and Rammers*. Harrisburg, PA: Stackpole, 1969.

Tucker, Spencer C. *Arming the Fleet: U.S. Naval Ordnance in the Muzzle-Loading Era*. Annapolis, MD: Naval Institute Press, 1989.

Flintlock

The flintlock was the basic individual firearm of the late 17th and 18th centuries. In widespread use by 1650, it was integrated into armies alongside the matchlock and wheel lock and replaced them in European armies, at least, by the end of the century. The flintlock remained the basic infantry firearm until the introduction of the percussion musket in the 1840s.

The flintlock was merely a refinement of the snaplock (snaphance) in which the steel and pan cover were of one piece. It proved to be simple and effective and far more reliable than its predecessors. It was also safer and far easier to load and could be carried for a distance. Firing procedure involved placing the weapon on half cock (safety, and the origin of the term "Don't go off half-cocked"); taking out the cartridge and biting off the paper at the top; pouring a small bit of powder into the pan; ramming the remaining powder, paper, and ball down the bore; placing the musket on full cock; and pulling the trigger.

Pressing the trigger allowed the lock to strike the flint, producing a spark in the powder pan. The cover (frissen) kept the powder dry and prevented it from falling out of the pan; it opened when the flint moved forward. (The term "flash in the pan," whereby there is a sign of something but not the desired result, comes from a misfire where there would be a flash only.) The resulting flash raced through the touchhole into the base of the bore, touching off the main charge.

The two most famous flintlock muskets of the 18th century were probably the French "Charleville" and the English "Brown Bess." The .69-caliber Charleville was the principal musket of the Continental Army in the American Revolutionary War (1775–1783). It was the basis of the first U.S. military musket, the Springfield

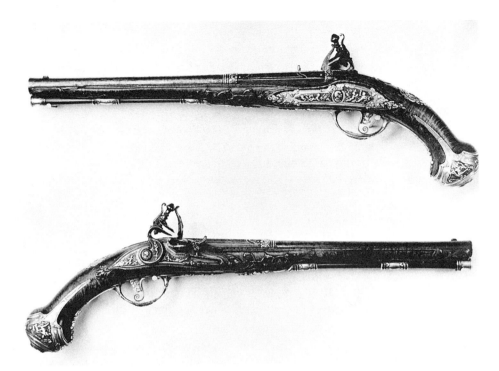

Two 17th-century flintlock pistols. (Bettmann/Corbis)

Model 1795. The Brown Bess was introduced into the British Army in 1720 and remained in service until the 1840s. All models were .75 caliber, but barrel length varied from 46 inches in the Long Land musket common in 1760 to 42 inches for the Short Land model or "Second Model" thereafter. The Brown Bess mounted a 17-inch socket bayonet, as did the Charleville.

A well-trained soldier could fire three or perhaps four shots a minute with the flintlock. Even so, it was a highly inaccurate and rather unreliable weapon. With the French flintlock musket, one misfire might be expected in every 9 shots and one hang fire in every 18. The flint was to be changed every 30 shots.

The main drawback to the flintlock musket was its lack of accuracy. The great windage (the difference between the diameter of the bore and the diameter of the ball being fired) meant that such weapons were inherently inaccurate. Soldiers could not reliably hit a man-sized target with them much beyond 80 yards. Windage was necessary because of the slightly irregular bullet and the considerable buildup of residue in the barrel from the burning of the black powder. As a result, the bullet actually bounded down the bore (balloting) and might actually take flight from the muzzle of the weapon at a wide angle.

This meant that most battles between infantry took place at near–dueling pistol range. Commanders sought to mass as many muskets as possible in a short length of firing line, expecting that sure volume of fire would overcome inaccuracy. The result could be frightful numbers of casualties. The large soft-lead bullet moving at a relatively low velocity had great knockdown power. As soon as it struck any resistant object, such as human flesh, it began to spread, creating frightful wounds. Because this so often removed chunks of bone, amputations were a common occurrence. Attacking infantry would press home the assault with the bayonet.

Further Reading

Blair, Claude, ed. *Pollard's History of Firearms.* New York: Macmillan, 1983.

Brown, M. L. *Firearms in Colonial America: The Impact on History and Technology, 1492–1792.* Washington, DC: Smithsonian Institution Press, 1980.

Lenk, Torsten. *The Flintlock: Its Origin and Development.* New York: Bramhall House, 1965.

Air Gun

The air gun is descended from the blowgun, the difference being that the air gun fires its projectiles by means of compressed air rather than by an individual blowing into a tube, as in the blowgun. In the air gun the pressure may be generated by a spring-piston, which is released on pulling the trigger. The degree of power provided is directly related to the difficulty of the cocking stroke. Guns of this type are of small caliber and fire either a BB, a small round shot usually formed of copper-coated steel, or a wasp-waisted lead diabolo pellet. Such guns are used for target practice or for hunting small game. Larger-caliber air guns, which are more lethal, operate from a compressed air reservoir. Multistroke pneumatic air guns require 2 to 10 pump-ups from an attached pump lever that then stores the compressed air in a reservoir. When the trigger is pulled, a valve briefly opens, releasing a set amount of air that then propels the projectile down the barrel. Some newer-cylinder air guns employ a purchased gas cylinder, usually with liquefied carbon dioxide.

Guns operating on compressed air are hardly new. In 18th- and 19th-century air guns the reservoir was often the butt of the gun. The operator removed the reservoir from the remainder of the gun and used a pump, similar to today's bicycle pumps, to fill it. A few Austrian Army sharpshooters employed the Girandonoi air rifle during 1793–1802 in the Wars of the French Revolution and the Napoleonic Wars. A 20-shot repeating rifle, it fired a round .51-caliber ball and had an effective range of about 130 yards. Nineteenth-century English sporting guns featured a ball-type reservoir under the stock.

The largest air guns were the three 15-inch guns on the U.S. dynamite cruiser *Vesuvius.* They saw service during the Spanish American War of 1898 when they were used to shell Morro Castle, Cuba.

While air guns have very high accuracy, their limited range usually restricts their use to hunting and target practice. The Crossman Corporation is the major U.S. firm manufacturing pump-up rifles and pistols. Most target practice air guns today are of .177 caliber (4.5mm).

Further Reading

The Diagram Group. *Weapons: An International Encyclopedia from 5000 BC to 2000 AD.* New York: St. Martin's, 1990.

Rifle (Muzzle-Loader)

The rifle is an individual shoulder-fired firearm. The first muzzle-loading rifles were identical in firing mechanism, means of loading, and general outward appearance to the smoothbore musket. The difference was that the rifle had a spiral twist of lands and grooves on the internal surface of the barrel. Known as rifling, these imparted spin to the round ball and gave it far greater accuracy at much greater distances. Ironically, rifling seems to have been designed not to improve accuracy but rather to collect fouling, which occurred with the black powder, and to ease the loading of the bullet, which had to be pushed down the bore with a ramrod. Rifling proved to be one of the most important inventions in the history of weaponry.

Thus, while the range at which an individual with a smoothbore musket would be expected to hit a man-sized target might be only 50–100 yards, the rifle had an effective range of up to 200 or even 300 yards. Such advantage, however, was offset by its much slower rate of fire because of the reduced windage (the difference between the diameters of the ball and of the bore) in order that the soft lead ball would take to the rifling. The difficulty of loading meant that the rifle could be fired only about one shot per minute as opposed to three to four shots per minute for a well-trained soldier with the smoothbore musket. Moreover, socket bayonets could not be mounted on rifles of that era; only "plug" bayonets, which prevented the weapon from being reloaded and fired, could be used. Hence, rifles were not suited for the military tactics of the day that stressed massed close-in fire followed by a bayonet charge.

Rifling was probably invented in Germany as early as the late 15th century, but it came into widespread use in the first quarter of the 16th century. The earliest extant rifle dates from 1547. Although spiral grooves and lands became the most accepted form of rifling, straight grooves and lands also existed.

The first centers of rifle manufacture were Scandinavia and Northern Europe, perhaps because the big game for which these weapons were especially useful in hunting were to be found chiefly in these regions. The Germans first employed rifles for military purposes in 1631. The men armed with rifles were known as jaegers, from the German word *Jäger,* meaning "hunter." Many riflemen were former gamekeepers and foresters. King Frederick II of Prussia (r. 1740–1786) raised the first permanent corps of jaegers.

Rifles were especially favored in America, where their long-range accuracy made them ideal for hunting game, especially on the frontier. They probably first arrived in America in the late 17th century and by the 1740s were being manufactured in

Pennsylvania and other, chiefly southern, colonies. Most colonists, however, preferred the more robust and less demanding musket, which provided sufficient accuracy for most hunting and effective self-defense.

American rifles of the period usually had octagonal barrels of greater than 40 inches in length. Calibers varied widely but most usually were .52 to .65, making them somewhat smaller than those of smoothbore muskets. Their stocks were often of maple with brass furniture. They also featured a wooden ramrod and patchbox cover. The rifle was loaded with loose powder, from a powder horn, that was poured down the barrel, followed by the ball wrapped in a greased cloth patch, which was then rammed home. The most common firing mechanism was the flintlock, also employed on the musket.

The importance of rifles in early American warfare has been exaggerated, but they were employed by some militia and used in the colonial wars, most notably the French and Indian War (1754–1763). Some Native Americans, notably the Shawnees and Delawares, also utilized them. Rifles were not equipped either with slings or with lugs for mounting the bayonet.

During the American Revolutionary War (1775–1783), the Continental Army boasted special units armed with the so-called Pennsylvania or Kentucky rifle as skirmishers to fire on British officers from long range. More limited numbers of opposing British and German soldiers also were armed with this weapon, although French troops who fought in America seem not to have been similarly equipped.

Further Reading

Blair, Claude, ed. *Pollard's History of Firearms.* New York: Macmillan, 1983.

Brown, M. L. *Firearms in Colonial America: The Impact on History and Technology, 1492–1792.* Washington, DC: Smithsonian Institution Press, 1980.

Blunderbuss

The blunderbuss was a short large-caliber individual firearm designed for close-range use. Almost all blunderbusses were flintlocks. Introduced to England from Holland in the mid-17th century, the blunderbuss had a short barrel and a distinctive expanding bore or flaring muzzle. Some blunderbusses had iron barrels, but many were of brass.

The blunderbuss was specifically designed to spray a large number of pellets at close range in the near certainty of hitting the intended target. The bell design of the muzzle of the barrel was based on the mistaken notion that this would increase shot dispersion. A large blunderbuss might be of .75-caliber bore at the breech end. Loaded with as many as 20 buckshot, it was fired with 120 grains of powder.

The blunderbuss was the preferred weapon of coach guards. It was also used in defense of close spaces such as buildings and in dealing with unruly crowds. Blunderbusses formed part of the regular armament of ships, where they were employed

An antique flintlock blunderbuss pistol. A favorite weapon of mail-coach guards, its bell-shaped muzzle caused the lead shot to spread widely in a short distance. (iStockphoto.com)

by boarding parties. At sea, large blunderbusses known as boat guns and mounted on swivels could fire up to one pound of shot.

Further Reading

Blair, Claude, ed. *Pollard's History of Firearms.* New York: Macmillan, 1983.

Brown, M. L. *Firearms in Colonial America: The Impact on History and Technology, 1492–1792.* Washington, DC: Smithsonian Institution Press, 1980.

Bayonet

The bayonet is a thrusting weapon attached to the muzzle of a firearm. With the introduction of individual firearms on the battlefield, pikemen were deployed to protect the musketeers from enemy cavalry attack during the period when the musketeers were reloading. In effect, attaching a long blade to the end of the firearm converted it into a pike and did away with the need for the pikemen.

The term "bayonet" probably originated from the French town of Bayonne. In any case, the French introduced the new weapon. The "bayonette" first appeared in 1647. The first were of the plug type; that is, their hilt or grip took the form of a long tapered plug to fit snugly into the musket barrel. It had the great disadvantage, however, of rendering the musket itself useless during its employment. The socket bayonet, usually credited to the great French military engineer and marshal Sebastien de Vauban, appeared in the 1680s and was attached by means of a socket that slipped over the muzzle end of the barrel and engaged a stud cast there. A later

A U.S. Army soldier undergoing bayonet training with a British Army sergeant major at Camp Dick, Texas, following the U.S. entry into World War I. (National Archives)

refinement was to cast the bayonet with a slot that fitted onto a bar on the outside of the muzzle.

With muzzle-loaders, the bayonet was positioned to the side. It could not be above the barrel, because that would interfere with aiming the musket, or below, because that was the location of the ramrod. With breech-loading weapons there was no ramrod, and so the bayonet was placed below the barrel bore and on its axis. Some early pistols were also fitted for bayonets.

All armies issued bayonets as standard infantry weapons. The British Army in particular considered the bayonet essential in battle. Theoretically, it was to be employed in the assault upon closing with an enemy. Arthur Wellesley, the Duke of Wellington, stressed its use as an offensive weapon. All armies conducted regular bayonet drill, and military leaders also believed that bayonet practice was essential in developing martial spirit and aggressive soldiers.

The bayonet was most employed in the 18th and 19th centuries. While it was thought to provide a psychological edge to attacking infantry, it was certainly obsolete by the end of the 19th century. The extra weight of the bayonet served to throw off the balance of the rifle and adversely affected accuracy of fire. Union medical records of the American Civil War (1861–1865) reveal that only one half of 1 percent of war wounds were inflicted with the bayonet, and no doubt many of these were self-inflicted.

With longer-fire weapons, bayonets fell into disuse but were part of the regular weaponry in World War I and World War II. Still issued to troops, the short bayonet of today serves primarily as a general-purpose knife and tool.

Further Reading

Kiesling, Paul. *Bayonets of the World.* Kedichem, Lingedijk, Netherlands: Military Collectors Service, 1973.

Stephens, F. J. *Bayonets.* London: Arms and Armour, 1968.

Wilkinson-Latham, R. J. *British Military Bayonets from 1700 to 1945.* London: Hutchinson, 1967.

Turtle Submarine

The *Turtle* was the world's first real submarine and was invented by American David Bushnell during the American Revolutionary War (1775–1783). Bushnell had already invented a mine, and he now came up with the means to deliver it, building at Saybrook on the Connecticut River in 1775 what he called a "submarine." It consisted of two tortoise-like shells made of oak staves similar to those of a barrel and clamped together by iron hoops. Resembling an egg in appearance, it rode upright in the water, with its smallest end facing down. An entry hatch at the top of the craft had small windows to provide light for the operator below, and a 900-pound keel provided stability. The 7.5- by 6-foot tar-coated craft was reinforced internally against water pressure. Two brass pipes with check valves to prevent flooding provided fresh air and a means of exhaust. A foot-operated valve in the keel admitted water to submerge, and a pump expelled water to ascend. The craft was driven forward and up and down by means of two sets of screwlike paddles manually operated by inside cranks, one on top of the craft and the other in front of the operator. It was steered by means of a rudder moved by a tiller. In an emergency the operator could detach 200 pounds of the lead keel, which could also be let down to serve as an anchor. The craft also had a depth gauge and a compass. Its appearance gave it the *Turtle* name.

The new craft's destructive power came in the form of a cask with 150 pounds of gunpowder. A long bolt attached it to the back of the submarine. When withdrawn, the bolt released the mine and activated the timer, which exploded the mine by means of a flintlock after about an hour.

The submarine was to dive beneath its target, and the operator would then screw an auger into the target vessel's hull. Once this was accomplished the auger was released, and the mine would float free against the target vessel's hull. The *Turtle*'s chief drawback was that the operator had only 30 minutes of air once it was submerged. This meant that an attack had to be mounted at night or in poor visibility in order to get as close as possible before submerging for the final run to its target.

Bushnell successfully tested the *Turtle* but was too frail to operate it in actual combat conditions and so recruited his brother. He fell ill, however, and a volunteer, Sergeant Ezra Lee, took his place for an attempt on the night of September 6–7, 1776, against Admiral Lord Richard Howe's flagship, the *Eagle,* at New York City. For various reasons the attack failed. Several other attempts to sink British ships in the Hudson were also unsuccessful. The *Turtle* was later destroyed, probably to prevent it from falling into British hands.

Further Reading

Miller, Nathan. *Sea of Glory: The Continental Navy Fights for Independence, 1775–1783.* New York: David McKay, 1974.

Roland, Alex. *Underwater Warfare in the Age of Sail.* Bloomington: Indiana University Press, 1978.

Sea Mines

The idea of using explosive devices to sink ships dates to at least the 16th century, but American and Yale University student David Bushnell developed the first practical sea mine. During the American Revolutionary War (1775–1783) he constructed floating contact mines in his workshop near Saybrook, Connecticut. These consisted of kegs of powder triggered by a flintlock. When the keg struck an object, the shock released the hammer and set off the main charge.

On January 5, 1778, Bushnell released his mines in the Delaware River in an effort to destroy British warships downstream. The current was slow, and the mines took more than a week to reach the British anchorage, by which time many of the ships had moved. Some boys spotted one of the kegs and tried to retrieve it, but the mine blew up and killed them. Thus warned, the British fired at anything floating in the water, initiating what became known as the Battle of the Kegs.

In 1801 during the Napoleonic Wars, American Robert Fulton tried to interest Napoleon Bonaparte in employing submarine-laid mines of his invention against English shipping in the Thames. After Bonaparte rejected his ideas, Fulton went to London in 1804 to try to sell his scheme there. Prime Minister William Pitt, worried about the concentration of French shipping across the English Channel for a possible invasion of England, arranged a contract for Fulton to build "submarine bombs."

Fulton carried out two attempts in 1804 and 1805 against French ships at Boulogne with floating mines set to explode on 10-minute fuzes. Deployed from cutters, the mines were secured together in pairs by means of a long line. Fulton hoped that these lines would catch on the cables of the vessels, causing the mines to come to rest against the ship's sides and there explode. Although many mines did explode, it was without significant result.

Mines in the Dardanelles Campaign

Some 310,000 sea mines were laid by belligerents in World War I, but one small mine-field may have altered the course of history. In early 1915 the Allies assembled a formi-dable naval task force to push through the Dardanelles and steam to Constantinople in an effort to force the Ottoman Empire from the war and open up a southern supply route to Russia. But on March 18 a small undetected Turkish minefield of 26 1880s-vintage German mines, laid only 10 days before and undetected by Allied seaplane patrols, brought the loss of three Allied battleships, causing Allied commander Admiral John de Robeck to break off the effort to force the Dardanelles by naval power alone. The failure to open up a supply corridor to Russia through the Mediterranean and the straits un-doubtedly prolonged the war and contributed to the Russian Revolution of 1917.

On October 15, 1805, Fulton demonstrated his mines in England against a 200-ton captured Danish brig, the *Dorothea*. This trial, of two mines secured to one another by a line and set to explode in 18 minutes, worked. This was the first time that a large vessel had been destroyed by a mine.

With Pitt's death in 1806, however, Fulton lost his chief patron. Fulton returned to the United States, where he conducted additional experiments with his "torpe-does," named for the electric ray fish that shocks its prey. In July 1807 he blew up a 200-ton brig in New York harbor, although this required several attempts before it was successful. He also advocated defensive mining to close American ports to an attacker in time of war. However, American attempts to blow up British ships with mines during the War of 1812 were not successful.

In 1839 Russian czar Nicholas I appointed Prussian émigré Moritz-Hermann Jacobi head of a scientific committee to conduct experiments on a galvanic (elec-tronic) mine. As early as 1782, Tiberius Cavallo had demonstrated that gunpowder could be detonated by means of an electric current. Building on work by Cavallo, Fulton and fellow American Samuel Colt, and Russian Baron Pavel L'vovich Schil-ling von Cannstadt, Jacobi developed working mines by the time of the Crimean War (1854–1856).

Jacobi's mines were zinc canisters filled with gunpowder and set off by a deto-nator, a glass tube filled with acid, that when broken ignited the main charge of gunpowder. The Russians employed chemical, contact, and electrical command-detonated mines in both the Baltic and Black Seas. Crimean War mines were, how-ever, too small to inflict major damage.

Mines came into their own during the American Civil War (1861–1865). Hoping to reduce the sizable Union naval advantage, the Confederacy employed them ex-tensively. Confederate Navy officer and scientist Matthew Fontaine Maury was an early proponent of mines and conducted extensive experiments with them. Civil War naval mines/torpedoes were of a variety of types but were essentially station-ary weapons, a sort of buoy held in place at an appropriate distance from the surface by a cable anchored to the sea bottom by a weight. There were two basic types of detonation: contact and electricity. Contact mines were detonated when the horns surrounding the charge were broken; this set off a chemical reaction that ignited the charge. Electricity mines were fired by means of electrical connections from batteries on shore. The first were more certain to explode but were unable to distinguish their victim and hence were dangerous to Confederate ships as well. The second type only could be used close to shore. More often than not, early mines failed to explode as a result of faulty detonating equipment or when they became waterlogged or were swept away by the current.

Mines discovered during the February 1862 Union assault on Fort Henry on the Tennessee River were sheet-iron cylinders some 5.5-feet long and pointed at the ends, each containing about 75 pounds of gunpowder. They were fired by contact-type detonators. All those recovered were waterlogged and harmless.

On December 12, 1862, the Union ironclad *Cairo* succumbed to a mine in the Yazoo River, but the first ship loss in actual battle was the ironclad *Tecumseh,* which went down during the August 5, 1864, Battle of Mobile Bay. Powder charges in Civil War mines ranged from approximately 50 pounds to up to a ton. One of the latter type, detonated electronically, sank the Union gunboat *Commodore Jones* in the James River on May 6, 1864.

Mines were also used offensively as spar torpedoes at the end of a spar or pole. The Confederates built a number of craft designed to operate very low in the water and carry such a spar torpedo in their bows to attack Union warships. The Union also employed such weapons, and on October 18, 1864. *Picket Boat No. 1* sank the Confederate ironclad ram *Albemarle.*

The largest ship sunk by a mine during the war was the Union steam sloop *Housatonic,* the victim on February 17, 1864, of a 90-pound spar torpedo from the partially submerged Confederate submarine *H. L. Hunley.* In all 50 ships, most of them Union vessels, were sunk or damaged by mines during the war.

In 1868 a German scientist named Hertz developed what became known as the Hertz horn to explode a contact mine. Such mines were typical of those deployed in both World War I and World War II. A half dozen horns extended outward from the top part of the mine in various directions. Each horn contained a glass tube with an electrolyte (potassium bichromate solution). This was connected to a carbon plate and a zinc plate. When a ship encountered the horn and broke it, the solution leaked out, connecting the two plates and forming a simple battery that generated sufficient current to ignite the mine's electric detonator.

In the second half of the 19th century, most naval powers pursued mine development. The most notable was the evolution of the spar torpedo into an automotive torpedo, or "fish." On the other hand, lesser and continental navies discovered static mines as a low-cost alternative to conventional coastal defense. Russia and Germany focused on the development of moored contact mines based on Hertz's and Jacobi's actuation mechanisms. By the turn of the century, both countries had sizable stocks of mines.

During the Russo-Japanese War (1904–1905), both sides made extensive use of mines. Russian mines claimed 10 Japanese warships, including 2 battleships—more ships than were lost to naval gunfire. During the war the Russians lost 6 ships, including 1 battleship, to mines. Encouraged by the results of mine warfare during their war with Japan, the Russians evolved their mine warfare capability with the addition to the fleet of the purpose-built minelayers *Amur* and *Jenissei* in 1906 and the launching of the world's first mine-laying submarine *Krab* in 1904.

World War I saw mine warfare at sea on a large scale by both sides. On October 14, 1914, the newly commissioned British battleship *Audacious* sank after having struck a single mine laid by a converted German liner. The most widely used mine in the war was the moored contact mine consisting of a spherical or cylindrical mine case, an anchor to secure the mine in place, and a mooring wire connecting the two to hold the buoyant mine case at a predetermined depth. Most powers relied mainly on the Hertz horn–type firing mechanism. The German E-Type moored contact mine was so reliable that the British copied it in 1917.

Both sides also deployed mines extensively as offensive weapons. The Germans used both submarines and surface vessels to lay mines off British ports, while the Allies sowed great belts of mines, known as barrages, to inhibit German access to the North Sea. Charge weights ranged from 60 to 600 pounds.

Mines and mine nets claimed 34 of the 178 German submarines lost to enemy action in the war. Of an estimated 310,000 sea mines deployed during the war, 260,000 were laid by the Allies. In return, German mines, mostly laid by submarines, claimed more than 1.5 million of a total of 12 million tons of Allied merchant shipping sunk during the war. On June 5, 1916, HMS *Hampshire* exploded and sank off the coast of Orkney Island after apparently striking a mine laid by a German submarine. Among the hundreds lost in the sinking was Britain's famed secretary of state for war Field Marshal Horatio Kitchener, perhaps the most famous military leader killed by a naval mine. Toward the end of the war the British developed the first magnetic influence mine. It was activated by the disruption of Earth's magnetic field generated by the passage of a steel ship.

Development of mines continued after the war. Experiments with acoustic mines, set off by noise, began in 1937. By World War II, mines were far more sophisticated and were capable of rising and falling with the tide or delayed-action release from the seabed. The Germans introduced air-laid magnetic mines with great effect in 1939. They continued to refine these influence mines throughout the war and ultimately incorporated magnetic, pressure, and acoustic firing mechanisms. The mines could be adjusted to detect the magnetic fields of even the smallest vessels, which made them a lethal enemy of Allied mine-sweeping forces. For the seaward defense of Europe the Germans also employed bottom contact mines, some of them simple antitank mines. These were laid offshore and on stakes to prevent landing craft from reaching shore.

The real operational value of mines lies in their disruptive effects on shipping. British aerial mining of the Kiel Canal and the Danube in 1944 severely disrupted the German material flow to the Western Front and oil supplies from the Romanian oil fields for brief periods of time. The most devastating mine-laying campaign of the war was perhaps the American Operation STARVATION that employed 15,000 air-laid mines in Japanese waters in 1945 and paralyzed what little Japanese maritime traffic remained at that stage.

Limpet mines, though technically time-fuzed demolition charges, were also employed. Small high-explosive charges, usually with small watertight compartments that gave them only the slightest negative buoyancy, limpet mines were usually carried by divers to the hulls of targeted ships and there affixed by magnets, hence the name for the mollusk limpet. Limpet mines were usually exploded by means of a timed fuze.

The Italians employed commandos to deliver the mines. So-called human torpedoes, electrically powered underwater vessels, delivered the combat swimmers and their craft's warhead charge to the targets. Just before the end of World War I, Italian commandos used such techniques to sink the Austro-Hungarian battleship *Viribus Unitis.* Continuing that tradition in World War II, Italian frogmen of the 10th Light Flotilla sank the British battleships *Valiant* and *Queen Elisabeth* in the port of Alexandria on December 18, 1941. A different mode of delivering the charges was selected by the Royal Navy in World War II when several midget submarines successfully placed explosive charges on the sea bottom underneath the German battleship *Tirpitz* at its anchorage in a Norwegian fjord on September 22, 1943.

Sea mines of the second half of the 20th century grew ever more sophisticated and remain an important weapon of naval warfare. Today most offensive mines are laid by aircraft, as in the case of the U.S. mining of Haiphong Harbor in North Vietnam during the Vietnam War. Among mines still in the U.S. inventory are the MK56 ASW (developed in 1966), the MK60 CAPTOR (for "encapsulated torpedo"), and the MK62 and MK63 Quickstrike and MK67 SLMM (for "submarine-launched mobile mine").

Mine-sweeping techniques were developed as early as 1900 by several nations. The preferred method usually involved a converted trawler (and later purpose-built minesweepers) to stream one or two steel wires held at the desired depth and angle by paravanes. Shears were mounted on the sweep wires to cut the mine's mooring wire. This is known as the Oropesa sweep. Team sweeps were also conducted in the form of a long wire run between two minesweeping vessels. Once the swept mines floated to the surface, they were exploded by rifle or shell fire.

During World War II, the Allies alone deployed 1,300 minesweeping vessels of all types. To counter magnetic mines, minesweeping vessels employed large electromagnets to try to explode them at a distance behind the vessels. Degaussing, or the wrapping of ships' hulls in cable to reduce their magnetic signature, and the use of wooden-hulled minesweepers assisted in efforts to stymie magnetic mines. Mine hunting, or actively searching for mines with sonar in front of the mine countermeasures vessel, is the standard measure today for hard-to-sweep influence sea mines. Once located, these are dispatched with explosive charges by divers or remote operated underwater vehicles.

Further Reading

Cowie, J. S. *Mines, Minelayers and Minelaying.* Oxford: Oxford University Press, 1949.

Hartmann, Gregory K., with Scott C. Truver. *Weapons That Wait: Mine Warfare in the U.S. Navy.* Annapolis, MD: Naval Institute Press, 1991.

Ledebur, Gerhard Freiherr von. *Die Seemine.* Munich: J. Lehmanns Verlag, 1977.

Roland, Alex. *Underwater Warfare in the Age of Sail.* Bloomington: Indiana University Press, 1978.

Balloons

French brothers Joseph-Michael Montgolfier (1740–1810) and Étienne Montgolfier (1745–1799), whose father owned a paper factory in Annonay in southeastern France, became fascinated by the rise of paper in updrafts in the chimney. The two were convinced that they could send aloft bags of paper by means of building a fire under them (although they mistakenly attributed the rise or levity to properties in the smoke). Their first known successful trial occurred on April 25, 1783, while the first public demonstration was in the Annonay town square on June 5. News of the event led to Étienne being called to Paris to meet with the members of the Academy of Sciences.

Before Étienne's arrival in Paris, French physicist Jacques-Alexandre-César Charles, believing that the Montgolfiers had employed hydrogen, caused to be built a balloon of silk, which he filled with that gas and launched from the Champ de Mars in Paris on August 27. The balloon ascended despite heavy rains that day, coming down some 15 miles from the launch point. Peasants, alarmed by the sight of the descending balloon, promptly ripped it to shreds with their pitchforks. Subsequently, hydrogen-filled balloons were known as Charlières, while hot-air balloons were Montgolfières.

The first human untethered flight took place on November 21, 1783, in a Montgolfier-built 70-foot tall balloon with a circular gallery below. Jean-François de Pilâtre de Rozier and François Laurent, the Marquis d'Arlandes, flew in it as the first aeronauts. Ascending from the grounds of the Chateau of Versailles, their flight lasted 23 minutes and covered a distance of some 10 miles. Most historians consider it to have been the first manned flight. Surprisingly, only one of the Montgolfier brothers ever ascended in a balloon, and then only once.

On December 1, 1783, Charles and Nicholas Robert ascended in a hydrogen-filled balloon from the Tuileries Garden in Paris. They flew for two hours and landed 27 miles distant. On January 7, 1785, Jean-Pierre Blanchard and John Jeffries crossed the English Channel in a hydrogen balloon.

The French soon used their invention for military purposes. In 1794 during the Wars of the French Revolution, French observers in balloons took part in the 1793 siege of Mainz, and the balloon *l'Entreprenant* proved invaluable in the French victory in the Battle of Fleurus in Belgium (June 26, 1794). Its crew continuously reported on Austrian movements. During the American Civil War (1861–1865), both the Union and Confederacy employed observation balloons, while in the siege of Paris during the Franco-Prussian War (1870–1871) the French sent balloons out of the city with communications and carrier pigeons (to carry back return messages). On October 7, 1870, French minister of the interior Léon Gambetta escaped from the city in a balloon in order to direct the war effort elsewhere. In all the French sent out 66 balloons from Paris (from mid-November 1870 only by night), 58 of them landing safely.

In 1877 France organized the special Aerial Communication Commission. Germany established the Balloon Corps in 1884, and Austria followed in 1893. The British employed observation balloons during the Boer War (1899–1902), while the Japanese used them during the Russo-Japanese War (1904–1905).

Balloons were of immense importance in artillery spotting and general observation during the fixed fighting that characterized warfare on the Western Front in World War I. Shooting them down became a primary task for opposing aircraft and antiaircraft artillery. This was not an easy task, for the balloons were protected by antiaircraft guns and machine guns. Wires strung between the balloons foiled low-flying enemy aircraft. Aircraft employed in balloon busting used special incendiary bullets to ignite the hydrogen.

Observation balloon duty was understandably hazardous for its participants. Although equipped with parachutes as early as 1915, the observers were authorized to put these on only when a balloon actually caught fire, but at that point chances of escape were slim.

Barrage balloons were also widely employed during World War II as a defense against low-flying aircraft. Tethered in large numbers over strategic locations, they trailed long steel cables, through which aircraft could not fly. The presence of barrage balloons forced attacking aircraft to fly at higher altitudes, reducing bombing accuracy.

In Operation FU-GO the Japanese sent some 9,000 hydrogen-filled paper balloons of 30-foot diameter against North America. Each balloon carried one 33-pound antipersonnel bomb or two 13.2-pound incendiary bombs. Of 258 reported incidents, there were only six fatalities—a woman and five children on a picnic. Reportedly some forest fires were started by the incendiaries.

Ironically, today's recreation balloons have returned to the Montgolfier hot air design, employing ripstop nylon for the envelope, with the hot air provided by propane gas burners.

Further Reading

Ege, Lennart A. T. *Balloons and Airships, 1783–1973.* Edited by Kenneth Munson. New York: Macmillan, 1981.

Manceron, Claude. *The French Revolution,* Vol. 3, *Their Gracious Pleasure, 1782–1785.* Translated by Nancy Amphoux. New York: Knopf, 1980.

Rolt, L. T. C. *The Aeronauts: A History of Ballooning, 1783–1903.* New York: Messner, 1958.

Popham's Signal System

Success in fleet actions at sea rested in large part on the ability of the overall commander to organize his ships and employ them effectively against an enemy. It was essential that individual captains promptly obey the commander's instructions.

The ancient Romans had employed a *sagum,* a scarlet cloak or banner, to announce to the ships of the fleet that an enemy force had been sighted and that they were to attack. Over time, naval signals by flags had become more complex, but communication by coded flags was time-consuming. In 1790 Royal Navy captain (later rear admiral) Sir Home Riggs Popham (1762–1820) developed a system of telegraphic signals employing numbered and eventually lettered flags. The system was published in *Telegraphic Signals or Marine Vocabulary,* in several editions between 1801 and 1812. Popham's signals replaced a system created by Admiral Richard Howe during 1776–1793 and could convey 30,000 real words. It established a workable signaling system for the Royal Navy.

Although the Admiralty did not formally adopt Popham's system until 1816, individual commanders made extensive use of it during the Napoleonic Wars (1803–1815). The French, meanwhile, slavishly followed an overly complicated system developed by the Vicomte de Morugues, the *Tatique Navale ou Traité des Évolutions et des Signaux* (1763).

Further Reading

Corbett, Julian S. *Fighting Instructions, 1530–1816.* London: Naval Records Society, 1905.

Nelson and the Battle of Trafalgar

British Vice Admiral Horatio Nelson was able to exploit Popham's system preceding and during the Battle of Trafalgar on October 21, 1805. Nelson arranged his frigates so that they could relay information to him over the horizon. This allowed him to maintain a loose blockade in order to entice the French and Spanish out of Cádiz, yet he was quickly and accurately informed when they did put to sea. Popham's system also enabled Nelson to control his ships perfectly in the resulting battle, which established Britain as the dominant power at sea for more than a century.

Popham, Hugh. *A Damned Cunning Fellow: The Eventful Life of Rear-Admiral Sir Home Popham, KCB, KCH, KM, FRS, 1762–1820.* Tywardreath, Cornwall, UK: Old Ferry Press, 1991.

Woods, David L., ed. *Signaling and Communicating at Sea.* 2 vols. New York: Arno, 1980.

Steam Warship

The steam engine revolutionized not only the construction of ships but also the entire practice of naval warfare, freeing ships from the vagaries of the wind and allowing captains to maneuver as the tactical situation required. Although primitive steam engines were known to the ancients, the modern type evolved from the late 17th century to the second half of the 18th century, when it was largely perfected by James Watt, an instrument maker at the University of Glasgow. He patented his steam engine in 1769, a date often given as the start of the Industrial Revolution.

In 1783 Frenchman Claude-François-Dorothée, Marquis de Jouffroy, constructed a practical small stern-wheel steamship, the *Pyroscaphe.* It plied the Sâone River near Lyons. In 1787 American John Fitch tested a steamboat on the Delaware River, and in 1788 Scottish banker Patrick Miller and engineer William Symington tested Britain's first steamboat, the *Charlotte Dundas,* on the Firth of Forth. In 1807 American inventor Robert Fulton built the first commercially successful steamboat, the *Clermont.* It carried passengers on the Hudson River between New York and Albany. Europe's first merchant steamer was Thomas Bell's *Comet* of 1812 on the Clyde River.

The first serious attempt at a steam-powered warship came in the 1790s in Britain, when the Earl of Stanhope built the *Kent.* It was powered by paddles (not paddle wheels), or "duck feet" as he called them, that feathered on the return stroke. Tested on the Thames in 1793, its engine proved a failure. In fact, the Royal Navy was slow to embrace a change that would render obsolete its sailing navy, the world's largest. The first steam warship in any nation was Robert Fulton's *Demologos* (later *Fulton I*) of 1815, but it was basically a floating battery to defend New York City.

All early steamers were hybrids, employing sail rigs as well as steam power. This practice continued late into the 19th century. Because of the inefficiency of the early steam engines, the first steamers relied on sail the vast majority of the time.

The first Royal Navy steamship was the *Comet* of 1822, employed as a tender and tug. The *Lightning* (1823) and *Meteor* (1824) followed. All three ships were rated at three guns each.

In fairness to their critics, early steam vessels had serious shortcomings. Their engines frequently failed, they were slow, and their high rate of fuel consumption reduced cruising range. Side wheels were an inefficient means of propulsion, and their drag inhibited speed when under sail. The large paddle wheels were also vulnerable to enemy fire and took up much room on the side of the vessel. This prevented standard broadside batteries, forcing location of fewer and larger longer-ranged guns on pivot mounts on the upper deck.

The first steam paddle warships were built for African service: the Royal Navy *Congo* in 1816 and the French *African* and *Voyager* in 1818. The first purpose-built war steamer actually known to have participated in high-intensity combat was the British-built Greek Navy *Karteria* (Perseverance) during the Greek War of Independence (1821–1832). Armed with four 68-pounders, in 1827 it captured or destroyed some two dozen Ottoman vessels and carried out shore bombardment.

Over time the numbers of steam warships grew. The *Dee* entered Royal Navy service in 1832. At 700 tons, it was twice the size of the previous steamers. Sometimes known as the first practical steam warship, it mounted two 32-pounders. The *Dee* and another steamer, the *Rhadamanthus,* proved their worth in 1832 during a Royal Navy blockade of the Netherlands coast to bring about the withdrawal of Dutch troops from Belgium. By 1837 nearly 30 steamers had been built expressly for the Royal Navy, with others purchased for minor duties.

Steam warships also grew larger and mounted more powerful armaments. The paddler frigate *Gorgon* of 1837 was 1,111 tons and mounted two 10-inch guns and four 32-pounders. It took part in the 1840 Syrian campaign. The paddle-wheel frigate *Cyclops* of 1838 mounted two 98-pounders and four 68-pounders. The Royal Navy built 18 *Gorgon* and 6 *Cyclops* derivatives through 1846.

France was the only other nation to make a serious commitment to steam in this period. The first effective French steam warship was the dispatch boat *Sphinx* of 1829. Of 777 tons, it took part in operations against Algiers in 1830. During the next 10 years France built 23 similar dispatch boats, and in the 1940s it also built a few larger paddle frigates to match the British Gorgon class.

The *Missouri* and *Mississippi* marked the real beginning of the U.S. steam navy. Launched in 1841, they displaced 3,200 tons and mounted two 10-inch pivot guns and eight 8-inch guns in broadside. The *Missouri* was destroyed by fire in 1843, but the *Mississippi* had a distinguished 20-year career.

The change from paddle wheel to screw propulsion was essential for steam-powered warships. Not only was the screw propeller more efficient, but it was concealed from enemy fire. Although there were a number of earlier experiments, in 1836 Francis Petit Smith and John Ericsson, working independently, took out patents for screw propellers. Smith's design was helical in shape. In 1839 Smith fitted his propeller to a ship of his design, the *Archimedes*. It became the first seagoing screw propeller vessel. In a series of races across the English Channel, it proved a match for the Dover paddle-wheel packets. Smith's propeller was also fitted on I. K. Brunel's Atlantic liner, the *Great Britain* of 1843, the first large commercial ship of iron construction.

Ericsson's first design consisted of a pair of contra-rotating drums aft of the rudder. It was tested successfully on the launch *Francis B. Ogdon*. Ericsson improved it by removing one of the drums and mounting the propeller before the rudder. One problem with the screw propeller was technical. The single expansion engine, in use until the 1860s, only worked at about 20 pounds per square inch. This slow-running engine was better suited to running the paddle wheel; to run the propeller with sufficient speed required considerable gearing.

The first screw-propeller warship in the world was the U.S. Navy steam sloop *Princeton* of 1843. Ericsson designed the engine and the six-blade propeller. The first Royal Navy screw-propelled vessel was the sloop *Rattler* of the same year. Of 888 tons, it mounted one 68-pounder bow gun and four 32-pounders. Doubts over which was the superior form of propulsion—the screw or the paddle wheel—were resolved by tests in 1845. In a series of races the *Rattler* proved faster than its rival, the paddle sloop *Alecto*. Proponents of the paddle wheel claimed that it had superior towing capabilities; this too was disproved in a tug-of-war between the two ships on April 30, 1845, which the *Rattler* won. The screw-propelled steamship was here to stay.

Further Reading

Brown, D. K. *Before the Ironclad: Development of Ship Design Propulsion and Armament in the Royal Navy, 1815–60.* Annapolis, MD: Naval Institute Press, 1990.

George, James L. *History of Warships: From Ancient Times to the Twenty-First Century.* Annapolis, MD: Naval Institute Press, 1998.

Lambert, Andrew D., ed. *Steam, Steel, and Shellfire: The Steam Warship, 1815–1905.* London: Conway Maritime, 1992.

Perlmutter, Tom. *War Machines, Sea.* London: Octopus Books, 1965.

Percussion Cap

The chief military invention of the first half of the 19th century was the percussion cap, made possible by the discovery of fulminate of mercury in 1800. In 1807 Scottish Presbyterian minister Alexander Forsyth patented a gun lock utilizing mercuric fulminates as a priming charge for firearms. The process brought reliability to the discharge of lethal projectiles.

Before this invention, all guns—individual firearms through the largest cannon—were discharged by lighting a priming charge of finely ground gunpowder. This was first accomplished by a burning rope and later by flint and steel, both outside the touchhole at the end of the bore. Mercury fulminate detonated when struck a sharp blow, and Forsyth's system employed what looked like a perfume bottle, known as the "scent bottle," that was mounted on the side of the gun at the breech. It contained sufficient fulminates for perhaps 20 shots and was connected by a fire hole that led to the base of the bore. To prime the scent bottle, it was turned upside down, causing some of the fulminates to drop down onto a flash pan. When the trigger was pulled, a hammer dropped down on top of a firing pin at the end of the scent bottle. It came down on the pan, exploding the small amount of fulminates there. The flash from this then passed into the bore of the gun, igniting the main charge.

Joshua Shaw, an English artist living in Philadelphia, simplified the process considerably by 1816. Shaw painted the fulminates on the inside of a small copper cap, which fitted over a nipple containing the fire hole over the base of the bore. When the hammer struck the percussion cap, the exploding fulminates ignited, and the fire raced down the touchhole to explode the main powder charge.

Percussion-cap sidearms could be reloaded and fired more rapidly than a flintlock and were reliable in all weather conditions. In 1834 the British Army tested a musket armed with the new percussion cap against the old Brown Bess flintlock. Each weapon fired 6,000 rounds. The percussion cap weapon failed 6 times, while the flintlock failed to fire nearly 1,000 times. As can be readily imagined, the new system produced a tremendous increase in firepower.

Muzzle-loading rifled muskets fired this way were in general service in the world's armies by 1850. The U.S. Army adopted the percussion cap system in 1842, paying Shaw for the use of it. The percussion cap muzzle-loading rifled musket was the standard infantry firearm of the American Civil War.

Further Reading

Blackmore, H. L. "The Percussion System." In *Pollard's History of Firearms,* edited by Claude Blair, 161–187. New York: Macmillan, 1986.

Tunis, Edwin. *Weapons: A Pictorial History.* New York: World Publishing, 1954.

Rockets, Early Types

The war rocket was actually the oldest of all explosively propelled projectiles. The Chinese used rockets, some of them quite sizable, as anticavalry weapons from the early 11th century. War rockets made their way into European arsenals by the 1300s. The French employed them in the Hundred Years' War against the English in the siege of Orléans in 1429.

The extensive use of rockets by Tippu Sultan of Mysore against the British during the siege of Seringapatam in 1799 gave British artillery officer Sir William Congreve the idea of improving on them. Congreve developed rockets for both land and naval use. These weighed as little as two ounces—"a species of self-moving musket balls"—to more than 300 pounds. In 1806 Congreve rockets were successfully tested at sea in an attack on the French port of Boulogne, and they were used with equal effectiveness in bombarding Copenhagen in 1807. In the latter instance the British fired thousands of Congreve rockets into the city, setting much of it on fire.

Congreve rockets were also employed in the War of 1812, both on land and at sea. Francis Scott Key's observations of the "rocket's red glare" in the bombardment of Fort McHenry at Baltimore, Maryland, provided the inspiration for his penning the "Star Spangled Banner." Rockets were also employed by the U.S. Army in the Mexican-American War during the Mexico City Campaign and in the American Civil War by Union forces on land in the bombardment of Yorktown and Richmond and at sea to drive off Confederate picket boats at night.

Continued experiments, however, failed to correct the rocket's problems of errant flight and instability. Because rockets often exploded prematurely, crews were reluctant to fire them. Rockets also tended to deteriorate in storage. Their promise as a weapon of war was not fulfilled until World War II, when rockets played a considerable role, especially in ground-to-ground and air-to-ground combat.

Further Reading

Baker, David. *The Rocket: The History and Development of Rocket & Missile Technology.* New York: Crown, 1978.

Carronade

The carronade was a new naval gun introduced late in the 18th century. Named for the Carron Company of Scotland, which produced the prototype in 1776, the carronade was a short, light gun of large bore. It appeared first in the Royal Navy beginning in the American Revolutionary War (1775–1783), was employed extensively in the French Revolutionary and Napoleonic Wars (1792–1815), and reached its greatest utilization during the War of 1812.

The true carronade had no trunnions (the lugs cast on the side of a long gun to support it in its carriage) but was mounted on its bed by means of a bolt through a loop cast on its underside. All carronades were short, only about 7 calibers (1 caliber being the diameter of the bore) in length. Carronades weighed about 50–70 pounds of metal for every pound of shot. This is in sharp contrast to as much as 150–200 pounds per 1 pound of shot in long guns.

The lightness of the carronade enabled it to be employed where a heavier gun could not be supported, as on the poop or forecastle. Savings in weight made it especially popular for smaller vessels, and it became the principal armament of brigs. Generally speaking, the carronade replaced the small 4- to 12-pounder long guns. At the turn of the century, carronades of up to 68-pounders in size had permeated the Royal Navy.

The French also employed the carronade. The French Navy first adopted the *caronade* in 1787 under the name of *obusiers de vaisseaux* (ship howitzers). The first French carronades were of bronze. Through 1856, the French Navy introduced new carronade models.

The carronade used approximately one-third the powder charge of the long gun. Owing to its low muzzle velocity, windage (the difference between the diameter of the shot and the diameter of the bore) was sharply reduced. The shot fired by the carronade moved at relatively slow velocity but produced a large irregular hole and considerable splintering.

While ideally suited for close actions, the carronade had its disadvantages. One was its excessive recoil; another was that because it was so short, burning powder from it might ignite the ship's side or rigging. Its chief weakness, however, was its lack of range. Carronades were employed at point-blank, which meant about 450 yards for a 68-pounder and 230 yards for a 12-pounder. If the fighting was at longer range, the carronade was a liability, as was revealed during the War of 1812. This led to the conclusion that vessels should not be armed exclusively with them.

While chiefly naval weapons, carronades were also employed on land, mainly in the defense of fortifications. The carronade did not automatically lead to the introduction of the shell gun but was an important step in that direction.

Further Reading

Caruana, Adrian B. *The History of English Sea Ordnance,* Vol. 2, *The Age of the System, 1715–1815.* Ashley Lodge, Rotherfield, East Sussex: Jean Boudriot Publications, 1997.

Tucker, Spencer C. *Arming the Fleet: U.S. Naval Ordnance in the Muzzle-Loading Era.* Annapolis, MD: Naval Institute Press, 1989.

Tucker, Spencer C. "The Carronade." *Nautical Research Journal* 42(1) (March 1997): 15–23.

Shell Gun

The introduction of a bursting projectile and a gun specifically designed to project it had tremendous impact on warship design and naval warfare. Solid shot had been the mainstay at sea for centuries. Shot was used to hole a vessel, damage and destroy spars and masts, and create crew casualties. But wooden warships with their thick oak sides could absorb a tremendous number of shot hits. Even if it penetrated, shot tended to leave regular rounded holes easily plugged by a ship's carpenter, especially as the wooden fibers tended to close after shot had passed through. In any case, it took a great many such holes to sink a large wooden warship. Occasionally ships were lost by a magazine explosion, but most captured vessels were disabled through damage to masts, spars, and rigging or from heavy personnel casualties that led to them being taken by boarding.

The antipersonnel effects of shot occurred when it exited the wood and produced showers of splinters. The effects of this were greatest when the force of the shot was only slightly more than that required to pass through the wood. But far too often shot failed to penetrate the wooden side of a ship at all.

Shell was designed not to penetrate. It moved at a slow velocity in order to lodge in the side of a ship and there explode, causing an irregular hole that would be difficult to patch and, in many cases, large enough that it might even sink the vessel. Shot had greater range, but shell was much more destructive.

With improvements in both shells and fuzing (crews firing early shells dreaded them because on occasion the shells exploded prematurely, bursting the gun), special guns were developed to fire it. The French took the lead because they had less to lose and more to gain than the British from the introduction of an entirely new system (the British had then the world's largest navy by far). In trials conducted in the 1820s, French colonel (later general) Henri Paixhans proved the effectiveness of explosive shell against wooden ships.

Shell guns had the great advantage of being lighter than shot guns, as shell was fired with smaller charges. This meant that the weight of metal that a warship fired in broadside might actually be increased at the same time the weight of its ordnance was reduced. In 1837 the French introduced the Paixhans 80-pounder shell gun as a part of every ship's regular battery. It weighed as much as a 36-pounder gun. A frigate armed with a few of the new guns could easily defeat a much larger ship of the line.

In the 1840s, shells and shell guns came into general use in the world's navies. In the United States, Lieutenant John Dahlgren (see Dahlgren guns entry) developed his own ordnance system for the U.S. Navy. In effect, explosive shell projected by special shell guns rendered wooden ships obsolete and led to the introduction of the ironclad warship. The irony is that with the appearance of the ironclad ship during the American Civil War, Dahlgren's shell guns fired solid shot rather than explosive shell against Confederate ironclads.

Further Reading

Hogg, Ivan, and John Batchelor. *Naval Gun.* Poole, Dorset, UK: Blandford, 1975.

Lambert, Andrew, ed. *Steam, Steel & Shellfire: The Steam Warship, 1815–1905.* Annapolis, MD: Naval Institute Press, 1992.

Tucker, Spencer C. *Arming the Fleet: U.S. Navy Ordnance in the Muzzle-Loading Era.* Annapolis, MD: Naval Institute Press, 1989.

Railroads

The first practical application of the steam engine to land transportation came in the locomotive designed by Richard Trevithick in England in 1801, but George Stephenson built the first true railway, between Stockton and Darlington, also in England, in 1825. The first U.S. rail line was constructed in 1828.

Prussia was the first nation to grasp the importance of the railroad in war. German writers were quick to point out how rail lines could help their nation in case of war against powerful neighbors. The railroad enabled Prussia, and later Germany, to use railroads in interior lines by which forces could be mobilized and then shifted about rapidly.

In 1846 the Prussians conducted the first major troop movement by rail, while in 1861 the American Civil War saw the first such movement by rail in war, when

Confederate forces were transported from the Shenandoah Valley to fight in the First Battle of Manassas (Bull Run). The much more developed Union rail net was an important factor in its victory in the Civil War, while railroads were critical in enabling Prussia to win a rapid victory over Austria in 1866. Armored trains and railroad artillery appeared in the American Civil War and in the Boer War.

At the beginning of World War I, France may have survived militarily because of its well-developed rail net that enabled rapid shifting of major units to meet the German foot-bound invasion of northeastern France in August 1914. Russia's ambitious program for a strategic railroad net would have rendered obsolete Germany's Schlieffen Plan for waging a near-simultaneous war against France and Russia and was a major factor in Germany's decision to declare war in 1914. German military leaders believed that five years later Germany would not be able to win a two-front war.

During World War I, railroads moved the bulk of the vast numbers of men and quantities of munitions and supplies to the front. Railroad artillery allowed rapid deployment of the heaviest guns, and railroad cars also served as mobile command posts. The inability of the Russian rail system to meet both civilian and military needs led to food riots in the cities and ultimately to revolution in March 1917.

Rail lines were also of immense importance in World War II, although modern aircraft rendered them much more vulnerable to attack. Disruption of the movement of the enemy's supplies by rail became a primary concern of both sides in war, as in the bombing and resistance activities prior to the Allied landings in Normandy in June 1944, and the rapid restoration of the French rail system thereafter was a top priority for the Western Allies.

Railroads continue to be a major factor in war.

Further Reading

Bishop, Denis, and W. J. K. Davies. *Railways and War before 1918*. London: Blandford, 1972.

Bishop, Denis, and W. J. K. Davies. *Railways and War since 1917*. London: Blandford, 1974.

Westwood, John N. *Railways at War*. San Diego: Howell-North Books, 1981.

Telegraph

Telegraph systems for the transmission of messages linked parts of the Roman Empire. Signaling stations set up at regular intervals on high ground or on towers could relay messages by flags, mirrors, fires, smoke, or other means. The English operated a system of warning beacons at the time of the Spanish Armada in 1588, while France and then Britain operated semaphore mechanical telegraph systems in the early 19th century. The French system could transmit simple messages across much of Europe in a matter of hours. Such systems were, however, subject to the vagaries of weather or actions by enemy troops and had only limited application at night. They were also costly to operate and maintain.

By about 1830, scientists determined that messages could be transmitted by means of an electrical impulse through wires. While a number of electric telegraphy systems were developed, American Samuel Morse created a system and a code for it that employed short and long breaks in the electrical current (dots and dashes). Morse received a patent for his invention in 1840, and in 1843 the U.S. Congress appropriated funds to build a pilot 40-mile telegraph line from Baltimore to Washington, D.C. In 1844 Morse transmitted his first message over this line: "What hath God wrought?"

The telegraph allowed messages to be transmitted over considerable distances within minutes. Applied initially to the control of railroad traffic, the combination of telegraph and railroad brought about great changes in military operations. The telegraph proved of immense military value in the rapid communication of messages and control of troops during the Crimean War in the 1850s, the American Civil War (1861–1865), and the Austro-Prussian War of 1866. Telegraph lines laid under the ocean by 1866 connected Europe with North America and within decades the rest of the world.

Telegraphy was widely applied in the Boer War (1899–1902) and was used by both sides in World War I. Indeed, the telegraph remained a means of military communication through World War II. Only after 1950 did telegraph usage decline in the face of competition from the telephone. Today few except radio ham operators use Morse code. The best-known telegraph signal is SOS, a call for assistance, consisting of three dots, three dashes, and three dots again.

Further Reading

Beauchamp, Ken. *History of Telegraphy.* London: IEE, 2001.
Wilson, Geoffrey. *The Old Telegraphs.* London: Phillimore, 1976.

Telephone

A communications device used to send and receive sound, usually speech, the telephone has also been adapted for data communication (telex, fax, and Internet). Telephone equipment consists of a bell, beeper, light, or other device so that the user is alerted to incoming calls and number buttons or (in earlier models) a rotary dial to enter a telephone number for outgoing calls. Work on telephone development was carried out by Innocenzo Manzetti, Antonio Meucci, Johann Philipp Reis, Elisha Gray, Alexander Graham Bell, and Thomas Edison. On March 7, 1876, Bell was granted a U.S. patent for "Improvement in Telegraphy," covering "the method of, and apparatus for, transmitting vocal or other sounds telegraphically . . . by causing electrical undulations, similar in form to the vibrations of the air accompanying the said vocal or other sound."

The telephone was adopted for military use more slowly than the telegraph. There were several reasons for this. The telephone left no physical record of a message, and until World War I, telephone signals were largely local. Yet the telephone could be easily used (no need for trained specialists), allowed fast transmission of messages without code, and encouraged two-way communication. Drawbacks included fragility and susceptibility to interference.

By the early 1880s, the British were using telephones over short distances in African colonial campaigns and in India, while the U.S. Army Signal Corps installed experimental telephones in 1878 and soon began to employ them at seacoast defenses for fire control. Following telegraph precedents, both man-carried and horse-borne means of laying wire in the field were developed. Hand generator and battery systems were both used, the former in combat conditions and the latter on individual posts.

Britain used telephones during the Boer War (1899–1902). During the Spanish-American war (1898), the U.S. Army Signal Corps established telephone networks within bases, and national military leaders in Washington, D.C., could call Tampa, Florida, the principal assembly point for Cuba. In the American West, telegraph lines that connected military posts slowly gave way to telephone networks.

By World War I, the military telephone was widely used. French civilian telephone networks were also utilized, but demand surpassed their capacity. The introduction of telephone repeaters allowed service over longer distances and use of thinner, lighter wire. Static trench warfare on the Western Front favored use of telephones, but even when buried deeply, massive heavy artillery fire repeatedly tore up lines. One important problem was security, and listening by induction to enemy telephone signals was widespread by 1915. For subsequent field operations, British and American forces used a combined buzzer and telephone—the British Fullerphone was the best-known example. The British manufactured more than 40,000 trench telephones that were used on all fronts, linked by manual switchboards. The U.S. Army standardized use of a field telephone based on commercial equipment. Dedicated telephone links were soon established between Allied headquarters and both London and Paris. After 1917 a cadre of some 200 women known as "Hello Girls" operated the switchboards. A huge dedicated network of some 20,000 miles of wire served both telegraph and telephone networks in France.

During World War II, telephones carried two-thirds of communications within the United States and some overseas sites (telegraphy remained the more secure long-distance communication mode). In combat theaters, redundant routing helped ensure communications continuity, although switchboards had changed little since World War I. Britain's Fighter Command connected more than 40 airfields and radar installations during the 1940 Battle of Britain with a dedicated telephone network that made use of redundant facilities to maintain connectivity despite battle damage. German and Japanese forces made extensive use of telephones, though the latter's Pacific islands made radio more practical. In order to improve security,

An officer of the U.S. Army 52nd Telegraph Battalion using a telephone at a switchboard in the Argonne Forest near Montfaucon, Meuse, France, in October 1918. (US Army/ Getty Images)

the Germans banned radio use in preparation for their massive Ardennes Offensive of December 1944, using only secure land lines instead. As a result, the Allied decoding ULTRA operation provided no advance warning of the German attack. During the war, British prime minister Winston Churchill and U.S. president Franklin Roosevelt communicated by secure transatlantic links.

By the late 20th century, telephone links were so common as to have become part of the military background—always available and ready—with a steady progression from analog to digital technology.

Further Reading

Fagan, M. D., ed. *A History of Engineering and Science in the Bell System: National Service in War and Peace (1925–1975).* New York: Bell Telephone Laboratories, 1980.

Lavine, A. Lincoln. *Circuits of Victory.* Garden City, NY: Country Life, 1921.

Scheips, Paul J., ed. *Military Signal Communication,* 2 vols. New York: Arno, 1980.

Ironclad Warships

While steam power was being applied to warships, experiments were also going forward with iron-hulled vessels. The boom in railroad construction in Britain reduced the price of iron and sharply increased the number of men skilled in its manufacture. The first iron vessels were canal boats at the end of the 18th century. In 1838 the British transatlantic liner *Great Britain* proved the durability of iron construction for larger ships, and the next step was to apply this to warships.

The British firm of Laird had already built several iron ships for the East India Company, and in 1839 Laird launched the first iron warship, the *Nemesis,* an iron paddler for the Bengal Marine, the naval arm of the East India Company. The world's first significant iron warship was the steam frigate *Guadeloupe,* built by Laird for Mexico in 1842. It and another Laird iron warship, the *Montezuma,* proved their worth in fighting against Texas. Under fire almost daily over a period of four to five weeks, the *Guadeloupe* was repeatedly hulled, but the shot passed through cleanly with few dangerous splinters (these caused the most personnel casualties in sea battles involving wooden warships), and the holes were easily patched. Royal Navy officers who served on the two ships thought them excellent fighting vessels.

Iron was brittle, however, and experiments revealed that it tended to fracture under the impact of shot, whereas wood merely absorbed it. This and the loss of the iron-hulled troopship *Birkenhead* on February 26, 1852, with the death of 455 people, resulted in a temporary move away from iron hulls.

The Crimean War changed this thinking. On November 30, 1853, at Sinop (Sinope), Turkey, a Russian squadron destroyed a Turkish squadron at anchor. The Russians fired both shot and shell, but shell did the most damage, tearing large irregular holes when it exploded in the wooden sides of the Ottoman ships. The effect of shell in the battle at Sinope was exaggerated—the Ottomans were simply overwhelmed in every category—but the battle renewed interest in iron as armor over wooden ships.

French emperor Napoleon III took the lead, the first ironclad vessels being literally ironclad in that iron armor was applied as plates over the wooden sides. The emperor, who was knowledgeable about artillery, wanted 10 such vessels for the 1855 campaign. But with French yards able to build only 5, he asked Britain to construct a like number. British chief naval engineer Thomas Lloyd meanwhile demonstrated that four inches of iron could indeed protect against powerful shot.

Virtually rectangular in shape so as to provide a more effective gun platform, the French ironclad floating batteries were some 170 feet by 43 feet in size and were protected by 4-inch iron plate backed by 17 inches of wood. Each mounted 16 50-pounder guns and 2 12-pounders and was capable of a speed of four knots under steam. Not seagoing vessels, they were specifically designed to batter Russian land fortifications.

On October 17, 1855, three of the French *batteries flottantes cuirassées* (armored floating batteries), the *Dévastation, Lave,* and *Tonnante,* took part in an attack on Russia's Kinburn forts in an estuary at the mouth of the Dnieper and Bug Rivers. The Russian fortifications, three of which were of stone and two of sand, housed 81 guns and mortars. From a range of between 900 and 1,200 yards in an engagement lasting from 9:30 a.m. until noon, the French vessels fired 3,177 shot and shell and reduced the Russian forts to rubble. Although they were repeatedly hulled, the vessels themselves were largely impervious to the Russian fire. The *Dévastation* suffered 67 hits and the *Tonnante* 66. Two men were killed and 24 wounded, but the casualties resulted from two hot shot entering gun ports and another through an imperfect main hatch. The vessels' armor was only dented. At noon an Allied fleet of ships of the line shelled what was left of the forts from a range of 1,600 yards, and in less than 90 minutes the Russians surrendered. Undoubtedly the success of the batteries was magnified because they were the emperor's special project, but many observers concluded that the Kinburn battle proved the effectiveness of wrought iron and marked the end of the old ships of the line.

Britain also built four floating batteries in 1856. Of the same general size as the French vessels, they were each armed with 14 68-pounder guns and were protected by four-inch iron armor, supported by six inches of oak.

Many observers now considered wooden warships to be obsolete, and the next step was to build true ironclad warships as opposed to mere floating batteries. France took the lead because it had far less to lose than the British, who maintained the world's largest wooden navy. The *Gloire* of 1860 began the naval revolution. The British responded with their *Warrior* of 1861, the first iron-hulled, armor-plated warship.

The American Civil War (1861–1865) saw the most extensive ironclad construction and helped prompt further ironclad construction. The U.S. Navy *Monitor* of 1861 was the most innovative, although not necessarily the most practical, of the early ironclad designs. During the war the North alone laid down 56 ironclads (52 of them of the turreted or *Monitor* type). The first clash between ironclad warships occurred in March 1862 during the Civil War when the *Monitor* and the Confederate ironclad *Virginia* fought to a stalemate in Hampton Roads, Virginia.

Further Reading

Baxter, James Phinney. *The Introduction of the Ironclad Warship.* New York: Archon, 1968.

George, James L. *History of Warships: From Earliest Times to the Twenty-First Century.* Annapolis, MD: Naval Institute Press, 1998.

Tucker, Spencer C. *Handbook of 19th Century Naval History.* Stroud, UK: Sutton, 2000.

Warrior, HMS

The Royal Navy armored frigate *Warrior* was the world's first seagoing iron-hulled warship. The Royal Navy was slow to introduce ironclad ships; after all, it had the world's largest wooden navy. The French decision in 1856 to build six seagoing ironclads brought action, however. News of the construction of the French *Gloire,* which reached Britain in May 1858, created something akin to panic. The British public need not have worried. Britain led the world in metallurgical techniques, and its armor plate was superior to that of France. The British also led in the development of rifled heavy ordnance.

Construction of the *Warrior* demonstrated the British determination to retain the technological lead at sea. As the Royal Dockyards lacked the experience and facilities to build large iron ships, the *Warrior* was ordered in May 1859 from the Thames Ironworks Company of Blackwall, London. The novelty of the construction and modifications to the design brought construction delays. The *Warrior* was launched in December 1860 and entered service in June 1862. At 9,210 tons and 380 feet in length and 58.5 feet in beam, the *Warrior* was larger than the *Gloire* and any wooden warship.

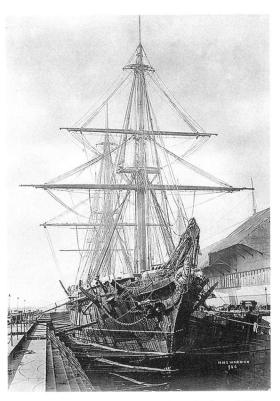

The warship *Warrior* in drydock at the Royal Navy Yard, Portsmouth, England, toward the end of its 1872-1875 refit. The *Warrior* was the world's first iron-hulled, armor-plated warship. (U.S. Naval Historical Center)

A quantum leap forward in ship design, the *Warrior* immediately made every other warship in the world obsolete. Whereas the *Gloire* was merely a wooden ship protected by iron plate, the *Warrior* was virtually an iron vessel. The ship was protected by a 4.5-inch band of iron bolted to .625-inch plating and 18 inches of teak running from 6 feet below to 6 feet above the waterline. The ends of the hull were divided into watertight compartments, a major innovation made possible by the iron construction. The heart of the design, however, was the citadel, a 210-foot-long armored box protecting the guns and machinery. Powered by a 1,250-horsepower engine (10 boilers and 40 furnaces), the *Warrior* nonetheless retained a full sail rig.

The *Warrior* had just one gun deck, but it carried a powerful battery of 10 Armstrong 110-pounder and 4 70-pounder Armstrong breech-loading rifled guns and 26 68-pounder muzzle-loading smoothbores. This was a heavier armament than wooden ships of the line, the guns of which could not penetrate its armor.

With its long, sleek lines, the *Warrior* was the prototype of the new warship. A true seagoing design, the ship was much faster than conventional ships of the line. The *Warrior* could make up to 13.75 knots under sail, 14.33 under steam, and 17.5

knots combined. Properly handled, with its superior speed, armor, and long-range guns, it could have destroyed any ship in the world.

Hulked in 1902, in 1923 the *Warrior* became a jetty at an oil terminal in Wales. Rescued in the 1970s, the ship was restored and in 1986 returned to Portsmouth as the largest historic ship in the dockyard complex. It can be toured there today.

Further Reading

Hamilton, C. I. *Anglo-French Naval Rivalry, 1846–1870.* Oxford: Oxford University Press, 1993.

Lambert, Andrew. Warrior: *The First and Last Ironclad.* London: Conway Maritime, 1987.

Naval Gun Turret

Following the decision to arm ships with a few large-bore pivot-mounted guns as their principal armament, the next step was an armored turret to protect the guns and their crews, especially during the lengthy reloading process. During the Crimean War (1853–1856), Royal Navy captain Cowper Coles designed two floating batteries to engage Russian shore batteries at close range. The second of these mounted a 68-pounder protected by a hemispheric iron shield, which during action proved largely impervious to hostile fire.

In March 1859 Coles patented the idea of turrets aboard ship. He advocated guns mounted on the centerline of the vessel so as to have wide arcs of fire on either side of the ship and halving the number of guns previously required for broadsides fire. Coles's persistence, coupled with the powerful support of Prince Albert, led the Admiralty in March 1861 to install an experimental armored turret on the floating battery *Trusty.* The test was a success, for 33 hits from 68-pounder and 100-pounder guns failed to disable it.

The Coles turret turned on a circumferential roller path set in the lower deck, operated by two men with a hand crank. Its upper 4.5 feet of armor came up through the main or upper deck and formed an armored glacis to protect the lower part. The crew and ammunition entered the turret from below through a hollow central cylinder.

The first British seagoing turreted ship was the Coles-inspired *Prince Albert* of 1864. It mounted four 9-inch muzzle-loading rifles, one each in four centerline circular turrets, turned by hand; 18 men could complete a revolution in one minute. The problem of centerline turrets in a ship of high superstructure and sail rig and very low freeboard (the latter the result of a design error) contributed to the disastrous loss at sea of the Coles-designed HMS *Captain* in 1870. Most of its crew drowned, Coles among them.

In the United States, John Ericsson's single revolving turret the *Monitor* entered service in March 1862. The *Monitor* and many follow-on types all had very low freeboard. This lessened the amount of armor required to protect the ship, allowing it to be concentrated in the turret. Unlike the *Captain,* however, the *Monitor* had no high superstructure or sail rig.

Ericsson's turret was all above the upper deck, on which it rested. Before the turret could be turned, it had to be lifted by rack and pinion from contact with the deck. A steam engine operating through gearing turned the turret around a central spindle. The *Monitor* was the first time that a revolving turret had actually been employed in battle, in its March 9, 1862, engagement with CSS *Virginia.*

Sharp disagreement continued between those who favored the revolving turret and supporters of broadside armament. Renewed interest in the ram—in consequence of the 1866 Battle of Lissa—and larger, more powerful guns helped decide this in favor of the turret. The ram meant that ships had to fire ahead as they prepared to attack an opposing vessel; heavier guns meant that ships needed fewer of them and that these should have the widest possible arc of fire. The elimination of sail rigs and improved ship designs heightened the stability of turreted warships.

Turrets continued to undergo design refinement and received new breech-loading guns as well as heavier armor, indeed the thickest aboard ship. Relatively thin top-of-turret armor on British battle cruisers, however, led to the loss of three of them to German armor-piercing shells in the Battle of Jutland (May 31–June 1, 1916). The battle cruiser turrets also lacked flash-protection doors and the means of preventing a shell burst inside the turret from reaching the magazines. The largest battleship ever built, the Japanese *Yamato* had 25.6 inches of steel armor protection on its turrets.

Further Reading

Hawkey, Arthur. *Black Night off Finisterre: The Tragic Tale of an Early British Ironclad.* Annapolis, MD: Naval Institute Press, 1999.

Hogg, Ivan, and John Batchelor. *Naval Gun.* Poole, Dorset, UK: Blandford, 1978.

Hough, Richard. *Fighting Ships.* New York: Putnam, 1969.

Padfield, Peter. *Guns at Sea.* New York: St. Martin's, 1974.

Tucker, Spencer C. *Handbook of 19th Century Naval Warfare.* Stroud, UK: Sutton, 2000.

Monitor, USS

The U.S. Navy *Monitor* was a revolutionary warship built during the American Civil War (1861–1865). Officials in Washington, D.C., were well aware that the Confederates were rebuilding the former steam sloop *Merrimack* as an ironclad, subsequently christened the *Virginia.* In consequence, in August 1861 Congress appropriated $1.5 million for U.S. ironclad construction. Swedish American engineer John Ericsson's design was by far the most revolutionary of the three considered and secured approval only because of the perceived threat from the *Virginia* and because Ericsson promised to complete the work quickly. The contract was highly unusual and reflected the serious government doubts about the ship, which some dubbed "Ericsson's Folly." Ericsson and his partners had to assume all the risk. If the ship failed in any way—with the navy to determine what constituted failure—then all sums advanced for its construction were to be returned to the government.

In contrast to the lengthy delays that marked construction of the *Virginia,* USS *Monitor* was completed in record time. Laid down in Brooklyn, New York, on October 25, 1861, the ship was ready for its trials on February 19, 1862. It was commissioned six days later.

The *Monitor* revolutionized naval warfare. Entirely of iron, it incorporated such innovations as forced draft ventilation. Of only 987 tons displacement, the ship was 179 feet long, with a beam of 41 feet 6 inches and a draft of only 10 feet 6 inches (half that of the *Virginia*). Its two engines delivered 320 horsepower to a single screw propeller. Design speed was nine knots, although actual speed was somewhat less.

For all practical purposes, the *Monitor* had two hulls: an upper or armored raft supported by a lower iron hull. The raft portion had 2 inches of iron on the deck and 4.5 inches on the sides. To shield the hull, the armor extended 3 feet 6 inches below the waterline. The *Monitor*'s most visible part was its 120-ton 9-foot-tall spindle-mounted turret amidships, with an interior diameter of less than 20 feet.

The turreted U.S. Navy ironclad *Monitor*, designed by John Ericsson. The light damage sustained in its May 9, 1862 fight with the Confederate ironclad ram *Virginia*—the first clash between two ironclad ships in history—may be seen in the slight dents in its revolving turret. (Library of Congress)

The turret had two side-by-side gun ports and mounted a pair of 9-inch Dahlgren smoothbores. Because the turret rotated, the ship's gun ports could be protected from enemy fire while the guns themselves were being reloaded. The turret and a small pilothouse (the command center of the ship) located forward and extending only 3 feet 10 inches above the deck were both heavily protected. The turret had eight layers of 1-inch plating, and the pilothouse nine layers. Most of the ship's machinery was below the waterline.

The turret was a great advantage in that it provided protection for the gun crews and could fire on an opponent with the ship in almost any direction, but because of the turret's great weight, Ericsson designed the *Monitor* with very low freeboard, only 18 inches. The *Monitor* thus came to be called "a hat on the water" or "a cheesebox on a raft." Ericsson simply ignored the contract requirement that the ship sport a sail rig. The *Monitor* and its offspring were coastal vessels rather than seagoing ships. They were also unsuited for blockade duties, as in rough seas the crews had no alternative but to batten down the hatches and remain below.

Following the success of the *Monitor* in its March 9, 1862, battle with the *Virginia* in Hampton Roads, the North was swept up in a so-called monitor mania. Of 56 ironclads laid down by the North during the war, 52 were of the *Monitor* or turreted type. The *Monitor* itself succumbed to a storm while under tow off the Atlantic coast on December 31, 1862. The wreck was located in 1975 and is now protected as the first U.S. National Marine Sanctuary Site. Parts of the ship, including its turret, can be seen at the Mariner's Museum in Virginia.

Further Reading

Baxter, James P. *The Introduction of the Ironclad Warship.* Cambridge, MA: Harvard University Press, 1933.

Bennett, Frank M. *The* Monitor *and the Navy under Steam.* Boston: Scribner, 1900.

Miller, Edward N. *U.S.S.* Monitor: *The Ship That Launched a Modern Navy.* Annapolis, MD: Leeward Publications, 1978.

Minié Ball

The minié system revolutionized military small arms in the 1850s. Others had experimented with similar ideas, but in 1849 Captain Claude Étienne Minié designed the bullet named for him. The French were particularly interested in developing a more rapidly fired rifle to deal with the Arabs in Algeria, who sniped at them from long range. The system proved effective, and in 1851 the British Army also adopted it, ordering 23,000 "Minié Rifled Musquets," many of which saw service in the Crimean War of 1854–1856. Ultimately any rifle with a similar bullet system became known as the "Minnie."

The minié ball (known as the Minnie ball during the American Civil War) was not a cylindrical ball at all but rather a cylindro-conoidal lead bullet that contained an iron plug set in a hollow in the base of the bullet, which was also cast in a diameter slightly smaller than the gun bore. When inserted into the rifle's muzzle, the bullet slid easily down the bore, but on the explosion of the gunpowder at the base of the bore, the base plug pushed forward a fraction of a second ahead of the rest of the bullet, expanding the soft lead to grip the rifling and cause the bullet to be fired on an accurate trajectory. A simpler form of the original minié bullet simply had a hollowed-out cone base. This had the same effect of expanding the bullet with the discharge of the powder and sealing the bore.

The Minié system combined the ease of loading of the smoothbore musket with the accuracy of the rifle. The new minié ball rifle could be loaded and fired as fast as the old smoothbore musket (perhaps three times a minute), but it had far greater effective range: at least 400 yards as opposed to 100–200 yards for the smoothbore musket. The two developments of the new bullet and reliable percussion primer ignition produced a tremendous increase in long-range defensive infantry firepower.

As is usually the case, tactics lagged behind technology. A great many lives would be lost in the wars of the mid-19th century, especially the American Civil War, to the failure to appreciate the effects of long-range rifle fire from defensive positions against charging troops.

Further Reading

Blackmore, H. L. "The Percussion System." In *Pollard's History of Firearms,* edited by Claude Blair, 161–187. New York: Macmillan, 1986.

Tunis, Edwin. *Weapons: A Pictorial History.* New York: World Publishing, 1954.

Revolver

The development of pistols paralleled that of muskets. Alexander Forsyth's patent of mercury fulminates as priming for firearms in 1807 was a great boon in pistol development.

Pistols proliferated in the 19th century. There were many types, but among notable designs were those of American Henry Deringer Jr. Deringer opened a business in Philadelphia in 1806 and routinely made flintlock muskets for the federal government. He was one of the first gun makers to embrace the new percussion cap system, although he did not receive his first government contract for percussion firearms until 1845. Deringer's muzzle-loading rifled percussion cap pistols were of varying bore size and had barrels that were one to six inches in length. The smaller pistols could easily be carried concealed and became de rigueur for many men and women, especially in the more lawless American West and South.

So-called pepperbox pistols were popular for defensive purposes. They had four to six barrels that were loaded separately from the muzzle end. Most often, the barrels were bored into a single piece of metal that then rotated on a long steel pin. In some of these pistols the barrels had to be turned by hand, but soon the barrels were turned by double action; that is, the action of pulling the trigger turned the barrel(s) and raised and dropped the hammer to fire the pistol.

In 1836 Samuel Colt of Hartford, Connecticut, formed the Patent Army Manufacturing Company in Paterson, New Jersey. Its first product was a small five-shot .28-caliber revolver, but its most famous early design was the 1838 Colt Holster Model Paterson Revolver No. 5. Better known as the Texas Paterson, it was .36 caliber, had five cylinders, and came in 4- to 12-inch barrel lengths. This was the first revolving cylinder pistol in general use. Each chamber was separately loaded from the muzzle end and had its own nipple for the copper percussion cap. The drum chamber moved each time the hammer was cocked. Colt revolvers were adopted by both the army and navy and saw wide service in both the Mexican-American War and the American Civil War as well as in fighting with American Indians in the West.

At the same time, breech-loading revolvers appeared. Screw-off barrels had appeared early in the development of firearms, but in 1812 Swiss national Samuel J. Pauly, working in Paris, developed a pistol in which the barrel swivelled downward to allow it to be loaded. It utilized a self-contained cartridge of Pauly's invention, surely one of the most important developments in the history of small arms. Several types of methods were used to fire it.

The development of metal cartridges led to a change from muzzle-loading to breech-loading firearms. Not only were muzzle-loading rifles turned into breech-loaders, but Colt revolvers were similarly transformed. Thus, in the 1870s the Colt Model 1861 navy revolver was converted to a breechloader. In the British .57-caliber aptly named "man-stopper" revolver of 1870–1880, the cylinder was removed for reloading.

There are three principal means of ejecting spent cartridge cases from the cylinder. In the side-gate method, the cartridge cases are pushed rearward out of the cylinder one at a time by means of a hand-operated rod alongside the barrel. In the break-open method, all cartridge cases are ejected at the same time by means of a star-shaped extractor when the revolver is opened. Finally there is the swing-out cylinder, in which all cases are ejected simultaneously by hand with a star-shaped extractor after the cylinder is opened.

The first breech-loading revolver designed specifically for metal cartridges was the Smith and Wesson Model No. 1. Manufactured during 1857–1860, it had a rifled barrel and seven chambers and was hinged at the top. It utilized .22-caliber rimfire ammunition. In 1869 Smith and Wesson produced a .44-caliber revolver for the army. Probably the most famous early revolver in U.S. history was the Colt .45 Peacemaker. Still in production, it was widely used in the American West in fighting against the Indians. The cavalry version had a 7.5-inch barrel and was officially known as the Single Action Army Revolver, Model 1873 Six-shot Caliber .45in Colt. Colt also produced another famous sidearm during 1898–1944, the Colt New Service Double Action Revolver, in .45 caliber.

For the most part, at the end of the 19th century .38 was the standard army caliber. It remained thus until after the Philippine-American War of 1898–1902 when the army sought a caliber with greater stopping power. Competition led to adoption of the Colt semiautomatic .45-caliber pistol, which became the standard sidearm of the U.S. military for the next 70 years.

Among other notable revolvers were designs in the United Kingdom by both Webley and Enfield, produced chiefly in .38 and .455 calibers. During World War II, Britain purchased some 1 million Smith and Wesson .38-caliber revolvers. In 1953 Colt introduced its new, more powerful Colt Python in .357 caliber, and a number of other manufacturers followed suit.

Further Reading

Blair, Claude, ed. *Pollard's History of Firearms.* New York: Macmillan, 1985.

Kinard, Jeff. *Pistols: An Illustrated History of Their Impact.* Santa Barbara, CA: ABC-CLIO, 2003.

Myatt, F. *Illustrated Encyclopedia of Pistols and Revolvers.* London: Salamander Books, 1980.

Taylorson, A. *The Revolver.* 3 vols. London: Arms and Armour, 1966–1970.

Napoleon Gun

The U.S. 12-pounder smoothbore Napoleon gun—the standard fieldpiece of the Union and Confederate Armies in the American Civil War (1861–1865)—was in effect the epitome of five centuries of field artillery development. Officially known in the U.S. Army as the "light 12-pounder gun," this fieldpiece was most often referred to on both sides in the war as the "Napoleon." The gun was named not for French emperor Napoleon I but for his nephew, Emperor Napoleon III (r. 1852–1870). A perceptive student of artillery, Napoleon III conceived a lightweight weapon of uniform caliber that would replace guns and howitzers of differing calibers for field service. Such a weapon would have the great advantage of standardization in ammunition. The new weapon was basically a gun without the powder chamber of the howitzer but able to fire shells at howitzer trajectories if need be. By 1856, so-called gun howitzers had been adopted by France, Prussia, Russia, and other European countries.

The first American Napoleon gun was produced in 1857 by the Ames Manufacturing Co. of Chicopee, Massachusetts. During the war five foundries in the North cast it. By the time production ceased in 1864, they had produced 1,157 guns, of which almost 500 survive. Seven Confederate arsenals cast some 535 Napoleons during the Civil War, of which 133 survive.

There were dozens of varieties of Napoleons. Although some were rifled (of surviving Union Napoleons, only five are rifled), the vast majority were smoothbores of bronze (at the end of the war with bronze in short supply, the Tredegar

An African-American soldier guards a 12-pounder Napoleon gun attached to its limber ready for travel. The Napoleon was the favored artillery piece during the American Civil War. (Library of Congress)

foundry in Richmond cast some Napoleons in iron). Napoleons had a bore diameter of 4.62 inches and a bore length of approximately 64 inches or 14 calibers (the bore being 14 times as long as its bore diameter).

Napoleons were characterized by a smooth exterior appearance without the rings of older guns and with only a slight muzzle swell (the best-known Confederate version had no muzzle swell). The guns weighed about 1,200 pounds, or 100 times the weight of their round shot. Several dozen of the earliest Union Napoleons had handles over their trunnions for lifting the guns, but these were eliminated in late 1861.

Napoleons fired a variety of ammunition, including solid shot, shell, spherical case, grapeshot, and canister. A powder charge of 2.5 pounds gave its solid-shot projectile a range of 1,600 yards, more than sufficient for the line-of-sight firing in mixed country that characterized most Civil War battles. Grapeshot fired at intermediate ranges was especially effective against cavalry charges, while canister from the Napoleon fired at close ranges proved deadly against attacking infantry.

The Napoleon gun was extraordinarily safe for its crews, with few if any recorded instances of them bursting. By the end of the Civil War, Napoleons accounted for four-fifths of Union artillery. The remaining guns were Parrott rifles.

Further Reading

Hazlett, James C., Edwin Olmstead, and M. Hume Parks. *Field Artillery Weapons of the Civil War.* Cranbury, NJ: Associated University Presses, 1983.

Ripley, Warren. *Artillery and Ammunition of the Civil War.* New York: Van Nostrand Reinhold, 1970.

Parrott Guns

Parrott guns were the most widely used rifled gun of the American Civil War (1861–1865). Designed by Robert P. Parrott, superintendent of the West Point Foundry, they were easy to operate, reliable, accurate, and relatively inexpensive to manufacture. Both sides produced them during the war. The Parrott gun was essentially a cast-iron rifled gun with a wrought-iron band shrunk over the breech, the point of greatest strain. The band was equal in thickness to half the diameter of the bore.

Parrott's first rifled gun was a 2.9-inch (land diameter) 10-pounder. Prior to the Civil War, Parrott also produced a 3.67-inch (20-pounder) and a 4.2-inch (30-pounder). Neither the army nor the navy adopted the Parrott guns until after the start of the Civil War. During the war Parrotts were produced in bore diameters of 2.9-inch, 3-inch, 3.3-inch, 3.67-inch, 4.2-inch, 5.3-inch (60-pounder), 6.4-inch (100-pounder army; 80-pounder navy), 8-inch (200-pounder army, 150-pounder navy), and 10-inch (300-pounder army, 250-pounder navy). The guns had spiraled rifling, with from 3 grooves and lands on the 1.9-inch to 15 grooves and lands on the 10-inch.

The smallest U.S. Navy Parrott gun was the 3.67-inch. The larger guns were better suited to naval service, where weight was also not as much a factor as in field artillery on land. The 6.4-inch Parrott, for example, weighed some 9,800 pounds. With a powder charge of 10 pounds and at 35 degrees of elevation, it could fire its projectile more than five miles. The U.S. Navy employed the 8-inch Parrott gun in the turrets of some of its monitors, alongside a smoothbore Dahlgren gun.

The Parrott gun fired an elongated projectile some 3 calibers in length. Cylindro-conical in shape, it had a bronze ring at a contraction in the base. On ignition of the powder charge, the gas expanded the bronze ring into the grooves of the bore, thus imparting a spin to the projectile. Parrott projectiles were fitted with both time and percussion fuzes, and there were also variations with hardened noses to pierce armor.

Both the army and the navy experienced problems during the war with Parrott guns bursting, most notably in operations against Charleston and Fort Fisher. Parrott blamed these on premature shell explosions rather than defects in the bore, but clearly these early rifled guns experienced greater problems than did the smoothbores, especially from grit and sand in the bores. Fewer navy guns burst, which was probably attributable to an order that all rifled projectiles be thoroughly greased before they were loaded. The navy did subsequently remove its heaviest Parrott guns from service, however.

From the beginning of the war through April 1864, nearly 2,000 Parrott guns were manufactured for the U.S. Army and the U.S. Navy, representing about one-fifth of Union guns on land and at sea. The Confederates produced their own Parrott guns at the Tredegar Iron Works in Richmond in 2.9-inch, 3-inch, 3.67-inch, and 4.2-inch sizes.

Further Reading

Hazlett, James C., Edwin Olmstead, and M. Hume Parks. *Field Artillery Weapons of the Civil War.* Newark: University of Delaware Press, 1983.

Olmstead, Edwin, Wayne Stark, and Spencer C. Tucker. *The Big Guns: Civil War Siege, Seacoast, and Naval Cannon.* Alexandria Bay, NY: Museum Restoration Service, 1997.

Tucker, Spencer C. *Arming the Fleet: U.S. Naval Ordnance in the Muzzle-Loading Era.* Annapolis, MD: Naval Institute Press, 1989.

Dahlgren Guns

Commander (later rear admiral) John A. Dahlgren developed a system of guns used extensively throughout the American Civil War (1861–1865) by both sides. In many ways, the Dahlgren gun marked the apogee of the heavy muzzle-loading gun at sea. Dahlgren first arrived at the Washington Navy Yard in 1844 as a lieutenant, assigned there to conduct ordnance-ranging experiments. Soon he was designing new firing locks for guns and had developed a new system of naval ordnance.

In 1849 Dahlgren produced a new boat howitzer for the navy. Cast of bronze, the howitzer appeared as a 12-pounder (light, 660 pounds, and heavy, 750 pounds) and 24-pounder smoothbore (1,300 pounds). There were also 3.4-inch (12-pounder, 870 pounds) and 4-inch (20-pounder, 1,350 pounds) rifles. Dahlgren boat howitzers were the finest guns of their time in the world and remained in service with the U.S. Navy until the 1880s. They were also copied by other navies.

Dahlgren is chiefly remembered, however, for the system of heavy smoothbore, muzzle-loading ordnance that bears his name. In January 1850 he submitted a draft for a 9-inch gun to the chief of ordnance. The first prototype Dahlgren gun was cast at the Fort Pitt Foundry and delivered to the Washington Navy Yard in May 1850. The original 9-incher had a more angular form and only one vent. Later the design was modified in favor of a curved shape and a double vent, and in 1856 the side vents were restored. The purpose of the second vent was to extend the life of the gun. Repeated firings enlarged the vent opening; when this occurred, the second vent, which had been filled with zinc, was opened, and the original vent itself sealed with zinc.

Dahlgren guns, with their smooth exterior, curved lines, and preponderant weight of metal at the breech, resembled in appearance soda water bottles and were

An 11-inch Dahlgren gun on a pivot mount aboard the U.S. Navy sidewheel gunboat *Miami* during the American Civil War. (Naval Historical Center)

sometimes so-called. Dahlgren designed them so as to place the greatest weight of metal at the point of greatest strain at the breech. The IX-inch Dahlgren smooth-bore (shell guns were identified by Roman numerals) remained the most common broadside, carriage-mounted gun in the U.S. Navy in the Civil War; the XI-inch, the prototype of which was cast in 1851, was the most widely used pivot-mounted gun. Its shell could pierce 4.5 inches of plate iron backed by 20 inches of solid oak.

Dahlgren guns appeared in a variety of sizes: 32-pounder (3,300 and 4,500 pounds), VIII-inch (6,500 pounds), IX-inch (12,280 pounds), X-inch (12,500 pounds for shell and 16,500 pounds for shot), XI-inch (16,000 pounds), XIII-inch (34,000 pounds), and XV-inch (42,000 pounds). There was even a XX-inch bore (97,300 pounds) Dahlgren, but it did not see service aboard ship during the war. The XV-inch Dahlgren was employed aboard Union monitors.

Dahlgrens also appeared as rifled guns, somewhat similar in shape to the smooth-bores. Some of these had separate bronze trunnion and breech straps. Dahlgren rifles appeared in these sizes: 4.4-inch/30-pounder (3,200 pounds), 5.1-inch/50-pounder (5,100 pounds), 6-inch/80-pounder (8,000 pounds), 7.5-inch/150-pounder (16,700 pounds), and 12-inch (45,520 pounds, only three of which were cast). Dahlgren's rifled guns were not as successful as his smoothbores, and in February 1862 most were withdrawn from service.

Apart from the rifles, Dahlgren guns were extraordinarily reliable. They remained the standard muzzle-loading guns in the navy until the introduction of breech-loading heavy guns in 1885.

Further Reading

Dahlgren, John A. *Shells and Shell Guns.* Philadelphia: King and Baird, 1856.

Olmstead, Edwin, Wayne Stark, and Spencer Tucker. *The Big Guns: Civil War Siege, Seacoast and Naval Cannon.* Alexandria Bay, NY, and Bloomfield, Ontario, Canada: Museum Restoration Service, 1997.

Tucker, Spencer C. *Arming the Fleet: U.S. Navy Ordnance in the Muzzle-Loading Era.* Annapolis, MD: Naval Institute Press, 1989.

Breech-Loading Rifle

The first guns were actually breechloaders, but the difficulty of effectively sealing the gases at the breech led to their abandonment and embrace of the muzzle-loader, both for cannon and for small arms. Improvements in metallurgical techniques and closer tolerances were one factor in changing this. The other factor was the change from a loose propellant charge in connection with the flint-and-steel method of firing to a metal cartridge case that contained both powder and projectile. Handmade cartridge cases, tailored to the gun so that their fire port matched one drilled through the gun breech, while possible for the very rich, were not practical for the equipment of mass armies.

The discovery of fulminate of mercury and the development of Alexander Forsyth's percussion cap did away with the necessity of striking fire outside the gun. The next step was to incorporate the percussion cap into a cartridge holding both gunpowder and the bullet, while a hinged-block or bolt opening made in the breech allowed the cartridge to be inserted there. Pulling the trigger released a steel pin that jabbed into the percussion cap and ignited it and thus the main charge. The first was the pin-fire cartridge in the 1840s, followed by the rimfire cartridge and then the central-fire cartridge by 1860. Prussia took the lead. In the 1840s it adopted the Dreyse breech-loading rifle, better known as the needle gun, a bolt-operated weapon that, however, utilized a paper cartridge.

The Spencer carbine of the American Civil War (1861–1865) was another important step forward. First issued to units of the Union Army, it featured a magazine, loaded through the butt of the rifle stock, that could hold seven metallic rimfire cartridges. These were fed to the breech by means of a compressed spring. When the trigger guard was lowered, the breechblock dropped down, ejecting the spent cartridge case. As the trigger guard was returned to its normal position, the breechblock moved up, catching a new cartridge and inserting it into the breech. Among the most important weapons utilizing this principle were the .44-caliber rimfire, lever-action, breech-loading rifle designed by American Benjamin Taylor

Henry in the late 1850s and the "improved Henry," the Model 1866 lever-action Winchester, its most notable improvement over the Henry being the addition of a patented cartridge-loading gate system that allowed for a closed magazine tube and a wood forearm. The Model 1866 fired the same .44-caliber rimfire round as the Henry rifle; however, cartridge improvements allowed a shorter carbine barrel length. Its follow-on was the Winchester Model 1873, the weapon that is said to have "won the West."

The breechloader could be loaded and fired three times as fast as the old muzzle-loader, but its chief advantage was that this could be easily accomplished in the prone position. By the 1870s breechloaders had magazines attached from which rounds could be fed to the breech as fast as the rifleman could aim, fire, and work the reloading mechanism that would eject the spent case, feed a new round into the breech, and cock the firing mechanism by either bolt or lever action.

By the first decade of the 20th century, such fine bolt-action repeating rifles as the German Mauser, the Austrian Mannlicher, the Russian Mosin-Nagant, the British Lee-Enfield, and the American Springfield provided riflemen with greatly enhanced firepower at ranges of up to 1,000 yards or more.

Further Reading

Blair, Claude, ed. *Pollard's History of Firearms.* New York: Macmillan, 1983.

Smith, W. H. B. *Small Arms of the World.* London: Arms and Armour, 1984.

Dreyse Needle Gun

Johann Nikolaus von Dreyse of Prussia is credited with the invention of the first practical bolt-action, breech-loading rifle. The Dreyse employed a paper cartridge with the primer situated at the base of the bullet. The charge was detonated by means of a long, sharp needlelike firing pin that pierced the cartridge and drove through the entire length to crush the primer against the base of the bullet. The Dreyse came to be known for its firing mechanism as the needle gun.

The Dreyse mechanism was for all intents and purposes the same as that employed in bolt actions today. A rigid arm on the bolt was raised and pulled back, exposing the breech. Once the cartridge was seated, the bolt was then pushed forward and down, closing the breech. Pulling the trigger released a spring that drove the needle forward into the cartridge, igniting the primer. The Dreyse cartridge had no extractor because the cartridge was paper and combustible.

Dreyse introduced his rifle in 1828. The Prussian Army began tests with it and officially adopted it in 1848, the first army in the world to go over exclusively to the breechloader. Despite serious problems—the Dreyse needle gun leaked gases from the breech, leading soldiers to fire it from the hip rather than the shoulder. Its high rate of fire of up to six times that of the standard muzzle-loader proved to be a tremendous advantage. The needle gun was in large part responsible for the success of Prussian arms against the Danes and the Austrians in 1864. It proved inferior, however, to the French chassepot of 1866, another needle-type gun that also utilized a combustible paper cartridge yet had more effective sealing at the breech. After the Franco-Prussian War, the Prussians modified captured chassepots for use by their own army.

Further Reading

Blair, Claude, ed. *Pollard's History of Firearms.* New York: Macmillan, 1983.

Cartridge

The cartridge is a case containing the charge for a gun. Later for small arms and most artillery it consisted of a single entity containing the powder charge, primer, and projectile. At first artillerists simply measured a loose amount of cannon powder to ladle into the bore of the gun. Cartridges came into general use in the second half of the 16th century. They offered the advantage of containing a precise amount of powder, which could vary and be so marked for the range desired. Once the desired sack of powder had been selected, it was rammed to the bottom of the bore and pierced by means of a sharp pick thrust through the touchhole of the gun. Fine gunpowder was then poured into the touchhole, and the gun was fired when this was ignited.

Cartridge cases were most usually of wool, paper, or parchment, but all left some residue in the bore, necessitating cleaning out the bore every few shots with a device known as a worm, which looked like a double corkscrew. The bore also had to be sponged out after every round, because burning residue might ignite the next powder charge as it was being loaded. Cartridges were usually made up by gunners in garrison on land or by a ship's gunner and his assistants at sea, to be stored until use.

Small-arms cartridges consisted of the entire round of cartridge case, powder, and ball. The individual ripped open the end of the cartridge case with his teeth and poured a small amount of powder into the flintlock's flash pan. He then poured the remaining powder down the barrel, to be followed by the ball and cartridge casing, which were seated at the base of the bore by means of a rammer. The cartridge case served as wadding to ensure that the ball did not move away from the powder charge when the weapon's muzzle was lowered into firing position.

In 1807 Scottish Presbyterian minister Alexander Forsyth patented a gun lock utilizing newly discovered mercuric fulminates as a priming charge for firearms. A percussion cap, the inside of which was coated with the mercuric fulminates, was placed over the touchhole of a firearm. When struck a blow by a hammer, it ignited and sent a flame down the touchhole to ignite the main charge in the bore. This system revolutionized the firing of small arms by sharply reducing misfires. It worked effectively with smaller individual firearms but not in large cannon with long touchholes. These guns continued to be fired by means of a loose fine powder poured into the touchhole or a quill arrangement containing such powder.

A number of individuals in different countries experimented with ways to combine the percussion cap with the cartridge and projectile into one unit. In 1812 Swiss national Samuel J. Pauly patented a cartridge incorporating a metal base with a cavity for detonating powder and a striker to ignite it. It was certainly one of the most important inventions in the history of small arms.

In 1828 Johann Nikolaus von Dreyse of Prussia invented the needle gun. The first practical bolt-action, breech-loading rifle, it employed a paper cartridge with the primer situated at the base of the bullet. The charge was detonated by a long, sharp needlelike firing pin that pierced the cartridge and drove through the entire length to crush the primer against the base of the bullet. It was adopted by the Prussian Army in 1841.

In 1829, meanwhile, Frenchman Clement Pottet designed a cartridge incorporating a depression at its base to receive a primer of fulminates. A metal cartridge case with priming on the inside of the rim of the base was patented in 1846. Such rimfire cartridges continue in those for the small-bore .22-caliber rifle of today. Pin-fire cartridges had a pin in the center of the base of the cartridge case that exploded the primer. Mass-produced metal cartridge cases appeared in the 1850s, while the French Schneider cartridge of 1858 with a paper upper section and a brass base was utilized in the shotgun shell.

The center-fire brass cartridge case won out. It had a primer situated in the center of its base. This helped facilitate the development of the modern bolt-action and semiautomatic rifles as well as the automatic-fire machine guns that appeared in a large number of types by the 1880s. Metal cartridge cases could also be retrieved, resized, fitted with a new primer, and reloaded.

Powder-bag cartridge charges continued for the largest naval and land guns, but brass fixed one-piece cartridge cases containing the primer, charge, and projectile became the norm for light artillery. These facilitated loading and made possible the so-called quick-firing guns that appeared at the end of the 19th century. Although there have been experiments with other types of cartridge cases, mostly plastics, the vast majority of subsequent changes in ammunition have been in the projectiles and in their propellant charges rather than the cartridge cases itself.

Further Reading

Blair, Claude, ed. *Pollard's History of Firearms.* New York: Macmillan, 1983.

Brown, G. I. *The Big Bang.* Stroud, Gloucestershire, UK: Sutton, 2005.

Hoyden, G. A. *The History and Development of Small Arms Ammunition.* Tacoma, WA: Armory, 1981.

Dynamite

Dynamite is a powerful explosive invented by Swedish chemist and engineer Alfred Nobel in 1866 and patented a year later. Nobel's involvement in heavy construction work in Stockholm led him to try to develop safer methods of blasting rock. In 1846 Italian chemist Ascanio Sobrero had invented nitroglycerine. It consists of a mix of sulfuric acid, nitric acid, and glycerine. A powerful explosive, nitroglycerine soon found application in commercial mining and blasting operations, but it suffered from the drawback of being highly volatile in its liquid state. Even a slight shock can cause nitroglycerin to explode, and it was thus very dangerous to transport and utilize.

Nobel discovered that nitroglycerin could be stabilized when absorbed in diatomaceous earth (kieselguhr). He named his invention dynamite after the Greek *dynamos* ("powerful"). It was the first safe and predictable explosive with a greater force than gunpowder and was certainly one of the great inventions of the 19th century.

Dynamite consists of three parts nitroglycerin and one part diatomaceous earth as well as a small amount of sodium carbonate. Dynamite most usually is formed into sticks about an inch in diameter and eight inches long and wrapped in paper. These sticks were so formed in order that they could be easily inserted in holes drilled into rock.

Dynamite is classified as a high explosive, meaning that it detonates instead of deflagrating. Nobel sold his explosive as "Nobel's Safety Blasting Powder." In order to detonate the dynamite, Nobel also developed a blasting cap, which he also patented. It was ignited by lighting a fuze.

Dynamite found wide application in such areas as construction, mining all sorts of materials, and digging canals and tunnels. Its military implications were also immense. Dynamite found its way into high-explosive fillers for artillery shells, bombs, and land mines. It was also used in satchel charges.

Nobel made a great fortune from his invention. The Republic of South Africa soon became the largest producer of dynamite, which was widely used in mining for gold. Nobel later used some of his money gained from the invention to establish prizes in the sciences, although the most recognized of these prizes is the Nobel Prize for Peace. Nobel's invention ended centuries of experiment with gunpowder and inaugurated a new era of vastly more powerful high explosives.

Further Reading

Brown, Stephen R. *A Most Damnable Invention: Dynamite, Nitrates, and the Making of the Modern World*. New York: St. Martin's, 2005.

Fordham, Stanley. *High Explosives and Propellents*. Oxford, UK: Pergamon, 1980.

Gatling Gun

The American Civil War (1861–1865) gave rise to a number of new weapons. Among these were several precursors to the modern machine gun, including Wilson Ager's "Coffee Mill." It took its name from the means of feeding the ammunition from the top of the weapon by a funnel and crank mechanism, all of which resembled a coffee mill.

Ager's gun had a single barrel. The ammunition was formed of a steel tube that contained powder and a .58-caliber bullet and a nipple at the end for a percussion cap. Steady turning of the crank dropped a round into the chamber, locked the breechblock in place, dropped a hammer that fired the round, and ejected the spent case. Ager claimed a firing rate of 100 rounds a minute, although the gun barrel could not have long withstood the heat thus generated.

Ager demonstrated his weapon before President Abraham Lincoln, and the U.S. Army eventually purchased 50 of them. The Coffee Mills proved unreliable, however, in combat use and were never employed en masse. Ultimately they were employed in the defensives of the city of Washington.

Confederate Army captain D. R. Williams also invented a mechanical gun. Mounted on a mountain-howitzer carriage, it was a 4-foot-long 1-pounder of 1.57-inch bore. Operated by a hand crank, it utilized paper cartridges and could fire 65 shots a minute. It tended to overheat, and it was also not a true machine weapon in that ammunition was fed into it by hand.

Other such weapons also appeared, but the most famous of mechanical guns was that invented by Richard Jordan Gatling in 1862. Well aware of problems from the buildup of heat, Gatling designed his gun with six rotating barrels around a central axis; each barrel fired in turn and each with its own bolt and firing pin. Thus, in a firing rate of 300 rounds per minute, each barrel would have been utilized only 50 times.

The Gatling gun employed a hopper for the ammunition similar to that of the Coffee Mill. The first Gatling gun employed steel cylinders with a percussion cap at the end, a round, and paper cartridges with the charge. The production model did away with the percussion cap in favor of a rimfire cartridge. Turning the crank rotated the barrels, dropped in the rounds, and fired each barrel in turn. The chief difference from the Coffee Mill was in the rotating multiple barrel design.

The U.S. Army's chief of ordnance Colonel John W. Ripley, who was well known for his opposition to innovative weaponry, blocked adoption of the Gatling gun. Gatling's North Carolina birth also seems to have worked against him. Despite Gatling's appeals to Lincoln, the army never adopted the gun. Its only use in the Civil War came when Major General Benjamin Butler purchased six of them at his own expense and employed them effectively in the siege of Petersburg at the end of the war.

In 1864 Gatling redesigned the gun so that each barrel had its own chamber, which helped prevent the leakage of gas. He also adopted center-fire cartridges. These and other refinements produced a rate of fire of about 300 rounds per minute. Finally in 1866 the U.S. Army purchased 100 Gatling guns, equally divided between 6-barrel models of 1-inch caliber and 10-barrel models of .50-inch caliber. Gatling worked out a licensing agreement with Colt Arms to produce the gun.

The Gatling gun provided effective service in the Indian Wars in the American West and in the Spanish American War. The V Corps' Gatling Gun Detachment played an important role in the campaign in Santiago, Cuba, especially in the U.S. victory in the Battle of San Juan Hill of July 1, 1898. They also were utilized in the Puerto Rico Campaign.

Gatling guns also served with the U.S. Navy. Tested by the British government in 1870, the Gatling gun outshot its competition by a wide margin and was adopted by both the British Army and the Royal Navy in .42 caliber and .65 caliber, respectively. It remained the standard mechanical rapid-fire weapon until the introduction of the Maxim gun, the first true machine gun.

During the Vietnam War era Gatling-type weapons returned, this time electrically driven. The 20mm M-61 Vulcan automatic cannon was first designed as an aircraft weapon but was also used as a ground-based antiaircraft weapon. The smaller 7.62mm M-134 minigun was primarily a helicopter-mounted weapon.

Further Reading

Berk, Joseph. *The Gatling Gun: 19th Century Machine Gun to 21st Century Vulcan.* Boulder, CO: Paladin, 1991.

Wahl, Paul, and Don Toppel. *The Gatling Gun.* New York: Arco, 1965.

Willbanks, James A. *Machine Guns: An Illustrated History of Their Impact.* Santa Barbara, CA: ABC-CLIO, 2004.

Mitrailleuse

In the 1860s and 1870s a number of inventors attempted to produce a truly automatic machine gun. Among them, Belgian engineer Joseph Montigny developed the *mitrailleuse* ("grape shooter" or "grapeshot shooter," today "machine gun"), a name that implied a weapon for the controlled dispersion of grapeshot on the battlefield.

Montigny's *mitrailleuse* incorporated first 37 barrels, later reduced to 25, in one tubular casing. Rather than single rounds being fed into a rotating breech from a hopper or magazine, the *mitrailleuse* incorporated a metal magazine plate. A long lever moved back the breechblock with its 37 firing pins. The metal plate holding the 37 cartridges was then inserted into a slot in the face of the block, which was then moved forward, pushing the cartridges into their chambers. Revolving a crank at the rear of the gun caused all the barrels to fire simultaneously. A later cam mechanism allowed selective volley fire.

A well-drilled crew with preloaded plates could keep up a rate of fire of 150–250 rounds per minute and even reach 400. The chief drawback to the new weapon was its weight, for the *mitrailleuse* mounted on its field carriage weighed 2,000 pounds without the ammunition. Montigny sold his new weapon to the Belgian government to use in fortress defense. He also managed to interest French emperor Napoleon III, himself an apt student of artillery, in his new weapon.

In 1869 the French began secret manufacture of the new weapon at the Meudon Arsenal under Montigny's direction. Meudon eventually produced 156 13mm 25-barrel *mitrailleuses*. Only its crews were allowed to see and use the new weapon, which was deployed in utmost secrecy.

The *mitrailleuse* proved to be a disappointment in the Franco-Prussian War of 1870–1871. The veil of official secrecy had prevented discussion in the military of its correct battlefield deployment. Perhaps in part because of its weight and transport problems, the French persisted in thinking of it as an artillery piece and located it with their artillery guns in the open with the plan of using it to provide covering fire for their infantry. The *mitrailleuse,* however, had a maximum range of 1,800 yards, while the Prussian artillery could range out to 2,500 yards. The result was predictable; as soon as the Prussians spotted the *mitrailleuse,* they opened fire on it with their artillery and destroyed it. If deployed forward using cover and concealment, the *mitrailleuse* could be very effective, as was demonstrated in the Battle of Gravelotte (August 18, 1870).

The war ended before the French Army had figured out the proper employment of the new weapon. Unfortunately, its failure on the battlefield led many European observers to denigrate the role and impact of the later machine gun and may well have caused the British and French to delay introducing the latter.

Further Reading

Howard, Michael. *The Franco-Prussian War.* New York: Routledge, 2001.

Wawro, Geoffrey. *The Franco-Prussian War: The German Conquest of France in 1870–1871.* New York: Cambridge University Press, 2003.

Willbanks, James H. *Machine Guns: An Illustrated History of Their Impact.* Santa Barbara, CA: ABC-CLIO, 2004.

Lebel Rifle

In 1886 France was the first nation to add a high-velocity, small-bore rifle to its arms inventory. It was also the first standard weapon to incorporate the spitzer bullet. Two years earlier French chemist Paul Vielle developed a successful nitrocellulose powder for small arms; his Poudre B was the first successful smokeless powder adopted by any nation. Weapons utilizing it also had a much higher muzzle velocity than those employing ordinary gunpowder cartridges.

The French government was not slow to capitalize on Vielle's work. Two years later it introduced the 8mm (.315-caliber) Lebel, based on the earlier 11mm Gras and officially known as the Fusil d'infanterie Modèle 1886. It was named for Colonel Nicolas Lebel, who chaired the committee that oversaw its development. Because the powder was more powerful, the French were able to reduce the caliber of the weapon and hence the weight of the ammunition, permitting individual soldiers to carry more rounds. With the Lebel, France captured the lead in small-arms development from Germany.

In 1898 the French introduced the spitzer boat-tail bullet in the Lebel. A more aerodynamic bullet, it had a tapered rear that looked a bit like a boat stern. The original bullet was 232 grains and had a flat nose and base. The spitzer was 198 grains. All military bullets are of this streamlined shape today.

The Lebel was an excellent long-range, high-velocity (2,380 feet per second) firearm but was also heavy, at 9 pounds 3.5 ounces, and in many ways an anachronism mechanically for its eight-round tubular magazine that was difficult to load with a stiff feed spring. Most new rifles were utilizing box magazines. The Lebel-Berthier 1907/1915 modification replaced the tubular magazine with a box magazine and Mannlicher clip, first for three rounds and then for five. The latter model had a weight of 8 pounds 8 ounces and remained in service until the 1950s.

The technological advances of the longer-range Lebel were obvious, and other nations quickly followed suit. Germany and Austria-Hungary produced an 8mm smokeless powder rifle in 1888. The standard German infantry rifle of World War I, the 7.92mm, 5-shot Mauser developed by Peter Paul Mauser, appeared in 1898 and incorporated the clip and magazine into one mechanism. Italy produced its first smokeless powder rifle in 1890. Britain was slower in this regard. Its .303-caliber smokeless powder Lee-Enfield, named for its designer, American James Lee, and its manufacturer, the Royal Small Arms Factory in Enfield, London, appeared only in 1895. The Short Magazine Lee-Enfield (SMLE) Mark III with which the British fought World War I was first produced in 1907. It incorporated a 10-round magazine and was suited to high-volume fire, as the well-trained professional British infantry showed in fighting at Mons in Belgium early in the war. An excellent weapon, it continued in service into World War II.

Perhaps three-quarters of the American troops in France in World War I were supplied with the M1917 American Enfield, which was chambered for .30-06 caliber. The remainder received the excellent M-1903 .30-06–caliber Springfield, manufactured at the Springfield Armory in Massachusetts. Comparable in performance to the Lee-Enfield, it utilized a Mauser-type action. Although the U.S. standard-issue rifle of World War II was the M-1 Garand, the M-1903A3 Springfield remained in service throughout World War II.

Further Reading

Blair, Claude, ed. *Pollard's History of Firearms*. New York: Macmillan, 1983.
Smith, W. H. B. *Small Arms of the World*. 9th ed. Harrisburg, PA: Stackpole, 1969.

Mauser Gewehr 98 Rifle

The German Mauser rifle Gewehr 98 (abbreviated as G98, Gew 98, or M98) was an extremely influential rifle design. Sold commercially to many nations, it was also widely copied. Designed by Peter Paul Mauser in 1895, it entered service in 1898 and remained a mainstay of the German Army until 1935 (when it was replaced by a shorter-barreled version, the Karabiner 98k) and with Volkssturm units through World War II.

The son of a gunsmith at the Württemberg State Arsenal, Mauser began working with the same firm and by 1866 had produced a self-cocking Dreyse needle gun. He then produced the Infanterie-Gewehr (Infantry Rifle) Model 1871, adopted by the Prussian Army in March 1872. It underwent modifications and ultimately became the Infanterie-Gewehr M1871/84.

With the introduction of new cordite smokeless gunpowder, Mauser modified his rifle to improve receiver strength because of the more powerful cordite and to incorporate a five-round box internal magazine. The result was the Gewehr 98 patented bolt-action rifle firing the powerful 7.92mm Mauser cartridge. In the opinion of many, Mauser had created the perfect infantry rifle. Rugged and easily operated, it is able to function effectively in adverse conditions. It is also considered extraordinarily safe for the user. The standard version was 4 feet 1 inch in length (barrel length 29.1 inches) and weighed 9 pounds 4 ounces.

The Mauser Model 1898 greatly influenced the development of a number of other infantry rifles, including the Anglo-American Pattern 1914 Enfield/M1917 Enfield, the Japanese Arisaka Type 38/Type 99, and the U.S. Model 1903 Springfield. Indeed, during the 1898 Spanish-American War, the U.S. Army secured a number of Spanish Model 93 Mauser rifles, and the Springfield utilized a Mauser-type action. Mauser brought suit, and the U.S. government was subsequently forced to pay royalties to him for patent infringement.

The Mauser Model 1898 remains highly sought after by collectors, and a great number have been converted to sporting use.

Further Reading

Ball, Robert W. D. *Mauser Military Rifles.* Iola, WI: Krause, 1996.

Blair, Claude, ed. *Pollard's History of Firearms.* New York: Macmillan, 1983.

Smith, W. H. B. *Mauser Military Rifles and Pistols.* Harrisburg, PA: Military Service Publishing, 1946.

Mauser C96 Pistol

The Mauser Pistol Model 1896 (C96) developed by German Peter Paul Mauser was the first practical self-loading (semiautomatic) pistol. Manufactured beginning in 1896, it remained in service until 1937. During that period, the Mauser factory in Oberndorf am Necker manufactured more than 1 million C96 pistols. Germany issued some 135,000 to its forces during World War I, and the Mauser also saw World War II service as well as wide use by other countries. China was by far the largest foreign user, with Chinese workshops turning out hundreds of thousands of them during the fighting between nationalist and communist forces in the Chinese Civil War (1927–1949).

The distinctive shape of the Model 1896 pistol's grip led to the nickname "Kuh-fusspistole" (Cow-Foot Pistol) by German soldiers and the "Broomhandle" by English speakers. The C96 is a recoil-operated, locked-breech pistol. Its magazine is located in front of the trigger guard. Magazines for the pistol are both fixed and detachable and of various capacities from 6-, 10-, and 20- to even 40-rounds. Most of the C96 pistols were chambered for the 7.63mm round. Both fixed and adjustable rear sights were available.

Pulling the bolt back cocked the exposed hammer. Releasing the bolt allowed the spring to carry it forward, stripping a round from the magazine and seating it in the chamber. The C96 also introduced a bolt-open device whereby the bolt remained open when the last cartridge had been fired. This feature also allowed the pistol to be reloaded more quickly.

The most common of the many types of the C96 issued to the German Army was the 5.5-inch model with a 10-round magazine and weighing only 3 pounds. It had a tangent leaf sight marked out to 1,000 meters. The pistol could be fitted with a combination wooden shoulder stock/holster that in effect turned the C96 into a carbine.

The Model 1932, the last in the series, was a selective-fire weapon permitting both semiautomatic and automatic fire. A switch on the left side of the pistol allowed the operator to select the mode of fire. In automatic fire it was a true machine pistol and was therefore often known as the "Schnellfeuer" (Quick Fire).

Further Reading

Blair, Claude, ed. *Pollard's History of Firearms.* New York: Macmillan, 1983.

Kinard, Jeff. *Pistols: An Illustrated History of Their Impact.* Santa Barbara, CA: ABC-CLIO, 2003.

Smith, W. H. B. *Mauser Military Rifles and Pistols.* Harrisburg, PA: Military Service Publishing, 1946.

Maxim Gun

If any one weapon symbolized World War I, it was the machine gun. Efficient manually operated rapid-firing small arms were in service in the 1860s and 1870s, including the Agar "Coffee Mill" (ca. 1860) and the Gatling gun (1862) employed at the end of the American Civil War (1861–1865). The French utilized the 25-barrel *mitrailleuse* (1869) in the Franco-Prussian War (1870–1871). But the Maxim gun

Maxim Gun at the Battle of Omdurman

In 1898 under orders from the British government, Major General Sir Horatio Kitchener, commander in chief of the Egyptian Army, led a sizable force of some 26,000 British, Egyptian, and Sudanese troops southward to reconquer the Sudan. On September 1 Kitchener and his men arrived at Omdurman on the west bank of the Nile across the river from Khartoum to face the main Mahdist army.

After some preliminary skirmishing, the next morning at dawn some 35,000–52,000 Sudanese attacked the British lines. Perhaps 15,000 had rifles; the remainder of the men were armed with spears and swords. In a series of charges against the British position, the Sudanese were simply annihilated. The British employed their magazine rifles and Maxim guns to kill perhaps 10,000 Dervishes and wound as many more, with 5,000 taken prisoner. The cost to the British side was 48 dead and 434 wounded.

Kitchener, surveying the battlefield from horseback, is said to have announced in a considerable understatement that the enemy has been given "a good dusting." For all practical purposes, the Battle of Omdurman gave the British control of the Sudan. It also led Hilaire Belloc to write:

Whatever happens we have got
The Maxim gun and they have not.

of 1884, named for American Hiram Maxim, was the first truly automatic machine gun. Development of the metallic cartridge made possible rapid loading at the breech.

Maxim's innovation was to use some of the energy of the firing to operate the weapon. Using the recoil energy, which he called "blowback," Maxim designed a fully automatic rifle fed by a revolving magazine. He then applied the same principle to a machine gun, which fired as long as the trigger was depressed. In the Maxim gun, the firing of the cartridge drove back the bolt, compressing a spring that in turn drove the bolt forward again, bringing a new round into position for firing. The Maxim gun was both self-loading and self-ejecting.

Maxim demonstrated his prototype machine gun in 1884. The gun weighed 60 pounds (the *mitrailleuse* had weighed 2,000 pounds because it was mounted on a towed field carriage, like an artillery piece). The Maxim gun was both belt-fed and water-cooled. It fired a .45-caliber bullet at a rate of up to 600 rounds per minute and could be operated by a crew of only five men. The gun was fired principally by a single gunner. The other crew members assisted in carrying it and in bringing up belts of ammunition for it. Aided by the British firm of Vickers, Maxim had his gun largely perfected before the end of the 1880s.

The British employed the Maxim gun with great success against the Zulus in South Africa and the Dervishes in the Sudan. Maxim was later knighted by Queen Victoria for "services to humanity," in the false assumption that the machine gun would make wars shorter and thus more humane. Despite the experiences of the

Boer War (1899–1902) and the Russo-Japanese War (1904–1905), almost all armies had failed to come to terms with the new lethality of the increased firepower by the start of World War I in 1914. At 450–600 rounds per minute, one machine gun could equal the fire of 40 to 80 riflemen. It also had greater range than the rifle, enabling indirect fire in support of an attack. In the German Army machine guns initially were deployed in companies as opposed to dispersing them among infantry formations, but as the war progressed the Germans altered their tactics and organization to make the light machine the centerpiece of the German infantry squad. Light machine guns, such as the excellent Lewis gun, appeared later and saw widespread service in World War I.

Further Reading

Goldsmith, Duff L., and R. Blake Stevens. *The Devil's Paintbrush: Sir Hiram Maxim's Gun.* 2nd ed. Toronto: Collector Grade Publications, 1993.

Willbanks, James H. *Machine Guns: An Illustrated History of Their Impact.* Santa Barbara, CA: ABC-CLIO, 2004.

Steel Armor, Naval

Iron armor for ships, introduced in the Crimean War in 1854–1856, grew increasingly thicker in an effort to counter more effective naval ordnance. The first armor protection took the form of 4-inch wrought-iron plates bolted to the ship's wooden hull. The next step was rolled-iron armor on double layers of wood, the whole supported by iron girders and an inner iron plate. In 1870, sandwich iron appeared. It consisted of layers of rolled iron plates alternating with wood and inner layers of sheet iron. Compound armor was introduced in 1877; it consisted of steel-clad wrought-iron plates. But improved armor-piercing projectiles of tremendous striking energy could penetrate test plates of 24-inch wrought iron, the maximum armor thickness on the British battleship *Inflexible* of 1876.

The new process of steel manufacture, introduced in warship construction in the mid-1870s, expanded to armor. Steel enabled ship constructors to build thinner yet tougher armor plating. At the end of the 1880s the French Schneider works added some 3–4 percent nickel to its steel armor plates, which reduced the tendency to crack. In 1890 American H. A. Harvey improved on this process by introducing what became known as Harvey plate: nickel steel alloy armor that was face hardened by a carbonizing process that raised the carbon content of the outer inch or so of the armor from .02 percent to more than 1 percent.

In 1895 Krupp engineers in Germany introduced KC, or Krupp-cemented, plate steel. It involved heating the plate to 2,000 degrees Fahrenheit and playing coal gas across its face. The heat broke up the gas and deposited carbon on the face, which was then ingested into the armor to form a hard skin. This process took some three weeks to complete, but the resulting armor was stronger than Harvey plate.

Chromium and manganese were also added to nickel steel, further increasing the hardness of the face of the armor and the toughness and elasticity of its back; all major navies of the world adopted it.

Harvey, Krupp, Armstrong in Britain, and Creusot in France all experimented with combinations of nickel, carbon, chromium, and manganese in their steel to produce ever more effective rolled armor plate that also yielded significant savings in weight and thickness.

By World War II, the U.S. Iowa-class battleships employed maximum 18-inch armor (on the turret face plates), while the largest battleship ever built, the Japanese Yamato class, had maximum armor protection of 25.6 inches on its turrets.

Further Reading

George, James L. *History of Warships: From Earliest Times to the Twenty-First Century.* Annapolis, MD: Naval Institute Press, 1998.

Tucker, Spencer C. *Handbook of 19th Century Naval Warfare.* Stroud, UK: Sutton, 2000.

Armor-Piercing Projectiles

In the ongoing race between guns and armor at sea, naval ordnance designers developed armor-piercing projectiles to overcome armor in warships. In 1881 Hadfield of Sheffield in England began manufacturing cast-steel projectiles. In 1885 that same firm patented a "Compound Armour Piercing Shell." As with compound armor, it combined a hardened steel point and a resilient body (a completely hardened shell would shatter on impact). Other types of hardened projectiles followed, including one of chrome steel. But most broke up when they struck the new armor.

In 1878 a Captain English of the Royal Engineers came upon capping the tip of the projectile. During tests of shells and armor at Woolwich Arsenal, a number of shells had broken up when fired against steel plate. Quite by accident, a 2.5-inch iron plate was left in front of a steel armor plate. In consequence, a 9-inch Palliser shell passed through the iron plate and penetrated 13 inches into the steel-faced plate. English then proposed manufacturing a shot with a wrought-iron cap of approximately the thickness of the plate that the other shell had passed through. When this was done and the shell was fired, it went entirely through the compound armor. Strangely, nothing was done to exploit this discovery, and it was left to the Russian admiral Stepan Makarov to reinvent the capped projectile in 1890.

When the capped shell struck its target, the cap received the full shock of the initial impact and distributed it over the length of the shell. The cap also served to lengthen the time during which the shock was distributed to the shell and acted as a support for the point at the beginning of penetration, softening the plate slightly so as to give the point a better opportunity for penetration.

The U.S. Navy came up with the Johnson capped shell. The French improved on this in their 1896 Holtzer cap. In spite of evidence of the success of the capped shell, the Royal Navy resisted adopting it until 1905. Nonetheless, by World War I all the world's major navies employed capped armor-piercing projectiles for use against enemy ships. The same process was applied to armor-piercing projectiles for land artillery.

Further Reading

Hogg, Ivan, and John Batchelor. *Naval Gun*. Poole, Dorset, UK: Blandford, 1975.

Lambert, Andrew, ed. *Steam, Steel & Shellfire: The Steam Warship, 1815–1905*. Annapolis, MD: Naval Institute Press, 1992.

Quick-Firing Naval Gun

The development of relatively small-caliber 4- to 6-inch quick-firing guns was of great importance to naval warfare at the end of the 19th century. All navies utilized machine guns, but they were of limited range and effectiveness. The quick-firing gun was a larger-caliber weapon specifically developed to deal with the threat of torpedo boat attack and to be able to riddle the unprotected portions of ships.

The quick-firing gun operated on the principle of fixed ammunition, cartridge cases utilized in small arms that contained propellant, primer, and projectile. Fixed ammunition had the advantages of ease and rapidity of loading, protection of the powder charge, the reduction of erosion on the chamber of the gun, and the sealing of the breech. Quick-firing guns had sliding breechblocks and a recoil mechanism that rapidly returned the gun into firing position with a minimum of displacement. Besides their rapid rate of fire, such guns required smaller crews—only three men each for the lesser calibers.

The quick-firing gun resulted from an 1881 Royal Navy advertisement for a gun to fire 12 aimed shots a minute. The 47mm revolving Hotchkiss gun, which fired a 2.37-pound high-explosive shell out to 4,000 yards, was subsequently adopted by several major navies. The 53mm Hotchkiss fired a 3.5-pound shell out to 5,500 yards but failed to achieve the popularity of the smaller model.

In 1886, 57mm (2.24-inch) 6-pounder single-barrel guns by Hotchkiss and Nordenfelt were introduced in Britain. Later the quick-firing gun was made larger to deal with armored vessels. A 4.7-inch quick-firing gun was tested and proven successful on the cruiser *Piemonte,* constructed in Britain for Italy in 1887. By the end of the decade Hotchkiss had built a 33-pounder and had a design for a 55-pounder; Armstrong had 4.72-inch, 5.5-inch, and even 6-inch rapid-fire guns. Such larger quick-firing guns soon became standard secondary armament on British battleships.

Because of the short battle ranges that prevailed in pre–range finder days, the quick-firing 6-inch gun could easily riddle the unarmored sections of the old battleships. Henceforth to use wood as material for a ship's superstructure was to invite disaster, as the Chinese learned during their war with Japan in 1894.

Further Reading

Brodie, Bernard. *Sea Power in the Machine Age.* Princeton, NJ: Princeton University Press, 1941.

Hogg, Ivan, and John Batchelor. *Naval Gun.* Poole, Dorset, UK: Blandford, 1975.

Lambert, Andrew, ed. *Steam, Steel & Shellfire: The Steam Warship, 1815–1905.* Annapolis, MD: Naval Institute Press, 1992.

Tucker, Spencer C. *Handbook of 19th Century Naval Warfare.* Stroud, UK: Sutton, 2000.

Torpedo

The success of stationary mines in the Crimean War (1854–1856) but primarily in the American Civil War (1861–1865), when mines were known as "torpedoes" for the torpedo fish that gives a shock to its prey, led to efforts to develop a self-propelled mine. The first modern automotive mine or torpedo was developed by Captain Johannes Luppis of the Austro-Hungarian Navy in 1865 and perfected two years later by the Scottish engineer Robert Whitehead, who managed an engine works in Fiume.

The Luppis-Whitehead torpedo was a long cylinder, streamlined for movement through the water. It had an 18-pound dynamite warhead and was powered by an engine that ran on compressed air. The torpedo moved just below the surface at a speed of six to eight knots and had an effective range of only several hundred yards. Its secret was a balance chamber that enabled the torpedo to keep a constant depth beneath the surface. The Austrian government, strapped financially by the 1866 war against Prussia and Italy, declined to buy the exclusive rights to the invention.

Whitehead then traveled to Britain to demonstrate the weapon. In 1870 the Admiralty was sufficiently impressed that it purchased rights to his invention for £15,000. Two years later Whitehead opened a torpedo factory in England. The British concentrated on a 16-inch, 1,000-yard-range version driven by contra-rotating screws at a speed of 7 knots, or 300 yards at 12 knots.

The torpedo was first employed in combat in 1877, when the British frigate *Shah* attacked the Peruvian monitor *Huascar.* The *Shah* launched its torpedo within 600 yards, but the *Huascar* easily changed direction and escaped.

Whitehead made improvements in his torpedo, further streamlining it and fitting it with fins to stabilize its movement toward the target. He also increased the explosive charge threefold by replacing gunpowder with guncotton. A three-cylinder, gas-powered engine dramatically improved torpedo speed to 18 knots, making it more difficult for a targeted vessel to escape. The addition of a gyroscope, adapted for torpedo use by the Austrian Ludwig Obry, made the torpedo more accurate. Range also increased so that by 1877, torpedoes could reach 800 yards.

Disappointment over the performance of torpedoes in the Russo-Japanese War (1904–1905) led to a new propellant to replace compressed air. In 1904–1905 both the Whitehead factory at Fiume and the Armstrong Whitworth works at Elswick in Britain came up with heaters to produce hot gas. This had a dramatic effect on both speed and range. A typical 18-inch torpedo driven by compressed air ranging out about 800 yards had a speed of 30 knots. The new hot gas torpedo of the same size could travel more than 2,000 yards at 34 knots, or 4,400 yards at 28 knots. By 1909, the British Mk VII "18-inch" (actually 17.7-inch) torpedo reached 3,500 yards at 45 knots, or 5,000 yards at 35 knots. Torpedoes also grew in size. The German 500mm (19.7-inch) Type G of 1906 could reach 6,000 yards at 36 knots, and its charge of 440 pounds was double that of an 18-inch weapon. The British Mk II 21-inch torpedo of 1910 carried a 400-pound charge some 5,000 yards at 35 knots.

The first successful torpedo attack in warfare occurred during the Russo-Turkish War of 1877–1878. On January 26, 1878, off Batum on the Black Sea, the Russian torpedo boat *Constantine* fired two torpedoes at a range of some 80 yards to sink the Ottoman patrol boat *Intikbah* in Batum Harbor. Torpedoes had a more spectacular result during the Indo-China Black Flag/Tonkin Wars (1882–1885). On August 23, 1884, at the Chinese naval base at Fuzhou (Foo Chow), French torpedo boats *No. 45* and *No. 46* sank the Chinese flagship cruiser and damaged a second vessel. Torpedoes found their natural delivery system in the submarine, and in World War I they wreaked havoc on both warships and merchant ships.

Torpedoes increased in both size and speed. In 1908 a 21-inch-diameter torpedo appeared. This soon became the standard size. The British Weymouth Mark II torpedo of 1914 weighed 2,794 pounds, could travel at 29 knots, and had a range of 10,000 yards. To pierce torpedo nets, swung out by ships when they were stationary, some torpedoes were equipped with net-cutting devices. Propellers underwent improvement, and the air-blast gyroscope improved stability at long ranges.

The finest torpedo early in World War II was the Japanese Long Lance. Torpedo improvements in World War II included the magnetic pistol, which set off the explosive charge when the torpedo was under a ship; electric drive; acoustic torpedoes that homed in on sound; and a system developed by the Germans whereby the torpedo would circle after its initial straight run in order to improve the chances of hitting a ship in a convoy.

Torpedo developments in the early Cold War period included smaller, lighter-weight models for aircraft use, although the standard heavy torpedo was still 21 inches in diameter. The U.S. Mary 44 torpedo was powered by a seawater battery and had active sonar to seek out its target. Most torpedoes employ acoustic homing. Active acoustic torpedoes generate sound and then home in on the echoes, while passive acoustic types are attracted by sound. Torpedoes have also been developed specifically to operate against other submarines.

Modern torpedoes utilize a variety of drive mechanisms, including electric motors and gas turbines. Some, such as the Russian VA-111 Shkval, utilize supercavitation to produce speeds of more than 200 knots. The U.S. Mark 48 heavy torpedo is 21 inches in diameter and 19 feet in length. It weighs 3,695 pounds, with a warhead of 650 pounds. It has wire guidance and passive and active sonar homing and is detonated by a proximity fuze, and its swash-plate piston engine gives it a speed of some 55 knots and a range of more than 23 miles.

Further Reading

Gray, Edwyn. *The Devil's Device: Robert Whitehead and the History of the Torpedo.* Revised and updated ed. Annapolis, MD: Naval Institute Press, 1991.

Jenkins, E. H. *A History of the French Navy: From its Beginnings to the Present Day.* Annapolis, MD: Naval Institute Press, 1973.

Torpedo Boats

Development of the automotive torpedo meant that for the first time in naval history, small vessels could threaten large ships. Torpedo boats launched their "fish" (torpedo) from the bow, presenting the smallest silhouette to enemy fire. All navies developed such small, fast boats specifically to launch torpedoes, leading to some discussion in the 1880s as to whether the battleship had been rendered obsolete.

The first purpose-built torpedo boat was the Royal Navy *Lightning* built by the firm of John I. Thornycroft in 1877. Displacing just 27 tons, it was 84.5 feet long and 11 feet in beam. Powered by a 478-horsepower engine, it could make 19 knots and was fitted with a bow-launching tube for a single 14-inch torpedo. The French were almost first. Their *Torpilleur No. 1* was actually ordered in 1875 but not completed until 1878. Heavily influenced by the thinking of the so-called Jeune École that emphasized smaller ships, France built the largest number of torpedo boats. By 1890 France had 220, Britain had 186, Russia had 152, Germany had 143, and Italy had 129. But torpedoes became standard armament on all classes of warships. All Royal Navy ships launched after 1872 carried them.

Early torpedo boats were too small to be effective. Their poor performance during maneuvers led to the construction of larger vessels. Torpedo boats were made about 50 percent longer, while at the same time preserving their slim, narrow lines. These craft were technically capable of ocean work, although their crews often did not think so. In 1889 France ordered larger boats of about 125 tons each to accompany squadrons at sea. In 1895 the 136-ton 144.4-foot *Forban* reached 31 knots, a world record.

The threat posed by torpedo boats was partially countered by the development of quick-firing Nordenfelt and Gatling machine guns, which became part of the standard armament of even the largest warships. At night these were paired with the newly developed searchlight. The torpedo boat destroyer (later simply known as the destroyer) also appeared; its task was to search out and destroy the torpedo boats before they could close within range. During World War I the Italian Navy operated nearly 300 torpedo-armed motorboats in the Adriatic Sea against the Austro-Hungarian Navy. The Royal Navy also employed coastal motor boats in home waters and in raids against Ostend and Zeebrugge, Belgium, in April 1918.

The major powers continued to employ torpedo boats during World War II. For the most part these small, fast, highly maneuverable wooden-hulled, shallow-draft vessels operated in coastal waters. The Germans had E boats, while the British employed motor torpedo boats.

Perhaps the best known of all these craft, however, were the U.S. Navy patrol torpedo boats, popularly known as PT boats. They were 77 feet long with an average speed of 27.5 knots in rough waters and mounted two 21-inch torpedo tubes. They also carried two .50-caliber machine guns in twin turrets. During the war the U.S. Navy deployed 350 PT boats in the Pacific theater, 42 in the Mediterranean, and 33 in the English Channel. They were not very effective against Japanese ships because early U.S. torpedoes proved defective and because of the difficulty of firing them accurately while maneuvering at high speed. PT boats were much more effective in coastal work, where they attacked and destroyed large numbers of Japanese landing craft, landed small forces, and—armed with rockets, mortars, or a 40mm gun—provided support to troops ashore.

The successors of such craft were effectively employed in riverine operations during the Vietnam War, while North Vietnamese torpedo boats triggered the Gulf of Tonkin Incident of August 1964.

Further Reading

Bulkley, Robert J., Jr. *At Close Quarters: PT Boats in the United States Navy.* Washington, DC: Naval Historical Division, 1962.

Nelson, Curtis L. *Hunters in the Shallows: A History of the PT Boat.* Washington, DC: Brassey's, 1998.

Preston, Anthony. *Destroyers.* Englewood Cliffs, NJ: Prentice Hall, 1977.

Ropp, Theodore. *The Development of a Modern Navy: French Naval Policy, 1871–1904.* Edited by Stephen S. Roberts. Annapolis, MD: Naval Institute Press, 1987.

Tucker, Spencer C. *Handbook of 19th Century Naval Warfare.* Stroud, UK: Sutton, 2000.

Destroyer

Destroyers are relatively small lightly armed and armored (even unprotected) warships capable of high speed. They were specifically developed to deal with the threat posed to the battle fleet by torpedo boats. First known as the torpedo boat destroyer, later the new ship was called simply a destroyer. The precursor was probably the Royal Navy *Polyphemus* of 1881. Known as a torpedo ram, it displaced 2,640 tons, was 240 by 40 feet in size, and was capable of 18 knots. It carried a 2-pounder gun and 18 torpedoes for its five torpedo tubes.

To counter the large number of torpedo boats built by the rival French and Russian Navies, in 1898 the Royal Navy contracted for what became known as a torpedo boat destroyer. Early types, however, lacked the speed to hunt down and destroy torpedo boats. That changed with the *Havock* of 1893, generally regarded as the first modern torpedo boat destroyer. At 275 tons, it was 180 by 19 feet in size and capable of nearly 27 knots. It was armed with a 12-pounder and three 6-pounder guns as well as three 18-inch torpedo tubes.

Each subsequent design registered improvements. Typical of British destroyers were the 34 River-class (later E-class) destroyers. They averaged 550 tons and were 225 by 24 feet in size and armed with four 12-pounders and two 18-inch torpedo tubes. Such ships were capable of sustained operations with the battle fleet.

With their excessive vibration, wet conditions, and excessive rolling, destroyers were difficult ships for their crews. Some of these negatives were mitigated in later designs that altered both superstructure and weight displacement. HMS *Viper*, launched in 1899, was the world's first naval vessel powered by the new turbine engine. This 440-ton destroyer was 210 by 21 feet. Armed with one 12-pounder and five 6-pounder guns and two torpedo tubes, it was, at 37 knots, the fastest ship in the fleet.

The U.S. Navy destroyer *Bainbridge* (DD-1), completed in 1902, began the U.S. Navy numbering system for destroyers. (The last in this numbering system was DD-997, the Spruance-class *Hayler* in 1983.) In 1914 destroyers were the most numerous warships of the world's navies, with Britain operating 221, Germany 90, France 81, Russia 42, and the United States and Japan about 50 each. Destroyers assumed the role of torpedo boats in attacking the capital ships of an enemy fleet, but they also were charged with providing perimeter protection for one's own capital ships against enemy destroyers. During World War I, Allied destroyers provided protection for the vital convoys.

With the advent of the submarine, destroyers became the primary antisubmarine vessel. Equipped with depth charges and hydrophones in 1917 and ASDIC (sonar) in 1918, they proved highly effective submarine hunters. They also provided gunfire support for amphibious operations.

Destroyers continued in these same roles in World War II, in addition to a new role as antiaircraft platforms. Probably the best known of World War II destroyers were the 150 U.S. Navy Fletcher-class ships. Launched during 1942–1945 and displacing 2,325 tons, they were 376 by 40 feet in size and capable of 38 knots. They carried an armament of five single-mount 5-inch guns along with four 40mm and four 20mm guns and 10 21-inch torpedo tubes. They had a crew complement of 273 men. Considered some of the best destroyers ever built, the Fletchers played an important role in the Pacific theater.

Destroyers remained in service after World War II and fought in the Korean War. In 1957 the United States launched the *Coontz,* the first purpose-built guided missile destroyer. The Soviet Union followed the American lead in 1958. In August

1964 during the Vietnam War, two U.S. destroyers were the focus of the Gulf of Tonkin Incident. During the 1982 Falklands War, British destroyers protected troopships from Argentine submarine and air attack.

In the first decade of the 21st century, destroyers are the heaviest surface combatants in general use, with only four navies—those of the United States, the Russian Federation, France, and Peru—still operating cruisers and none having battleships in active service. Modern destroyers, also known as guided missile destroyers, are equivalent in tonnage but substantially superior in firepower to World War II–era cruisers.

Further Reading

George, James L. *History of Warships: From Ancient Times to the Twenty-First Century.* Annapolis, MD: Naval Institute Press, 1998.

Lambert, Andrew, ed. *Steam, Steel & Shellfire: The Steam Warship, 1815–1905.* Annapolis, MD: Naval Institute Press, 1992.

Preston, Anthony. *Destroyers.* Englewood Cliffs, NJ: Prentice Hall, 1977.

Smith, Peter. *Hard Lying: The Birth of the Destroyer, 1893–1913.* Annapolis, MD: Naval Institute Press, 1971.

Tucker, Spencer C. *Handbook of 19th Century Naval Warfare.* Stroud, UK: Sutton, 2000.

Dynamite Gun

The dynamite gun utilized compressed air for launching its projectile. In 1882 D. M. Mefford in the United States patented a compressed-air gun "for discharging projectiles filled with dynamite or other detonating powders." Hoping to provide a less jarring initial shock for the projectile to enable it to have a dynamite filler, in 1884 Mefford demonstrated a 2-inch–caliber gun made from brass tubing. It fired a 5-pound solid shot for half a mile, where it penetrated 26 inches into a concrete target. Mefford believed that some redesign of the gun was necessary, but before he could do this, G. H. Reynolds patented a design taken from Mefford's work but sufficiently different to avoid patent infringement. U.S. Army lieutenant E. L. Zalinski, present at the Mefford trial, resigned from the service and teamed up with Reynolds to form the Pneumatic Dynamite Gun Company.

Eventually the company produced a 15-inch–caliber smoothbore gun that fired a variety of dynamite-filled projectiles, from a 12-inch of 966 pounds to an 8-inch of 298 pounds. The projectiles had fins to aid in stability in flight, and the smaller ones had wooden sleeves to bring them up to the gun caliber.

The U.S. government purchased a number of these guns for coast-defense purposes, and the navy fitted three 15-inch dynamite guns aboard the "dynamite cruiser" *Vesuvius,* authorized in 1886 and completed in 1890. Mounted at fixed angle on the fore deck, its three dynamite guns were aimed by turning the ship; range was

A dynamite gun field piece in Cuba during the 1898 Spanish-American War. Dynamite guns employed compressed air to project shells charged with dynamite and were utilized by both the U.S. Army and Navy with mixed results during the war. (Paine, Ralph D. *Roads of Adventure*, 1922)

regulated by the amount of air pressure on the shell. All the necessary compressing equipment left little room for anything else.

The dynamite gun's chief failing was its relatively short range. Advances in slower-burning powder that produced longer pressure on the projectile quickly brought its eclipse. The only use of this weapon in warfare came during the Spanish-American War of 1898, when the *Vesuvius* shelled Morro Castle, Cuba, without significant effect.

In 1897, a Zalinski dynamite gun was also mounted on the first American submarine, the *Holland* (SS-1), but was removed in 1900. The government also purchased 16 Sims-Dudley fieldpieces for use by the army, one of which saw service—with mixed results—during the siege of Santiago in the Spanish-American War. Its chief advantage seems to be that it did not give away the firing location. During 1894–1901, the U.S. Army also purchased several 15-inch dynamite guns to be used as coastal artillery pieces. These had a range of 2,000–5,000 yards, depending on the weight of the projectile (from 50 to 500 pounds). The equipment to operate the guns, including the steam boiler, compressor, and other equipment, weighed more than 200 tons. The batteries were scrapped in 1904.

Further Reading

Gardiner, Robert, ed. *Conway's All the World's Fighting Ships, 1860–1905.* Annapolis, MD: Naval Institute Press, 1979.

Hogg, Ivan, and John Batchelor. *Naval Gun.* Poole, Dorset, UK: Blandford, 1978.

Smokeless Gunpowder

Black powder was the standard propellant for firearms, large and small, from its introduction into Europe in the 13th century up to the late 19th century. Its principal liabilities were the residue it produced on burning, known as fouling, that necessitated considerable windage (the difference between the diameter of the bore and the projectile) and the dense cloud of smoke it gave off on firing. The latter immediately revealed the weapon's location on the battlefield. After a half dozen shots, the smoke also obscured observation of the target. With the development of rapid-firing firearms and artillery, this became a serious liability.

Attempts were made to develop a substitute for black powder, especially after the mid-19th century. In 1846 the French government appointed a commission to report on the feasibility of using nitrated cotton, which was found to burn without smoke and might be suitable for small-arms use. In 1884 French chemist Paul Vielle produced a successful nitrocellulose powder for small arms. His next type, which came to be designated Poudre B, was the first successful smokeless powder adopted by any nation. Weapons utilizing it also had a much higher velocity than those with ordinary gunpowder.

Similar experiments were carried out by Alfred Nobel in Sweden with what came to be known as *ballistite,* a compound of nitroglycerine and nitrocellulose. Nobel employed camphor to harden the powder grains. The British were aware of Nobel's work and sought to develop a powder using nitroglycerine and acetone as a solvent for guncotton but without using camphor. British scientists used petroleum jelly to help with stabilizing and antifouling. The British powder, formed in pale brown stands, came to be called cordite. The chief problem with cordite was a more rapid erosion of the weapon's bore. These new powders also proved less dangerous in bulk than the old black powder.

Smokeless powder proved its worth in the Boer War (1899–1902). Using it in new German Krupp artillery and long-range Mauser rifles, the Boers were able to open fire at long range on the British positions without revealing their own. This development greatly influenced tactics and led to renewed interest in camouflage.

Further Reading

Blair, Claude, ed. *Pollard's History of Firearms.* New York: Macmillan, 1983.

Cocroft, Wayne. *Dangerous Energy: The Archaeology of Gunpowder.* London: English Heritage Publications, 2000.

Kelly, Jack. *Gunpowder: Alchemy, Bombards, and Pyrotechnics: The History of the Explosive That Changed the World.* New York: Basic Books, 2004.
Partington, James Riddick. *A History of Greek Fire and Gunpowder.* Baltimore: Johns Hopkins University Press, 1998.

Trinitrotoluene

Trinitrotoluene, more commonly known as TNT, is a pale yellow crystalline hydrocarbon high-explosive compound. Its chemical formula is $C_7H_5N_3O_6$. TNT is today part of many explosive mixtures. German chemist Joseph Wilbrand invented TNT in 1863, although it was not an immediate success because it was hard to detonate and not as powerful as some other high explosives. TNT is much more stable than nitroglycerine, however, and unlike dynamite does not absorb water and thus can be safely stored over long periods. Because of its low melting point (81°C), TNT could be easily melted by hot water and then poured in liquid form into shell casings. TNT is, however, quite toxic. Munitions workers handling it during World War I developed a number of serious health problems until they were equipped with respirators and protective skin grease.

The Germans first adopted TNT as a filler for artillery shells in 1902, and the British followed suit in 1907. TNT is mixed with 40–80 percent ammonium nitrate to form amatol. Mixed with about 20 percent aluminum powder, it forms minol, which the British used in both mines and depth charges. The explosive force of TNT is today the standard measurement for the energy released in nuclear weapons blasts.

Further Reading
Cook, Melvin A. *The Science of High Explosives.* New York: Reinhold, 1958.
Fordham, Stanley. *High Explosives and Propellents.* Oxford, UK: Pergamon, 1980.

Bicycle

German baron Karl Drais von Sauerbronn is credited with inventing the bicycle. In 1817 he came up with the *Laufmaschine* (running machine), which he patented the next year. It was also known as the Draisine, the Draisienne, and the Hobby Horse. The first bicycle had two in-line wheels and the ability to steer. The operator straddled the wheels and propelled the bicycle by pushing his or her feet against the ground.

In 1860 French carriage maker Pierre Michaux connected crank arms and pedals directly to the front wheel. The new form of the bicycle was known as the Vélocipède (Fast Foot) and was the first to be ridden without the operator's feet touching the ground. Made almost entirely of wood, its extraordinarily rough ride on cobblestone streets led to it also being known as the "Boneshaker."

In 1871 British engineer James Starley came up with the Penny Farthing, also known as the "high" or "ordinary" bicycle. It was probably the first really efficient bicycle. It had a small rear wheel and a large front wheel pivoting on a simple tubular frame with tires of rubber. It also had double-spoke wheels. Other refinements followed, including inflatable tires.

The bicycle proved to be a tremendous boon for inner-city transportation. In general use in Europe's cities by the 1880s, it also allowed workers to escape the city to the countryside when free time allowed. The bicycle also went to war.

The first recorded use of the bicycle for military purposes seems to have been when the Italian Army employed it on maneuvers in 1875. By the end of the 1880s the British Army had organized some cycle companies. The British employed four-wheel tandem bicycles, with wheels that could fit railroad tracks, in the 1889–1902 South African (Boer) War. Most of the warring powers also utilized units of bicyclists during World War I.

During World War II, both the Germans, who were chronically short of motor transport, and the Japanese used bicycles widely. They were also employed by the Viet Minh during the Indochina War (1946–1954). Bicycles played a key role in the supply of Viet Minh forces by tens of thousands of porters during the 1954 siege of Dien Bien Phu and during the Vietnam War along the Ho Chi Minh Trail from North Vietnam to South Vietnam.

Further Reading

Herlihy, David V. *Bicycle: The History.* New Haven, CT: Yale University Press, 2004.

McGonagle, Seamus. *The Bicycle in Life, Love, War and Literature.* New York: A. S. Barnes, 1968.

Breech-Loading Field Artillery

Dramatic improvements in artillery occurred in the second half of the 19th century. The most important of these occurred in the change from muzzle-loading to breech-loading guns. This was made possible by greatly improved manufacturing techniques and tremendous advances in metallurgy, especially steel alloys. Steel guns appeared, machined to close tolerances.

Two efficient means of sealing the breech developed. The first of these employed a brass cartridge case, in effect itself the seal. This became the established process for smaller fieldpieces employing what was known as fixed ammunition, with projectile, charge, and primer all contained in one case. The second method of sealing the breech was the De Bange system. In it, the projectile, the bag or bags of powder, and the primer (the vent tube) were all loaded separately. This system was used in the larger guns and had the advantage of being able to vary the range depending on powder charge utilized. In the De Bange system, a

---

Indirect Artillery Fire

Through the 1860s, artillery was essentially a direct-fire antipersonnel weapon. This was its primary employment in the American Civil War. During that conflict, artillery-men usually fired only at what they could actually see. If infantry were out of sight, they were generally safe from enemy artillery fire.

An important change occurred with the advent of aimed indirect fire. In 1882 Russian Carl Guk published a system for firing on an unseen target using a compass, an aiming point, and a forward observer. Ironically, the Japanese refined Guk's method and employed indirect fire with great success against the Russians in the Russo-Japanese War (1904–1905).

The new breech-loading artillery with independent recoil systems and the use of wire (telephone) and later radio communication for forward observers, along with the accurate calculation of firing data, revolutionized the employment of artillery. By the 1890s most European armies had standardized the new techniques of artillery fire, allowing for the massing of fire on remote targets.

New smokeless powders also meant that a gun's position was more difficult to locate when it was fired. At the same time, new slower-burning powder also produced more thrust against the shell and less pressure on the gun itself, allowing greater ranges. All of these changes greatly increased the lethality of artillery. Artillery fire and not the rifle or machine gun was the great killer of World War I; estimates claim that artillery fire caused up to 70 percent of battlefield deaths in the war.

---

mushroom-shaped piece was driven back by the force of the exploding gunpowder against a soft obturator ring in front of the breechblock. The obturator ring expanded, sealing the breech.

Sliding breechblocks were developed for quick-firing guns. These moved to one side or downward and allowed the breech to be quickly opened and then closed again. Another system employed an interrupted screw breech. In it, the breechblock had a screw thread but with a section cut away. Turning it through a few degrees would either lock or unlock the breech, permitting rapid reloading. Usually the interrupted screw breech was used with the De Bange system.

One of the first modern breech-loading guns was the British 12-pounder Armstrong field gun of 1859. In this 3-inch–caliber gun, shell and propellant were loaded separately. Some 12-pounder Armstrongs saw service on the Confederate side in the American Civil War (1861–1865). In 1891 both France and Germany developed recoil systems in which the gun recoiled in a slide against springs or hydropneumatic buffers that returned it to its original position. This meant that the artillery piece did not have to be reaimed after each round, which produced far more rapid rates of fire as well as improved accuracy. There were also new mechanical fuzes, steel-jacketed projectiles, and new high-explosive fillers. Such guns were quick-firing and highly accurate. The howitzer also increased in importance. This midtrajectory weapon could fire at longer ranges than mortars. It came to be the preferred artillery piece in World War I because its high arc of fire allowed highly accurate plunging fire against enemy entrenchments.

Notable light field artillery pieces going into World War I included the French 75mm, the Russian 76.2mm, the British 13-pounder (3-inch) and 18-pounder (3.3-inch), and the German 77mm. One trend during the war, however, was the increasing use of heavier guns, which were found necessary to smash through concrete bunkers. Such pieces included the British 4.5-inch and 9.2-inch howitzers and 60-pounder (5-inch) gun; the French howitzer and gun, both of 155mm caliber; the Russian 122mm gun; and the German 105mm howitzer, 150mm long gun, and 210mm howitzer. In World War II the standard German and American field howitzers were of 105mm. Heavier guns included the 155mm M2 "Long Tom" used by the Americans and a number of their allies.

In modern artillery, caliber means two different things. It is first the diameter of the bore and second the length of the barrel. Thus, a 16-inch/50-caliber naval gun would have a bore 16 inches in diameter and a gun tube length of 16 inches x 50 or 66.67 feet.

Further Reading

Hogg, Ivan V. *The Guns, 1914–1918*. New York: Ballantine, 1971.

Hogg, Ivan V. *The Illustrated Encyclopedia of Artillery*. London: Quarto, 1987.

Jobé, Joseph, ed. *Guns: An Illustrated History of Artillery*. New York: Crescent Books, 1971.

French 75mm Gun

The Canon de 75 Mle Modèle 1897, adopted by the French Army in March 1898, was history's first truly modern artillery piece and the most advanced field gun in any army at the start of World War I. Produced at the Bourges Arsenal under the direction of Colonel Emile Rimailho, it featured a revolutionary new hydropneumatic recoil system. That system, developed at the Puteaux Arsenal, allowed the tube of a firing gun to recoil backward while the carriage remained firmly in position on the ground. After the tube recoiled, the system then moved it back forward into battery. The great tactical advantage of this system was that the gun did not have to be relaid every time it was fired.

The French 75mm combined the new recoil system with other innovative features, including a rapid-acting, screw-type breech mechanism; a fixed round of ammunition that could be loaded in a single movement; an independent line-of-sight gun-laying system; and shields to protect the gun crew from enemy small-arms fire. These were all the signature features of what became known in World War I as quick-firing artillery. Along with machine guns, quick-firing artillery introduced a previously unimaginable level of lethality to the battlefield.

Weighing only 2,700 pounds, the French 75mm was towed by a team of six horses. It fired a 75mm round weighing 15.8 pounds to a range of 7,500 yards. Its seven-man gun crew could produce a sustained rate of fire of six rounds per minute. The U.S. Army adopted the French 75mm in 1917.

The French 75mm did have its shortcomings. Its single-pole trail extended directly back from and underneath the breech end of the tube, limiting the gun's ability to elevate to only 18 degrees. This in turn drastically limited the maximum range, which is normally achieved at an elevation of 45 degrees. After World War I the French 75mm was retrofitted with a split trail that permitted greater elevation. As with the light field guns of all the other armies of the times, the French 75mm was also too light to have any real effect against well-prepared field fortifications. Once the war started and machine-gun fire forced all artillery to move back off the front lines, the French 75mm and all the other light guns lacked the higher trajectories necessary for indirect fire, especially in rougher terrain.

Prior to the war, the French Army made the mistake of putting all its faith in the French 75mm. Rejecting heavier guns and howitzers almost completely, the French believed that the French 75mm could accomplish any artillery mission on the battlefield. Whatever the gun lacked in hitting power could be more than compensated for by its high rate of fire. The main problem with this approach was that the French entered the war with only 1,300 rounds for each of their 75mm guns, which was sufficient for somewhat less than four hours of firing per gun at the sustained rate. Almost as soon as the war started, the French ran into an ammunition supply crisis that lasted more than a year. In August 1914, the French Army had 3,840 75mm guns but had a grand total of only 308 guns larger than 75mm. By November 1918, the French artillery had 4,968 75mm field guns and 5,128 guns and howitzers above 75mm.

Further Reading

Bailey, Jonathan B. A. *Field Artillery and Firepower.* 2nd ed. Annapolis, MD: Naval Institute Press, 2003.

Hogg, Ivan V. *The Guns, 1914–1918.* New York: Ballantine, 1971.

Zabecki, David T. *Steel Wind: Colonel Georg Bruchmüller and the Birth of Modern Artillery.* Westport, CT: Praeger, 1994.

Breech-Loading Heavy Guns at Sea

Ordnance experiments in the 1870s involving testing pressures in gun bores revealed that performance could be significantly enhanced by utilizing slower-burning gunpowder and longer barrels. Slow-burning large-grain powder, known as prismatic powder, prolonged the length of time that the charge acted on the projectile and thus increased both muzzle velocity and range. The problem with this was that the projectile left the barrel before all the powder was consumed. This could be solved by longer barrels, but that made muzzle-loading next to impossible. The slower-burning powders also required a powder chamber of diameter larger than that of the bore. All these factors, and the need to protect gun crews during the loading process, prompted a renewed search for an effective breech-loading gun.

Although breechloaders had been tried at sea in the modern era, beginning in 1858 in the French *Gloire* and later in the British *Warrior*, problems led to them being discarded. In 1864 the Royal Navy reverted definitively to muzzle-loading ordnance, but other nations, especially the French, moved ahead with breechloaders.

The old problem of ineffective sealing at the breech was only slowly overcome. In 1872 a French Army captain named de Bange came up with a "plastic gas check" that helped prevent escape of gases at the breech, and in 1875 France adopted the breechloader. At the same time brass cartridge cases, already used for small arms, came into use for the smaller breech-loading guns.

An accident aboard HMS *Thunderer* in the Sea of Marmora in January 1879 helped prompt the Royal Navy's return to breechloaders. Simultaneous firing was under way, with the main guns fired in salvo; during this, one of the battleship's 12-inch muzzle-loading guns misfired. This was not detected from the force of the discharge of the one gun, and both guns were run back in hydraulically to be reloaded. When they were again fired the double-charged gun blew up, killing 11 men and injuring 35 others. This could not have happened with a breech-loading gun, and in May the Admiralty set up a committee to investigate the merits of breech-loading versus muzzle-loading guns. In August 1879 after a committee of officers examined new breechloaders built by Armstrong in Britain and Krupp in Germany, the Royal Navy decided to utilize the breechloader in three battleships entering service in 1881–1882.

Another change in the period was to guns of steel, which accompanied enormous increases in gun size. Krupp in Germany began producing cast steel rifled guns in 1860. The change to steel guns was made possible by the production of higher-quality steel. At the same time that the Royal Navy went to the breechloader it adopted the all-steel gun, in which a steel jacket was shrunk over a steel tube and layers of steel hoops were then shrunk over this. The system of jackets and hoops over an inner steel tube was followed by one in which steel wire was spun on under tension varying with the distance from the bore. This helped eliminate barrel droop. Such "wire guns" continued in British service until the 1930s. Bore lengths of the guns increased from 35 to 45 calibers and even from 40 to 45 calibers.

The larger guns of the period required mechanized ammunition hoists and complex breech-loading gear. Their metal carriages recoiled on inclined metal slides that pivoted under the gun port. The slides were trained laterally by means of transverse truck wheels moving on racers, iron paths set into the ship's deck.

Further Reading

Hogg, Ivan, and John Batchelor. *Naval Gun*. Poole, Dorset, UK: Blandford, 1978.

Lambert, Andrew, ed. *Steam, Steel & Shellfire: The Steam Warship, 1815–1905.* Annapolis, MD: Naval Institute Press, 1992.

Padfield, Peter. *Guns at Sea.* New York: St. Martin's, 1974.

Tucker, Spencer C. *Handbook of 19th Century Naval Warfare.* Stroud, UK: Sutton, 2000.

Dumdum Bullet

"Dumdum" is the name given to expanding, hollow-point, and even exploding small-arms bullets. It has come to be a generic term for any ammunition that is illegally altered to cause it to expand on impact. The dumdum bullet takes its name from the location of a British small-arms Dum Dum factory near Kolkata (Calcutta), India.

With the introduction of new and more powerful smokeless powder in the 1880s and semiautomatic and automatic firearms, armies substituted harder metal jacketed bullets for those entirely of lead, which tended to leave significant residue behind in the weapon's chamber and bore. This was particularly important in the smooth functioning of new self-loading firearms. The new full metal jacket bullets, while of higher velocity, inflicted less damage on striking human flesh than the old lead bullets, which flattened on impact, creating larger wound channels and removing chunks of bone.

In the early 1890s the superintendent at the Dum Dum arsenal, Captain N. S. Bertie Clay, designed a new bullet to inflict maximum damage against Afridi

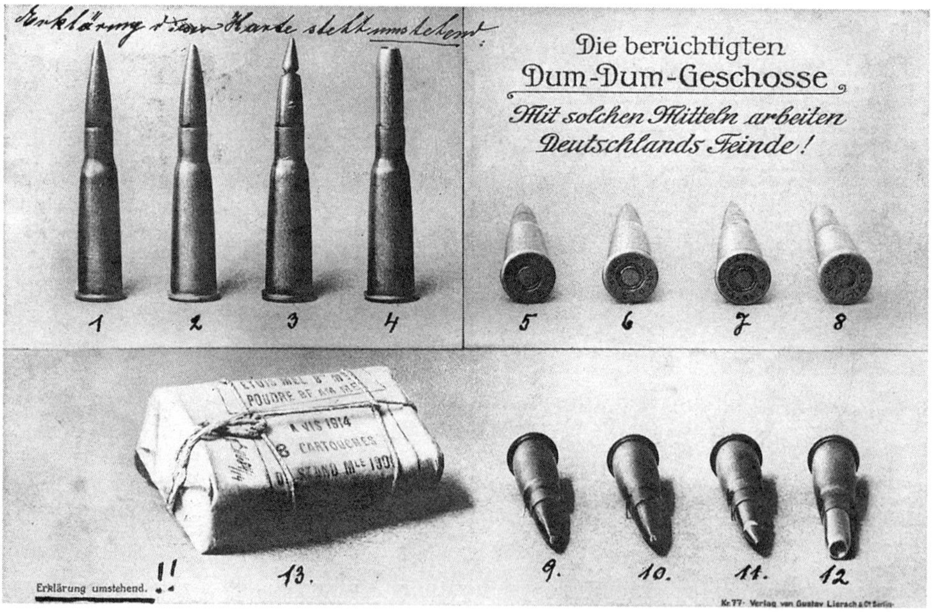

Germany propaganda illustration of various rifle cartridges employing expanding bullets allegedly used by the French Army. Bullets that flattened or expanded on impact, causing frightful wounds, were known as dum dums. (Rykoff Collection/Corbis)

Islamic rebels at Khyber Pass in northwestern India. Clay removed the bronze tip of the jacket covering the lead. The now soft-nosed bullet then expanded on contact. Because this might leave the jacketing behind in the barrel as an obstruction for the next round with possible dire consequences, later that same decade the British Army produced bullets of a hollow-point design, which had the same expanding effect.

The Hague Convention of 1899 banned the military use of "explosive" (expanding) bullets as well as asphyxiating gases, and Britain abandoned the dumdum altogether in 1902. Controversy continued, however, as during World War I (and thereafter) charges were leveled about the use of blunt-nosed or mutilated bullets in order to cause more horrific wounds. For the most part armies had eschewed dumdum bullets because of their greater tendency to jam in the new high-volume weapons.

Further Reading

Hogg, Ivan V. *Jane's Dictionary of Military Small Arms Ammunition*. London: Jane's, 1985.
Sellier, K. G., and B. P. Kneubuehl. *Wound Ballistics*. Amsterdam: Elsevier, 1894.

Hollow or Shaped Charge

The hollow charge or shaped charge principle was discovered in the late 1880s by American physicist Charles Munroe. In the Munroe Effect, the detonation of a shaped explosive charge around an open-ended cavity concentrates the blast in that direction. Placing a hollow cone at the front of a projectile with a high-explosive filler produces on impact a small perforation tunnel for the blast to pass through. In the 1920s German scientist Egon Neumann discovered that metal liners magnify the effect of the shaped charge. The deepest penetrations occur with a dense ductile metal, with the common choice being copper. In the 1930s Swiss immigrant Henry Mohaupt, working for the U.S. War Department, carried out further research in this principle to armor-piercing weapons.

Such charges are extraordinarily useful against tanks and fixed defenses such as pillboxes. In an antitank round, molten droplets of armor and metal from the lining are propelled into the targeted vehicle, and the superheated jet of gas sets off ammunition and fuel inside the tank and kills the crew.

During World War II the Germans used shaped charges in their capture of the great Belgian fortress of Eben Emael in May 1940, and the Americans employed the hollow charge in the development of the Bazooka antitank rocket. Hollow charges are also used in rifle grenades.

Hollow charges have their greatest effect when they detonate some two to three diameters from the target and when there is little rotation of the missile or the shell in which the explosive is carried.

Further Reading

Gander, Terry. *Anti-Tank Weapons*. Marlborough, UK: Crowood, 2000.

Margiotta, Franklin D., ed. *Brassey's Encyclopedia of Land Forces and Warfare*. Washington, DC: Brassey's, 1996.

Browning (Colt) .45 Semiautomatic Pistol

Identified as Automatic Pistol, Caliber .45, M1911, and one of the most famous firearms and probably the most enduring pistol in history, the Browning .45-caliber pistol was designed by American John M. Browning for Colt Patent Firearms Manufacturing Company and was actually a semiautomatic, firing one shot each time the trigger was pulled. Born in 1855 the son of a gunsmith, Browning was perhaps the most innovative and prolific firearms designer in history. In addition to the .45-caliber semiautomatic pistol, he also designed, among many others, the M2 .50-caliber machine gun and the Browning Automatic Rifle (BAR).

By the 1890s, Browning had developed a self-loading pistol, initially in .38 caliber, that he demonstrated for officials at Colt. In 1896 the two parties agreed that Colt would develop, manufacture, and distribute Browning's designs in the United States, while Browning struck a similar deal with the Belgian firm of Fabrique Nationale in Europe.

Browning's first Model 1900 semiautomatic pistol was the basis of the later M1911 .45. It fired a .38-caliber rimless cartridge and had a seven-round detachable box magazine. The barrel was attached to the receiver with corresponding grooves and lugs. When the weapon was fired, the barrel moved to the rear just slightly and simultaneously pivoted downward slightly, which caused the locking grooves to disengage. The slide continued moving back to the rear. As it did so, it ejected the spent cartridge and cocked the exposed hammer. It continued rearward until it hit the positive stop on the receiver, when the operating spring then returned the slide into the battery, stripping a new round from the magazine as it did so.

The Model 1902 and a shorter-barrel Model 1903 followed. The Model 1903 .32 pistol, with a 4-inch (later 3.75-inch) barrel, was highly successful. With its slide lock, concealed hammer, and weight of only 23 ounces, it remained in production until 1946. Browning also designed a Model 1908 .38 caliber and a .25 caliber that was produced until 1941.

But Colt and other firearms manufacturers were most interested in winning the competition for a new U.S. government sidearm. The army's experience during the Philippine-American War (1899–1902) and the Moro Rebellion (1899–1913), in which its .38-caliber pistols had not been able to halt hard-charging Moro insurgents, led to the decision by the Ordnance Bureau that the new weapon could be no less than .45 caliber. Following extensive tests, including those in the field and

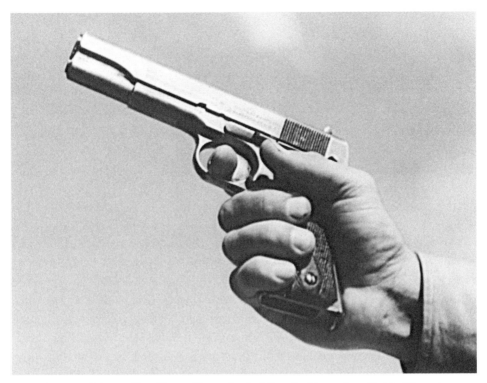

A soldier in training at Fort Knox, Kentucky, holding the Browning (Colt) .45 semi-automatic pistol in June 1942. (Library of Congress)

against cadavers and animals, it won out over a half dozen other designs to enter service in May 1911. It replaced a wide range of revolvers and semiautomatic pistols to equip all the U.S. armed forces.

Although heavy at 39 ounces with an empty magazine and having a hefty recoil, the .45 was absolutely reliable and accurate. It also had great knockdown power, thanks to the large 230-grain relatively slow-moving bullet (muzzle velocity of 830 feet per second). Magazine capacity was eight rimless .45 rounds. The M1911 also featured both a thumb-operated and a grip safety.

With World War I, demand for the pistol increased tremendously, and 380,000 were manufactured between April 1917 and November 1918 alone. In 1927 the M-1911 was improved slightly and redesignated the M-1911A1. During World War II, the U.S. government ordered 1.9 million of them. The M-1911 and M-1911A1 remained in service with the U.S. military (and many foreign militaries) from 1911 until 1985 and the changeover to the standard 9mm NATO model Beretta.

Further Reading

Kinard, Jeff. *Pistols: An Illustrated History of Their Impact.* Santa Barbara, CA: ABC-CLIO, 2004.

Smith, W. H. B. *Small Arms of the World.* 9th ed. Harrisburg, PA: Stackpole, 1969.

Lewis Gun

By 1910, machine guns shared the basic characteristics of being belt-fed, water-cooled, and tripod-mounted. The Maxim and Vickers machine guns had a minimum three-man crew, however, and there was a persistent need for a light machine gun capable of being carried in the attack by one man. The first true light machine gun, the Madsen, which was employed by the Russians in the Russo-Japanese War of 1904–1905, demonstrated the important role that such a weapon could play in offensive operations. Hotchkiss in Paris developed a light machine gun, subsequently adopted by both the French and British cavalry. The U.S. Army also purchased some. A lighter version of the regular Hotchkiss design, it remained in service in some reserve units until 1949.

The most significant new light machine gun design, however, was advanced by Americans Samuel McClean and U.S. Army lieutenant colonel O. M. Lissak. The two developed several gas-operated designs, which they described as automatic rifles. Unable to interest the army in their work, they sold the patents to the Automatic Arms Company of Buffalo, which in turn approached U.S. Army lieutenant colonel Issac Lewis about turning the designs into a workable product. Lewis took the McClean design and transformed it from a water-cooled, tripod-mounted medium gun into an air-cooled, shoulder-fired light model. By 1911 he had developed a number of working models and demonstrated them before U.S. Army officials, who then turned them over to the Board of Ordnance for testing.

Here Lewis ran up against the obstacle of General William Crozier, who took umbrage at the fact that Lewis had worked on the gun while in the army. Although Lewis resigned his commission in 1913, he could not overcome Crozier's opposition. Lewis then set up his own company in Belgium, Armes Automatiques Lewis, to produce the gun.

The gas-operated, air-cooled Lewis gun was an excellent weapon. Weighing 27 pounds and chambered for a .303-caliber round, it was easily carried into battle by one man, although all machine guns have at least an assistant gunner. The Lewis gun had a 47-round circular, horizontally mounted drum magazine. Cooling was effected by a tubular jacket over the barrel covering aluminum fins. When the gun was fired, muzzle draft drew air forward over the fins, cooling the barrel. Lewis licensed the Birmingham Small Arms Company (BSA) in Britain to make the weapon. The Lewis gun was easy to manufacture, with six produced in the time it took to make one Vickers. At the beginning of World War I in 1914, the BSA could not keep up with demand, and the Savage Arms Company in the United States also produced the Lewis gun.

The Lewis gun was the best light machine gun of its time and became standard issue with the Royal Army and the Belgian Army. The gun was also widely used by U.S. forces when they entered the war and was modified to use .30-06–caliber ammunition. In 1915 British infantry battalions on the Western Front each had 4

A test of the Lewis machine gun by the U.S. Marine Corps in 1917. The air-cooled Lewis was an excellent light machine gun that saw extensive service on the ground and in aircraft in World War I. The British also employed it in World War II. (Library of Congress)

Lewis Guns; by 1917 each battalion was equipped with 46. The Germans referred to the gun as the "Belgian Rattlesnake."

The Lewis gun also saw extensive use in aircraft, both in fixed and flexible mountings, with a 97-round drum. In the air the cooling system was discarded, reducing the gun's weight to only 20 pounds. The Lewis gun was also used in armored cars, in tanks, and even on motorcycles.

During World War II the British returned 50,000 Lewis guns in reserve stocks to service, and the weapon also saw widespread use in the armies of other nations. In the U.S. Army, the Lewis Gun was replaced by the Browning Automatic Rifle.

Further Reading

Skennerton, Ian. *.303 Lewis Machine Gun.* N.p.: Arms and Armour Militaria Press, Australia, 2001.

Truby, J. David. *The Lewis Gun.* 2nd ed. Boulder, CO: Palladin, 1978.

Willbanks, James H. *Machine Guns: An Illustrated History of Their Impact.* Santa Barbara, CA: ABC-CLIO, 2004.

Browning Automatic Rifle

Based on its experience in World War I, the U.S. Army determined that each infantry section (squad) should be armed with an automatic weapon. The Browning

Automatic Rifle (BAR), M1918A1, first produced in 1917, saw service with the U.S. Army Expeditionary Forces (AEF) in France in 1918 and was developed to meet that need. The gas-operated BAR was basically a light machine gun with a bipod at the muzzle end. Machine guns, however, are classified as crew-served weapons, while automatic rifles are individual weapons.

The BAR fired the same .30-caliber round as the U.S. infantry Springfield and later Garand rifles but did not enjoy wide popularity among troops in the field because of its size and weight (19.4 pounds) and speed with which it emptied its 20-round box magazine. The World War II version M1918A2 had two rates of automatic fire (300–350 and 500–600 rounds per minute). The BAR saw extensive service with a number of Allied armies in World War II and is still employed in some armies today.

Further Reading

Gander, Terry J. *The Browning Automatic Rifle.* London: PRC Publishing, 1999.

U.S. Army. *Browning Automatic Rifle: Caliber .30 M1918A2.* Washington, DC: U.S. Government Printing Office, 1951.

Willbanks, James H. *Machine Guns: An Illustrated History of Their Impact.* Santa Barbara, CA: ABC-CLIO, 2004.

MP18 Submachine Gun

The German MP18 was the first true submachine gun. Bolt-action infantry rifles were slow to operate and often proved unwieldy in the close confines of World War I trench warfare. What was required was a lightweight portable weapon capable of short bursts of high-volume fire, and beginning in 1915, the German Rifle Testing Commission at Spandau began development of such a weapon.

Tests with the Luger pistol, converted to automatic fire and fitted with a shoulder stock, proved unsuccessful. It had too high a rate of fire and was too light and difficult to keep on target. An entirely new weapon was necessary, and the commission selected a design by Hugo Schmeisser, working for Waffenfabrik Theodor Bergmann. It was designated Maschinenpistole 18/1 (more commonly known as the MP18 or simply the Schmeisser).

The German government placed an order for 50,000 of the new weapons. The MP18 proved its worth in the great German Spring Offensive of 1918. Yet only 10,000 MP18s had been placed in service by the end of the war.

The MP18 weighed 11.5 pounds. It fired the common 9mm Parabellum pistol ammunition from a left side–loading 20-round magazine (32 rounds from a small drum magazine). Its cyclical rate of fire of 450 rounds per minute made it in effect a machine pistol or small submachine gun.

The MP18 proved to be simple to operate and maintain and was generally reliable. Inaugurating a new era of simplification in small-arms design, it had but 34 parts

Hutier Tactics

The MP28 submachine gun was ideally suited to the new German infiltration tactics, introduced in the capture of Riga on the Eastern Front on September 1, 1917. These were named by the Western Allies "Hutier tactics" for German general of infantry Oscar von Hutier, who had employed them in his capture of the Russian city of Riga in September 1917. The tactics had been developed by Captain Willy Rohr, who in August 1915 had taken command of the Assault Detachment (Sturmabteilung) on the Western Front. Russian general Aleksei Brusilov had by necessity also employed somewhat similar tactics with great success in his 1916 offensive against Austro-Hungarian forces on the Eastern Front.

The new tactics were centered on highly trained assault forces, massed at the last moment by night. A short, intense barrage firing a mix of high explosive, gas, and smoke shells to mask enemy strongpoints, cause confusion, and disrupt the enemy replaced the old, long preliminary bombardment. The artillery preparation was immediately followed by an infantry assault led by specially trained elite forces. Armed with rapid-fire small arms and supported by light artillery, they bypassed enemy strongpoints and created corridors rather than trying to advance along an entire front.

Such tactics proved very successful in the German Spring (Ludendorff) Offensives (March 21–July 18, 1918), although a lack of reserves brought their failure.

(counting the magazine but not screws). The front half of the receiver tube around the barrel was perforated for cooling purposes and to act as a hand guard. The MP18 operated on the blowback principle and was fired from an open bolt. When the trigger was pressed, the weapon's powerful recoil spring drove the bolt forward, stripping a round from the magazine and chambering and firing it. Some of the propellant gases forced the bolt rearward, ejecting the spent cartridge case, whereupon the spring drove it forward again. The weapon continued to fire as long as the trigger was depressed.

Although the Treaty of Versailles of 1919 specifically banned German possession of machine pistols, the MP18 continued to be produced thereafter. The next German submachine guns were the MP38, introduced in 1938, and the MP40 of 1940.

Further Reading

Götz, Hans Dieter. *German Military Rifles and Machine Pistols, 1871–1945.* Translated by Edward Force. West Chester, PA: Shiffer, 1990.

Smith, W. H. B. *A Basic Manual of Military Small Arms.* Harrisburg, PA: Military Service Publishing, 1945.

Willbanks, James H. *Machine Guns: An Illustrated History of Their Impact.* Santa Barbara, CA: ABC-CLIO, 2004.

Barbed Wire

From the first domestication of animals, men sought to find effective barriers to contain them. Fences of both wood and stone appeared, but by the second half of

---

Barbed Wire in the Battle of the Somme

Accurate reports from the front lines just before the start of the Somme Offensive on July 1, 1916, that the lengthy British preliminary bombardment had failed to destroy the barbed wire in front of the German positions and that it was still intact were not believed at headquarters, where the reports were attributed to a reluctance to attack. When the attack went forward on schedule and the soldiers scrambled out of the trenches, lined up abreast, and began their advance across no-man's-land, the largely intact wire broke up the British formations and canalized them to the few gaps in the wire, making the attackers easy prey for the surviving German machine-gunners. On this bloodiest day in British military history, the British sustained 57,470 casualties, 19,240 of whom were killed or died of their wounds.

---

the 19th century ranchers in the vast expanse of the North American West employed fences of smooth wire strung between posts. Wire was easily erected, relatively inexpensive, would not rot, and was unaffected by fire. Smooth wire was not terribly effective as a barrier, however, as cattle could push through it. By the 1860s, manufacturers experimented with adding sharp points to the wire. In 1868 Michael Kelly invented a wire with points that was used in quantity until 1874, when Joseph Glidden of DeKalb, Illinois, came up with a process whereby barbs were placed at intervals on smooth wire and fixed in place by a twisted second wire. Subsequently, hundreds of patents were issued on thousands of varieties of barbed wire on this principle.

The British used barbed wire to protect their military encampments during the Boer War (1899–1902), but World War I saw its extensive employment. Once the front lines on the Western Front stabilized at the end of 1914, both sides erected wire barriers to break up enemy attacks and prevent trench raids and to secure prisoners.

Wire became a ubiquitous feature of no-man's-land. Almost every night parties of soldiers ventured forth to lay additional wire and repair breaks in existing wire that had been cut by enemy sappers. At first the wooden stakes holding the wire had to be hammered into the ground. The noise from this, however, alerted opposing troops, with obvious ill effects for the wire layers. Someone then came up with the idea of a metal stake with a corkscrew tip that allowed it to be screwed into the ground noiselessly.

The wire was laid not singly but in belts. The Germans, who were for the most part standing on the defensive on the Western Front, laid particularly thick bands of wire. These were often more than 50 feet deep, and in some places on the Hindenburg Line they were 100 yards in depth. A properly organized mile-long defensive position might require 900 miles of barbed wire.

The belief that artillery could blast holes in the wire proved false. More often than not, even prolonged shelling merely rearranged the entanglements. Barbed wire thus contributed greatly to the heavy casualties of the war. The need to deal with barbed-wire obstacles was one of the motives behind British and French development of the tank. Specialized explosive charges, such as the bangalore torpedo, were also developed and were used extensively in World War II to blast holes in a defender's wire.

During World War II, barbed wire was a feature of concentration camps and prisoner-of-war facilities. More lethal razor wire was developed and utilized during the Vietnam War and other late-20th-century conflicts.

Further Reading

Ellis, John. *Eye-Deep in Hell: Trench Warfare in World War I.* New York: Pantheon Books, 1977.

McCallum, Henry D., and Frances T. McCallum. *The Wire That Frenched the West.* Norman: University of Oklahoma Press, 1965.

Simpson, Andy, ed. *Hot Blood and Cold Steel: Life and Death in the Trenches of the First World War.* London: Tom Donovan, 1993.

A Russian soldier killed in a barbed-wire entanglement during an infantry assault in World War I. The difficulties of storming an enemy position were vastly increased by the use of such obstacles in the war. (Wallace, Duncan-Clark, and Plewman, *Canada in the Great War*, 1919)

Sandbags

Sandbags, most often thought of as a means of containing rivers and streams from overflowing their banks and flooding towns and cities, also are an important passive defensive weapon. A sandbag is a bag or sack of cotton ducking, burlap, or any number of other materials that is then filled with sand or soil, most usually in situ. They are inexpensive but also labor-intensive. Generally, shovels are utilized to fill them. Sandbags are most usually about 14 by 26 inches in size, making them relatively easy to move and to form an interlocking wall.

In war, sandbags are found in field fortifications and used to protect civilian structures. Because the bags themselves are inexpensive, large protective barriers can be erected cheaply. Sandbags can help dissipate the effects of shell explosions. Sandbags may be utilized in a revetment, or, if there is a low water table, as free-standing walls aboveground.

Sandbags have been used since at least the late 18th century. They are known to have been used by Loyalists defending Fort Ninety Six in South Carolina during the American Revolutionary War (1775–1783) and have been ubiquitous in almost every war since. They are much identified with trench warfare in World War I. As soon as possible, sandbags were brought up to be filled with earth. These bags were then compressed into a wall of earth in front of the trench, forming a parapet. A properly constructed defensive trench line might require as many as 6 million sandbags per mile.

Further Reading

Bull, Stephen. *Trench: A History of Trench Warfare on the Western Front.* London: Osprey, 2010.

Griffith, Paddy. *Fortifications of the Western Front, 1914–18.* Illustrated by Peter Dennis. Oxford, UK: Osprey, 2014.

Saunders, Anthony. *Dominating the Enemy: War in the Trenches 1914–1918.* Phoenix Mill, UK: Sutton, 2000.

Trench Fortifications, 1914–1918: A Reference Manual. Uckfield, East Sussex, UK: Naval and military Press, 2014.

Camouflage

Camouflage is a method of deception whereby men and their equipment are concealed from enemy observation, both on and off the battlefield. This process had existed since ancient times, with individuals wearing animal skins and employing foliage to conceal their location. With the development of mass armies maneuvering on the battlefield in compact formations, however, camouflage seemed of little worth.

The arrival of the long-range rifle in the second half of the 19th century changed all that. Its bullets were able to reach much farther into the battlefield than ever before, and personal concealment now became a major concern. Also, the development of smokeless powder meant that firing a rifle did not mean the immediate appearance of a telltale cloud of black powder smoke. It was thus much more difficult for opposing forces at greater range to detect an enemy position. Both developments heightened interest in cover and concealment. Uniforms, heretofore brightly colored in part to instill confidence in one's own side and intimidate an opponent, soon gave way to drab khaki and gray that blended in with the landscape. Cheap and fast chemical dye processes aided the process. Aerial observation, which came into its own in World War I, heightened the need to conceal one's own dispositions, even well behind the front lines.

Camouflage, first widely practiced by the Boers against the British in the Boer War (1899–1902), really took on major importance in World War I. Camouflage seeks to reduce the effect of color and blend an object into the background. Properly applied, it also transforms shapes, changing them from rectangular man-made forms to the indiscriminate. Camouflage also involves removing the shine from metal equipment. Faces too might be colored, either by burnt cork or by mud. White suits were introduced for alpine troops so that they would blend in against the snow.

Screens of green canvas with different-color shapes applied to them and the netting were also widely employed beginning in World War I. Dummy tree trunks and other common objects also appeared overnight, replacing real tree trunks on the battlefield. These concealed snipers and observation outposts. At the same time, dummy heads and body shapes were used to attract enemy fire where it could do no harm to real troops.

Ships and aircraft were not immune from this process. Experiments revealed that aircraft were less prone to observation from above if they were painted in a disruptive pattern in matt colors, mainly olive green and very dark green, while the same was true from below if the undersides of fuselages and wings were painted a

U.S. soldiers wearing camouflage clothing during World War II. Such uniforms helped the soldiers avoid detection by helping them to blend in with the landscape. (Library of Congress)

sky blue or light gray. Aircraft while on the ground were parked in revetments with their own camouflage netting.

At sea, attempts were made to disrupt the silhouette of a vessel by painting it in alternating dark and light gray blocks of color. This type of dazzle camouflage was intended not to conceal the presence of a vessel, which was impossible, but to obscure its size, type, and orientation.

Camouflage, which saw its first wide-scale use in World War I, reached new levels of sophistication in World War II. Painted screens and face blackening, especially among elite raiding troops, came into frequent use, as did helmet nets to hold foliage. Uniforms varied in color depending on the battlefield, from jungle to desert. Factories received paint schemes that appeared to alter their shape when viewed from the air, while painted forms could give the impression of a bomb crater on an otherwise undamaged runway. Lights at night in open, uninhabited positions were used to attract enemy aircraft, while night-fighter aircraft were painted black to render them more invisible. Aircraft also dropped aluminum strips, known as chaff, to give false readings on radar. Today there are stealth aircraft and even stealth ships designed so as to be invisible to conventional radar.

As infrared sights and observation equipment came into wider use, new materials were introduced for uniforms and camouflage netting that absorbed, rather than reflected, the infrared rays. Special paint for vehicles and equipment also absorbs infrared. Camouflage continues to be an important element of modern war.

Further Reading

Hartcup, Guy. *Camouflage: A History of Concealment and Deception in War.* New York: Encore Editions, 1980.

Hodges, P. *Royal Navy Warship Camouflage.* London: Almark, 1973.

Stanley, R. M. *To Fool a Glass Eye: Camouflage versus Photoreconnaissance in World War II.* Shrewsbury, UK: Airlife, 1998.

Pillbox

A pillbox is a small protective fortification, so-named because it resembles the medicine pillbox in form. Modern pillboxes had their predecessors in blockhouses, the fortified buildings of colonial North America that provided protection against Indian attack and structures erected by the British Army to guard against Boer guerrillas during the Boer War (1899–1902). Modern pillboxes are usually of concrete, reinforced by steel and built with embrasures, or small openings, for the purposes of observation and employment of weapons.

After the advent of static trench warfare on the Western Front in World War I, the Germans employed concrete pillboxes as an important element of their elaborate defensive scheme. Known as *Mannschaftsunterstände aus Eisenbeton* (reinforced concrete personnel dugouts), they housed one or more machine-gun crews and were spaced at irregular intervals as part of a defense in-depth. The Allies, who were seeking to drive the Germans from France and thus were not as interested in defensive works, nonetheless built pillboxes of their own, including a design with a steel cupola.

Pillboxes were incorporated into the French Maginot Line prior to World War II, in the German Atlantic Wall (where they can be inspected today) and on Japanese-held Pacific Islands of World War II, and in the French De Lattre Line during the Indo-China War. Pillbox strongpoints are still employed to protect airfields and other strategic locations.

Further Reading

Oldham, P. *Pillboxes of the Western Front*. London: Leo Cooper, 1995.
Wills, H. *Pillboxes*. London: Leo Cooper, 1985.

Hand Grenades

Hand grenades date from at least the 16th century, and most probably take their name from the Spanish word *granado*, meaning "pomegranate," which the weapon resembled in form. Although it had a long life and was often employed by specialized troops (grenadiers), the hand grenade proved to be a significant weapon in trench warfare during World War I. Hand grenades have seen widespread use ever since, particularly in attacking bunkers and in close-quarter urban warfare.

Hand grenades consist of three basic parts: the body, which contains the filler and, in the case of most hand grenades, also provides the fragmentation; the explosive filler; and the fusing mechanism. Hand grenades have appeared in a vast number of types: antipersonnel (both fragmentation and concussion), specialized (such as smoke, incendiary, riot control, stun, and chemical), and antitank. They are fuzed to explode either by time (usually only four to five seconds so as not to allow time for the grenade to be hurled back) or by impact. Because of the blast effect beyond maximum short throwing distance, individuals utilizing grenades need to throw them from behind barriers or to utilize the delay of the fuze to take immediate cover themselves.

Most early grenades were round or oblong in shape with a powder train fuze at the top. The Ketchum grenade used during the American Civil War was of oblong shape with an impact/percussion fuze at the top and a finned tail for stabilization. Early in World War I, troops fastened high explosives and a fuze to a wooden handle, wrapped it with wire for fragmentation effect, lit the fuze, and hurled it into an enemy trench. The British "jam tin" grenade of 1915 improved on this

A German soldier hurls a Model 24 Stielhandgranate (stalk hand-grenade) usually called a stick hand-grenade or "potato masher" at Soviet troops during the German invasion of Russia, July 1941. (National Archives)

process. It was in essence a tin can filled with guncotton and metal scraps, set off by a fuze with a friction igniter.

Perhaps the three most famous hand grenades have been the British No. 36 Mills bomb, the American M2 "pineapple," and the German "potato masher." The British No. 36 hand grenade, first introduced in 1915, was known in World War II as the Mills bomb. It and the U.S. M2 had the similar pineapple shape with deep serrations in the metal casing to assist in fragmentation. They differed in that much of the M2's fusing mechanism extended from the top of the grenade body. In both grenades, pulling the ringed safety pin and releasing the handle (known as the "spoon" for its shape) either before or upon throwing allowed a spring striker to strike the percussion cap, igniting the fuze.

The German "potato masher" grenade took its name from its shape of a can holding high explosive at the end of a wooden stick used to hurl it. This *Stielhandgranate 24* contained a TNT bursting charge and relied on blast effect rather than fragmentation. It could, however, be fitted with a fragmentation sleeve. The thrower activated the igniter by pulling the porcelain bead found at the end of the handle behind a metal cap.

Further Reading

U.S. Department of the Army. *Hand and Rifle Grenades: FM 23-30.* Washington, DC: U.S. Government Printing Office, 1949.

U.S. War Department. *Handbook on German Military Forces.* 1945; reprint, Baton Rouge: Louisiana State University Press, 1995.

Rifle Grenade

Rifle grenades are grenades that use a rifle as their launch mechanism as opposed to being hurled by hand. Rifle grenades considerably increase the projection range of the grenade and have been in use since the 18th century, when a cup discharger was fitted over the muzzle of a flintlock musket. The grenade was inserted into the cup and projected by means of the gases from a blank cartridge.

The modern rifle grenade dates from the first years of the 20th century and is usually attributed to Englishman Martin Hale. He came up with the rod-projection grenade. In it, a grenade was cast with a steel rod, which was then inserted into the muzzle. It was fired by means of blank cartridge. The Hale grenade could be hurled up to 200 yards. In addition to cup and rod projection, there is a third type of rifle grenade, the spigot grenade. It had a fin-stabilized tube that fitted over the muzzle of the rifle, the fins helping to improve accuracy. It also employed a blank cartridge. Most such systems required a special muzzle adaptor to be fitted over the muzzle of the rifle before it could be used to launch rifle grenades. Blank cartridges also produced inadequate pressure and were soon replaced by special gas cartridges specifically designed for launching rifle grenades.

Similar grenade launcher systems were employed by the Germans and other powers in World War I. The most popular British hand grenade of the war, the Mills bomb, was also fitted with a detachable base plate to allow for use with a rifle discharger cup. The French VB model, also employed by U.S. forces, utilized the cup device but could be fired with a regular cartridge in which the bullet passed through a channel in the grenade, launching it and igniting its fuze.

A wide variety of rifle grenades appeared in World War II, especially for anti-tank use. Grenades were also adopted to be projected by flare pistols. Rifle grenades come in a wide range of types, including antipersonnel, antitank, smoke, and antiriot gas. Some are time fuzed, while others, such as antitank grenades, are designed to explode on impact.

Because of the excessive recoil, normal firing positions for a rifle firing a grenade were usually with the rifle butt on the ground and the rifle held at approximately a 45-degree angle. For flatter-trajectory fire, the grenadier tucked the rifle butt under his armpit. Firing higher than a 45-degree angle might be used to drop grenades into an opposing enemy trench or foxhole, while flatter-trajectory fire might be employed to project the grenade through the window of a building or against an enemy tank.

During the Cold War specialist grenade launchers appeared, most notably the U.S. M79, which saw extensive use in Vietnam. The contemporary U.S. M203 is a M16 rifle with a grenade launcher permanently affixed below its barrel.

Further Reading

Hogg, Ivan V. *Infantry Weapons of World War II*. London: Bison, 1977.

Hogg, Ivan V., ed. *Jane's Infantry Weapons, 1991–1992.* New York: Jane's Information Group, 1991.

U.S. Department of the Army. *Hand and Rifle Grenades: FM 23-30.* Washington, DC: U.S. Government Printing Office, 1949.

Stokes Mortar

High-angle–fire (45 degrees and greater) mortars appeared in large numbers during World War I. They proved to be the ideal heavy firepower weapon in support of frontline infantry in the trench warfare that characterized combat in World War I. Lighter and more compact than other artillery, they had the great advantage of being able to fire from the most forward trench positions without requiring the space needed by artillery systems with long recoils. The high angle of their fire made it easier to attack targets behind defensive positions.

The Germans started the war with the largest number of mortars. German observers in the Russo-Japanese War (1904–1905) recognized the great potential of both hand grenades and mortars. These observations were greatly reinforced by the Balkan War of 1912. By the start of World War I the German Army fielded more than 2,000 trench mortars and by the end of the war were fielding 10,000.

The German trench mortar (*Minenwerfer,* or "mine thrower") was of three types. The light 76mm trench mortar weighed 300 pounds and had a range of up to 1,300 meters. German medium trench mortars weighed 1,100 pounds and fired a 170mm round at a maximum range of 1,100 meters. German heavy trench mortars weighed 1,500 pounds and fired a 250mm round as far as 1,000 meters. Convinced in the early fighting in World War I of the great utility of this weapon, the Germans began mass production of it, yet these weapons had more in common with the earliest mortars than with those of today.

The French were caught by surprise by the reappearance of the mortar. They even pressed some early-19th-century mortars into service while pushing development of modern types. The British, while lagging far behind the Germans in mortar development, had at least experimented with mortars during the Boer War (1899–1902). In late 1915, however, the British not only caught up with the Germans but surpassed them with the introduction of the Stokes mortar.

The Stokes mortar was of very simple design and was the forerunner of all modern muzzle-loading, gravity-fed mortars. Developed in January 1915 by Wilford Stokes (later knighted for his services), the approximately four-foot-high "stovepipe" metal tube had no rifling, sighting, or recoil mechanism. It had a simple metal base plate to absorb recoil against the ground and a light bipod mount. To fire the mortar, an infantryman simply dropped the mortar shell (known to the British as a "bomb") into the tube. It slid down the tube and struck a fixed firing pin in the bottom, detonating the propellant charge in the shell and hurling it skyward.

The Stokes mortar fired a 3-inch approximately 10-pound shell to a range of about 1,200 yards.

In addition to the light Stokes mortar, the British subsequently introduced larger models: the 4-inch medium Stokes and a 9.45-inch heavy Stokes-Newton mortar (the shells of which were known as "Flying Pigs"). These operated on the same principle of automatic ignition.

The first shells had time fuzes, but these were subsequently changed to point-detonating fuzes. Shells included high-explosive, smoke, incendiary, and gas. By 1918 each British division had 24 light, 12 medium, and several heavy mortars.

Mortars were used to take out such enemy positions as machine-gun nests and sniper posts. Large mortar shells were also utilized to try to cut barbed wire. Mortars were also an integral part of the creeping barrage that preceded the attacking infantry.

Further Reading

Bailey, Jonathan B. A. *Field Artillery and Firepower.* 2nd ed. Annapolis, MD: Naval Institute Press, 2003.

Hogg, Ivan V. *The Guns, 1914–1918.* New York: Ballantine, 1971.

Hogg, Ivan V. *The Illustrated Encyclopedia of Artillery.* London: Quarto, 1987.

Big Bertha Mortar

The German siege howitzer known as the "Big Bertha" was officially designated the 42cm Mörser (Mortar) L/14. The gun's nickname came from Bertha Krupp von Bohlen und Halbach, the daughter of gun manufacturer Alfred Krupp. Despite being designated a mortar, it was actually a howitzer. It fired a 420mm round weighing 1,719 pounds with a high degree of accuracy out to a range of 10,253 yards. Its specially designed projectile had a hardened conical nose with the fuze at the base of the round, which made it especially effective for penetrating reinforced ferroconcrete fortifications.

Introduced in 1914, the Big Bertha was designed as a more mobile field version of the huge 420mm Gamma H coastal defense howitzer, introduced in 1906. Weighing 93,720 pounds in action, the Big Bertha had to be moved in five separate pieces and assembled on-site using a crane carried by one of the prime mover tractors. At just more than 19 feet, the gun's relatively short barrel was only 14 times as long as the diameter of the bore. Only two Big Berthas were manufactured and fielded. Together they comprised a unit called Kurz Marin Kanone Batterie Nr. 3, manned by 200 gunners and 80 mechanics and drivers. On August 12, 1914, the battery opened fire against the Belgian forts at Liège. Four days later Liège surrendered.

Big Bertha's relatively short range made it increasingly vulnerable to Allied counterbattery fire as the war progressed, and by 1917 the Germans withdrew the guns from service.

156 | Paris Gun

A captured German "Big Bertha" 420-mm siege howitzer displayed on the Champs-Élysées in Paris, in 1919. (Bettmann/Corbis)

Further Reading

Hogg, Ivan V. *The Guns, 1914–1918.* New York: Ballantine, 1971.
Hogg, Ivan V. *The Illustrated Encyclopedia of Artillery.* London: Quarto, 1987.

Paris Gun

German long-range cannon of World War I. The "Paris gun" is one of the most remarkable artillery pieces in military history. Its maximum range of 130,000 meters (about 75 miles) by far exceeded any gun ever built to that time. Even today, very few conventional artillery pieces actually fired in war have been able to achieve even half that range. Often incorrectly called the "Big Bertha," the official name of the Paris gun was the *Wilhelmgeschütz* (Kaiser Wilhelm Gun). It was designed by Krupp managing director Professor Fritz Rausenberger, a brilliant ordnance engineer who also designed the 42cm Big Bertha siege howitzer.

The Paris gun was constructed by inserting a 210mm liner tube into a bored-out 380mm naval gun barrel. The liner extended some 39 feet beyond the muzzle of the base barrel. A 19-foot smoothbore extension was then added to the front of the extended liner, giving the composite barrel a length of 130 feet. The entire assembly required an external truss system mounted on top of the barrel to reduce the droop of the tube. The carriage consisted of a steel box assembly with a pivot in the front

The German "Paris Gun" undergoing test firing. Officially named the Kaiser Wilhelm Gun and built by the firm Krupp, it had the remarkable range of 75 miles. Although they had little military impact, several of these guns shelled the city of Paris during World War I. (Hulton-Deutsch Collection/Corbis)

and wheels in the rear that ran on a rail track. The gun could only be fired from a prepared concrete firing platform. The barrel alone weighed 200 tons, the carriage weighed 250 tons, and the turntable-type firing platform weighed 300 tons.

Despite being a technical marvel, the Paris gun was a relatively impractical combat weapon. The long and drooping barrel that produced its great range also meant that the fall of shot had a very large circular probable error, which meant wide inaccuracy. The huge and corrosive 400-pound propellant charge caused several centimeters of metal erosion on each shot fired. This meant that the firing chamber volume increased with every round, and each subsequent propellant charge had to be calibrated accordingly. The wear produced by the round as it moved down the tube also caused the bore diameter to grow, meaning that every subsequent round had to be slightly larger than the last. Thus, every barrel and its ammunition had to be supplied as a unit set, with the projectiles and propellant charges precisely numbered. Each barrel was good for a maximum of 60 rounds, after which it had to be replaced. Reportedly, a round loaded out of sequence caused one of the guns to explode on its firing platform.

Virtually all artillery pieces achieve their maximum range when the barrel is elevated to an angle of 45 degrees. Anything over 45 degrees is classified as high-angle fire, and as the elevation increases the range then decreases. The Paris gun, however, appeared to defy the normal laws of ballistics by achieving its maximum range at an elevation of 50 degrees. The reason is that at 50 degrees elevation, the round from the Paris gun went significantly higher into the stratosphere than at 45 degrees elevation. The reduced air density at the higher altitudes caused far less drag on the body of the projectile, which resulted in the far greater horizontal range.

There were at least three Paris guns, and there may have been a fourth. The guns were actually manned by naval gunners, with a vice admiral in command of the battery. In early 1918 the Germans emplaced three of the guns in the Forest of Crépy, just northwest of Laon, and between March and July the battery fired 303 rounds at Paris. Only 183 of the 265-pound 210mm rounds actually landed in the city, causing 256 deaths and 620 injuries.

The Germans withdrew the guns from action in August 1918 as the Allies were advancing. The guns were taken back to Germany and presumably destroyed to prevent their capture. The Allied Disarmament Commission was never able to find their remains or determine their exact fate. As with the V-1 and V-2 rockets of World War II, the Paris gun proved to be little more than a long-range terror weapon that had little influence on the outcome of the war. If the Germans had used the guns to target the Dover ports, through which the British Expeditionary Force was supplied, rather than randomly shelling Paris, they just might have achieved some operational effect.

Further Reading

Bailey, Jonathan B. A. *Field Artillery and Firepower.* 2nd ed. Annapolis, MD: Naval Institute Press, 2003.

Bull, Gerald V., and C. H. Murphy. *Paris Kanonen: The Paris Guns (Wilhelmgeschütze) and Project HARP.* Herford, Germany: Verlag E. S. Mittler and Sohn, 1988.

Hogg, Ivan V. *The Guns, 1914–1918.* New York: Ballantine, 1971.

Miller, Henry W. *The Paris Gun.* New York: Jonathan Cape and Harrison Smith, 1930.

Poison Gas

Poison gases were first extensively used during World War I. With the advent of modern chemistry, the major industrial powers anticipated the possible employment of poison gases in warfare, and signatories to the 1899 Hague Convention agreed not to deploy projectiles the sole use of which would be "the diffusion of asphyxiating or harmful gases." As a consequence, the German use of poison gas in World War I came as a great shock to the Allies and was regarded as an atrocity.

At the end of October 1914 the Germans had fired shells with an irritant gas in the Neuve Chapelle sector of the Western Front but without apparent effect. They first used tear gas, xylyl bromide (code-named "T-Stoff"), on the Eastern Front on January 31, 1915, when they fired some 18,000 gas shells against the Russians at

---

First Successful Use of Poison Gas

The first successful use of poison gas in World War I occurred on the Western Front and began the Second Battle of Ypres (April 22–May 25, 1915). Despite specific warnings from German deserters and prisoners of an imminent gas attack, Allied commanders dismissed the possibility and did nothing to prepare.

German chemist Fritz Haber had charge of the new weapon. Certain of its success, he urged his army superiors to prepare accordingly. Skeptical of it, short of manpower, and regarding this largely as an experiment, they refused to allocate reserves to exploit any breach that the gas might effect.

At about 5:30 p.m. on April 22 with the wind in the correct direction and following their brief artillery bombardment, the Germans released 168 tons of chlorine gas from 4,000 cylinders. With the trenches as close as 100 yards apart, the resultant yellow cloud wiped out the two French divisions on a four-mile section of front, killing and incapacitating the defenders or causing them to flee. By the end of the day 15,000 Allied soldiers were casualties, 5,000 of them dead.

Allied reserves were able to slow the German advance and ultimately sealed the breach. A second German gas attack on April 24 was less successful, with Canadian troops employing handkerchiefs soaked in water or urine as crude respirators. The Allies subsequently adopted more effective countermeasures and their own chemical weapons.

Bolimov. The weather was so cold that the gas failed to vaporize; it froze and sank into the snow.

The first successful employment of poison gas in the war occurred on April 22, 1915, when the Germans used chlorine gas to initiate the Second Battle of Ypres (April 22–May 25). The Allies thereafter developed their own poison gases; the British employed gas for the first time at Loos on September 25, 1915.

Both sides developed gas shells to disperse the gas by artillery fire. The most effective way to release the gas, however, was by gas projectors. These were large-bore, lightweight mortars, with the best known the Livens projector. These did not have to depend on perfect weather conditions, as was the case in releasing gas from cylinders. For the most part, only the Allies made wide use of gas projectors because of their short range and the fact that the prevailing winds on the Western Front were against the Germans.

Although there were other types, most World War I gases were of three main categories: chlorine; phosgene, which attacked the lungs and caused them to fill with fluid, drowning the victim; and mustard gas. The latter, introduced in 1917, burned and blistered the body, resulting in great pain and in some cases blindness.

World War I poison gases incapacitated or wounded far more men than they killed. From the standpoint of the attacker, this was an advantage because each wounded enemy soldier neutralized additional other soldiers and increased the burden on the

British machine gunners wearing anti-phosgene gas masks during the Battle of the Somme in 1916. A colorless gas and powerful respiratory agent, phosgene was one of many types of chemical weapons employed during World War I. (Universal History Archive/UIG via Getty images)

enemy logistical and medical systems. Although poison gas claimed a number of casualties in the war, the development of gas masks and their general issue by 1916 reduced the tactical effects of poison gas, and it became just another of many threats that soldiers had to endure. Poison gas never came close to being a decisive weapon.

Despite the Geneva Protocol of 1925 prohibiting its use, the Italians employed poison gas in the Italo-Ethiopian War (1935–1936), and the Japanese used it during the Sino-Japanese War (1937–1945). The most notorious employment of poison gas in World War II, however, was Zyklon B, which the Germans used in the death camps during the Holocaust to kill millions of Jews. Undoubtedly, the fear of retaliation and mass civilian deaths inhibited the widespread military use of poison gases in the war. Irritant gases, such as tear gas, were employed, however.

Colorless, odorless nerve agents such as sarin, soman, and tabun appeared, and after the war the major military powers built up considerable stockpiles of all types of chemical weapons. They were only rarely used, however. Exceptions occurred, as when Iraqi dictator Saddam Hussein authorized poison gas against Iranian forces in the Iran-Iraq War (1980–1988) and against his own people, the Kurds. During the Syrian Civil War (2011–), Syrian government forces early on August

21, 2013, fired rockets containing the chemical agent sarin against an opposition-controlled area around Damascus. Estimates of the death toll range from 281 to 1,729, the vast majority of whom were civilians.

Further Reading

Haber, L. F. *The Poisonous Cloud: Chemical Warfare in the First World War.* Oxford: Oxford University Press, 1986.

Moore, William. *Gas Attack: Chemical Warfare, 1915 to the Present Day.* London: Leo Cooper, 1987.

Tucker, Jonathan B. *War of Nerves: Chemical Warfare from World War I to Al-Qaeda.* New York: Pantheon Books, 2006.

Livens Projector

The Livens projector was a large-bore chemical mortar used by the Allies on the Western Front to fire poison gas at the German lines. Developed in late 1916 by Captain F. H. Livens of the British Army Engineers, it was in essence a metal pipe about a yard long with a baseplate. The projector was most usually set in the soil at a 45-degree angle. Large numbers of projectors were arranged in banks, and each was loaded with a drum containing 30 pounds of poison gas. The projectors were then fired remotely and simultaneously by electronic means, whereupon the drums tumbled through the air before landing up to a mile distant. Each had a small bursting charge that released the gas when the drum struck the earth.

The advantage of the Livens projectors was that poison gas could be fired at the opposing lines with little warning and before the Germans had time to don protective gear, thus maximizing casualties. The Livens projector was inexpensive to manufacture and extremely effective. The British first employed it on April 9, 1917, in the Battle of Arras, firing 2,340 drums at the German lines. They landed 20 seconds later and released nearly 50 tons of phosgene gas.

The British subsequently developed a number of different projectiles for the Livens projector, which in effect gave the British an advantage in gas warfare over the Germans. With the prevailing winds against the Germans, the relatively short range of the Livens projector was not a disadvantage for the Allies. The Germans, however, were severely limited in using a similar system and generally had to fire chemical projectiles using artillery at much greater range against the Allies.

Further Reading

Cook, Tim. *No Place to Run: The Canadian Corps and Gas Warfare in the First World War.* Vancouver: University of British Columbia Press, 1999.

Haber, Ludwig Fritz. *The Poisonous Cloud.* Oxford, UK: Clarendon, 1986.

Palazzo, Albert. *Seeking Victory on the Western Front: The British Army and Chemical Warfare in World War I.* Lincoln: University of Nebraska Press, 2000.

Richter, Donald. *Chemical Soldiers: British Gas Warfare in World War I.* Lawrence: University Press of Kansas, 1992.

Flamethrowers

Ancient warfare included the projection of fire against enemy targets, as in Greek fire at sea. Modern flamethrowers date from World War I, however. In 1901 a Berlin chemical engineer presented plans to the German Army for a man-portable flame-projecting device, leading to the testing of a prototype flamethrower (*Flammenwerfer*) in 1908. The Germans improved the design and developed plans to employ pioneer infantry (combat engineer) troops with flamethrowers in support of assaulting infantry. The Germans also developed a larger nonportable device for the defense of trenches.

Flamethrowers utilize a pressure tank filled with flammable liquid that is ignited as it exits the nozzle. In man-portable flamethrowers, the individual operator controls the direction of the flame and its ignition by means of a handheld wand or tube terminating in the nozzle and ignition device. World War I flamethrowers generally projected flame out to about 30 yards.

The first flamethrower assault of the war occurred on February 26, 1915, when the single German flamethrower unit attacked and routed French troops just north of Verdun. The success of this operation led the Germans to expand the flamethrower unit tenfold to 800 men. The Germans employed flamethrowers in fighting most notably against the British in the Second Battle of Ypres in 1915 and against the French in the Battle of Verdun in 1916. Although the Allies initially criticized the Germans for employing a barbarous new weapon, the British and French soon fielded their own flamethrowers. Most flamethrowers utilized heavy oil, but the French employed a mixture of gasoline and naphtha.

Flamethrowers were used extensively in World War II in city and jungle fighting. During the war not only were new man-portable flamethrowers developed, but a number of tanks were converted to that use to attack bunkers and tunnels. More than 50 U.S. M4 Shermans were converted into flamethrower tanks and used with considerable effectiveness in the Battle of Okinawa (April 1–June 22, 1945). Flamethrowers, even on vehicles, still have relatively short ranges, are prime targets for enemy fire, and are vulnerable to explosion.

Virtually all of the major warring powers employed flamethrowers in the war. Flamethrowers continued to be a part of post–World War II arsenals and saw action in the Korean War and the Vietnam War. During the Vietnam War, the M-113 armored personnel carrier (APC) was retrofitted with a flame turret and internal fuel tanks and redesignated the M-132. The troops called the flamethrower APCs "Zippos," after the iconic cigarette lighter.

Further Reading

Langer, William L. *Gas and Flame in World War I*. New York: Knopf, 1965.

Mountcastle, John W. *Flame On! U.S. Incendiary Weapons, 1918–1945*. Shippensburg, PA: White Mane, 1999.

Motor Transport

In the development of vehicle transport over roads, the breakthrough in terms of a practical power plant came with the invention of the internal combustion engine. Destined to revolutionize war, this small, reliable, and much more efficient power plant utilized oil as a fuel. The internal combustion engine produced one of the most profound paradigm shifts in the history of warfare, as machine power replaced human and animal muscle power as the primary source of battlefield mobility.

In 1882 German Gottlieb Daimler invented the first successful lightweight gasoline engine, and to him belongs principal credit for the development of the automobile. In 1895 another German, Rudolf Diesel, invented an engine that helped to solve the fuel problem by using low-grade fuel oil. The diesel engine proved to be a tremendous boost to the submarine, which needed an internal combustion engine that did not give off dangerous explosive fumes.

These developments led armies to begin to experiment with motorized transport. In August 1914 at the start of World War I, however, all armies still relied on the horse to a considerable degree (as was indeed the case for many armies, including that of Germany, in World War II), and on the battlefield most infantrymen moved on foot.

World War I provided the first major test for military trucks and demonstrated the importance of motor transport in modern warfare. In September 1914 General Joseph S. Galliéni commandeered some 600 Parisian taxicabs to rush 6,000 French troop reinforcements to the front, where they helped turn the tide of the First Battle of the Marne in favor of the Allies. Two years later some 3,500 French trucks braved German artillery fire to transport men and supplies along the 35-mile Voie Sacrée (Sacred Way) to the French fortress of Verdun and then carry out the wounded.

By war's end, the major warring powers boasted a combined total of more than 200,000 trucks. The French built the most; by 1918 they had almost 70,000 trucks and steam tractors in military service. World War II completed the revolution in transport.

Further Reading

Green, Michael. *Military Trucks.* New York: Grolier Publications, 1997.

O'Malley, T. J. *Military Transport: Trucks and Transporters.* London: Greenhill Books, 1995.

Armored Car

Armies soon made use of the internal combustion engine in motorcycles for communication and trucks for the movement of men and supplies, but it was inevitable that some sort of internal combustion engine–powered fighting machine would also appear. In 1902 Englishman F. R. Simms demonstrated his fully armored Simms Motor War Car, armed with two machine guns and a 1-pounder gun. In 1906 the German firms of Daimler and Ehrhardt and the French firm Charron-Girardot et Voigt each produced armored cars, the latter design being a four-wheeled lightly armored truck topped by a rotating turret that was sold to Russia.

In the United States, Colonel R. P. Davidson designed an armored weapons carrier in 1898, but it elicited little interest from the army. In 1915 Davidson led a column of eight Cadillac combat vehicles by road from Chicago to San Francisco. These included the first U.S. fully armored car. Capable of a speed of 70 miles per hour, it mounted a .30-caliber machine gun. The vehicles also included a kitchen car, a hospital car, a quartermaster car, and a balloon-destroyer car with an upward-firing machine gun. Although the trip brought Cadillac considerable publicity, the army was not interested, and Davidson's efforts seem to have accomplished little more than eliciting interest in improving the quality of the national road system.

The Italians were the first to use armored cars in war. Their Bianchi armored cars saw service in the Italo-Turkish War of 1911–1912 and the Balkan Wars of 1912–1913. The Isotta Fraschini, another Italian armored car, was a large boxlike vehicle with a revolving turret mounting a single machine gun.

The Belgians were the first to use armored cars in World War I: two Minerva Tourers armored and employed in scouting and reconnaissance. Their success encouraged the Belgians to armor other cars, but it was the British who led the way in the development of armored cars and ultimately the tank.

Royal Navy commander Charles Samson partially armored both a Mercedes and a Rolls-Royce belonging to the Royal Navy Air Service. They were the first armored cars to see action in the war. Each mounted a rearward-facing machine gun. The Rolls-Royce weighed 3.9 tons, had 8mm armor and a crew of three men, and was armed with a Vickers machine gun.

Armored cars continued to undergo refinement and performed a variety of functions during the war, including reconnaissance, convoy protection, and serving as mobile strongpoints. Armored cars were also occasionally employed to rescue downed fliers in no-man's-land. Some, including a truck equipped with a 3-pounder gun, took part in infantry operations. Armored cars proved particularly useful in the flat, open terrain of the Middle East.

The Germans also produced armored cars. Despite a lack of encouragement from the German General Staff, Ehrhardt produced a turreted armored car in 1915, and Daimler built a *Panzer Wagen*. Both saw action, principally on the Eastern Front.

For a variety of reasons, chiefly their inability to cross torn-up ground and their light armament and armor, armored cars were not the answer to the impasse of trench warfare. That came in the tank. Armored cars nonetheless possessed certain advantages. Along good roads and on firm ground, they were much faster than tanks. They were also much cheaper to produce.

A French Renault Model 1915 armored car, complete with tree-branch camouflage, operating in support of British forces in the area of Ypres, Belgium, on the Western Front in World War I. (National Archives)

Armored cars also saw action in World War II, when some received larger guns and were employed as tank destroyers. During the war the U.S. M3 scout car, which shared many characteristics with the M2/M3 half-truck, saw considerable service. Some 21,000 were produced, a number of which were sent to the Soviet Union under Lend-Lease. The M8 (Greyhound in British service) was perhaps the best medium armored car of the war. Weighing 7.68 tons and powered by a 110-horsepower engine, it could reach speeds of 60 miles per hour. It had a four-man crew and mounted one 37mm (1.46-inch) gun and two .30-caliber machine guns. By war's end, 8,523 had been built.

Cold War–era U.S. armored cars include the V-100 Commando, which saw extensive Vietnam War service in convoy and base protection. The M1117 armored security vehicle entered service with the U.S. Army only in 2000. Armored cars have also proven useful in riot control.

Further Reading

Foss, Christopher F., ed. *The Encyclopedia of Tanks and Armored Fighting Vehicles*. San Diego: Thunder Bay, 2002.

Hunnicutt, R. P. *Armoured Car: A History of American Wheeled Combat Vehicles*. Novato, CA: Presidio, 2002.

Terry, T. W., et al. *Fighting Vehicles*. London: Brassey's, 1991.

Tanks, Early

Armored vehicles existed in ancient times, but the idea of joining firearms with an armored vehicle found fruition in the early 15th century when Bohemian John Žižka, a follower of the Protestant revolutionary John Hus, modified four-wheeled, horse-drawn farm carts to carry small guns. Hundreds of Žižka's so-called battle wagons served effectively in the Hussite Wars (1419–1434).

The internal combustion engine made possible the modern tank, which arose from the need to break the military deadlock of the Western Front. While the Germans relied on tactical innovation, the British and French sought to break the impasse through technology. Armored cars were not the answer. They were unsuited to rough terrain and lacked a trench-spanning capability. Some means had to be found to smash through enemy lines and overcome the barriers of barbed wire and trenches defended by rifles, machine guns, and artillery. The solution lay in a vehicle powered by an internal combustion engine but one that was tracked and armored as opposed to wheeled. Tracking was essential both for traversing the battlefield and distributing the heavy weight of an armored vehicle over a greater area.

In 1915 both Britain and France began development of armored and tracked fighting vehicles. Neither coordinated with the other, and the result was a profusion of different types and no clear doctrine governing their employment. Only Great Britain, France, and Germany manufactured such machines that saw combat service in World War I, and Germany produced but few.

Britain and specifically first lord of the Admiralty Winston Churchill took the lead. Churchill had discussed with retired rear admiral Reginald Bacon, former director of Naval Ordnance and then general manager of the Coventry Ordnance Works, building large 15-inch howitzers to be moved in sections by large field tractors. Such weapons were indeed built and took part in the Battle of Neuve Chapelle in March 1915.

Churchill and Bacon now discussed whether such tractors might be used to span trenches and carry guns and infantry. Bacon produced a design for a "caterpillar tractor" able to cross a trench by means of a portable bridge, which it would lay beforehand and retrieve thereafter. Early in November Churchill ordered Bacon to produce an experimental model. It showed promise, and in February 1915 Churchill ordered 30. The War Office tested the first of Bacon's machines in May 1915 but rejected it because it was unable to meet certain conditions, including climbing a four-foot bank or going through three feet of water (a feat not achieved by any tank to the end of the war).

Churchill's order had already been canceled by the time of the first test because a better design had appeared. Advanced by Lieutenant Colonel Ernest D. Swinton of the Royal Engineers, it was based on the Holt farm tractor with caterpillar tread.

Swinton, assistant secretary for the Committee of Imperial Defence, became the principal figure in British tank development. Churchill called for tractors with "small armoured shelters" for men and machine guns that were able to flatten barbed wire for following infantry and to span enemy trenches. Meeting with opposition from the War Department, in February 1915 Churchill formed the Landships Committee at the Admiralty. The next month on his own responsibility and at a cost of about £70,000, he ordered construction of 18 "landships."

Although Churchill was forced to resign as first lord in May 1915 over the failure of the Dardanelles/Gallipoli Campaign, his successor, Arthur Balfour, was sympathetic to the project, as was Minister of Munitions David Lloyd George. The Landships Committee at the Admiralty then became a joint army-navy group, chaired by the War Office director of fortifications.

Balfour approved construction of an experimental machine. The contract went to William Foster and Co. William Tritton, managing director of the firm, had already designed a 105-horsepower trench-spanning machine as well as models of other armored vehicles and howitzer tractors. The prototype for the British government contract became known as "Little Willie." Designed by Tritton and Major William Wilson, who was assigned as a special adviser, it had its first trial on December 3, 1915.

Little Willie, the first tracked and armored vehicle, bears a remarkable resemblance to its successors, or at least to armored personnel carriers, into the 21st century. It weighed 40,300 pounds, had a 105-horsepower gasoline engine and a road speed of 1.8 miles per hour, and was protected with 6mm steel plate. Its set of trailing wheels, designed to provide stability in steering, proved unsuccessful. Although *Little Willie* was never armed and served only as a training vehicle, the top of the hull sported a ring with the intention that it would mount a turret.

At the same time, William Foster and Co. was already completing work on a war version. Tritton and Wilson designed a lozenge-shaped design with a long upward sloping high hull and all-around tracks that carried over its top. This design maximized trench-crossing ability. Because a turret would have made the machine too high, its designers mounted the guns in sponsons, or half turrets, one on either side of the hull. The resulting machine was first known as *Centipede,* then *Big Willie,* and finally *Mother.*

Mother first moved under its own power on January 12, 1916. Some 32 feet long and weighing 69,400 pounds, it met expectations placed on it, even crossing a 9-foot trench with ease. Although British secretary of state for war Field Marshal Horatio Kitchener found it little more than "a pretty mechanical toy," he was in the minority, and shortly thereafter the British government ordered 100 of them, a number later increased to 150.

Unfortunately, the perceived need to rush the new weapon into production meant that design flaws remained largely uncorrected. For one thing, *Mother* was underpowered. With its 105-horsepower Daimler engine, it had only 3.7 horsepower per ton of weight. Also, half of the crew of eight men were engaged simply in driving and steering the vehicle through the clutch and brake method of controlling the tracks. The remaining four men manned two 6-pounder (57mm) guns and two machine guns. The new machine was also insufficiently armored.

The Mark I production model that first saw combat was almost identical to *Mother.* It weighed 62,700 pounds and had a top speed of only 3.7 miles per hour (half that over rough ground) and a range of some 23 miles. Its two-wheeled trailing unit assisted with steering, but this was ineffective over rough ground and in any case was vulnerable to enemy fire. While it could span a 10-foot trench, the Mark I was only lightly armored in the (mistaken) belief that this would be sufficient to protect its crew against rifle and machine-gun fire. Armor thickness varied from 6mm to 12mm.

The Mark I came in two types. Half mounted four machine guns as well as two 6-pounder naval guns in sponsons on the sides, which provided a considerable arc of fire. These were known as the "Males." The "Female" version mounted only five machine guns and was intended to operate primarily against infantry.

The name "tank," by which these armored fighting vehicles became universally known, was intended to disguise the contents of the large crates containing the vehicles when they were shipped to France. The curious would draw the conclusion that the crates held water tanks. The French dubbed their new weapon a *char* (chariot).

The Mark I was the mainstay of tank fighting in 1916 and early 1917, but it had notable defects. The stabilizer tail proved worthless, its fuel tanks were in a vulnerable position, the exhaust outlet on the top emitted telltale sparks and flame, and there was no way for a ditched tank to retrieve itself. Some of these deficiencies were addressed in Marks II and III that appeared in early 1917. Produced in the same versions and almost identical to the Mark I, they differed only in details such as wider treads and improved armor. The Mark IV model was a slightly better-armored and more powerful version.

The French built many more tanks than did the British (4,800 to 2,818), but unfortunately for the Allies there was no design coordination or joint plan for their use. In December 1915 French artillery colonel Jean E. Estienne suggested that the French build caterpillar-type vehicles similar to the Holt tractors used by the British to move about their artillery. Estienne proposed an armored box that would mount a quick-firing gun. Throughout, the French regarded their tanks as "portable artillery" operating in support of infantry.

The first French tank was the Schneider Char d'Assaut 1 (CA1). Ordered in February 1916, a total of 400 were produced. Weighing 32,200 pounds and powered by a 70-horsepower 4-cylinder gasoline engine, it was capable of 3.7 miles per hour. It had a crew of six men, was armed with a 75mm main gun and two machine guns, and had maximum 11.5mm armor protection. The CA1 had poor cross-country mobility and trench-spanning ability, and its gasoline tanks were vulnerable to enemy fire. The CA1 first saw action on April 16, 1917, during the Nivelle Offensive.

The best French medium tank was the St. Chamond of 50,700 pounds, with a 90-horsepower engine and a maximum speed of 5.3 miles per hour. It too entered service in the April 1917 Nivelle Offensive. The St. Chamond mounted a 75mm main gun and four machine guns and had 17mm armor.

The French had already shifted priority to a light tank to accompany assaulting infantry. This new tank, the Renault FT-17, was the simplest, least expensive, and most produced (4,000 ordered) of the war. The two-man Renault was powered by a 39-horsepower gasoline engine and was capable of five miles per hour. This was not deemed a problem, as it was designed to move at the pace of advancing infantry. It had maximum 22mm armor. The Renault also boasted a fully rotating turret, the world's first, mounting an 8mm Hotchkiss machine gun, later changed to a short 37mm gun. The Renault first saw action in May 1918. Throughout the remainder of the war the tiny Renault became the commonplace image of the World War I tank. The Americans began production of a Renault clone, but none was delivered in time to see action, and the American Expeditionary Forces in France were equipped with the FT-17. Other countries also produced variants, and it became the most common armored fighting vehicle between the two world wars.

The lone German production tank of World War I was the A7V *Sturmpanzerwagen.* The Germans dismissed the tank on the basis of the performance of British tanks as both unreliable and a waste of effort. The A7V was an armored box on top of a Holt-type tractor chassis. Although 100 were ordered, only 20 were ever built. Weighing 65,900 pounds and thoroughly unwieldy, the A7V was nearly 11 feet high. Powered by two 100-horsepower engines, it had an optimum speed of eight miles per hour and a crew of 18 men. It sported 30mm poor-quality plate armor and was armed with one 57mm main gun at the bow and six machine guns, two on each side and to the rear. It first went into action on March 21, 1918, the opening day of Germany's great Spring or Ludendorff Offensive. Total German tank strength never exceeded 40 tanks, and the majority of these were machines captured from the British.

Further Reading

Chamberlain, Peter. *Tanks of World War I: British and German.* New York: Arco, 1969.

Crow, Duncan, ed. *AFV's of World War I.* Windsor, UK: Profile Publications, 1970.

Macksey, Kenneth, and John H. Batchelor. *Tank: A History of the Armoured Fighting Vehicle.* New York: Scribner, 1970.

Tucker, Spencer C. *Tanks: An Illustrated History of Their Impact.* Santa Barbara, CA: ABC-CLIO, 2004.

Antitank Rifle

The antitank rifle is essentially a large-caliber, high-velocity rifle utilizing special armor-piercing ammunition designed to penetrate thin-skinned armored vehicles. The contest between armor and projectiles has been a long one in history, and in the period from the introduction of the tank to about 1940, tank armor was as little as 6mm in thickness. Even the French Renault, the most widely produced tank of World War I, had only maximum 22mm armor protection. Generally speaking, special bullets had a fairly good chance of penetrating the armor of World War I tanks.

As they were the ones who first had to contend with the tank, the Germans developed a special steel-cored, armor-piercing bullet, the Patrone SmK Kurz 7.92mm. Its cartridge had a higher powder charge. This ammunition was generally issued only to snipers or to specially trained marksmen. The rounds posed some difficulties, including far greater wear on the rifle firing them.

Large-caliber high-powered rifles had appeared by the end of the 19th century for big-game hunting. They were also pressed into service. The first true antitank rifle was the German 13mm Mauser T-Gewehr of 1918. Other important antitank rifles included the Polish Karabin Przecipancerny wz 35 Ur, which incorporated a four-round magazine; the Soviet 14.5mm Simonov PTRS-41 and Degtyarev PTRD-41; the Swiss Sollothurn 20mm S-18/100; the German 7.92mm Pz B 39; and the Finnish 20mm Lahti L-39. The U.S. Browning M2 .50-caliber machine gun, introduced in 1933, proved highly effective against light-skinned vehicles. It remains in service today. The Japanese introduced the Type 97, which was a 20mm automatic rifle weighing nearly 116 pounds. In 1937 the British brought into service the .55-caliber Boys antitank rifle. It could penetrate up to 21mm of armor at 300 yards and was thus effective only against the thin-skinned German PzKpfw (*Panzerkampfwagen,* or tank) I and II early in World War II.

Although obsolescent by 1940–1941, the antitank rifle was subsequently used to touch off unexploded bombs and for long-range sniping. Other more effective antitank weapons appeared, including the rifle-fired antitank grenade, the German Panzerfaust, and the U.S. bazooka. The successor to the antitank rifle is today's antimaterial rifle.

Further Reading

Fleischer, Wolfgang. *Panzerfaust and Other German Infantry Anti-Tank Weapons.* Atglen, PA: Schiffer, 1994.

Gander, Terry J. *Anti-Tank Weapons.* Marlborough, UK: Crowood, 2000.

Antimaterial Rifle

The antimaterial (antimateriél or equipment) rifle is the successor to the antitank rifle of World War I and early World War II. Essentially a large-caliber, high-velocity rifle firing special armor-piercing ammunition, it is designed to operate against enemy equipment, such as thin-skinned and lightly armored vehicles. The weapon can also be used for long-range sniping. Antimaterial rifles are often favored by special operations military units.

The U.S. Army Browning M2 .50-caliber machine gun, which cam be fired single shot as a sniper rifle, fits in this category. The Austrian Steyr 25mm antimaterial rifle, with a claimed effective range of 1.2 miles, features both a muzzle brake and a hydropneumatic sleeve to lessen recoil. The weapon has a bipod and can be broken down for ease of transport by its crew. Among other such weapons is the South African Mechem NTW-20. This 20mm bolt-action rifle features a 3-round side-mounted box magazine. There is also a 14.5mm model. To reduce recoil, the NTW-20 utilizes a hydraulic double-action damper along with a double baffle muzzle brake. Among other such weapons are the U.S. Armalite AR50 and Barrett M82A1, both of which fire the 12.7mm NATO (.50-caliber) round; the British Accuracy International AW50F, firing the 12.7mm NATO (.50-caliber) round; the Hungarian Gerpard M1(B) and M2(B) 12.7mm rifles, which with changed barrel can also fire the .50-caliber round; and the Russian KSVK 12.7mm rifle.

Further Reading

Gander, Terry J. *Anti-Tank Weapons.* Marlborough, UK: Crowood, 2000.

Hogg, I. V., and J. Weeks. *Browning M2 Heavy Machine Gun.* London: PRC Publishing, 1999.

Hogg, I. V., and J. Weeks. *Military Small Arms of the Twentieth Century.* New York: Hippocrene, 1994.

Wright Brothers' Military Flyer

Although men had flown in gliders, balloons, and lighter-than-air ships, the first powered, manned, heavier-than-air flight was achieved by Wilbur and Orville Wright, two bicycle builders from Dayton, Ohio. In their accomplishment they owed substantial debt to others, most notably Samuel Langley, who made significant advances in aerodynamics. On December 17, 1903, at Kitty Hawk, North Carolina, Orville Wright accomplished the first manned powered flight. During a 12-second span, he flew the biplane Flyer a distance of 120 feet. (Since 1949, *Flyer I* has been displayed by the Smithsonian Institution's Air and Space Museum as the world's first piloted powered airplane in which man made controlled and sustained flight.)

The Wright brothers continued to improve their design. In 1908 they built the Military Flyer. Purchased by the U.S. Army Signal Corps in August 1909 for $30,000 ($25,000 and a $5,000 bonus, as it flew faster than the 40 miles per hour required), it was designated *Signal Corps Airplane No. 1* and was the world's first military heavier-than-air flying machine. Employed in pilot instruction, it was retired in March 1911 and is also in the Smithsonian Institution.

The Military Flyer has a wingspan of 36 feet 6 inches and a length of 28 feet 11 inches. A biplane, it has a double horizontal front rudder. It stands 7 feet 10.5 inches high and weighs 740 pounds. Powered by a 4-cylinder 30.6-horsepower engine, the Military Flyer was capable of a speed of 42 miles per hour and had a maximum endurance of approximately one hour.

Further Reading

Chandler, Charles deForest, and Frank P. Lahm. *How Our Army Grew Wings.* New York: Ronald, 1943.

McFarland, Marvin W., ed. *The Papers of Wilbur and Orville Wright.* New York: McGraw-Hill, 1953.

Aircraft, World War I

The first military heavier-than-air flying machine was the Wright brothers' Military Flyer of 1908, purchased by the U.S. Army Signal Corps in August 1909. Four years later the U.S. Army organized a squadron of aircraft. The United States was also the first to experiment with naval aviation. In 1910 Eugene Ely flew a plane off the cruiser *Birmingham,* and the next year he landed one on the cruiser *Pennsylvania,* the first time such feats had been accomplished.

Aircraft first went to war in the Tripolitan conflict of 1911–1912. Most were unarmed and employed for reconnaissance only, although some dropped handheld bombs. Although aviation made rapid strides, by 1914 generals and admirals still persisted in regarding aircraft, if useful at all, to be employed for observation and scouting. French Colonel (later marshal of France) Ferdinand Foch summed up the feelings of many when he remarked that "aviation is a good sport, but for the army it is useless." Nonetheless, all powers built aircraft. In August 1914, including seaplanes but not airships, Britain had 270, Germany had 267, Russia had 190, France had 141, Austria-Hungary had 97, and Belgium had 24.

Aircraft made an impact early in World War I. At first they were employed for reconnaissance, the value of which was shown early. On September 3 a French aviator provided critical intelligence to the Allies on German troop movements that played a key role in the subsequent Allied victory in the First Battle of the Marne. As aircraft proved their worth in observation roles, it became necessary for the other side to shoot them down. Pilots and observers on both sides began carrying small arms and taking occasional shots at enemy aircraft. Not long afterward, they also carried machine guns aloft. These were mounted either for an observer to fire or fixed in order that the pilot could aim the plane at a target. The machine gun became the key weapon of the air war.

Two-seater aircraft were the mainstay for observation purposes, with a pilot and an observer. There were also single-seater scouts, fighting scouts, or fighters as they came to be known. They were used to shoot down enemy aircraft in dogfights and were also used in ground attacks.

Fighter aircraft underwent rapid evolution during the war, and there were as many as five generations during the conflict. The first aircraft, still in service as late as September 1915, included prewar designs modified for air combat. Among them were the German Fokker Eindecker (monoplane) E.I through E.III, the French Morane-Saulnier Types L and N, and the British Vickers FB 5 and Royal Aircraft Factory FE 2b. Most of these aircraft used wing warping for lateral control rather than the more efficient ailerons.

All of the second-generation aircraft were biplanes. Designed from the outset as gun platforms, they included single- or two-seater tractor or pusher aircraft such as the French Nieuport 11 Bébé, the British Vickers FB 5 and de Havilland DH 2, and the Fokker D I, II, and III. Appearing as early as February 1915, they remained in service over the Western Front as late as August 1917.

A new generation of fighters appeared in the late spring and summer of 1916. They took advantage of lessons learned in early air combat over the Western Front. They were more powerful than their predecessors, of stronger structural design, and more aerodynamically streamlined. These aircraft were also effectively armed, including synchronization gear (first introduced by the Germans) to enable a machine gun mounted on the front of the fuselage to fire through the arc of the propeller. Two-seater aircraft featured rotating or ring-type mounts for a machine gun that could be fired by an observer.

These third-generation fighters entered service beginning in April 1916, and many continued in use until the end of the war, although they were clearly obsolescent by then. Among these were the excellent French Nieuport 17 through 27; the German Albatros series; Halberstadt D II, III, and V and Spad VII; and the British Sopwith 1½ Strutter and Pup and the de Havilland DH 5. The Germans were the first to use large numbers of aircraft specifically to strafe enemy ground troops, during the Third Battle of Ypres or Passchendaele Campaign of July–November 1917.

Excellent 1917–1918 designs included the British Bristol F 2B, Royal Aircraft Factory SE 5, and Sopwith F1 Camel and the German Albatros D III and V, Halberstadt CL II, Fokker D VII and VIII, and Siemens-Schuckert D III. Triplanes included the British Sopwith Triplane and the Fokker Dr. I.

The final fighter aircraft of the war included two German monoplanes—the Junkers D I and CL I—and the biplanes Roland D II and Pfaltz D XII. The Austrian Phönix D I also appeared in 1918. On the Allied side, the last aircraft of the war included the British Sopwith 7F Snipe (probably the best Allied fighter in service at the time of the armistice) and Austin-Ball AFB 1, the Ansaldo A1 Balilla (the first Italian-designed fighter of the war), and the U.S. Packard Le Père-Lusac (designed by French Air Service captain G. Le Père, it appeared too late to see combat in the war). In addition to more powerful engines and better designs, some of the final aircraft of the war saw metal replace wood and fabric as the aircraft skin.

Bombers developed later than fighters. Early bombing more often than not was random. The British Royal Naval Air Service may have conducted the first effective strategic bombing raids of the war in September and October 1914, when planes carrying 20-pound bombs flew from Antwerp to strike zeppelin sheds at Düsseldorf and there destroyed one airship. During the March 1915 Battle of Neuve Chapelle, the British were the first to use bombers as an extension of the land campaign. Hoping to disrupt the flow of men and supplies to the fight in progress, the British sent bombers against railway installations.

The planes used for these missions were former observation aircraft adapted for that purpose. The French were the first to form units of aircraft specifically dedicated to bombing missions. Most early bombing was, however, extraordinarily inaccurate, and problems grew with increases in antiaircraft guns and fighter aircraft.

Actually, the Russians were the first to introduce large bomber aircraft. Their four-engine Bolshoi Bal'tisky (Great Baltic) Type B first flew in 1913 and achieved excellent results. It was followed by the two-engine Sikorsky Ilya Mourometz A in 1914 and the four-engine Sikorsky Ilya Mourometz V in 1915. The first French bomber aircraft appeared in 1915 in the Caudron G 4, Breguet BR M5, and Voisin 5. Bombers of 1916 included the British Sopwith 1½ Strutter and the French Voison 8. Heavy bombers of 1916 intended for strategic bombing included the German Allgemeine Elektrizitätis Gesellschaft GI V and the British Short Bomber and Handley Page O/100. In 1917 the Allies introduced a number of light bombers, including the French Breguet 14, the Italian Caprioni Ca 5, and the British Airco DH 4. Heavy German bombers of 1917 included the workhorse Gotha G IV and V, the Friedrichshafen G III, and the Zeppelin Staaken R VI. In the last year of the war, the French brought on line the Caudron R 11, while the Italians brought the Caproni Ca 42 and the British brought the Vickers Vimy and Blackburn Kangaroo and the Handley Page V/1500.

Purpose-built ground-attack aircraft also appeared at the end of World War I. The Germans led in this. Their Junkers J 1 was not only the world's first practical all sheet-metal aircraft but also the first purpose-built for ground attack. Another purpose-built ground-attack model was the Hanover C-III. By 1918 the Germans had entire ground-attack squadrons, called Schlachtstaffeln, that were distinct from Jagdstaffeln (fighter squadrons) and Kampfstaffeln (bomber squadrons).

By the end of the war, the airplane had proved its worth. During the conflict, the warring powers built more than 161,000 aircraft of all types. April 1918 saw the world's first independent air force, the Royal Air Force. Formed of the Royal Navy Air Service and Royal Flying Corps, it had 22,000 aircraft and 291,175 personnel, a far cry indeed from the 270 planes of 1914.

By 1918, military aircraft had not only undergone great evolution but were fulfilling virtually all the major roles of nearly a century later. From a military curiosity dismissed by most generals, the airplane had become a major weapon of war that could provide reconnaissance and adjust artillery fire, attack enemy command centers and ground installations, and provide close air support to ground forces. Strategic bombing had also begun, with raids mounted on major civilian centers.

At sea, aircraft helped locate enemy ships and adjust naval gunfire and even attacked enemy ships. Land- and sea-based aircraft would reach their full potential in World War II.

Further Reading

Hallion, Richard P. *Rise of the Fighter Aircraft, 1914–1918.* Annapolis, MD: Nautical and Aviation Publishing Company of America, 1984.

Kennett, Lee. *The First Air War, 1914–1918.* New York: Free Press, 1991.

Munson, Kenneth. *Bombers 1914–19: Patrol and Reconnaissance Aircraft, 1914–1919.* New York: Macmillan, 1968.

Fokker E.I Eindecker Fighter Aircraft

The German Fokker E.I Eindecker (monoplane) was the world's first true fighter aircraft. Closely resembling in appearance the French Mourane-Saulnier monoplane in both structure and appearance, the E.I was powered by an 80-horsepower 7-cylinder Oberursel U O rotary engine that gave it a speed of 80 miles per hour. It entered service on the Western Front in June 1915. E series aircraft were armed with one fixed Spandau 7.92mm machine gun forward, offset to starboard of the fuselage centerline and equipped with interrupter gear designed by Anthony Fokker that enabled the machine gun to fire through the propeller arc without damaging the blades. This yielded a tremendous increase in firepower.

An improved, slightly stronger Eindecker entered service in September 1915, but only several dozen of this model were built. The most important E series model was the E.III. Powered by a 100-horsepower Oberusel U.I 9-cylinder rotary engine, it had a maximum speed of 87.5 miles per hour, a ceiling of 11,500 feet, and a flight duration of 1.5 hours. Although never deployed in large numbers, the Fokker E series aircraft enjoyed great success.

Eindecker pilots relied on tactical surprise, attempting to attack Allied aircraft from behind. During the winter of 1915–1916, E series aircraft wreaked havoc against Allied two-seat reconnaissance aircraft, especially the British B.E. types with the observer in the front cockpit. These planes became known as "Fokker Fodder." This period was known to the Allies as the Fokker Scourge.

The Allies then developed their own practical synchronization gear, but it was not until the spring of 1916, when the British FE 2b and DH 2 and the French Nieuport 11 Bebe were deployed in sufficient numbers, that the Allies regained air superiority. In all, Fokker built approximately 423 E-type aircraft.

Further Reading

Angelucci, Enzo. *The Rand McNally Encyclopedia of Military Aircraft, 1914–1980.* New York: Military Press, 1983.

Fredriksen, John C. *International Warbirds: An Illustrated Guide to World Military Aircraft, 1914–2000.* Santa Barbara, CA: ABC-CLIO, 2001.

Gray, Peter, and Owen Thetford. *German Aircraft of the First World War.* London: Putnam, 1992.

Hallion, Richard P. *Rise of the Fighter Aircraft, 1914–1918.* Annapolis, MD: Nautical and Aviation Publishing Company of America, 1984.

Interrupter Gear

Interrupter gear allowed a fixed machine gun to fire through the arc of a rotating airplane propeller without damaging its blades. A typical World War I propeller rotated at about 1,200 rounds per minute, and since the usual rate of fire for a machine gun was 400 to 600 rounds per minute, some mechanism was required to ensure that a bullet did not damage the propeller blades.

Before the war, several engineers had worked independently on the concept of an interrupter gear. In July 1913 Franz Schneider, a Swiss national working for the German aircraft manufacturer L.V.G. (Luft-Verkehrs Gesellschaft), patented an idea for an interrupter mechanism but experienced some difficulty in making it work. A synchronization mechanism of his design was eventually fitted to a single L.V.G. E.IV monoplane in 1915, but the aircraft was destroyed in an accident on its way to the front. In 1914 Frenchman Raymond Saulnier of the firm of Morane-Saulnier almost certainly invented the first successful synchronization mechanism and had some success with static trials, but he was hampered by an unsuitable weapon and faulty ammunition.

French fighter pilot Roland Garros suggested fitting steel plates to the propeller blades to deflect stray bullets that would otherwise hit the blades. Garros had a Morane type L aircraft fitted with a Hotchkiss machine gun and the triangular-shaped deflector plates and scored three victories in two weeks during April 1915. The French press made much of his success, and he was the first pilot to be labeled an ace. On April 18, 1915, however, Garros's aircraft suffered engine failure. He was forced to land behind German lines and was unable to destroy the aircraft before capture.

The Germans investigated Garros's mechanism and took it to the Fokker works in Schwerin, where they discovered that the firm already had such a device completed. Anthony Fokker subsequently claimed to have personally designed and built a working synchronization mechanism in just 48 hours, but as he had no prior experience of automatic weapons, it is almost certain that the actual design of the mechanism was the work of Fokker's engineering staff at Schwerin sometime before April 1915. Indeed, in 1917 Franz Schneider successfully sued Fokker for patent infringement, but Fokker refused to pay.

In common with all successful mechanisms, Fokker's interrupter gear was actually a synchronization gear; it used a cam driven from the engine to actuate a plunger on the gun that, when tripped, fired a round if the mechanism was ready to fire. From mid-1915, Fokker E.I Eindecker fighters were fitted with the mechanism and began to shoot down increasing numbers of Entente aircraft, leading to what became known as the Fokker Scourge through the winter of 1915–1916.

Other designers quickly followed suit, and there were many variations of synchronization mechanism, the most advanced and reliable of which was probably the British Constantinesco-Colley hydraulic synchronizing gear that was eventually adopted as standard by the Royal Flying Corps, later the Royal Air Force.

Further Reading

Grosz, Peter M. *Windsock Datafile 91, Fokker E.I/II.* Berkhamsted, UK: Albatros Productions, 2002.

Munson, Kenneth. *Fighters, Attack and Training Aircraft, 1914–19.* Poole, UK: Blandford, 1976.

Woodman, Harry. *Early Aircraft Armament.* London: Arms and Armour, 1989.

De Havilland DH 2 Fighter Aircraft

The fragile in appearance yet rugged de Havilland 2 biplane was the first true British fighter aircraft. Its arrival over the Western Front early in 1916 marked the beginning of the end of the so-called Fokker Scourge of the winter of 1915–1916, when German Fokker E series Eindecker (monoplane) aircraft had ruled the skies. Designed by Geoffrey de Havilland, the single-seater DH 2 evolved from his earlier DH 1 single-seat observer aircraft. The rotary pusher engine and propeller were immediately to the pilot's rear. Booms beyond the propeller arc connected the wings and fuselage to the tail section.

Whereas the Eindecker had been conceived as an observation aircraft, the DH 2 was intended from the beginning as a fighter to carry a machine gun. Powered by a pusher 100-horsepower Gnôme Monosoupape rotary engine, the DH 2 had a maximum speed of 93 miles per hour, a ceiling of 14,000 feet, and a range of 250 miles. The plane was built around a pusher engine because the British still lacked the synchronization gear to enable a machine gun to fire through the propeller. Armament consisted of a single .303-caliber Lewis machine gun. At first the gun was mounted to the left side of the fuselage forward, but it was later moved to a rotating centerline mount. Because it was so difficult to fly the plane and fire the machine gun at the same time, most pilots chose to regard the gun as semifixed, turning the aircraft rather than the gun to aim.

Highly maneuverable and as fast as the Eindecker, the DH 2 nonetheless suffered from the problem of entering a sudden spin during abrupt maneuvers. Nonetheless, the DH 2, along with another British pusher fighter, the Royal Aircraft Factory FE 2b, and the French Nieuport 11 Bébé, ended the reign of the Eindecker. The DH 2 remained in service into 1917 and the appearance of the German Albatros D Is and DII fighters, which greatly outclassed it.

Further Reading

Angelucci, Enzo. *The Rand McNally Encyclopedia of Military Aircraft, 1914–1980.* New York: Military Press, 1983.

Fredriksen, John C. *International Warbirds: An Illustrated Guide to World Military Aircraft, 1914–2000.* Santa Barbara, CA: ABC-CLIO, 2001.

Hallion, Richard P. *Rise of the Fighter Aircraft, 1914–1918.* Annapolis, MD: Nautical and Aviation Publishing Company of America, 1984.

Nieuport 17 Fighter Aircraft

The French Nieuport 17 single-seater biplane was one of the outstanding fighter aircraft of World War I. Designed by Gustave Delage as an improvement on his Nieuport 16, it was manufactured by the Société Anonyme des Etablissements Nieuport. Improvements over the Nieuport 16 included greater wing area, strengthened lower wing, and more streamlined appearance. The Nieuport 17 was powered by a Le Rhône 9J 9-cylinder air-cooled rotary 110-horsepower engine that produced a maximum speed of 110 miles per hour, a ceiling of 17,390 feet, and a range of 186 miles. It was armed with a single 7.7mm fully synchronized machine gun on the fuselage centerline forward of the cockpit.

Entering service in the summer of 1916, the Nieuport 17 easily handled the remaining German Fokker E.III Eindecker fighters and could hold its own against the newer Albatros and Halberstadt D I fighters appearing that fall. The Nieuport 17 remained a frontline aircraft until 1917, when it was superseded by the SPAD VII. The Italians manufactured the Nieuport 17 under license, while both the Belgians and Russians imported and flew it. It also served as the principal aircraft of the American volunteer squadron in France, the famous Lafayette Escadrille.

Further Reading

Angelucci, Enzo. *The Rand McNally Encyclopedia of Military Aircraft, 1914–1980.* New York: Military Press, 1983.

Fredriksen, John C. *International Warbirds: An Illustrated Guide to World Military Aircraft, 1914–2000.* Santa Barbara, CA: ABC-CLIO, 2001.

Hallion, Richard P. *Rise of the Fighter Aircraft, 1914–1918.* Annapolis, MD: Nautical and Aviation Publishing Company of America, 1984.

Sopwith F.1 Camel Fighter Aircraft

The Sopwith Camel was probably the finest British fighter aircraft of World War I. Designed by Herbert Smith of the Sopwith Aviation Company, the prototype first flew in December 1916 and entered service in July 1917. Smith placed the heaviest

A Sopwith F.1 Camel. Entering service in July 1917, this highly maneuverable aircraft had a top speed of 115 mph and was probably the best British fighter of World War I. (National Archives)

elements of the aircraft very close to the nose section. That and its powerful engine provided excellent turning capability. The name came from the humped shape of the fairing that covered the two machine guns.

The Camel had a single 130-horsepower Clerget 9B 9-cylinder air-cooled rotary engine that gave it a maximum speed of 115 miles per hour, a ceiling of 19,000 feet, and an endurance of 2.5 hours. It was also the first British aircraft to mount two machine guns (Vickers .303 caliber) that fired through the propeller arc. The Camel was not an easy aircraft to fly because of the great torque from its rotary engine, but at the hands of an experienced pilot it could outmaneuver all opposing aircraft, except possibly the German Fokker Dr.I triplane. A naval version had shorter wings and disassembled for ship storage. Camels flown by the Royal Flying Corps as well as the Royal Navy destroyed some 1,294 German aircraft in little more than a year of operation, more than any other Allied fighter. A total of 5,490 Camels were built. The aircraft remained in service only until 1919, when it was superseded by the Sopwith Snipe.

Further Reading

Angelucci, Enzo. *The Rand McNally Encyclopedia of Military Aircraft, 1914–1980*. New York: Military Press, 1983.

Fredriksen, John C. *International Warbirds: An Illustrated Guide to World Military Aircraft, 1914–2000*. Santa Barbara, CA: ABC-CLIO, 2001.

Hallion, Richard P. *Rise of the Fighter Aircraft, 1914–1918*. Annapolis, MD: Nautical and Aviation Publishing Company of America, 1984.

Sikorsky Ilya Mourometz Heavy Bomber

The Sikorsky Ilya Mourometz was the world's first four-engine bomber. Ultimately produced in a half-dozen models, it both preceded World War I and was built in Russia, whose industrial base was the least advanced of the major aeronautical powers. The plane was designed by brilliant young aeronautical engineer Igor Sikorsky, chief designer for RBVZ, the Russo-Baltic Railway Factories. Sikorsky envisioned a large multiengine transport aircraft. The resulting two-engine design first flew in May 1913 but was found to be underpowered. Fitted with four 100-horsepower Argus engines in separate gondolas between the wings and known as the Russkyi Vitiaz, it was test flown in July 1913 and proved a success.

Sikorsky then designed a larger four-engine aircraft with new fuselage. With Sikorsky himself at the controls, in February 1914 it carried aloft over Moscow 16 men and a dog. The plane reached 6,560 feet on a flight of five hours, averaging 62 miles per hour. The military implications of the giant plane (wingspan of 113 feet and length of 67 feet) were obvious, and the Russian government immediately ordered 10 (subsequently increased to 80), to be adapted for military use.

Named the Ilya Mourometz for the legendary medieval Russian folk hero, the aircraft was produced in a number of different versions. The A model went to the Russian Navy as a floatplane. The B model was a land type with more powerful engines. Thirty bomber-variant Mourometz Vs were built in 1915, followed by 30 G Model aircraft with stronger wings and enhanced armament. The Type E had a smaller (124 feet) wingspan and engines mounted in tandem. The final variant was the most successful, with the E model receiving four more powerful Renault engines, built under license in Russia.

The Ilya Mourometz E of 1917 had a crew of seven. Its four Renault 12-cylinder, liquid-cooled, in-line, 220-horsepower engines provided a speed of 85 miles per hour. It had a ceiling of 13,120 feet and endurance of five hours aloft. Armed with seven machine guns, it could carry 1,760 pounds of bombs.

Employing the Ilya Mourometz V, the first Russian bomber squadron carried out a bombing raid from Poland into East Prussia on February 15, 1915. From that point until Russia left the war at the end of 1917, Ilya Mourometz bombers mounted more than 400 raids into Germany and Lithuania. Amazingly, only 3 of the big bombers were lost. The bomber squadron claimed to have downed 10 German aircraft, possibly the only time in history when a bomber aircraft held a positive kill ratio to fighter aircraft.

Further Reading

Angelucci, Enzo. *The Rand McNally Encyclopedia of Military Aircraft, 1914–1980*. New York: Military Press, 1983.

Fredriksen, John C. *International Warbirds: An Illustrated Guide to World Military Aircraft, 1914–2000*. Santa Barbara, CA: ABC-CLIO, 2001.

Gotha G IV Bomber

The Gotha G IV and G V bombers were no doubt the best-known bombers on the Central Powers side in World War I. Along with the Friedrichshafen G III, the Gothas conducted the bulk of German strategic bombing during the war.

The Germans carried out their first air raids against London with zeppelins, but by 1916 these large airships were taking prohibitive losses from British defenses, and the German high command called for production of large bomber aircraft to replace them. The German firm of Gothaer Waggonfabrik had already been working on the design of such aircraft. The Gotha G I first flew in July 1915 and was both a land plane and a seaplane. The twin-engine G I had a crew of three and two machine guns. Gothas G II and G III differed only in their interior details. Appearing in 1916, they were tested on the Western Front but were found to have inadequate range and bomb payload. Only 25 production-model G IIIs were built.

The first major Gotha production bomber, the G IV, proved to be a success, however. It entered service in the spring of 1917. This large biplane G IV was a two-engine pusher aircraft constructed largely of wood with plywood covering. Powered by two 260-horsepower Mercedes D IVa 6-cylinder, in-line, water-cooled engines, it was capable of a maximum speed of 87.5 miles per hour, a ceiling of 21,320 feet, and a range of 305 miles. It carried from 660 to 1,100 pounds of bombs on external racks and was armed with two 7.92mm Parabellum machine guns.

A German ground crew attaching a 220-lb bomb to a Gotha G IV bomber. The G IV was the principal German strategic bomber of World War I. (Corbis)

The G IV had a crew of three (the pilot and two gunners). As with the GI, the front gunner occupied his own cockpit in the nose of the aircraft and had an unparalleled range of fire, while the rear gunner was able to fire his machine gun upward and backward but also downward through a special opening in the bottom of the fuselage. Bombs were carried externally in removable racks. The bomber's chief drawbacks were that the landing gear and fuselage were weak. About 230 G IVs were built. The G V entered service late in 1917. It received a front pair of wheels to prevent the plane from nosing over in night landings.

G IVs carried out the first daylight aircraft raids on London on May 25, 1917. The normal bomb load for these raids was six 110-pound bombs. Their usual high flying altitude of 15,000 feet made it difficult for British interceptor aircraft to attain sufficient altitude before the Gothas had departed. Although Gotha raids killed hundreds of people, they caused little physical damage and hardly affected the British war effort. Their principal effect was to cause the British to relocate some fighter squadrons from France for home defense.

When they began taking unacceptable losses, Gothas switched to night attacks. Their last daylight raid was on August 22, 1917. Their first night attack occurred on September 3. Gotha raids against Britain were halted altogether from May 1918, when the giant bombers were switched to supporting the German ground effort in France. Altogether, the Gothas dropped nearly 187,000 pounds of bombs over England in 22 raids. Twenty-four Gothas were shot down, while another 37 were lost in accidents. Some Gotha-built aircraft were provided to Austria-Hungary.

Further Reading

Angelucci, Enzo. *The Rand McNally Encyclopedia of Military Aircraft, 1914–1980.* New York: Military Press, 1983.

Fredriksen, John C. *International Warbirds: An Illustrated Guide to World Military Aircraft, 1914–2000.* Santa Barbara, CA: ABC-CLIO, 2001.

Gray, Peter, and Owen Thetford. *German Aircraft of the First World War.* London: Putnam, 1992.

Handley Page O/100 and O/400 Bombers

The Handley Page O/100 was Britain's first strategic bomber. In December 1914 the Admiralty issued a requirement for a strategic bomber, a "bloody paralyser of an aeroplane." Specifications called for a two-seater with a speed of at least 75 miles per hour and a minimum bomb load of six 112-pound bombs. Forty of the aircraft were ordered before the first flight in December 1915.

The Handley Page O/100 entered service with the Royal Naval Air Service on the Western Front in December 1916. This twin-engine biplane had a long box-like fuselage and a large biplane tail section. The O/100 was powered by two Rolls-Royce Eagle II, 250-horsepower, 12-cylinder, liquid-cooled, in-line engines.

A British Handley-Page O/400 bomber. Entering service in 1917, some 607 were built in Britain and the United States. It remained with the Royal Air Force until 1920. (National Archives)

Mounted between the wings, they provided a speed of 85 miles per hour. The plane had a ceiling of 7,000 feet, only one-third that of its German Gotha G IV counterpart, but its endurance time of eight hours was twice that of the German bomber. The O/100 had a crew of four, was armed with four to five machine guns, and could carry a bomb load of 1,792 pounds.

The Royal Naval Air Service initially used the planes in daytime reconnaissance missions off the Flanders coast. Losses, however, forced a shift in April 1917 to night bombing of major German targets, such as submarine bases and railroad centers. Most flew with the Royal Flying Corps. Several saw service against Ottoman forces in Palestine, and one took part in a raid on the German battle cruiser *Goeben* at Constantinople. In all, 46 O/100s were built, and a number were still in service at war's end.

The Handley Page O/400 entered service in France in April 1917, concurrent with the shift of the O/100 to night bombing operations. The O/400 was itself shifted to night bombing that October. The chief difference of the O/400 compared to the O/100 was the shift of fuel storage from the engine nacelles to the fuselage. The O/400s also received successively higher-powered engines, chiefly the Rolls-Royce Eagle IV, VII, and VIII. The VIII of 360 horsepower produced a speed of 97.5 miles per hour, a ceiling of 8,500 feet, and eight-hour endurance. Nearly 800 O/400 aircraft were ordered, with 550 actually built in Britain to November 1918. Another 107 were assembled in the United States by the Standard Aircraft Corporation and powered with the 350-horsepower Liberty 12N engine.

From September 1918, the Royal Flying Corps carried out both day and night raids with 40 or more O/400s each. They carried bomb loads up to a single 1,650-pound bomb against industrial targets in the Rhineland. The Handley Page O/400 remained in service until 1920.

A far superior and good deal larger Handley Page O/1500, Britain's first four-engine aircraft, was armed with up to six machine guns, including for the first time one located in the tail. It had a bomb load of up to 30 250-pound bombs or two giant 3,300-pound bombs, and it could stay aloft for 12 hours. Although 250 O/1500s were ordered, only 35 left the factory by the end of the war. Three were being readied for a raid on Berlin when the armistice intervened. Had the war continued into 1919, the Allies would have launched massive bombing raids against Germany.

Further Reading

Angelucci, Enzo. *The Rand McNally Encyclopedia of Military Aircraft, 1914–1980.* New York: Military Press, 1983.

Fredriksen, John C. *International Warbirds: An Illustrated Guide to World Military Aircraft, 1914–2000.* Santa Barbara, CA: ABC-CLIO, 2001.

Munson, Kenneth. *Bombers: Patrol and Reconnaissance Aircraft, 1914–19.* New York: Macmillan, 1968.

Zeppelins

"Zeppelin" is the generic term for rigid lighter-than-air airships. Developed in Germany before World War I, zeppelins proved useful for reconnaissance purposes and were the world's first strategic bombers. They were named for retired German Army general Count Ferdinand von Zeppelin (1838–1917), who established a company to manufacture airships.

The first Luftschiff Zeppelin (Airship Zeppelin), *LZ 1,* took to the air on July 2, 1900. Early designs were both slow and difficult to maneuver. Improvements enhanced speed and control, and by the beginning of World War I the German Army and the German Navy operated 20 of them for aerial reconnaissance. Most World War I zeppelins were 500–600 feet in length and weighed up to 12 tons. They were cylindrically shaped, with rigid steel frame hulls holding bags filled with 400,000 cubic feet of hydrogen to keep them aloft. Gondolas carried crews and equipment. Propelled by twin engines, most zeppelins had a maximum ceiling of 14,000 feet and a speed of 55 miles per hour.

The *L-70,* commissioned in July 1918, was 694 feet long, powered by seven engines developing 1,715 horsepower, and attained a speed of 81 miles per hour. It had a useful lift of 97,100 pounds.

On August 6, 1914, zeppelin *L-6* inaugurated a 20th-century practice when it flew from Köln (Cologne) to Liège, Belgium, and there dropped bombs, killing

Flight of Zeppelin *L59*

The most notable zeppelin flight of the war occurred in November 1917, when the Imperial German Navy *L59* (known as *Das Afrika-Schiff*, the Africa Ship) attempted to transport supplies 2,000 miles across the Mediterranean and Allied-held Africa to German East Africa. After a 29-hour flight from Friedrichshafen, the *L59* arrived at Yambol (Jambol) in Bulgaria on November 4. As no hydrogen was available in Africa, the Germans planned to dismantle the zeppelin there and cannibalize it, with the outer fabric to be used for tents, muslin linings for bandages, etc. The *L59* carried 15 tons of cargo, including machine guns, spare parts, ammunition, and medical supplies.

Two earlier attempts were halted by bad weather, but the *L59* set out on November 21. Despite mechanical problems, including the inability to send radio messages, it reached as far as Khartoum in the Sudan, where on November 23 it was recalled by an "abort" radio message owing to the inability of German African forces to secure a suitable landing site. Surviving a loss of buoyancy over Asia Minor, the *L59* returned to Yambol on November 25, having covered more than 4,200 miles in 95 hours.

The *L59* succumbed to an accident on April 7, 1918, while on its way to attack the British base at Malta. None of its crew of 21 survived.

nine civilians. Holed by ground fire, it later crashed near Bonn. Low-flying zeppelins proved to be easy targets for antiaircraft fire. Not deterred, the Germans then sent zeppelins against French and British strategic sites, hoping to intimidate the civilian populations.

The first German aerial raid against Britain occurred on the night of January 19–20, 1915, and involved two airships. During the war, zeppelins carried out 51 separate attacks (208 sorties) against England, dropping 196 tons of bombs that killed 557 people and wounded 1,350. By mid-1916 British defenders had gained the upper hand. Countermeasures included searchlight batteries, antiaircraft guns, and aircraft firing incendiary bullets, to which the hydrogen-filled zeppelins were especially vulnerable. Although the zeppelin campaign diverted British air defense resources from the Western Front (12 fighter squadrons of 110 aircraft and 2,200 men, plus antiaircraft units with more than 17,000 additional personnel), its actual military effect was slight.

Navy use of zeppelins for scouting was frequently negated by bad weather, as when dense mist prevented two airships from participating in the May 31–June 1, 1916, Battle of Jutland. In the war the German Navy lost 53 of its 73 airships, while the army lost half of its fleet of 52. Heavy losses to multiple causes, including lightning and storms, led the army to abandon them entirely in June 1917, although the navy continued to fly zeppelins for observation and reconnaissance purposes until the end of the war.

Following the war, zeppelins became peacetime luxury passenger aircraft. The catastrophic explosion of the *Hindenburg* on May 6, 1937, at Lakehurst, New

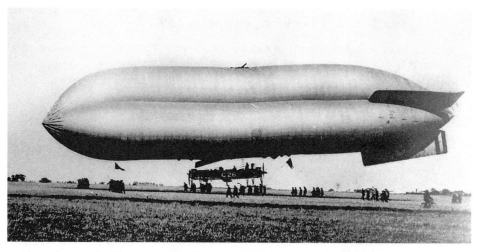

A German navy airship or zeppelin. The rigid lighter-than-air zeppelin was history's first strategic bomber, and the Germans used them to bomb London in World War I. The navy also employed zeppelins in reconnaissance missions. (National Archives)

Jersey, however, ended their popular use. In recent years, there have been efforts to revive airships for cargo transportation.

Further Reading

Cross, Wilbur. *Zeppelins of World War I.* New York: Paragon House, 1991.

De Syon, Guillaume. *Zeppelin! Germany and the Airship, 1900–1939.* Baltimore: Johns Hopkins University Press, 2001.

Rimell, Raymond L. *Zeppelin! A Battle for Air Supremacy in World War I.* London: Conway Maritime, 1984.

Director Fire Control and New Range Finding at Sea

The Battle of Tsushima Straits in May 1905 demonstrated that the big gun was the key at sea; only the largest shells could inflict crippling damage on an armored ship's superstructure. Navies therefore paid increasing attention to gunnery practice and methods, and during the next decade naval gunnery was transformed. Range finders of longer base length appeared, capable of accurate range measurement out to 10,000 yards, and early analogue computer systems helped solve the considerable problem of calculating the precise location of the target ship when the shells arrived. Such systems took into account range, drift, speed of the ship and of its target, deflection (lead angle), gun elevation, and forces exerted on the projectile.

The most important figure in the dramatic change in naval gunnery practice was Royal Navy captain Percy Scott, known as "the pocket Hercules." In 1898 while commanding the cruiser *Scylla* in the Mediterranean, Scott invented a technique of continuous aiming. In the Mediterranean Fleet annual firing competition, the average for the ships participating was only 30 percent hits, but the *Scylla* scored 80 percent. Scott also introduced salvo firing.

Then in 1905 Scott perfected a system of director firing. Taking advantage of new electrical circuitry, he came up with a system that concentrated control of all the big guns in the hands of the director, or first gunnery officer. The director and his assistants were located in a director tower high in the foremast to remain clear of funnel and gun smoke, blast, and sea spray. From this observation platform with its master sight, cables ran to a central transmitting station, which produced firing data for the director and to the individual turrets. The director controlled laying and firing all the main guns. In emergency circumstances or if the director tower was out of action, individual turrets could still fire on their own.

The Admiralty long resisted this change, but in November 1912 the superdreadnought *Thunderer,* fitted for director firing, achieved a hit ratio six times that of its sister ship, *Orion,* which employed the older independent method. Nonetheless, the Admiralty moved so slowly that at the beginning of World War I, only a third of Royal Navy dreadnoughts were fitted with director towers. The Royal Navy also turned down a privately developed fire-control computer system, an early analogue computer designed by civilian Arthur Pollen, in favor of an inferior, less sophisticated system developed by Admiral Sir Frederic Dreyer.

By World War I nonetheless, capital ships could engage their opponents at ranges out to five miles or more, double that of Tsushima. Elevation in ship guns reflected this change. In the Royal Navy maximum gun elevation was 13.5 degrees until 1909, when in new ships it became 15 degrees. In 1911 it became 20 degrees, and in 1915 it was increased to 30 degrees.

By 1912 with assistance from instruments to plot range changes (the dumaresqs or trigometric slide rule developed in 1902 by Royal Navy Lieutenant John S. Dumaresq), Vickers range clocks to determine changes of range rate, and new Barr & Stroud range finders, British capital ships could conduct firing practice out to 14,000 yards. If ships during World War I scored about the same number of hits as the U.S. Navy had registered at Manila Bay and Santiago during the Spanish-American War of 1898, it was in considerably more difficult circumstances and at up to 10 times the range.

Further Reading

Brown, David K. *The Eclipse of the Big Gun: The Warship, 1906–45.* Annapolis, MD: Naval Institute Press, 1992.

Hogg, Ivan, and John Batchelor. *Naval Gun.* Poole, Dorset, UK: Blandford, 1978.

Padfield, Peter. *Guns at Sea.* New York: St. Martin's, 1974.

Tucker, Spencer C. *Handbook of 19th Century Naval Warfare.* Stroud, UK: Sutton, 2000.

Wrigley, Walter, and John Hovorka. *Fire Control Principles.* New York: McGraw-Hill, 1959.

Dreadnought, HMS

The name "dreadnought" was given to at least 11 different British warships. The most famous was that of 1906, which gave its name to a new type of superbattleship. The first all-big-gun capital ship, it revolutionized ship design and made obsolete every other battleship in the world, including those of Britain. The *Dreadnought* was the British Admiralty's answer to a massive increase in German battleship strength. The ship is forever associated with first sea lord Admiral John A. "Jackie" Fisher. This is ironic, because he opposed its construction and sought a new class of heavy gunned armored cruisers, what became the battle cruiser.

Until the *Dreadnought,* battleships had mixed armaments. The Japanese *Mikasa,* completed in Britain in 1902 and rated at the time as the largest and most powerful of the world's warships, had 4 12-inch guns in two turrets but also 14 6-inch and 20 3-inch guns to enable it to fight at long, intermediate, and close ranges. The Battle of Tsushima Straits in May 1905, however, confirmed the belief of many experts that a mixed battery was less efficient than one of single caliber. One battleship mounting 10 12-inch guns would be the mathematical equivalent of two and a half *Mikasa*s. With central gunnery control and presenting a smaller target, it might even be the equivalent of four or five.

Clearly, it was not in Britain's interest to introduce the all-big-gun ship and render obsolete its own large number of capital ships, but there was little choice because other powers were contemplating such a step. In March 1905 the U.S. Congress authorized building two such ships, the future *South Carolina* and *Michigan.* Italy, Russia, Germany, and Japan were also considering such a step.

In March 1905, the Board of Admiralty approved plans for both a new battleship and a new armored cruiser with all-big-gun armament. One of Fisher's favorite expressions was *totus porcus* (whole hog), and he went furiously at the project. All materials were collected in advance, some from other ships then building, and nothing was allowed to delay construction.

The *Dreadnought* was laid down at Portsmouth on October 2, 1905. Completed with astonishing speed on October 2, 1906, it displaced 17,900 tons and was 490 feet in length (527 feet overall) and 82 feet in beam. It was the first all-big-gun, turbine-powered, fast battleship. Its new lighter and more durable turbine engines (the first in a battleship) drove it at 21 knots, 2 knots faster than its nearest competitor. Its 10 12-inch guns in five turrets could all be centrally controlled and aimed at a single target. It also had 27 12-pounders and some smaller guns to deal with the threat of torpedo boats, and it mounted five 18-inch torpedo tubes (four in broadside and one in her stern). The *Dreadnought* had 11-inch armor plate below the waterline and an 8-inch belt above it. Bow and stern were protected with 6- and 4-inch armor, respectively.

The *Dreadnought* saw active service in World War I, although it was then outclassed by even more powerful superbattleships. It sank only one vessel during the

HMS *Dreadnought*. Commissioned in 1906, it was the first all-big-gun battleship and forced a technological revolution in battleship design. (Topical Press Agency/Getty Images)

war, a German submarine that it sent to the bottom by ramming. The *Dreadnought* was sold out of the service in 1921 and broken up in 1923.

Further Reading

Brown, David K. *The Eclipse of the Big Gun: The Warship, 1906–45.* Annapolis, MD: Naval Institute Press, 1992.

Massie, Robert K. *Dreadnought: Britain, Germany, and the Coming of the Great War.* New York: Random House, 1991.

Parkes, Oscar. *British Battleships* Warrior *(1860) to* Vanguard *(1950): A History of Design, Construction, and Armament.* London: Seeley Service, 1970.

Roberts, John. *The Battleship* Dreadnought. Annapolis, MD: Naval Institute Press, 1992.

Invincible-Class Battle Cruisers

The Royal Navy *Invincible* was the first battle cruiser. Royal Navy first sea lord Admiral Sir John "Jackie" Fisher had been forced to introduce the first superbattleship, the *Dreadnought,* but his chief interest lay in a new class of heavy cruisers that would incorporate the dreadnought principles of higher speed, greater armament, and larger size. The new ships would employ battleship armament on a high-speed cruiser hull. Fisher reasoned that this new ship type, known first as the battleship cruiser and then as the battle cruiser, would be able to use its superior speed to keep a range sufficient to avoid enemy torpedoes and gunfire while at the same time relying on both larger guns and enhanced gunnery equipment to hit its opponent before it could be struck in return.

The first three British battle cruisers were the *Invincible, Inflexible,* and *Indomitable.* Authorized in 1905, the ships were completed in 1907. Displacing 17,250 tons and having an overall length of 567 feet and a beam of 78 feet 8.5 inches, the *Invincible* incorporated new turbines that allowed it to achieve sustained speeds of up to 27 knots. It mounted a main battery of 8 12-inch guns. The turrets forward and aft were on the centerline. The other two turrets were offset: the No. Two turret was to port, and the No. Three turret was to starboard. Secondary battery included 12 4-inch guns.

The Invincible-class ships had only 2 fewer 15-inch guns than the *Dreadnought.* The standard armored (heavy) cruiser had 12 8-inch guns, whereas the new battle cruiser had 8 12-inch guns. But an 8-inch shell weighed only 250 pounds, whereas a 12-inch shell weighed 886 pounds and was fired at greater range. The battle cruisers could also outrun the 22–23–knot armored cruisers. In theory, what the battle cruiser could not destroy it could outrun. The proof of the superiority of the new design was shown in the Battle of the Falkland Islands in December 1914 when two British battle cruisers stood off at long range and sank two German armored cruisers without the loss of a single man on the British ships.

The flaw in the design was the sacrifice of armor protection to resist battleship shells for speed. Whereas the *Dreadnought* had an 11-inch armor belt, the *Invincible*-class ships had only 6 inches. The battle cruiser had battleship guns but could not stand against them; because of their guns, the tendency was to place the battle cruisers against battleships in fleet engagements.

The British battle cruisers also suffered from serious design flaws in a lack of sufficient armor on the tops of their turrets and inadequate flash protection for their magazines. These shortcomings became all too apparent in the Battle of Jutland of May 31–June 1, 1916, when the *Invincible* and other battle cruisers—the *Indefatigable* and *Queen Mary*—were sunk with terrible loss of life.

The Germans and other naval powers also built battle cruisers, and the ship type continued into World War II. Its design deficiencies were again demonstrated in May 1941 when the German battleship *Bismarck* sank the British battle cruiser *Hood.* The last two of this ship type constructed were the U.S. Navy's *Alaska* and *Guam,* completed in 1944.

Further Reading

Brown, David K. *The Eclipse of the Big Gun: The Warship, 1906–45.* Annapolis, MD: Naval Institute Press, 1992.

Osborne, Eric W. *Cruisers and Battle Cruisers: An Illustrated History of Their Impact.* Santa Barbara, CA: ABC-CLIO, 2004.

Furious, HMS

The Royal Navy aircraft carrier *Furious* occupies a prominent place in the history of naval aviation. It was the best-known carrier of World War I. A growing recognition of the need for fighter aircraft to operate with the Grand Fleet in the North Sea led to aircraft being carried on platforms mounted on battleships and cruisers. The next step was hybrid conversions such as *Campania* and *Furious,* ships that would have the necessary speed to operate with the fleet but also be able to carry a number of fighters.

Built by the firm of Armstrong Whitworth, HMS *Furious* was a conversion from a Courageous-class battle cruiser. Laid down in June 1915, it was commissioned in June 1917. The ship was 786 feet 6 inches in overall length by 88 feet in beam. It displaced 19,100 tons standard load and had a speed of 31.5 knots.

As designed, the *Furious* was intended for service in the Baltic and to mount 2 18-inch 40-caliber guns (1 gun in each of two turrets fore and aft) and 11 5.5-inch guns. Commander in chief of the Grand Fleet Admiral David Beatty established a special committee of the navy to address problems in the seaplane carriers then in service, namely their slow speed and small number of aircraft carried. In February 1917 the committee recommended alterations to the *Furious,* then nearing completion. The modifications were approved and easily effected. The forward turret was removed and replaced with a hangar sufficient for eight seaplanes. The *Furious* also received a planked wooden flight deck forward and two derricks—one on each side of the ship. The ship's crew numbered 796 men, along with 84 Royal Navy Air Service personnel.

Following trials and the death of one pilot trying to land his Sopwith Pup aircraft on the ship, the *Furious* underwent additional modification. Completed by November 1917, this work added a flight deck aft. A second hangar was located underneath it, doubling the complement of aircraft carried. Electric lifts fore and aft were added, as was primitive arresting gear. The ship's superstructure remained, rising in the middle.

The *Furious* made history when it carried out the first air strike ever from an aircraft carrier. On July 19, 1918, it launched seven Sopwith Camels, each carrying two 50-pound bombs, in a raid against the zeppelin base at Tondern that destroyed two of the German airships.

Retention of the superstructure made landing difficult for pilots, and during 1922–1925 the *Furious* was rebuilt and the superstructure removed. The flight decks then ran four-fifths of the ship's length up to the forward section. Although the *Furious* was now a flush-deck carrier, the decks were seen as separate: the forward for launch and the aft for recovery. Conning positions were to either side of the flight deck. The ship retained 10 5.5-inch guns for antiaircraft protection.

The *Furious* saw extensive World War II service, primarily in antisubmarine warfare and convoy protection, but it also took part in the Allied invasion of North

Africa and in strikes against the German battleship *Tirpitz*. Placed in reserve in September 1944, the *Furious* was sold for scrap in 1948.

Further Reading

Chesneau, Roger. *Aircraft Carriers of the World, 1914 to the Present: An Illustrated Encyclopedia*. Annapolis, MD: Naval Institute Press, 1995.

Friedman, Norman. *British Carrier Aviation: The Evolution of the Ships and Their Aircraft*. Annapolis, MD: Naval Institute Press, 1988.

Hobbs, David. *Aircraft Carriers of the Royal and Commonwealth Navies: The Complete Illustrated Encyclopedia from World War I to the Present*. London: Greenhill Books, 1996.

Argus, HMS

HMS *Argus* was a British aircraft carrier, notable as the first clear-deck carrier. Laid down in a British yard in 1914 as the passenger liner *Conte Rosso* for an Italian firm, all work on the ship halted with the outbreak of World War I. Purchased by the British government in 1916 and intended as a cruiser, it underwent another conversion, into an aircraft carrier. The *Argus* underwent sea trials in October 1918.

The *Argus* was 565 feet in overall length with a flight deck of 550 feet and a beam of 68 feet. The ship displaced 24,000 tons and had a maximum speed of 21 knots and a normal complement of 495 Royal Navy and Royal Air Force personnel. The *Argus* had two electrically powered elevators for raising aircraft from the hangar deck below and carried 20 Sopwith Cuckoo aircraft. Armament in 1918 was two 4-inch/50-caliber and two 4-inch antiaircraft guns.

Completed too late to see World War I service, the *Argus* served in the Atlantic Fleet. Refitted in 1925–1926, it was placed in reserve status in 1930. Returned to duty during World War II, the *Argus* served effectively in the Mediterranean theater during 1939–1940 and with Force H in 1942. Again placed in reserve in 1944, it was scrapped in 1947. The ship's clear-deck design formed the basis of all other aircraft carriers to follow.

Further Reading

Chesneau, Roger. *Aircraft Carriers of the World, 1914 to the Present: An Illustrated Encyclopedia*. Annapolis, MD: Naval Institute Press, 1984.

Friedman, Norman. *British Carrier Aviation: The Evolution of the Ships and Their Aircraft*. Annapolis, MD: Naval Institute Press, 1988.

Hobbs, David. *Aircraft Carriers of the Royal and Commonwealth Navies*. Mechanicsburg, PA: Stackpole, 1996.

Submarine Development to 1914

Submarines became important weapons of war during World War I, but the concept was not new. In the 1620s Charles von Drebbel, a Dutch physician living in

Sinking of the *Aboukir, Cressy,* and *Hogue*

The importance of the submarine as an offensive weapon was revealed early in World War I, on September 12, 1914. The *Aboukir, Cressy,* and *Hogue*—three British 12,000-ton cruisers of the 1900 Bacchantes class—were patrolling in the North Sea south of the Dogger Bank. Contrary to orders, the ships were not zigzagging when the German submarine *U-9* under Commander Otto Weddigen arrived. The *Aboukir* was the first to be torpedoed and sunk (at 6:30 a.m.). The other two cruisers immediately attempted to rescue members of the *Aboukir*'s crew in the water. Standing dead in the water to launch and recover lifeboats, first the *Hogue* and shortly thereafter the *Cressy* were also sunk. Although two small Dutch ships appeared more than an hour after the last of the three ships went down and rescued 840 men, more than 1,400 (most of them reservists with families) were lost in the disaster. The *U-9* survived the war.

London, built a combination wood and greased leather craft that could submerge and was propelled by oars fitted in watertight sleeves. The first real submarine was American David Bushnell's *Turtle* during the American Revolutionary War (1775–1783), but an attempt by it in 1776 to sink a British ship of the line failed. In 1800 American Robert Fulton built another submarine, the *Nautilus,* for the French government. Despite its apparent success, Fulton was displeased with the design and dismantled it.

In 1850, Bavarian Wilhelm Bauer invented *Le Plongeur Marin*. Powered by an internal handwheel that turned a screw propeller, it submerged by letting water into a double bottom; to rise, a pump expelled the water. Weights moved forward and aft adjusted the trim. In 1856 Bauer constructed a larger 56-foot-long submarine in Russia. This *Diable-Marin* was powered by a treadmill and could transport a 500-pound mine.

During the American Civil War, both sides—but especially the Confederates—built submarines. In February 1864 the Confederate submarine *H. L. Hunley* employed a spar torpedo (a mine on the end of a long pole) to sink the Union screw sloop *Housatonic* off Charleston, South Carolina. This was the first time in the history of warfare that a submersible craft had sunk a ship. The unstable *H. L. Hunley* went down as well.

In 1862 Frenchmen Siméon Bourgeois and Charles Marie Brun designed the *Plongeur*. Launched in 1863, it was some 140 feet long and displaced 153 tons. Its propeller was driven by compressed air, and the submarine incorporated watertight bulkheads. In 1875 English clergyman George William Garrett developed a steam-powered submarine, the *Resurgam*. Swedish cannon founder Thorsten Nordenfelt worked with Garrett to produce a twin-screw, steam-propelled, 64-foot-long, 60-ton submarine. This *Nordenfelt No. 1* of 1885 could dive to 50 feet and was operated by three men. It was the first submarine to carry an automotive torpedo, the

Whitehead. Nordenfelt later built and sold submarines of this design to Turkey, Russia, and Germany, but they suffered from control problems.

In 1877 Polish-born Stefan Drzewiecki constructed a submarine less than 10 feet long, propelled by means of pedals by its single occupant. Two years later he built a 19.67-foot version that had a crew of five and incorporated a periscope to be used when the submarine was submerged. Air was brought into the submarine by means of a pump connected to a tube extending above the surface of the water. Hand pumps emptied the ballast tanks, and the diving angle was adjusted by moving weights along overhead beams. The Russian Navy ordered 50 of these submarines.

In 1886 Englishmen Andrew Campbell and James Ash designed a submarine powered by electric engines operating on a 100-cell storage battery. Their *Nautilus* was capable of 6–8 knots and had a cruising range of 80 miles.

In France, Gustave Zédé designed the *Gymnote*. Launched in 1888, it was some 59 feet long and displaced 31 tons. It had a steel hull and was powered by an electric motor. Internal ballast tanks and hydroplanes facilitated submerging and surfacing. A much larger French submarine, the *Zédé* of 1893, was also electrically powered but had a bronze pressure hull. It was 159 feet long, displaced 366 tons, and mounted a torpedo tube with space for two reload Whitehead torpedoes.

One of the first practical designs was the French submarine *Narval* of 1900. It displaced 200 tons submerged and was 111.5 feet long with a double hull. The first heavier hull could withstand pressure underwater; the second lighter hull provided buoyancy and improved surface seaworthiness. The space between the two was used for water ballast for diving. The *Narval*'s other novel feature was that it was powered by two motors on the same shaft. A steam motor for surface cruising also turned an electric motor acting as a dynamo that in turn charged storage batteries. The electric motor powered the submarine underwater. The *Narval* was armed with four 17.7-inch-diameter torpedoes.

The first really practical submarine, however, was invented by Irish immigrant to the United States John P. Holland. His sixth design, the *Holland VI* (usually known simply as the *Holland*) of 1898, was purchased by the U.S. Navy. The forerunner of all modern submarines, it was powered by an internal combustion engine for surface cruising and an electric motor for underwater operation. It mounted a single 18-inch torpedo tube and could carry two reload torpedoes. The navy soon signed a contract with Holland for six additional boats, the Adler class.

Simon Lake, Holland's principal American competitor, experimented with submarines off New York. His *Argonaut First* of 1897 displaced 59 tons submerged, was 36 feet long, and was built of ⅜-inch steel plate. Operated by a crew of five men, it was powered by a 30-horsepower gasoline engine. The *Argonaut* also had a double hull, with the space between flooded on diving. It also featured intake and exhaust pipes for air while submerged, a forerunner of the German snorkel of World War II. Lake also built other submarines.

Rudolph Diesel's new engine in the 1890s solved a major problem for the submarines. Early gasoline combustion engines emitted dangerous fumes, which meant that the danger of an explosion was always present. Diesel engine burned a fuel far less volatile than gasoline. Diesel engines also had the advantages of being cheaper to run and more efficient in fuel consumption, particularly important when space was at such a premium. The world's first diesel-powered submarine was the French *Aigrette* of 1904. The *A-13* was the first British submarine with a diesel engine; it was working by 1905. The United States adopted the diesel for its submarines in 1911. The *U-19,* launched in 1912, was the first German diesel-powered submarine.

Originally the submarine was conceived to be most useful for picket and observation duty to provide information on enemy fleet movements. Even when fitted with a small deck gun, the submarine on the surface was no match for anything other than an unarmed merchant ship. The automotive torpedo was, however, ideally suited to submarine use, and by World War I torpedoes powered by electric motors with stubby vanes to control their running depths could travel 7,000–8,000 yards at up to 36 knots and deliver a 500-pound charge of TNT.

Fitted with a periscope, powered by a diesel-electric power plant, and armed with torpedoes and 4- to 5-inch deck guns, the submarine could challenge the largest surface ship. Its only real limitation was the length of time it could remain submerged operating on its electric engine. The maximum was only about 48 hours. Running on the surface, the submarine was vulnerable to attack by ships or aircraft.

Germany entered the war with few submarines because minister of marine Admiral Alfred von Tirpitz was busy building a surface fleet, centered on dreadnoughts, in order to contest Britain for world naval mastery. He saw submarines not as a means of reducing Britain's advantage in surface ships or as commerce destroyers but instead primarily as defensive weapons. Germany did not order its first submarine, the *Unterseeboot 1 (U-1)* until 1906.

Britain was also slow to embrace the submarine. Admiral Sir A. K. Wilson described the new weapon as "underhand, unfair, and damned un-English"; Lord Charles Beresford dismissed it as a useless weapon, "always in a fog." But with the French and Germans building them, the British had to enter the race. In December 1900 London made arrangements with the Holland Torpedo Boat Company in the United States to build five of its boats, referred to as Type Number VII, in Britain.

Soon the British had developed their own submarines. The 13 190-ton A class boats, launched beginning in 1902, were more powerful than any of the Hollands. By 1904, the Royal Navy had reluctantly accepted submarines as a part of its naval armament; that year it began the B class, building 11 of these 287-ton boats. B class submarines continued in service into World War I, and of these the *B-11* penetrated the Dardanelles to sink the Turkish battleship *Messudieh* in December 1914. Beginning in 1906 the British launched 38 238-ton C class submarines, and in 1910 they completed the first of 8 490-ton diesel-powered D-class boats.

By September 1914 the British had 13 E-class 700-ton submarines with four 18-inch torpedo tubes. Capable of 16 knots on the surface and 10 knots submerged and with a range of 1,500 miles, these were the first true oceangoing submarines. France also kept in the race, with 20 70-ton Naïde-class submarines in 1904 and 18 398-ton Pluviôse-class submarines beginning in 1907.

By 1914, submarine design had reached a plateau and, in fact, changed little in the course of World War I. Naval leaders were slow to realize the submarine's offensive potential, simply because the last sinking of a ship by a submarine had occurred 50 years earlier, and no surface ship had yet to be sunk by a submarine-launched automotive torpedo. A Greek submarine, the *Delfin,* had hit an Ottoman cruiser with a torpedo during the First Balkan War (1912–1913), but it was a dud. The admirals therefore persisted in thinking of the submarine primarily for observation duties and mine laying.

On the eve of World War I, Britain had the most submarines, 73. France had 55, the United States had 38, Russia had 24, and Italy had 24. Germany, the great practitioner of submarine warfare during the war, had only 35 in 1914. Nonetheless, the Germans probably had the best submarines qualitatively. The newest German submarines were superior in range and more modern than those of Britain or France. During World War I, however, Germany built 332 additional submarines, almost three times the number built by Britain, the second leading submarine builder, with 128. German submarines had the best diesel engines in the world and also the best periscopes. Functionally, World War I boats (and also World War II boats for that matter) were submersibles rather than true submarines. They were designed for optimal operation on the surface and had only limited capabilities submerged.

The submarine phase of World War I did not begin well for Germany, however. On August 9 in the North Sea the British cruiser *Birmingham* rammed and sank the *U-15,* which was then on the surface for engine repair. On September 5, however, the *U-21* sank the British destroyer *Pathfinder* off the Firth of Forth, the first warship sunk by a submarine in the war. The *Pathfinder* went down with 259 men.

Further Reading

Fontenoy, Paul E. *Submarines: An Illustrated History of Their Impact.* Santa Barbara, CA: ABC-CLIO, 2007.

Hutchinson, Robert. *Jane's Submarines: War beneath the Waves from 1776 to the Present Day.* New York: HarperCollins, 2001.

Depth Charge

Depth charges are an important antisubmarine warfare (ASW) weapon. They are explosive devices designed to sink a submarine by detonating in its vicinity. The depth charge traces its roots to the Royal Navy's 1910 experiments with towed explosive sweeps. Prior to 1916, the Royal Navy relied on these to engage submerged enemy submarines. The single sweep was an 80-pound charge towed astern of a vessel and supported at a depth of 40 feet by a hydroplane. When the cable fouled a submarine, the charge was detonated electrically. A modified sweep was a large loop towed vertically. Floats supported the upper section 24 feet below the surface and nine 80-pound charges hung at 100-feet intervals along the lower section, maintained 24 feet deeper by kites. The charges carried contact pistols or could be fired electrically. Both the French and Italian Navies developed similar devices, but none was particularly successful. Explosive sweeps may have sunk two U-boats during World War I.

The British introduced depth charges in January 1915. These carried charges of either 33 or 100 pounds and were triggered by a pull-off pistol: a float with a lanyard that pulled out a firing pin when the charge reached its designated depth. Too small to be effective, they were replaced a year later by one with a 300-pound charge. It used a hydrostatic pistol set for depths of either 40 or 80 feet. The French had depth charges in service in mid-1916. The U.S. Navy soon adopted a modified British type that could be set for 300 feet, while one in September 1918 had a 600-pound charge.

Depth charges resembled oil drums in appearance and could thus be rolled off a ship. The British also developed a variety of howitzers and bomb throwers that could project charges between 50 and 80 yards to the side. The combination of racks and throwers allowed antisubmarine ships to fire patterns of charges around a submarine and thus greatly increase the danger zone. Despite inadequate detection methods, Allied depth charges sank 30 German U-boats between 1916 and 1918.

Budget cuts during the interwar years led most countries to terminate research and development of antisubmarine weapons. The depth charge was considered adequate, a belief that was

Crewmen of the British Navy Captain-class frigate *Holmes* observing the plume of water from the explosion of a depth charge dropped against a suspected German U-boat off the coast of Normandy, France, June 7, 1944. (Photo by Mansell/Time & Life Pictures/Getty Images)

reinforced in most Western countries by the advent of active sonar, ASDIC in Britain. The 1930s led to a resumption of their production, however. Britain introduced one utilizing amatol explosive instead of TNT and a simpler, more reliable hydrostatic fuze. Germany was the first to develop specifically designed aircraft depth charges. The Luftwaffe modified bombs for antisubmarine work by developing a hydrostatic device that detonated them at a depth of 40 feet. This was intended for use against diving submarines or those whose periscopes had been sighted.

World War II revealed shortcomings in the depth charges in service. Newer submarines could dive deeper and maneuver more quickly underwater. Britain responded in 1940 with a depth charge that had a 150-pound cast iron weight in the nose to increase its sink rate. Maximum engagement depths were also increased as the war advanced. By 1942, Allied depth charges had a maximum depth setting of 900 feet, and Britain experimented with settings of 1,492 feet. Additionally, some 3,050-pound depth charges were introduced into service in 1943. Launched from 21-inch torpedo tubes, they were intended to engage deep-running submarines below 620 feet.

Both the United States and Britain experimented with proximity-fuzed depth charges. Both tried magnetic-activated fuzes, but these were not successful. Britain also tested one that was detonated by the submarine's underwater electronic potential, but it never went into service. Smaller depth charges were also introduced for use against frogmen and midget submarines. The United States and Britain focused on accelerating the descent rate of depth charges. One U.S. design had a teardrop shape, giving it a 50 percent faster sink rate.

In 1942, the United States also introduced specifically designed aircraft depth charges. The first had a charge of 234 pounds of TNT. Its teardrop shape not only reduced drag when carried on the wings but gave it a faster sink rate. A heavier model, with 252 pounds of torpex explosive, began to replace the Mark 44s in 1944. Other modified designs followed.

Despite these advances, the depth charge increasingly gave way to longer-ranged guided ASWs. The Hedgehog was developed by the British in 1942. Suggested by Royal Navy lieutenant commander Charles F. Goodeve in 1941, the Hedgehog utilized a spigot mortar shell ("bomb" in British parlance) developed to project wire devices against aircraft attacking ships. The spigot mortar worked against a rod (the spigot) set in a baseplate at a fixed angle. The tubular tail of the mortar shell fit over the spigot. The Hedgehog launcher mounted 24 mortar shells, each 7 inches in diameter with 31 pounds of torpex explosive.

The Hedgehog was mounted forward on the ship (first on a fixed mount and later on one gyro-stabilized to compensate for the movement of the vessel). Fired simultaneously, the charges threw the mortar shells in a 130-foot circular pattern 215 yards in advance of the ship. Firing the shells forward gave an enemy submarine less chance to take evasive action. The charges exploded on contact. The

Hedgehog got its name because when empty, the rows of empty spigots resembled the spines of a hedgehog.

The Hedgehog joined the fleet at the end of the year, deployed on small convoy escort vessels such as destroyers and destroyer escorts. U.S. Navy escort vessels were later similarly armed.

The Hedgehog had several advantages over the depth charge. There was no warning of the attack, and because the charges went off only on contact, the depth did not have to be known. Also, if there was no explosion and no settling down period thereafter, the submarine could still be tracked on sonar. The Hedgehog was deployed on small convoy escort vessels such as destroyers and destroyer escorts. The U.S. Navy developed a smaller version of the Hedgehog, known as the Mouse-trap. It fired four or eight similar rockets.

The Royal Navy introduced an entirely new weapon in the so-called Squid depth charge mortar in September 1943. Known as the Squid, it fired three 12-inch 390-pound shells with a 207-pound minol charge. The charges were set to explode at specified depths, and the pressure waves created could crack open a submarine hull. Each corvette carried a 3-barreled Squid mortar that fired its three shells in a triangular pattern some 275 yards in front of the ship. The mortar was automatically fired by the sonar range recorder. The Squid had the fastest sink rate of any unpowered ASW weapon of World War II at 43.5 feet per second, more than double that of any standard depth charge. A Squid sank the *U-333* in the Atlantic on July 31, 1944. Reportedly, the Hedgehog and Squid together accounted for some 50 Axis submarines.

By 1944, the Hedgehog and air-dropped Mark 24 antisubmarine torpedo had become the Western Allies primary submarine killers. The trend toward guided antisubmarine torpedoes has continued into the 21st century. Both the United States and the Soviet Union developed rocket-thrown nuclear depth charges for use by both submarines and surface ships. Airborne versions were also developed. However, the environmental and political implications of using such weapons make their employment problematic. Depth charges continue to be important ASW weapons, although they primarily are viewed as shallow-water ASW weapons and are most often thrown from ASW mortars, rockets, or guns. Few navies use stern-dropped depth charges today.

Further Reading

Campbell, John. *Naval Weapons of World War II*. Annapolis, MD: Naval Institute Press, 1985.

Friedman, Norman. *World Naval Weapons Systems*. Annapolis, MD: Naval Institute Press, 1991.

Messimer, Dwight R. *Find and Destroy: Antisubmarine Warfare in World War I*. Annapolis, MD: Naval Institute Press, 2001.

Pawle, Gerald. *The Secret War*. London: G. G. Harrap, 1956.

Hydrophone

A hydrophone is a passive underwater listening device employed by surface ships to detect submarines and by submarines to detect the presence of surface vessels. The hydrophone converts sound to electricity. U.S. naval architect Lewis Nixon is credited with the invention in 1906 of the first operating hydrophone using this principle. The sinking of the British liner *Titanic* from striking an iceberg in 1912 spurred further interest in underwater navigation. That year Alexander Belm in Austria described an underwater ranging device, while Lewis Richardson in Britain secured a patent for echo ranging, the forerunner of sonar.

Although the development of sonar and hydrophones is essentially linked, passive hydrophone technology led in terms of practical application. The first working active and passive hydrophone system was developed in 1914, but it was 1918 before the British were able to translate the pioneering work of French physicist Paul Langévin and Russian scientist Constantin Chilowsky in the field of high-frequency ultrasonic echo-listening devices into a working experimental sonar.

Meanwhile, work on passive hydrophones continued. Early work focused on shore-based systems for controlled minefields. The connection to submarines was only made after the war began. The drawback of early hydrophones was that they could determine the presence of an object within their listening range but could not determine precise direction. Nevertheless, hydrophones for escort vessels evolved from simple nondirectional devices hung over the side of the ship to towed, then hull-mounted, and ultimately hull-contained systems capable of establishing the direction of a contact. By 1918, 54 out of 255 attacks on submarines by Allied escort vessels were carried out with some degree of assistance by hydrophones. Although others may have been sunk earlier, the first submarine confirmed lost in consequence of hydrophonic detection was the German *UC-49* on August 8, 1918.

Hydrophones have the advantage of being passive devices, not themselves liable to detection. They are still widely employed to target a variety of sound emissions from submarines and surface ships, including the noise of propellers. Germany's GHG (Gruppen-Horch-Gerät) bow array for submarines, first installed in 1935, could detect a single surface ship at a distance of 12 miles and a convoy at up to a distance of 60 miles. Conversely, surface vessels in World War II used passive listening devices to detect lurking submarines, which would then be homed in on by active range finding with the characteristic pinging sonar.

During the Cold War, the U.S. Navy employed a large number of sophisticated, passive hydrophonic listening devices positioned on ocean floors. This network, known as SOSUS (for *so*und *su*rveillance *s*ystem), was vital for tracking and identifying Soviet submarines. Through triangulation, SOSUS sensors could even provide reasonably accurate position data. Greatly improved hydrophones are today part of every modern submarine's sonar sensor suite. They are able to detect and identify targets hundreds of miles away. Other naval applications for hydrophones today include hydrophonic sensors for detonating so-called underwater influence mines and swimmer detectors for naval base defense.

Further Reading

Brodie, Bernard. *Sea Power in the Machine Age.* Princeton, NJ: Princeton University Press, 1944.

Levert, Lee J. *Fundamentals of Naval Warfare.* New York: Macmillan, 1947.

Messimer, Dwight R. *Find and Destroy: Antisubmarine Warfare in World War I.* Annapolis, MD: Naval Institute Press, 2001.

Miller, David, and John Jordan. *Modern Submarine Warfare.* London: Salamander Books, 1987.

Radio

Both the telegraph and then the telephone had major impacts on the conduct of war. The follow-on communications method of wireless telegraphy, or radio, produced a communications revolution. In the 1870s Briton James Clerk Maxwell first theorized that electrical waves traveled over distances, and German Heinrich Hertz then demonstrated that these waves traveled in straight lines and could be reflected. Italian Guglielmo Marconi is, however, generally credited with the invention of radio around 1895. By 1896 Marconi had developed or adapted the equipment to enable a Morse code radio message to be beamed across the English Channel, and in 1901 he managed to send the Morse code signal, three dots for the letter "S," across the Atlantic.

The implications of radio in war were not immediately apparent to many military leaders, but in 1899 the Royal Navy used radio between ships and shore during

---

Battle of Tannenberg

Sometimes new technologies can be a double-edged sword. Before World War I the Russians acquired radios and, with the start of the war, used these for communication between Stavka (the high command) and the armies in the field. As early as 1913 the Germans had been using their own powerful radio at Königsberg to intercept the Russian communications. The poor training and illiteracy of Russian radio operators precluded mastering codes, and Russian Army communications were broadcast in the clear. Thus, the Germans knew the orders from Stavka as soon as the Russian field commanders. Coupled with information gathered via aircraft reconnaissance and cavalry patrols, the Germans had an accurate picture of Russian plans and dispositions and were able to capitalize on this. The result was the Battle of Tannenberg of August 26–31, 1914, one of the worst defeats in military history. It claimed 122,000 Russian casualties, including some 90,000 prisoners. The Russians also lost 500 guns. German losses were on the order of 10,000–15,000 men.

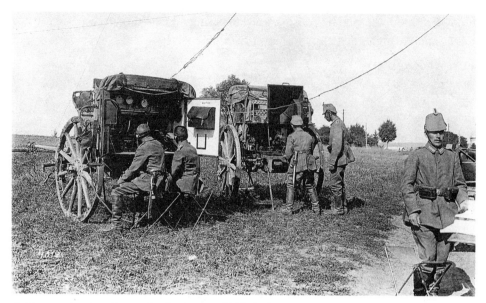

A German Army radio station in August 1917 during World War I. Radio became increasingly important in military communications during the course of that war. (National Archives)

fleet maneuvers. Despite its limited initial range, however, the world's navies eventually adopted radio for communication. For the first time in naval history, communications could be effected between vessels over the horizon from one another. The first operational application of wireless in war came during the 1904–1905 Russo-Japanese War.

Progress in adapting wireless to land warfare was slower because the first radios were very bulky and prone to malfunction. In the course of World War I, however, radios were adopted to use in both tanks and aircraft communicating with the ground. Improved modes of transmission allowed the use of voice signals and not merely code. By World War II all major armies had developed man-portable radios that accompanied troops in the field. During the first two postwar decades, the transistor and then integrated circuits miniaturized radios and made them far more durable. So-called burst transmissions also make it more difficult for enemy forces to detect the location of the sending source.

In addition to helping commanders control events on the battlefield, radios have also greatly aided search and rescue operations. Radio also became an important propaganda tool in the hands of governments, a means to communicate policy objectives at home and abroad. The great importance of radio in war led to the development of so-called jamming to interrupt communication by this means.

Further Reading

Burns, Russell W. *Communications: An International History of the Formative Years.* London: Institute of Electrical Engineers, 2004.

Hezlet, Sir Arthur. *Electronics and Sea Power.* New York: Stein and Day, 1975.

Snyder, Thomas S., ed. *Air Force Communications Command, 1938–1991: An Illustrated History.* Scott Air Force Base, IL: Office of History, 1991.

Wedlake, G. E. C. *SOS: The Story of Radio Communication.* North Pomfret, VT: David and Charles, 1973.

Antiaircraft Artillery

With the advent of balloons and aircraft for reconnaissance and adjustment of artillery fire, armies sought to deny air space over the battlefield to the enemy. One way of accomplishing this was sending aloft one's own aircraft, while another was by ground fire from specially designed antiaircraft (AA) guns. During the course of two world wars, antiaircraft artillery became ever more powerful and accurate. Dramatic improvements were registered in the guns themselves; in their projectiles; in techniques of spotting such as by sound location, searchlights, and radar; and in control of the guns and crew training. During the last half century, guns have been joined by surface-to-air missiles (SAMs). Despite SAMs, guns have proven the most effective means of dealing with enemy aircraft at the lower operating altitudes. This was the case during the U.S. strategic bombing of Germany in World War II and continued to be true through the Vietnam War, when communist guns downed far more U.S. aircraft than did SAMs or aircraft.

The Germans knew antiaircraft guns as "flak," an acronymn for *Fliegerabwehrkanone* (aircraft defense cannon). The British called it "ack-ack" from the World War I phonetic alphabet for AA or "archie" (believed to come from a line by British comedian George Robey). Americans might refer to it as "flak" or "Triple A," for antiaircraft artillery.

Machine guns were widely employed in an AA role, but these are ineffective above 3,000 feet and are also highly inaccurate. Still, as late as the Vietnam War, the Democratic Republic of Vietnam (North Vietnam) relied on large numbers of rifles and machine guns in the defense of Hanoi. Alerted by loudspeakers, ordinary citizens would take up assigned positions and there be ordered to concentrate their fire on one selected low-flying aircraft.

For longer-range fire, a variety of medium-caliber guns appeared, with 20mm, 37mm, and 40mm (2-pounder "pom-pom" in British service) being the most popular calibers. Such weapons were particularly favored for the defense of ships against attacking aircraft, but they saw wide service over land and water in both world wars. By 1945, the navy deployed aboard ship some 13,000 20mm guns along with some 5,000 40mm guns of Swedish design in single, dual, and quad mounts.

But only the higher-caliber heavy guns could hope to reach high-flying bombers by the standards of World Wars I and II. The heavy guns included 75mm, 3-inch, 80mm, 88mm, 90mm, and even larger sizes. By the time of the Vietnam War,

U.S. soldiers firing an antiaircraft machine gun at a German observation plane over the Chemin des Dames on the Western Front in France, March 5, 1918. Antiaircraft guns were introduced to deal with the new threat posed by aircraft. (National Archives)

however, AA guns could not reach the big Boeing B-52 Stratofortress bombers flying at maximum altitude. Over time muzzle velocities steadily increased, along with gun calibers. Higher muzzle velocities meant less time for the projectile to reach its target and quicker response times to changing aircraft flight.

When World War I began, the implications of aircraft were not understood, and neither side had given great attention to AA weapons. France had two armored cars mounting the 75mm field gun, while Britain fielded a few motorized 3-inch guns. Germany had more AA guns than any other power: 18 77mm. It continued to lead in AA artillery during the war. Its principal AA gun was the 77mm. Germany also fielded a few 80mm guns, but in 1917 it introduced the 88mm gun, forerunner of the famed "88" that was employed in so many roles during World War II. The Germans also relied on captured artillery, especially the French 75mm, which they bored up to take German 77mm shells. In 1918 nearly half of German AA artillery consisted of captured guns.

France relied on its 75mm gun throughout World War I. The most common British AA gun was the 3-inch. When the United States entered the war, its forces also employed this weapon. It remained in U.S. service into World War II.

Fuzes, new types of shells, searchlights, sound detectors, tethered balloons, and fire-control devices all played key roles. By 1917, AA projectiles incorporated mechanical time fuzes set to explode at a predetermined altitude, while incendiary shells proved highly effective against German zeppelin airships. Searchlights illuminated German zeppelins and bombers conducting night bombing raids over

London. Sound detectors provided warning of approaching aircraft, while tethered barrage balloons trailing cables were employed in both world wars to defend sensitive targets against low-flying aircraft. New optical sights also appeared.

Despite such improvements, it took a tremendous expenditure of ammunition to bring down an enemy aircraft. During World War I, the Germans shot down more enemy aircraft than any other power, but in 1914 the Germans were firing on average 11,500 shells to down a single Allied plane. By 1918 this had shrunk to 5,040 shells, still a considerable number.

Development of antiaircraft artillery continued after World War I. Perhaps the most famous heavy gun of the war was the German 88mm. Building on the 1917 model, the 88mm of 1935 had a maximum effective altitude of 35,000 feet. The Germans also fielded a 105mm gun and in 1942 brought on line a 128mm gun. At war's end they had under development a 150mm AA gun. The Germans also employed lighter 20mm, 37mm, and 55mm AA guns on motorized platforms, but the effectiveness of their AA system was marred by the absence of the proximity fuze for their projectiles and precision radar control (PRC) systems.

The British relied on their highly effective 3.7-inch gun of 1938, which had a ceiling of 28,000 feet. Its effectiveness was greatly increased by the introduction of PRC in 1944. The British also led in radar detection, and in October 1940 they began to equip their AA forces with gun-laying radar. The Germans followed suit in 1941 and also began employing incendiary shells and more lethal projectiles against aircraft.

The U.S. Army introduced a 90mm AA gun beginning in 1940. It was often mounted on a multipurpose carriage for antiaircraft or field artillery employment. In early 1944 the army adopted a 120mm antiaircraft stratosphere gun. The U.S. Navy, meanwhile, relied on the 5-inch/38-caliber dual-purpose (AA and antiship) gun. Some 3,000 were eventually mounted on U.S. Navy ships. Coupled with the new proximity fuze in 1944, it proved to be a highly effective antiaircraft weapon.

The Soviets copied the Swedish Bofors 25mm and 40mm guns, reworking the latter to fire a 37mm round. The Soviet 76.2mm gun was their largest field AA weapon, while the principal weapon for the defense of cities and industrial sites remained the 85mm. As with the German 88mm, both guns also served as main tank armament.

Technological improvements included the conversion of projectiles from powder to mechanical fuzes, the introduction of flashless propellants, and automatic fuze setters that increased both accuracy and rate of fire. In 1944 the Germans introduced combination contact and timed fuzes in their shells. By then, however, the Allies were employing proximity fuzes, a technology never successfully developed by the Axis side.

In major urban centers the Germans constructed special flak towers. Some covered an entire city block and were over 130 feet high, with reinforced concrete walls up to 8 feet thick and turreted corners. Heavy AA guns were mounted on their rooftops.

The Italians utilized a wide range of antiaircraft guns up to 90mm in size. The standard Japanese World War II AA gun remained the 75mm introduced in the 1920s. The navy relied on the 25mm as its light AA gun and the 5-inch as its standard heavy gun.

Development of AA artillery continued after 1945. Early in the Cold War, the U.S. Army deployed batteries of 90mm and 120mm radar-controlled guns as a means to defend major cities against air attack. The army also came up with the 75mm Skysweeper AA system. With the advent of SAMs, however, larger antiaircraft guns for the most part disappeared. Today, armies and navies rely on a combination of guns, antiaircraft missiles, and friendly aircraft for defense against enemy aircraft.

Of contemporary antiaircraft weapons, mention should be made of the Soviet Union's Shilka ZSU-23/4 (ZSU = Zenitnaya Samokhodnaya Ustanovka, Antiaircraft Self-Propelled Gun). It was employed extensively by the People's Army of Vietnam (North Vietnamese Army) during the Vietnam War and by the Arab states in the Arab-Israeli Wars. The ZSU-23/4 is a self-propelled antiaircraft gun featuring a radar dish that can be folded down. The system is mounted on a modified PT-76 tank chassis. The ZSU 23/4 Shilka can acquire, track, and engage low-flying aircraft as well as engage ground targets, to include antitank missile launch sites and tube-launched, optically tracked, wire-guided missile (TOW) vehicles, taking them under fire while either stationary or on the move. Its armament consists of four 23mm cannon with a maximum range of 3,000 meters. Ammunition is normally loaded with a ratio of three high explosive rounds to one armor-piercing round. Resupply vehicles carry additional ammunition.

Further Reading

Chamberlain, Peter, and Terry Gander. *Anti-Aircraft Guns of World War II.* New York: Arco, 1976.

Hogg, Ivan V. *Anti-Aircraft: A History of Air Defense.* London: MacDonald and Jane's, 1978.

Routledge, N. W. *History of the Royal Regiment of Artillery: Anti-Aircraft Artillery, 1914–55.* London: Brassey's, 1994.

Werrell, Kenneth P. *Archie, Flak, AAA, and SAM.* Maxwell Air Force Base, AL: Air University Press, 1988.

Westermann, Edward B. *Flak: German Anti-Aircraft Defenses, 1914–1945.* Lawrence: University Press of Kansas, 2001.

Browning M2 .50-Caliber Heavy Machine Gun

The iconic Browning M2 .50-caliber heavy machine gun was first produced in 1921 as the M1921 antiaircraft weapon. It evolved into the M2 and has appeared in a wide variety of heavy machine gun guises, all utilizing the same mechanisms but serving in a variety of installations and with differing barrels.

Known affectionately by its gunners as "Ma Deuce," the M2 was employed by every service of the U.S. armed forces in every theater of World War II. The water-cooled barrel model was used as an antiaircraft weapon on U.S. Navy vessels, while almost 1.5 million air-cooled M2s were produced during the war for U.S. aircraft. The M2 was also widely employed on tanks and other vehicles and on ships and patrol craft.

The M2 remains in service today with the U.S. Army and the U.S. Marine Corps. It is the primary heavy machine gun of North Atlantic Treaty Organization (NATO) countries and is in use in many other armies. The official U.S. designation for the current infantry type is Browning Machine Gun, Cal. .50, M2, HB, Flexible. Weighing approximately 64 pounds and fed by a metal-link belt, it can be fired in single-shot mode and has an automatic rate of fire of 450–550 rounds per minute, depending on tactical conditions.

The M2 has been in production longer than any other machine gun. Indeed, it has been in use longer than any other small arm in the U.S. military inventory except the .45 ACP M1911 pistol, also designed by John Browning. The M2 is currently manufactured in the United States by General Dynamic and U.S. Ordnance and in Belgium by FN Herstal.

Further Reading

Gander, Terry J. *Browning M2 Heavy Machine Gun.* London: PRC Publishing, 1999.

U.S. Army. *FM 23–65: Browning Machine Gun Cal. 50 HB, -2.* Washington, DC: U.S. Government Printing Office, 1944.

Willbanks, James H. *Machine Guns: An Illustrated History of Their Impact.* Santa Barbara, CA: ABC-CLIO, 2004.

Molotov Cocktail

The Molotov cocktail is an improvised gasoline bomb. The gasoline, sometimes with additives such as motor oil to make it stick to its target, is placed in a glass bottle, which is then stopped with a cork or other airtight sealer. A wick or cloth rag is fixed securely to the neck of the bottle, soaked in gas, and lit before the bottle is thrown. The glass shatters on impact, and the gas immediately ignites. In war, the Molotov cocktail was used against personnel and vehicles.

The Molotov cocktail first appeared during the Spanish Civil War (1936–1939). It was widely used by the Finns against Soviet forces during the Finnish-Soviet War (1939–1940) and the so-called Continuation War between the same two states (1941–1944). The Soviets also employed it against German vehicles on the Eastern Front during World War II. The weapon is named for Vyacheslav Molotov, Soviet foreign minister during 1939–1949. The Finns gave it that name during the Finnish-Soviet War after Molotov claimed in a radio broadcast that the Soviets were not dropping bombs but rather delivering food to the starving Finns.

The British also produced a hand grenade during World War II, known as a sticky bomb, that was in essence a Molotov cocktail. More recently, improvised Molotov cocktails have been employed against the British Army during the Troubles in Northern Ireland and by rioters against police and troops.

Further Reading

Mountcastle, John W. *Flame On! U.S. Incendiary Weapons, 1918–1945.* Shippensburg, PA: White Mane, 1999.

Biological Weapons

Biological warfare, also known as germ warfare, is the use as weapons of biological agents such as bacteria, viruses, and disease-causing organisms. Biological warfare has been practiced since ancient times with the poisoning of an adversary's wells.

There are also numerous examples of besiegers catapulting the carcasses of dead animals or the bodies of humans who had died of the plague into an enemy city. During the North American colonial wars, the British gave smallpox-infested blankets to unsuspecting Indians, who had no resistance to this infectious disease. The endemic diseases inadvertently spread by the colonizers to the natives decimated the tribal populations and were a major factor in the successful European colonization of the Americas.

Despite widespread concerns over biological warfare and poison gas and their prohibition in the 1925 Geneva Protocol, many governments conducted research into this method of warfare, and the Japanese actually implemented it. In 1936, 3,000 members of Japanese Army Unit 731 began a series of horrific experiments on human beings in Harbin, Manchuria. The Japanese subsequently carried out a series of attacks on the Chinese, employing by various methods such biological agents as anthrax, cholera, shigellosis, salmonella, and plague, killing an unknown number of Chinese.

In 1943 the United States initiated its own biological warfare program at Camp Detrick in Frederick, Maryland. Except for the secret Japanese program in China, the threat of retaliation largely inhibited the use of biological weapons during World War II, however. During the Cold War, both the United States and the Soviet Union manufactured and stockpiled biological weapons. By 1969, the United States had weaponized agents causing anthrax, botulism, tularemia, brucellosis, Venezuelan equine encephalitis, and Q fever. During the Vietnam War, the Viet Cong used human and animal feces to coat punji stakes used in booby traps, which instantly infected any wound created by that weapon.

Scientific advances in the fields of genetics enable contemporary scientists to produce new forms of such viruses as influenza. Biological weapons, such as anthrax and swine fever, may also be used indirectly to attack animals and plants, devastating an enemy nation's food supply. The extreme danger of biological agents, which do not discriminate between friend and foe, in addition to the ability of an enemy to retaliate and the delayed nature of the effects of such weapons have thus far largely contained their use.

The threat of terrorist attack with biological weapons remains very real, however. Cholera, diphtheria, typhus, Rocky Mountain fever, and dysentery could all be devastating to civilian and military populations alike. They are therefore considered likely weapons in the hands of terrorists, who do not fear and might even welcome retaliation.

Further Reading

Barnaby, W. *The Plague Makers.* London: Vision, 1999.

Harris, Sheldon. *Factories of Death.* London: Routledge, 1994.

Mayor, Adrienne. *Greek Fire, Poison Arrows, and Scorpion Bombs: Biological and Chemical Warfare in the Ancient World.* New York: Overlook Duckworth, 2003.

Williams, Peter, and David Wallace. *Unit 731.* New York: Free Press, 1989.

German 88mm Gun

The German 88mm gun was quite possibly the best-known and most feared artillery piece of World War II. It appeared in a wide variety of guises: an artillery piece in support of infantry, an antitank and tank weapon, and as an antiaircraft gun.

With the dramatic increases in altitude achieved by aircraft in the years after World War I, the world's armies sought to develop more powerful antiaircraft guns. The German answer appeared in the form of the 88mm *Flugabwehrkanone* (antiaircraft gun) developed in 1936 but building on a 1918 design. It was officially designated the 8.8cm Flak 18, 36, or 37; follow-on but somewhat different weapons were the Flak 41 and 43.

The prototype 88 was first produced in 1928. It weighed 5.2 tons, had a 56-caliber barrel length, and was mounted on a cross-shaped gun carriage that permitted fire in any direction. A semiautomatic loading system enabled a very high firing rate for that era of 15–20 rounds per minute. With its effective ceiling of up to 32,000 feet, it posed a significant threat to enemy bombers.

The 88 was first employed in actual warfare by the German Kondor (Condor) Legion during the Spanish Civil War (1936–1939) and was immediately recognized as the best antiaircraft gun of that conflict. The Germans also discovered by 1933 that the 88 was highly effective as an antitank weapon.

Improvements, including a two-piece barrel for easier replacement of worn liners and a new trailer that facilitated faster setting up of the gun, led to the Flak 36 model. The Flak 37 was somewhat lighter and also incorporated gun-laying improvements. The Flak 41 had an improved range (a ceiling of 48,000 feet rather than 32,000) and a higher firing rate (20–25 rounds per minute). The Flak 41 appeared in a dedicated antitank role as the Pak (for *Panzerabwehrkanone,* or "antitank gun") 43.

The 88 saw wide-ranging service in a variety of roles during World War II. First purposely employed in an antitank role in the Polish campaign of September 1939, it proved highly successful then and in the Battle for France against the more heavily armored British and French tanks. Its most extensive service came in North Africa and on the Eastern Front, where the flat terrain allowed its long effective range full play. Antitank-role 88s were often provided with armored frontal shields to provide some protection for the gunners.

Its two chief roles were as an antiaircraft and antitank weapon, but late in the war the 88 was utilized as a powerful tank gun, such as on the PzKpfw VI *Tiger* and *Nashon* tank destroyers. The *Tiger* took a heavy toll of Allied tanks through the end of the war. The Soviets learned through the hard experience of tank-on-tank combat that the only way they could nullify the *Tiger*'s longer-range 88mm gun was to close the distance before firing. In the close quarters of the Stalingrad fighting, for example, distances hardly mattered. Maximum armor penetration for the 88 was 150mm. Armor-piercing shell weight was 20.9 pounds, and muzzle velocity was some 2,660 feet per second.

The 88 was also used in a coast-defense role. Although Germany fielded more than 10,000 88mm guns in 1944, there were simply too few to go around, and interservice debate (the Luftwaffe had charge of air defense) raged regarding their use.

Further Reading

Norris, John. *German 88 mm Flak 18/36/37 and Pak 43 1936–45.* London: Osprey, 2002.

Werner, Muller. *The 88 mm Flak in the First and Second World Wars.* West Chester, PA: Schiffer, 1998.

M-2A1/M-101A1 105mm Howitzer

The M-2A/M-101A1 105mm howitzer was one of the most successful artillery weapons in U.S. history. A signature weapon, it was for World War II what the French 75mm gun was for World War I and remained the principal light artillery piece of the U.S. military for more than 50 years.

Following World War I, in 1919 the U.S. Army convened the Westervelt Board to undertake a study of its artillery and make recommendations. The board called for a 105mm gun capable of 65 degrees of elevation that would utilize semifixed ammunition to fire a 35-pound shell to a range of 12,000 yards (6.8 miles). Development of the new weapon began in 1920, and in 1928 it was officially designated the 105mm Howitzer M-1. Lean defense budgets prevented it from entering production, however.

The design was modified in 1933 to allow it to be towed by motor vehicles. Further modified in 1934 to accept a fixed shrapnel round, it was officially designated the 105mm Howitzer M-2. In March 1940 with a modified carriage, it became the

M-2A1. It was towed by a 2.5-ton truck, which also carried its eight-man crew and ammunition.

The M-2A1 had a two-wheel carriage with trail. The trail was split for firing, then joined and locked together for travel. A shield provided limited protection for the crew from small-arms fire. The gun and carriage weighed 4,475 pounds. The gun tube was short, just over 100 inches (22.5 calibers), and could be elevated to 65 degrees, depressed to minus 4 degrees, traversed a total of 45 degrees (22.5 degrees either left or right), and operated with a hydropneumatic recoil system. It fired a 33-pound high-explosive projectile to a maximum range of 12,200 yards.

The M-2A1's maximum rate of fire was 10 rounds per minute, but the sustained rate of fire was 2–4 rounds a minute. The gun was fired by a continuous pull firing lock system, operated by a lanyard. The M-2A1 was relatively lightweight, mobile, easy to operate, accurate, reliable, and robust.

Mass production of the M-2A1 commenced in March 1940, first at the Rock Island Arsenal in Illinois and then at a number of other plants. The M-2A1 formed the standard field artillery support for U.S. infantry and armor divisions during World War II. It also appeared in the armor divisions on a self-propelled mount as either the M-7B on a modified Sherman tank chassis or, after 1945, as the M-37 on a modified Chaffee tank chassis. A lightened version of the M-2A1 with an even shorter barrel was produced for airborne units. Known as the M-3, it was not a successful design, however. The M-2A1 served with the U.S. Army and the U.S. Marine Corps in all theaters of the war.

The M-2A1 also served effectively with U.S. and allied units in the Korean War. In 1958 it was modified slightly and redesignated the M-101A1. It remained in service in the Vietnam War. In 1966 it began to be replaced by the lighter M-102 105mm, although this conversion was not completed until the early 1980s. The M-2A1 continued in service with U.S. National Guard and reserve units into the early 1990s. Supplied to the militaries of some 45 other countries, it continues in service with many of them. Between 1940 and 1953, a total of 10,202 M-2A1s and M-101A1s were produced.

Further Reading

Seelinger, Matthew J. "M2/M101 105 mm Howitzer." *On Point: The Journal of Army History* 2(4) (Spring 2006): 6–7.

Zabecki, David T. "Artillery Types." In *The Encyclopedia of World War II: A Political, Social, and Military History,* edited by Spencer C. Tucker, 136–41. Santa Barbara, CA: ABC-CLIO, 2005.

Long Lance Torpedo

The Japanese Shiki Sanso Gyorai Type 93 torpedo, known as the "Long Lance" for its range, was developed in 1933, inspired by 24-inch torpedoes on HMS *Nelson* and *Rodney*. At the beginning of World War II the Long Lance was superior to those of any other nation.

The Long Lance had a diameter of 24 inches, a length of 29 feet 4 inches, and a weight of 6,107 pounds and carried a 1,100-pound warhead. Powered by liquid oxygen that did not leave a wake, it had a range of 24,000 yards (almost 14 miles) at 48 knots; at 36 knots its range was a phenomenal 43,744 yards (nearly 25 miles). The U.S. 21-inch torpedo had a 780-pound warhead and a range of 16,000 yards; turbine powered, it left a wake.

In 1934 the Japanese developed a smaller 21-inch version of the Long Lance for naval aircraft. Known as the Type 94, it weighed 3,245 pounds and had a maximum speed of 41 knots and a range of 4,900 yards. In the December 7, 1941, attack on Pearl Harbor, Japanese torpedo-bombers carried the earlier (ca. 1931) Type 91 torpedo; considerably lighter than the 21-inch Long Lance, it weighed only 1,847 pounds and had a 425-pound warhead. In 1935 a submarine version of the Long Lance appeared. It also had a diameter of 21 inches and was fueled by an enriched oxygen propellant. It had a speed of 50 knots, a maximum range of 13,000 yards, and a warhead of 900 pounds. An improved 21-inch submarine model had a maximum range of 8,200 yards and a warhead of 1,210 pounds.

The Long Lance figured prominently in Japanese naval planning. Carried by destroyers and cruisers, it was to be a key element to weaken the American battle

---

Torpedo Attack at Taranto

The success of the Japanese attack on Pearl Harbor of December 7, 1941, owed much to the November 11, 1940, British attack on the principal Italian naval base at Taranto. Twenty-one Swordfisah biplanes carried out the attack, 11 of them armed with torpedos and the remainder carrying bombs and flares. The torpedoes were modified to negate the effects of porpoising in the harbor's shallow water.

The attack was a great success, with the battleships *Conte di Cavour*, *Littorio*, and *Caio Duilio* all hit. In the two attacks, the *Conte di Cavour* and *Caio Duilio* each took one torpedo, and the *Littorio* took three torpedoes. The *Conte di Cavour* was the only one to sink, and it went down in shallow water. Italian tugs towed the other two damaged battleships to shore. The British lost only two of the Swordfish, and the crew of one was rescued. The *Conte di Cavour* was later raised and towed to Trieste to be repaired, but the work was not completed, and it was never recommissioned. The other two were ultimately overhauled in 1941 and returned to service.

The Taranto raid deprived Italy of its naval advantage and at least temporarily altered the Mediterranean balance of power. The raid also underscored the effectiveness of naval aircraft and was immensely useful to the Japanese, who were already working on techniques to employ air-dropped Long Lance torpedoes in shallow water. Taranto provided both further information and confirmation for the Japanese plan to strike Pearl Harbor.

line prior to the great fleet battle that each side anticipated would be fought in the western Pacific for mastery of that ocean. While the U.S. Navy planned for a daylight Jutland-type battle fought primarily by long-range naval gunfire (most U.S. cruisers did not carry torpedoes), the Japanese hoped to savage the American battle fleet through night attacks, at which they excelled, making use of torpedoes. In order to conserve expenditure of these important weapons, Tokyo imposed strict guidelines governing targets and the number that could be fired. The Long Lance played a key role in the 1942–1943 battles off the Solomon Islands.

Further Reading

Boyd, Carl, and Akihiko Yoshida. *The Japanese Submarine Force and World War II*. Annapolis, MD: Naval Institute Press, 1995.

Gray, Edwyn. *The Devil's Device: Robert Whitehead and the History of the Torpedo*. Revised ed. Annapolis, MD: Naval Institute Press, 1991.

Thompson MIAI Submachine Gun

The Thompson is probably the most famous submachine gun in history. It arose from the desire to develop an individual firearm with a high rate of fire for the trench warfare of World War I. While it was not the first firearm to utilize pistol ammunition automatically, the term "submachine gun" was apparently first applied to the Thompson. The weapon was named for retired U.S. Army brigadier general Taliaferro Thompson, but it was actually designed by Theodore Eickhoff and Oscar Payne. U.S. Navy commander John B. Blish came up with the important breech-locking mechanism.

Thompson had helped in tests that led to adoption of the Colt M1911 .45-caliber automatic pistol, and on his retirement from the army in 1914 he went to work for the Remington Arms Company. He remained interested in developing an automatic weapon, but gas, recoil, and blowback operation all posed different problems for a shoulder-fired individual firearm. Utilization of a powerful military cartridge in a blowback system was overcome by Blish's design and patent of 1915 for a delayed blowback breech system. It employed a sloping metal wedge interlocking the breechblock with the body of the gun.

In 1916 Thompson formed the Auto-Ordnance Company, offering Blish shares in exchange for his patent. Eickhoff, Payne, and George E. Goll all helped design the new weapon, which Thompson wanted to fire high-powered rifle ammunition. It, however, produced jamming and wore out the lock. Tests revealed that the relatively low-velocity .45-caliber pistol round worked perfectly with the Blish lock. Because it fired pistol ammunition, the new weapon was not accurate beyond 50 yards or so, but Thompson referred to it as a "trench broom."

The Thompson submachine gun had a finned barrel, two pistol grips, and a short butt. The first Thompson models incorporated different ammunition-loading systems. The first Thompson, known as the "Persuader," was belt-fed, but its rate of fire proved too great, so it was given a box magazine. The new version became the "Annihilator." The third model of 1919, known as the tommy gun, utilized a 50-round drum magazine. Thompson's Auto-Ordnance Corporation lacked manufacturing facilities, so he subcontracted the components for 15,000 of the weapons to Colt, which delivered them in 1921.

World War I had ended three years earlier, and Thompson sought to market his new weapon for police work. Because no U.S. laws then banned the sale of automatic weapons, Thompson also sold it to private citizens. It became widely favored by gangsters in the 1920s and 1930s and was known as the "Chicago Piano."

The U.S. Navy purchased 500 of the Model 1928 Thompson. Some of these were used by U.S. marines in the intervention in Nicaragua and in China. With World War II, there was a great demand for the weapon. France, Britain, and Sweden placed large orders. The M1, simplified for mass production, entered service in 1942. A final version of the next year, the M1A1, incorporated a firing pin modification.

The Thompson provided the high-volume firepower that was so important in the close-range street fighting of World War II. Ultimately 1.75 million tommy guns were produced, and the weapon saw widespread service in every theater of World War II. The Thompson submachine gun had a high rate of fire—700 rounds per minute—and its large .45-caliber bullet had tremendous stopping power. It was difficult to maintain, and its machined parts with their fine tolerances made it susceptible to jamming in field conditions. The Thompson was replaced by the much simpler, robust, and inexpensive to produce M-3, .45-caliber submachine gun, which is known as the "grease gun."

Further Reading

Hill, Tracie L., R. Blake Stevens, and Rick Cartledge. *Thompson, the American Legend: The First Submachine Gun.* Coburg, Ontario: Collector Grade Publications, 1996.

Willbanks, James A. *Machine Guns: An Illustrated History of Their Impact.* Santa Barbara, CA: ABC-CLIO, 2004.

MP40 Submachine Gun

The German MP40 submachine gun was one of the outstanding small-arms weapons of World War II. Designed at the firm of Ermawerk in 1938 before the war, its predecessor MP-38 was known as a machine pistol for its compact size. With an innovative folding metal stock, it was developed for use by tank crews and security personnel. Later it was issued to infantry units. The follow-on MP40, first produced in 1940, incorporated changes that made it more suitable for mass production. The 9-pound MP40 had a stamped metal body, spot welds, and grip areas of phenolic resin. Firing the 9mm Parabellum cartridge and utilizing a detachable

25- or 32-round box magazine, the MP40 had a rate of fire of 500 rounds per minute.

The Germans produced more than 1 million of the highly reliable MP40 during the war. Allied soldiers persisted in calling the MP40 the Schmeisser, despite the fact that Hugo Schmeisser, designer of the Bergmann MP18 of World War I, had nothing to do with either the MP38 or the MP40.

Further Reading

Bruce, R. *German Automatic Weapons of World War II*. Crowood, UK: Marlborough, 1996.

Götz, Hans Dieter. *German Military Rifles and Machine Pistols, 1871–1945*. Translated by Edward Force. West Chester, PA: Shiffer, 1990.

Willbanks, James A. *Machine Guns: An Illustrated History of Their Impact*. Santa Barbara, CA: ABC-CLIO, 2004.

Sten Gun

The British Army resisted introducing a submachine gun. Senior officers had long been advocates of long-range aimed rifle fire and regarded the submachine gun as both inaccurate and of limited application. That changed with World War II, when the British turned to inexpensive and easily made submachine guns as one answer to equipping quickly a large number of men, especially following the British abandonment of most of their equipment in France during the Dunkirk (Dunkerque) Evacuation of June 1940.

The British first adopted the Thompson submachine gun, but it and a British design by George Lancaster proved too expensive to manufacture and difficult to maintain in the field because of closely machined tolerances. The army then called on the Enfield Royal Small Arms Factory to come up with a weapon that could be produced quickly, inexpensively, and in large numbers and that would serve a variety of needs, including home defense. In a few months, Major R. Vernon Shepherd and Harold John Turpin produced a solution. The weapon's name combined the first letters of their own last names and the first two letters of the factory producing it.

The Sten gun borrowed much from the German Schmeisser MP28. A straight blowback weapon, firing from an open bolt with a fixed firing pin, the Sten gun utilized the 9mm Parabellum round at 550 rounds per minute from a 32-round magazine extending laterally from the left side. Easily and inexpensively produced, it weighed 6.5 pounds unloaded and was entirely of metal. It employed welded stampings, with the only machined parts being the bolt and barrel.

The Royal Small Arms factory produced 4 million Sten guns during 1941–1945, although users complained of its inaccuracy and its tendency to fire accidently (a design hazard of all open-bolt systems) and jam during battle. Resistance groups favored the Sten gun for its ease of assembly, disassembly, and reassembly. They even produced on their own copies of the design.

Further Reading

Huff, Rolland. *The Sten Submachine Gun.* El Dorado, AR: Desert Publications, 1991.

Willbanks, James H. *Machine Guns: An Illustrated History of Their Impact.* Santa Barbara, CA: ABC-CLIO, 2004.

M1 Garand Rifle

The M1-Garand semiautomatic rifle was the standard U.S. infantry rifle during all of World War II, the Korean War, and, in the hands of American allies, the Vietnam War. It replaced the five-shot bolt-action Springfield Cal .30-06 M1903 rifle with which the United States had fought World War I.

Canadian-born John C. Garand of the Springfield Armory designed the weapon named for him. He first produced his semiautomatic, gas-operated rifle in .276 caliber, but the army wanted to employ the standard .30-06–caliber Springfield round, and Garand redesigned the rifle accordingly. In 1936 the army officially adopted it as the Rifle, Semi-Automatic, M1, but it was widely known simply as the "Garand."

The United States became the only country in World War II to have a semiautomatic rifle as a standard infantry weapon. A pull of the trigger not only fired the round, but also gas moved the bolt back, ejecting the spent round. A powerful spring then drove the bolt forward again, stripping a new round from the internal magazine mechanism and chambering it. The Garand's semiautomatic functioning gave it a higher rate of fire over bolt-action rifles and also made it easier for riflemen to keep it on target.

The rugged Garand weighed 9 pounds 8 ounces (unloaded). It fired its ammunition from an 8-round spring steel clip, which was fed en bloc (as a single unit) into the internal magazine mechanism. The clip was automatically rejected on the last round being fired. The butt stock contained a rifle-cleaning kit.

Designed for long-range fire, the Garand had rear sights fully adjustable for windage and elevation. The Garand had a muzzle velocity of 2,800 feet per second, an effective range of 440 yards, and a maximum range of 3,200 yards. The Garand was well liked by the men who used it. General George S. Patton Jr. called it "the greatest battle implement ever devised." The chief problems of the Garand were its weight and unpleasant recoil, the consequence of it firing the same cartridge as the Springfield.

Some 4.04 million Garands were produced, including a large number of specialized models to include sniper rifles (the M1C) and match rifles. The M1 was the standard U.S. infantry firearm from 1936 to 1957, when the army adopted the M14 rifle. The Garand remains a favorite among American competitive shooters and gun collectors.

Further Reading

Duff, Scott A. *The M1 Garand, World War II: History of Development and Production, 1900 through 2 September 1945.* Export, PA: Scott A. Duff, 1996.

Hogg, Ivan. *Military Small Arms Data Book.* Philadelphia: Stackpole, 1999.

Thompson, Jim. *The Complete M1 Garand.* New York: Paladin, 1998.

MG42 Machine Gun

The German MG34 machine gun introduced in 1934, while a superbly engineered weapon, was largely machined and expensive to produce. With a general European war looming, Germany rearming apace, and factories unable to keep up with demand for the MG34, the German government called for a design competition for a new light machine gun. The MG34 had extremely fine tolerances, and one condition of the new design was that it be more suited to operations in less than ideal conditions.

Among the firms entering the competition was Grossfuss, which had no previous experience in weapons production. Ernst Grunow, an engineer with Grossfuss, used the same basic gas-operated system as the MG-34 but introduced an innovative roller-locked breech mechanism. The government conducted extensive tests in 1941 on the new weapon, first designated the MG39/41. It entered service in 1942 as the MG42.

Designed for inexpensive manufacture, the MG42 incorporated metal stampings along with rivets and welds. Not only was it much less expensive to manufacture than the MG34, but production time was cut by 35 percent. Its enhanced ability to operate in less than ideal circumstances made the MG42 one of history's best machine guns. The barrel was also easily changed; this could be accomplished in combat in mere seconds.

The MG42 fired the 7.92mm round from a 50- or 250-round link belt. With its bipod mount, the MG42 weighed only 25.25 pounds. At 1,200 rounds per minute, its rate of fire was far higher than its contemporaries. This meant increased inaccuracy, but German machine-gun doctrine accepted this because it was believed that machine-gunners had only a few seconds of opportunity in combat. In addition to serving as the primary German infantry weapon of high-volume fire of the war, the MG42 was also used on virtually all German armored vehicles.

More than 400,000 MG42s were manufactured by a number of German firms during the war. The design proved so effective that virtually identical models are still in production. The German Army's present MG-3 machine gun is virtually a MG42 clone but with a somewhat slower rate of fire. The U.S. M-60 machine gun was patterned very closely on the MG-42.

Further Reading

Myrvang, Folke. *MG34-MG42: German Universal Machineguns.* Cobourg, Canada: Collector Grade Publications, 2002.

Willbanks, James H. *Machine Guns: An Illustrated History of Their Impact.* Santa Barbara, CA: ABC-CLIO, 2004.

Mortars, Post–World War I

Mortars are high-angle, plunging-fire weapons. Relatively small in size and man-transportable, modern mortars are in effect frontline artillery. The U.S. 60mm mortar, for example, weighs only 42 pounds, while the medium 81mm weighs 136 pounds. Mortars can fire a variety of shells, including illumination. Their high-angle fire enables mortars to overcome forward-facing defenses, and because its shell ("bomb" in British parlance) descends from the near vertical, unlike the low-angle gun artillery shell it produces a 360-degree blast and shrapnel effect. Mortars can also be fired rapidly, about 18 rounds per minute for the 60mm and 81mm. Mortars consist of a tube, a base plate, an adjustable bipod, and sight and fire-control equipment. They are relatively inexpensive to produce. Mortars came into their own in the trench warfare of World War I and were also employed in large numbers in World War II.

During World War II the Allies stressed range, shell, and accuracy improvements, leading to rifled mortars, proximity-fuzed and rod-detonated shells, and complex sighting systems. Fighting on the Eastern Front led to sharp increases in mortar calibers and multibarreled mortars, which were deemed essential to engage large numbers of attacking infantry.

Germany, Japan, and the Soviet Union employed light mortars of 50mm caliber. These fired shells of 1.75 to 2.25 pounds out to 500–550 yards. The British mortar was comparable, at 2-inch caliber. The U.S. light mortar was larger. At 60mm, it was based on the same caliber French weapon of 1937. Its shell weighed 3–4 pounds, depending on type, and could range out as far as 2,000 yards.

Medium mortars were undoubtedly the most important type in the war. The Germans issued the 80mm Granatwerfer-34 at the battalion level. It fired a 7.72-pound shell out to 2,625

U.S. soldiers firing a mortar against a Japanese position on Attu in the Aleutian Islands, June 4, 1943. (Library of Congress)

yards. The Japanese medium mortar was of similar caliber. The Soviets placed more reliance on the mortar than any other power, in part because these weapons provided artillery support to frontline units at little cost and with ease of production. The Soviet medium mortar was the 82mm Type M36 and its successors. It fired a 6.72-pound shell out to 3,400 yards. The British medium 3-inch mortar fired a 10-pound shell out to 2,800 yards. The U.S. medium 81mm mortar fired a shell weighing from 7 to 15 pounds as far as 3,290 yards.

The Soviet 120mm heavy mortar was so successful that the Germans copied it in their GrW-42. The 120mm GrW-42 fired out to 5,900 yards. The Soviets even developed a 160mm weapon that fired a 89.7-pound shell. Its explosive filler weighed a whopping 72 pounds, whereas that for the 82mm was only 4.5 pounds. The U.S. heavy mortar was of 107mm (more commonly known as the 4.2-inch mortar). Operated by a crew of seven men, it had a range of 5,400 yards.

Both sides in the Korean War found mortars especially useful in the hilly and mountainous terrain that was typical in that conflict. The U.S. Army allocated three 60mm mortars per rifle company, three 81mm mortars per infantry battalion, and six 4.2-inch mortars per infantry regiment. The North Koreans and Chinese employed the standard Soviet World War II 61mm, 82mm, and 120mm mortars. These had the advantage of being able to utilize the slightly smaller U.S. ammunition, whereas the slightly smaller-bore U.S. weapons could not fire the larger Soviet ammunition.

Mortars continue in widespread use today. Among recent improvements are guided mortar projectiles, the use of new lightweight alloys, and projectiles with submunitions.

Further Reading

Hogg, I. V. *Mortars.* Marlborough, UK: Crowood, 2001.

Jane's Infantry Weapons, 2000–2001. Coulson, Surrey, UK: Jane's Information Group, 2000.

Norris, John. *Infantry Mortars of World War II.* London: Osprey, 2002.

Ryan, J. W. *Guns, Mortars and Rockets.* London: Brassey's, 1982.

T-34 Soviet Medium Tank

The Soviet Union introduced a new medium tank, the T-32, in 1939. It weighed 41,800 pounds, had a crew of four, and was armed with a 76.2mm gun and two 7.62mm machine guns. Combat experience in Mongolia against Japanese and then in Finland, however, led the Soviet Defense Committee to order an up-gunned and heavier-armored T-32 into production in December 1939.

At the same time, Soviet designers were at work on a redesign of the T-32. This resulted in the T-34 medium, the most widely produced Soviet tank of the war and perhaps the single most important weapons system in the Soviet arsenal on the

Eastern Front. The first T-34 test models were ready in 1940, with the production model entering service in 1941.

Simple in design and easy to mass-produce, the T-34 also had heavier (maximum 45mm) sloped armor than the T-32. Low in silhouette, the T-34 retained the basic Christie suspension system, with five large road wheels per side and wide (18.7-inch) tracks for improved traction in mud or snow. The initial T-34A model weighed 58,900 pounds and had a crew of four men, a 500-horsepower diesel engine, a speed of 33 miles per hour, a 76.2mm main gun, and two or three machine guns. Its diesel engine was safer than the gasoline engines on the German tanks, and its frontal armor could be penetrated only by 50mm antitank rounds at under 500 yards. The 76.2mm gun T-34 became known as the T-34/76.

The up-gunned T-34/85 weighed some 70,500 pounds and had a five-man crew (as opposed to four on the T-34/76), the same engine as the T-34/76, a speed of 31 miles per hour, and maximum 90mm armor and mounted in a larger turret an 85mm main gun adapted from the prewar 85mm Model 1939 antiaircraft gun. At a range of under 900 yards, the T-34/85 could penetrate the frontal armor of the German Panther and Tiger tanks. The T-34/85 also had a new five-speed gearbox. Apart from this, the chassis was much the same as for the T-34/76. The addition of a loader to the crew reduced demands on the commander and gunner and significantly enhanced the tank's combat efficiency. The T-34/85 entered service in early 1944 and gradually replaced the T-34/76, although not completely. Able to hold its own against the most powerful German tanks, especially at close range, the T-34/85 may have been the best all-around tank of the entire war.

In all the Soviets produced some 53,000 T-34s of all types, along with 5,000 T-34 chassis for assault guns. Between 1943 and May 1945 alone, Soviet factories turned out 35,000 T-34s. During the same period the Germans manufactured only slightly more than 5,000 of the PzKpfw V Panther, the only real rival to the T-34. The Panther matched up well in capabilities, but it could not overcome the significantly greater numbers of T-34s.

The T-34 continued in service well after the war. An upgraded model, the T-34/85 II, appeared in 1947 and was produced in the Soviet Union and in Czechoslovakia and Poland until 1964. It remained the principal Soviet main battle tank into the 1950s. Exported widely, T-34s saw extensive combat during the Korean War and wars in the Middle East.

Further Reading

Bean, Tim, and William Fowler. *Russian Tanks of World War II: Stalin's Armored Might.* St. Paul, MN: MBI, 2002.

Hughes, M., and C. Mann. *The T-34 Tank.* Staplehurst, UK: Spellmount, 1999.

Tucker, Spencer C. *Tanks: An Illustrated History of Their Impact.* Santa Barbara, CA: ABC-CLIO, 2004.

M4 Sherman Medium Tank

The Rock Island Arsenal produced the design for a new U.S. medium tank that would mount a 75mm gun. Following approval by the Armored Force Board, production began in July 1942. The U.S. Army M4 medium tank first saw combat with the British, in the Battle of El Alamein in October 1942, and was known by its British name of German Sherman (more often simply Sherman) after Union Army general and later commanding general William Tecumseh Sherman.

The Sherman was the most important tank in service with British or U.S. forces in the war. Although not the best qualitatively (it was inferior in armor and armament to the best German and Soviet tanks), it was nonetheless the most widely produced and utilized American or British tank. During 1942–1946 a dozen U.S. factories turned out more than 40,000 M4 series tanks and modified-chassis armored fighting vehicles. The Sherman not only formed the backbone of U.S. armor divisions but also was the most important British and Canadian tank of 1943–1945. In Canadian service it was known as the Grizzly. The M4 served on virtually every fighting front of the war and had a long life thereafter, remaining in service until only recently in the armies of a number of nations.

The M4A1 weighed 66,500 pounds, had a crew of five men, and was protected by a maximum of 51mm armor. Initially powered by a Continental R-975 engine (300 horsepower subsequently improved to 450 horsepower), it was capable of 24 miles per hour. It mounted a 75mm main gun and had a .50-caliber machine gun on the commander's hatch and two .30-caliber machine guns.

The Sherman had two great advantages over the German tanks. Its powered turret enabled crews to react and fire more quickly than their German counterparts, and it was more reliable mechanically and easily repaired.

Rugged, fast, simple in design, easy to maintain, and highly maneuverable, the M4 went through a half dozen upgrades in armor, engine, and main gun during the course of the war. It also appeared in a vast number of variants including tank recovery, flamethrower, mine clearer, mobile assault bridge, and rocket launcher. The Sherman chassis also provided the basis for the M7B1 howitzer motor carriage with a 105mm howitzer, the M10 tank destroyer with a 3-inch gun, and the M36 series with a 90mm gun.

The major British innovation regarding the Sherman was to replace its 75mm main gun with a higher-velocity 17-pounder (76.2mm). This up-gunned M4, known as the Sherman Firefly, was the most powerfully armed British tank of the war. Among the many British Sherman variants was the duplex drive (DD), in which the tanks were waterproofed and fitted with a collapsible canvas screen around the hull to provide flotation. Sherman DDs constituted an entire brigade of the 79th Armoured Division in the Normandy landings and were the first British tanks ashore.

The Sherman had a number of disadvantages. Its track width was only 14 inches. With their 30- to 36-inch track widths, German tanks were not as easily bogged down. But the Sherman's two chief drawbacks were its engine and main gun. Its gasoline (vice diesel) engine led GIs to give it the nickname "Ronson" after the Ronson cigarette lighter, sold with the slogan of "lights first time every time." The Sherman was also consistently outgunned by the larger German tanks, which had heavier frontal armor. In February 1944, the Americans followed the British in giving the Sherman a high-velocity 76mm gun.

The answer to the German tanks was a heavy tank. The M26 Pershing, armed with a 90mm main gun, did not enter service until January 1945, and only a handful saw actual combat in World War II largely because the army assigned the destruction of enemy tanks to tank destroyers and because influential U.S. Army lieutenant general George S. Patton Jr. insisted that emphasis be placed on increasing the production of Shermans.

Further Reading

Chamberlain, Peter, and Chris Ellis. *British and American Tanks of World War Two: The Complete Illustrated History of British, American and Commonwealth Tanks, Gun Motor Carriages and Special Purpose Vehicles, 1939–1945.* London: Cassell, 2000.

Tucker, Spencer C. *Tanks: An Illustrated History of Their Impact.* Santa Barbara, CA: ABC-CLIO, 2004.

PzKpfw V Panther Medium Tank

Colonel General Heinz Guderian, generally recognized as the father of German armored forces in World War II, was so impressed with the Soviet Union's T-34 medium tank that he suggested that the Germans merely copy it. German leader Adolf Hitler rejected this idea outright as politically unacceptable, leading to two entirely new German tank designs: the PzKpfw V Panther and the PzKpfw VI Tiger heavy, perhaps the most feared tank of the war.

The Germans carefully studied the T-34 and incorporated in their new medium tank a number of its features. The resulting PzKpfw Panther was certainly one of the best tanks of the war. Production began almost immediately after testing in September 1942, with the first models appearing that November.

The PzKpfw V was instantly recognizable by its more elongated lower-silhouette turret. Indeed, the design heavily influenced that of countless turrets to come in the tanks of many nations. The PzKpfw V Ausf. D Panther weighed some 94,800 pounds. Crewed by five men, it had a 700-horsepower engine and was capable of a speed of 28 miles per hour. It had maximum 100mm armor protection, enhanced by the use of sloped surfaces in the turret and hull and sheet steel side skirts. It mounted a long high-velocity (L/70, or 70 calibers of the bore in length) 75mm gun and also had three machine guns (one each hull, turret, and antiaircraft).

Some observers rate the Panther as the best all-around tank of the war. It represented an excellent combination of armament, protection, and mobility. The Panther's high-velocity main gun had great striking power and could engage and knock out at long range all but the most powerful Allied tanks.

Panther production was set at 600 units a month, but this figure was never realized despite a consortium of manufacturers. The Panther remained expensive and difficult to manufacture, and its production was plagued by continued Allied bombing. Only 850 Ausf. D Panthers, the first production model, were manufactured between January and September 1943, and only some 5,000 were manufactured by the end of the war. Because Hitler insisted that the tank go into action immediately without proper testing, it experienced a series of functional problems, especially mechanical. Two subsequent Panther upgrades, Ausf. A and Ausf. G, featured thicker armor protection, strengthened road wheels, and changes to the hull to enhance the ease of production. Panther variants included armored recovery vehicles. Although a fine design, the German Panther never could overcome the far greater number of Allied tanks.

Further Reading

Chamberlain, Peter, H. L. Doyle, and Thomas L. Jentz. *Encyclopedia of German Tanks of World War Two: A Complete Illustrated Directory of German Battle Tanks, Armoured Cars, Self-Propelled Guns and Semi-tracked Vehicles, 1933–1945.* New York: Arco, 1978.

Hughes, M., and C. Mann. *The Panther Tank.* Staplehurt, UK: Spellmount, 2000.

Tucker, Spencer C. *Tanks: An Illustrated History of Their Impact.* Santa Barbara, CA: ABC-CLIO, 2004.

PzKpfw Tiger and King Tiger

The PzKpfw VI Tiger was easily the most feared German tank during the war. It resulted from an Ordnance Department order in 1937 for a heavy breakthrough tank that would be 50 percent heavier than the PzKpfw IV and protected by 50mm armor. First manufactured in March 1941, the Tiger went through several prototypes before production began in earnest in July 1942. The PzKpfw VI Tiger weighed some 125,700 pounds (it was the world's heaviest tank) and had a crew of five men, a 700-horsepower engine that produced a maximum speed of 24 miles per hour, and a powerful 88mm gun along with two 7.92mm machine guns. The Tiger had 100mm hull front armor and 120mm armor on the gun mantelet.

While the Tiger was not especially nimble and was in fact better suited to defense than offense, its gun could destroy any other tank in the world, while it in turn could be destroyed only by the heaviest Allied antitank guns and then only at much shorter ranges than the Tiger's main gun. General Heinz Guderian had urged that the Tiger be held back until sufficient numbers were available to enable it to effect a major victory, but German dictator Adolf Hitler insisted on trying the tanks out on the Leningrad sector that September in a situation where they fell prey to well-sited Soviet antitank guns. The result was not only heavy, unnecessary casualties but also the loss of surprise for future operations.

The Tiger was a complicated vehicle and thus difficult to manufacture and maintain. It also had an overlapping wheel suspension that tended to clog in muddy conditions or freeze up in cold weather, immobilizing the vehicle. Nonetheless, its superb 88mm main gun took a heavy toll of enemy tanks through the end of the war. The Soviets learned through hard experience of tank-on-tank combat that the only way they could nullify the Tiger's longer-range main gun was to close the distance before firing. In the close quarters of the Stalingrad fighting, for example, distances hardly mattered.

The final German tank of the war was the PzKpfw Tiger II, Königstiger (King Tiger). With a weight of some 149,900 pounds, it had a hull design similar to the Panther series and the same engine. Its frontal armor was well sloped to increase its effectiveness. Its far heavier armor (up to 180mm in the turret), however, rendered it slow (maximum of 21 miles per hour) and hard to maneuver. The King Tiger mounted the 88mm gun and two machine guns. Issued to training units beginning in February 1944, it did not begin to arrive in combat units until June. It proved in the fighting in Normandy that it was more than a match for any Allied tank. Although it could withstand most Allied antitank weapons, there were insufficient numbers of the King Tiger to either employ them in mass formations or erase the great deficit in numbers of Allied tanks. It also suffered from mechanical unreliability, and its considerable bulk was difficult to conceal from Allied aircraft, which by the time of its appearance enjoyed complete air superiority over the battlefield.

Further Reading

Chamberlain, Peter, and Hilary Doyle. *Encyclopedia of German Tanks of World War II.* Revised ed. London: Arms and Armour, 2001.

Foss, Christopher F., ed. *The Encyclopedia of Tanks and Armored Fighting Vehicles.* San Diego: Thunder Bay, 2002.

Tucker, Spencer C. *Tanks: An Illustrated History of Their Impact.* Santa Barbara, CA: ABC-CLIO, 2004.

Self-Propelled Guns and Artillery

Self-propelled guns are guns or howitzers that have their own integral propulsion systems capable of moving the gun about rather than having to be towed by a vehicle known as a prime mover. Generally this definition is restricted to fully tracked or wheeled armored fighting vehicles. In their broadest definition, self-propelled guns include not only mobile field artillery but also air defense artillery, assault guns specifically designed for the close support of attacking infantry, and tank destroyers: large high-velocity artillery designed specifically to defeat enemy tanks. Self-propelled artillery guns operate in the same fashion as conventional artillery and yet are able to move at the pace of advancing infantry. Self-propelled artillery, as opposed to tank destroyers, is expected to stand off at a distance and not directly engage enemy armor.

Perhaps the first self-propelled gun was the British gun carrier of World War I. It utilized a tracked tank chassis to mount a 6-inch howitzer. With the interest in motorization and mechanization in armies after the war, all major powers experimented with self-propelled guns. The British Birch gun with a 75mm howitzer was the world's first practical self-propelled artillery gun.

Self-propelled guns came into general use during World War II. This was especially true of the German Army, for in the blitzkrieg (lightning war), artillery and infantry had to be able to move at the same pace as the tanks. Among notable German self-propelled guns were the 105mm howitzer *Wespe* (wasp) and the 150mm *Hummel* (bumblebee). In addition to converting a wide range of captured Allied tanks into self-propelled guns, the Germans also mounted 75mm and 105mm guns on their own PzKpfw III chassis. They also developed a wide range of tank destroyers, including the 75mm Marder II and Marder III and the 88mm *Nashorn* (rhinoceros), *Elefant* (elephant), and *Jagdpanther* (hunting panther).

The U.S. Army preferred to delay introduction of a heavy tank, believing that this function should be left to self-propelled guns and tank destroyers. The self-propelled M7 Priest mounted a 105mm howitzer first on an M3 Grant/Lee medium tank chassis and then the M4 Sherman medium tank chassis. Nearly 3,500 were produced during the war. The heaviest U.S. self-propelled gun was the 155mm M12 howitzer. Similar in appearance, the 240mm howitzer motor carriage, popularly known as the "King Kong," came too late to see service in the war. The 155mm M40 self-propelled gun saw wide service in the Korean War. The first U.S. tank destroyer was the 76mm M10 Wolverine. It was followed by the highly effective 76mm M18 Hellcat.

Self-propelled guns continue in wide use. Among contemporary examples are the U.S. 155mm M109A6 Paladin, the British 155mm AS90, the French Giat Caesar 155mm, the German Panzerhaubitze (armored howitzer) 2000 155mm, and the Soviet/Russian 2S5 152mm.

Further Reading

Dunstan, J. *Self Propelled Howitzers*. London: Arms and Armour, 1988.

Foss, Christopher F., ed. *The Encyclopedia of Tanks and Armored Fighting Vehicles*. San Diego: Thunder Bay, 2002.

Hogg, Ivan V. *The Greenhill Armoured Fighting Vehicles Data Book*. Mechanicsburg, PA: Stackpole, 2000.

Birch Gun

The British Birch gun, although only experimental, was the world's first practical self-propelled artillery piece. Developed and built at the British Royal Arsenal, Woolwich, in 1925, it was named for General Sir Noel Birch, master general of ordnance during 1923–1927. The Birch gun consisted of a standard British 18-pounder (83.3mm) fieldpiece mounted on the chassis of a Vickers Mark II medium tank. Armament was changed to a 75mm gun in the Mark II Birch gun version. This enabled firing at a higher elevation and its employment in an antiaircraft role. The Birch gun had an open firing platform with the exception of a front shield with 6mm steel armor. It had a crew of six men.

Weighing 11.9 tons, the Birch gun was 19 feet in length, 7 feet 10 inches in width, and 7 feet 7 inches in height. Its Armstrong Siddeley 90-horsepower eight-cylinder gas engine gave it a maximum speed of 28 miles per hour. It had an operational range of 119 miles.

Only five of the Birch guns were built. They saw service both with the Experimental Mechanized Force and its successor Experimental Armoured Force, which unfortunately for the British Army was disbanded in 1929 owing to opposition to it from tradition-bound senior British generals. All five Birch guns were withdrawn from service in 1931, and the British were then forced to scramble to come up with improvised self-propelled guns during World War II.

Further Reading

Bailey, Jonathan B. A. *Field Artillery and Firepower.* 2nd ed. Annapolis, MD: Naval Institute Press, 2003.

Zabecki, David T. "Great Guns! Benchmark Artillery Pieces That Shaped Military History." *MHQ* (August 2014): 76–84.

Jeep

One of the most famous of World War II military vehicles and officially designated the ¼-ton 4x4 truck, the U.S. jeep was described in its training manual as a "general purpose, personnel, or cargo carrier especially adaptable for reconnaissance or command." The term "jeep" has been attributed to "GP" for "general purpose" but most probably was named by Willys Overland engineers after a popular comic strip character, Eugene the Jeep.

In 1940 the U.S. Army Ordnance Department sent out invitations for bids for a 1,300-pound, 4x4, rugged, fast vehicle capable of operating cross-country. The American Bantam Car Company in Baltimore and Willys Overland were the only companies to submit bids. The Bantam design was well received, but it suffered from mechanical problems. Willys, meanwhile, took much of the Bantam design, ignored the specification stressing lightness, and concentrated on performance and ruggedness. The light design could not meet the requisite requirements for durability and strength, whereupon the army increased allowable weight to 2,160 pounds.

In November 1940 Bantam, Willys, and the Ford Motor Company (which had developed its own design) all received contracts for 1,500 vehicles, which then underwent tests. The 60-horsepower Willys easily won out over its two rivals, both with 45-horsepower engines. The Willys engineers also managed to trim 263 pounds from their vehicle, just meeting the allowable limit. Willys Overland got the lead order, but U.S. Army quartermaster general Edmund B. Gregory persuaded Edsel Ford of the Ford Motor Company to build the Willys design as well. Wartime production at both Willys and Ford plants totaled some 650,000 units. The Willys jeep carried a model designation of MB, and the Ford jeep had a model designation of GPW.

The jeep was capable of a speed of 55 miles per hour. It could climb steep grades and ford streams up to 18 inches deep and could also easily transport four men and 800 pounds of equipment and tow a 37mm antitank gun or transport additional cargo in a specially designed trailer.

The jeep symbolized the total mobility that marked the U.S. Army of World War II. The United States produced a sufficient number of vehicles to allow all the men and women of the armed forces to ride at the same time and still have room left over. Indeed, thousands of jeeps (perhaps as many as 30 percent of those produced during the war) were provided as Lend-Lease equipment to other Allied nations, notably Britain and the Soviet Union.

Widely copied overseas, the jeep remained with modifications in the U.S. military inventory during World War II, the Korean War, and the Vietnam War, serving until the mid-1980s. The Korean War–era jeep was the M-38, and the Vietnam War–era jeep was the M-151.

Further Reading

Colby, C. B. *Military Vehicles: Gun Carriers, Mechanical Mules, Ducks and Super Ducks.* New York: Coward McCann, 1956.

Perret, Geoffrey. *There's a War to Be Won: The United States Army in World War II.* New York: Random House, 1991.

Truck, 2.5-Ton

The U.S. 2.5-ton truck, affectionately known as the "deuce-and-a-half" or "Jimmy" (for its maker General Motors Corporation, or GM) is one of the most important military vehicles in history. It played a vital role in the Allied victory in World War II. Unlike the jeep's convoluted development process, the 2.5-ton truck arrived fully developed by the Yellow Truck Company in 1940. The 2.5-ton rating meant that it could carry a load of that weight over rough terrain. On improved roads, it could carry double that load.

Red Ball Express

Following the Allied breakout from Normandy in late July 1944, there was an urgent need to supply the troops now advancing rapidly across France. Because most of the French railroads had been destroyed, beginning on August 24 the U.S. Army Quartermaster Corps began the Red Ball Express, a massive road operation to bring forward critically needed supplies. At its peak, it involved 132 truck companies of some 23,000 men operating 5,958 vehicles.

Without ammunition, rations, medical supplies, and gasoline, the Allied advance would have to grind to a halt. Most truck runs were overnight operations that allowed the drivers little sleep. African Americans, who constituted only about 10 percent of the U.S. Army, made up three-quarters of the drivers on the Red Ball Express, which officially lasted until November 16, 1944, when much of the French rail system had been restored. By that date, the trucks were moving 7,000 tons a day. In all, they transported 412,193 tons of matériel from Normandy to the front and had also met the gasoline demands of the U.S. First and Third Armies, a total of 800,000 gallons a day.

Of relatively simple design and using standard automotive construction, the 2.5-ton truck was rugged and absolutely reliable. With its three axles and six-wheel drive it could go cross-country and, fitted with breathing apparatus, through water. The truck was in fact well ahead of any other military truck of its time. It underwent numerous small improvements and appeared in a variety of models, including short and long wheelbases. Truck types included basic cargo, dump truck, water tanker, gasoline tanker, air compressor, and wrecker. GM produced 412,385 2.5-ton cargo trucks and another 48,345 dump trucks.

The 2.5-ton truck was supplied in large numbers to the Soviet Union under Lend-Lease and helped bring to that nation battlefield logistics mobility. The large number of U.S.-supplied trucks also allowed Soviet industry to concentrate on producing tanks and artillery pieces. The 2.5-ton truck was the primary vehicle in the Red Ball Express, the logistics system that supplied Allied armies pushing across France following D-Day until the French railroads could be restored to service. The deuce-and-a-half was also the prime mover and ammunition carrier for almost all Allied divisional-towed artillery. Large numbers of 2.5-ton trucks remain in service overseas, including the Philippines and Vietnam.

Further Reading

Berndt, Thomas. *Standard Catalog of U.S. Military Vehicles, 1940–1965.* Iola, WI: Krause, 1993.

Doyle, David. *Standard Catalog of U.S. Military Vehicles.* 2nd revised ed. Iola, WI: Krause, 2003.

Landing Craft

Since ancient times the world's armies have employed boats and ships to move forces over water. During the Mexican-American War (1846–1848) the U.S. Navy employed special surfboats for its amphibious landing at Veracruz. During the Gallipoli Campaign in World War I, the British modified craft to move men and equipment to and from the shore. Landing craft, however, reached a new level of sophistication and numbers during World War II.

Both the Axis and Allied powers conducted amphibious operations during that conflict, and landing craft were widely employed in the Mediterranean, European, and Pacific theaters. In consequence, the war saw the development of purpose-built craft to land troops and equipment on a hostile shore. These craft allowed an attacker to land larger numbers of men and equipment faster and in a smaller area than would otherwise be possible. Only the United States, however, built large numbers of amphibious wheeled and tracked vehicles that allowed transport of men and equipment from ship to shore and then inland.

Landing craft came in a wide variety of forms. They were armored and unarmored and designed to transport both personnel and vehicles. Some had bow ramps, while others were of fixed bow configuration. Most landing craft, however, had a blunt bow, were powered by diesel engines acting on twin screws, were anchored at the stern, and had a shallow draft forward, a flat bottom, and a bow ramp. The bow ramp allowed rapid unloading of men and cargo.

While Germany, Italy, and Japan all built landing craft, the Western Allies, and essentially the United States, constructed by far the largest number. This was because the Allies had to invade and secure areas in the Mediterranean and then invade Northwestern Europe. In the Pacific, the Allies also had to recapture the Japanese-held Pacific islands.

Many Allied landing craft were quite large and carried smaller landing craft on their decks. Landing craft were identified by number, not name. Almost all were designated by a series of letters followed by the particular number. The most common U.S. Navy designators from largest to smallest vessels were the following:

LSV	Landing Ship, Vehicle
LSD	Landing Ship, Dock
LST	Landing Ship, Tank
LSM	Landing Ship, Medium
LCI(L)	Landing Craft, Infantry (Large)
LCS(L)	Landing Craft, Support (Large)
LCT	Landing Craft, Tank
LCM	Landing Craft, Mechanized
LCVP	Landing Craft, Vehicle or Personnel

Two U.S. Coast Guard–manned Landing Ship Tank (LST) supply vessels, bows open in the surf to disgorge their cargoes during the U.S. landing on Leyte Island in the Philippines beginning on October 20, 1944. (National Archives)

In 1941 the British pioneered development of the LST and the LCT. Both were intended to be seagoing craft in order to deliver vehicles and bulk supplies directly to the shore. The United States altered the original British designs and then produced them for both nations.

The LST was undoubtedly the most well-known larger landing vessel of the war, a staple of later landings in the Pacific theater and during the Korean War. The most common version of the LST was 328 feet in overall length with a 50-foot beam and a displacement fully loaded of 4,080 tons. LSTs were unarmored and only lightly armed (8 40mm and 12 20mm antiaircraft guns). The bow of the ship opened, allowing the front ramp to drop and the crew to land cargo directly on a shore. The LST could carry smaller LCTs and was configured with davits to lower LCVPs over its sides. Some LSTs carried only two LCVPs in this fashion, while others carried six. The LST crew complement was 111 officers and men.

The LCS(L) was developed to provide support to amphibious landings. With a crew complement of 71, it was armed with 1 3-inch/.50-caliber gun, 2 twin 40mm guns, 4 20mm guns, 4 .50-caliber machine guns, and 10 rocket launchers.

The smaller LCT carried trucks, tanks, or cargo directly to an invasion beach. The LCVP, developed by New Orleans entrepreneur Andrew J. Higgins and popularly known as the "Higgins boat," was of wood. With a crew of 3 men, it was designed to land 36 troops (or one 6,000-pound vehicle or 8,100 pounds of cargo) directly on the beach. Developed for ease of mass production, more than 23,000 were manufactured by the end of the war. The Allies also developed true amphibians capable of transporting men and equipment from ship to shore and then inland, the best known of these being the DUKW.

Landing craft were immensely important to the Allies in the war, so much so that U.S. Army chief of staff George C. Marshall stated in 1943, "Prior to the present war I never heard of landing craft except as a rubber boat. Now I think of nothing else." The availability of landing craft dictated timetables for Allied amphibious landings, and the shortage of them precluded simultaneous landings in northern France (Operation OVERLORD) and southern France (Operation ANVIL-DRAGOON). Far less glamorous than combatant vessels, landing craft were nonetheless an essential element in the Allied victory in World War II, and they continue to be an integral part of naval operations today.

Further Reading

Baker, A. D., III. *Allied Landing Craft of World War Two*. Annapolis, MD: Naval Institute Press, 1985.

Gardiner, Robert, ed. *Conway's All the World's Fighting Ships, 1922–1946*. London: Conway Maritime, 1980.

DUKW Amphibian Truck

The DUKW amphibian truck was one of the most innovative logistical developments of World War II. Based on the highly successful Yellow Truck 2.5-ton truck, the new vehicle was developed to meet the need for an amphibian vehicle capable of delivering men and supplies over the beaches on remote islands without dock facilities in the Pacific theater.

When approached about the possibility, General Motors, which had bought out Yellow Truck, took little more than a month to produce four pilot models. The new vehicle took its name from the company code of D for the year (1942), U for utility, K for four-wheel drive, and W for two rear-driving axles. The "Duck," as it became known, weighed 7.5 tons empty; was 31 feet long and 8 feet wide; was powered by an 8-cylinder, 91-horsepower engine; and could transport up to 50 troops or 2.5 tons of supplies.

Buoyancy was provided by giving it a body composed largely of sealed, empty tanks. On land the DUKW employed its six driving wheels, while in the water it used its marine propeller and rudder. On land it could reach road speeds of 45 miles per hour, while its maximum water speed was 5 miles per hour. In order to

---

The Army Rescues the Navy

There was some objection to the DUKWs as a waste of resources. The first were shipped to Cape Cod, where they joined the U.S. Army's 1st Engineer Amphibian Brigade. That winter when a Coast Guard boat foundered in high winds and a DUKW rescued its seven-man crew, Secretary of War Henry L. Stimson informed President Franklin D. Roosevelt at a cabinet meeting that "Two nights ago on Cape Cod, an army truck rescued the men from a stranded naval vessel." This ended any opposition to the new vehicle, which was then sent to war.

---

prevent the DUKW from becoming bogged down in sand, tire pressure was kept low. Once the vehicle was on a solid surface, the driver used a device to inflate the tires from an air compressor and air storage tank. The DUKW entered the U.S. military inventory in October 1942. The DUKWs entered the Pacific fighting in operations against Nouméa in New Caledonia. In the European theater, DUKWs were employed most notably in the Sicily landings and at Normandy, where in the first 90 days after the initial landings they moved ashore 18 million tons of supplies.

A number of DUKWs remain in service to transport tourists. They have also been used to rescue civilians stranded by natural disasters, such as flooding.

Further Reading

Berndt, Thomas. *Standard Catalog of U.S. Military Vehicles, 1940–1965.* New York: Krause, 1993.

Doyle, David. *Standard Catalog of U.S. Military Vehicles.* 2nd revised ed. London: F&W Publications, 2003.

Mulberry

Mulberry was the Allied code name for two artificial harbors constructed in Britain and towed across the English Channel to France to support Operation OVERLORD, the Normandy Invasion of June 6, 1944. The Allies knew that once having secured a beachhead, they would require immense quantities of men and supplies to sustain operations and that it would be impossible to land such amounts over the beaches. The Germans well understood this and, anticipating the Allied invasion attempt, fortified the major French ports and readied vital facilities there for demolition in the event of attack.

Well aware from the French underground of German defensive preparations, Allied leaders assumed that they would not be able to capture a major port in the initial invasion. They would have to build their own. The result was one of the greatest engineering feats in military history. The British War Office initiated planning, and the Combined Chiefs of Staff officially approved the concept during the Quebec Conference of August 1943. Two mulberries were planned: Mulberry A was intended to support the American invasion beaches, and Mulberry B was intended to support those of the British and Canadians.

The operation was immensely complicated and centered on construction of five artificial anchorages, two of which served as foundations for the mulberries. Immediately after the landings of June 6, Allied engineers worked to establish the anchorages by scuttling expendable ships as breakwaters. Completing that, the engineers set to work constructing piers and causeways to the mulberries.

The mulberries began operation 10 days after the landings. Unfortunately, on June 18 the largest channel storm in half a century hit the French coast, halting all landing operations for three days and destroying Mulberry A. Mulberry B, although damaged, remained in operation, and parts of Mulberry A were used to complete it.

Mulberry B became known as the Harbor at Arromanches. By October it enclosed two square miles of water and could handle seven Liberty ships and 23 coasting vessels simultaneously. Meanwhile, the Allies secured Cherbourg. In the fighting for this key French port, the Germans destroyed much of its facilities, but the Allies worked feverishly to place them back into operation.

Mulberry B continued in service until closed on November 19. Disassembly commenced at the end of December. By the end of October 1944, the Allies had moved through it 25 percent of their stores, 20 percent of personnel, and 15 percent of vehicles. The remains of Mulberry A can still be seen off the Normandy coast.

While the mulberries failed to live up to expectations because of the destruction of one of them, DUKW amphibious trucks and LSTs proved more effective than anticipated in moving supplies over the beaches. All this ensured the success of the Allied invasion, leading to the liberation of France and invasion of Germany from the west.

Further Reading

Bykofsky, J., and H. Larson. *The U.S. Army in World War II: Transportation Corps Operations Overseas.* Washington, DC: Center of Military History, 1957.

Hartcup, Guy. *Code Name Mulberry: The Planning, Building and Operation of the Normandy Harbours.* New York: Hippocrene Books, 1977.

PLUTO

PLUTO, the acronym/code word for "*p*ipe*l*ine *u*nder *t*he *o*cean" or "*p*ipe*l*ine *u*nderwater *t*ransport of *o*il," was designed to ship petroleum to France following the Normandy Invasion of June 1944. General Dwight D. Eisenhower identified PLUTO as second in importance only to the mulberry artificial harbors for the success of the invasion and subsequent liberation of France. A sustainable and considerable supply of petroleum was essential in order to maintain the highly mechanized and motorized Allied forces in their drive across France.

Not one pipeline but a network of high-pressure pipelines, PLUTO carried vital petroleum products. The three-inch pipelines were of two types. HAIS (for Hartley-Anglo-Iranian-Siemens) was of lead with an outer steel winding, and HAMEL (for the two chief engineers, H. A. Hammick and B. J. Ellis) was of steel. Each mile of HAIS pipe incorporated 24 tons of lead, 7.5 tons of steel tape, and 15 tons of steel outer armor, in addition to other materials such as cotton tape and jute serving. In all, PLUTO incorporated nearly 800 miles of pipe, of which the vast majority came from British manufacturers. PLUTO pumping stations were carefully disguised as buildings and gravel pits and even an ice cream shop.

The pipe was laid from large floating steel bobbins known as "conundrums," for "cone ended drum." Each weighed 1,600 tons and carried 60 miles of pipeline. The first pipe-laying ship was the converted coastal freighter HMS *Holdfast*. As it and the other three pipe-laying ships towed one of the five conundrums across the channel, the cable unrolled from its bobbin and sank to the seabed. In all a total of 34 pipe-laying ships and 600 officers and men were involved in the operation.

The two principal pipelines were Bambi, from the Isle of Wight to Cherbourg, and Dumbo, from Dungeness in Kent to Boulogne. Bambi ultimately had 4 lines totaling 280 miles, while Dumbo came to number 17 lines totaling 500 miles of pipeline capable of pumping 1.35 million gallons a day. Supplementing these were Tambola ship-to-shore pipelines.

PLUTO made it possible to dispense with a large number of tankers and removed them as possible targets. It also sharply reduced congestion at Mulberry B and the French ports once the latter were back in operation. By the end of the war in Europe, PLUTO had delivered 172 million gallons of petroleum to France. The vast majority of the PLUTO pipelines were salvaged after the war. PLUTO was just another example of the superior Allied logistics in the war.

Further Reading

Knight, Bob, Harry Smith, and Barry Barnett. *PLUTO: World War II's Best-Kept Secret.* Bexley, UK: Bexley Council, 1998.

Moore, Rufus J. "Operation PLUTO." *United States Naval Institute Proceedings* 80(6) (1954): 647–653.

Searle, Adrian. *PLUTO: Pipe-Line under the Ocean.* Isle of Wight, UK: Shanklin Chine, 1995.

Destroyer Escort

Destroyer escorts consisted of a class of ships developed in World War II specifically for convoy escort duties. The Royal Navy Hunt-class vessels are generally acknowledged as the first of the type. Planning for these ships began in October 1938 with an Admiralty directive for a new "Fast Escort Vessel" of the small destroyer type intended to protect convoys against submarine and air attack. Although soon reclassified as Hunt-class destroyers, the ships lacked the high speed and strong torpedo armament of standard destroyers.

Displacing approximately 1,500 tons at full load, the Hunts carried four to six 4-inch dual-purpose guns; some had two or three torpedo tubes, but all carried a heavy antisubmarine armament of 50 to 110 depth charges. Eventually, 86 of four subtype destroyer escorts were commissioned. The class saw hard service. The *Whaddon,* for instance, steamed 64,689 miles while escorting 140 convoys. War losses totaled 19 ships.

The Hunts inspired substantial early interest in the U.S. Navy, although that service preferred initially to stick with the more capable destroyer designs already in serial production. In 1941 the Royal Navy appealed to the United States for escorts; in August, President Franklin Roosevelt approved the construction in U.S. yards of 50 destroyer escorts for Great Britain. This relatively modest start was followed by a flood of U.S. Navy orders, with a peak of 1,005 destroyer escorts under contract, of which 563 were commissioned.

Officially divided into six classes, all were variants on a single design and were distinguished from each other principally by armament or machinery differences. Some ships had conventional steam boilers, while others were fitted with diesels. Some ships mounted three 3-inch dual-purpose guns; others had two 5-inch dual-purpose guns. Antisubmarine armament was optimized, with some units carrying 100 depth charges; those ships with a set of triple torpedo tubes frequently substituted for one torpedo a single one-ton depth charge.

With the tide clearly turning against the U-boats by the summer of 1943, mass cancellations sharply pruned the destroyer escort program. Ninety-five were converted while under construction to fast light transports; 7 were modified to serve as radar pickets. During the war, American destroyer escorts sank 29 U-boats (and helped capture *U-505*) and 29 Japanese submarines (6 by USS *England* alone) while losing 7 of their number to submarine attack, 1 to surface gunfire, and 1 to a mine. Four were damaged beyond repair by torpedoes or kamikazes.

Following World War II, the destroyer escorts were only marginally fast enough to cope with the new high-speed Soviet submarines. Many of the U.S. escorts were retained for amphibious operations; others went to friendly nations. In 1953 a modest building program yielded the new Dealey class, which could be built rapidly in an emergency. Although retaining the designation "DE" in the U.S. Navy, all the destroyer escorts were officially redubbed "escort vessels" or "ocean escorts" until 1975, when they became frigates with the designation "FF."

Further Reading

Friedman, Norman. *U.S. Destroyers: An Illustrated Design History.* Annapolis, MD: Naval Institute Press, 1982.

March, Edgar J. *British Destroyers: A History of Development, 1893–1953.* London: Seeley Service, 1966.

Whitley, M. J. *Destroyers of World War Two: An International Encyclopedia.* Annapolis, MD: Naval Institute Press, 1988.

Yamato-Class Battleships, Japanese

The Imperial Japanese Navy Yamato-class battleships were the largest battleships ever built. Withdrawing from the 1935 London Naval Agreements, the Japanese were free to construct capital ships of any size. Japanese Navy doctrine centered on one big decisive action at sea, and with these superbattleships the Japanese expected to be able to defeat any possible opponent.

The battleships were built under extraordinarily tight security, and U.S. intelligence had no idea of their size or capabilities. The keel of the lead ship, the *Yamoto,* was laid down at the Kure Navy Yard in November 1937, and the ship entered service in December 1941. The *Musashi* was completed in 1942, and the *Shinano* was completed in 1944 (but as an aircraft carrier). The fourth ship in the class was never finished.

The *Yamato* and *Musashi* carried the largest naval guns ever to go to sea: 9 18.1-inch guns, capable of firing a broadside some 20 percent heavier than that of any contemporary U.S. battleship. Additional armament consisted of 12 6.1-inch and 12 5-inch antiaircraft (AA) as well as 24 1-inch (25mm) and 8 .5-inch (23mm) AA guns. The number of AA guns increased with the demonstrated vulnerability of capital ships to air attack, and by 1945 the *Yamato* mounted as many as 150 25mm guns. Maximum armor protection was 25.6 inches on the turrets.

The *Yamato* and *Musashi* displaced nearly 70,000 tons fully loaded. They had an overall length of 862 feet 10 inches and a beam of 127 feet 6 inches. Their 12 boilers delivered some 150,000 horsepower to four shafts, producing a maximum speed of nearly 28 knots. Since spotting was so important, the *Yamato* carried seven floatplanes to be launched from two catapults. The wartime crew complement was approximately 2,500 men.

On its commissioning the *Yamato* became the flagship of Combined Fleet commander Admiral Yamamoto Isoroku, but both the *Yamato* and *Musashi* spent most of the war at anchor. They were such powerful national symbols that the Japanese leadership was unwilling to put them at undue risk. While the *Yamato* took part in the Battle of Midway (June 3–6, 1942), it saw no action. It might have been decisive in Solomon Islands fighting in a shore bombardment role but was not utilized. A shortage of oil curtailed subsequent operations. The *Yamato* was hit by a U.S. submarine-fired torpedo in December 1943 and did not return to service until April 1944.

Not until the Battle of Leyte Gulf (October 26–29, 1944) did the two battleships fire their guns in combat. In that battle the *Musashi* was sunk by prolonged U.S. carrier aviation attack. The *Yamato* escaped destruction but was sunk, also by U.S.

carrier aviation, on April 7, 1945, in a suicidal sortie against the Allied invasion fleet off Okinawa.

Further Reading

Skulski, Janusz. *The Battleship* Yamato. Annapolis, MD: Naval Institute Press, 1988.

Spurr, Russell. *A Glorious Way to Die: The Kamikaze Mission of the Battleship* Yamato. New York: Newmarket, 1981.

Yoshida, Mitsuru, *Requiem for the Battleship* Yamato. Annapolis, MD: Naval Institute Press, 1965.

Iowa-Class Battleships, U.S. Navy

The four U.S. Iowa-class battleships were the last U.S. battleships commissioned and the largest U.S. and last world battleships in service. Six were scheduled: the *Iowa* (BB-61), *New Jersey* (BB-62), *Missouri* (BB-63), *Wisconsin* (BB-64), *Illinois* (BB-65), and *Kentucky* (BB-66). The last two were never completed.

Apart from the two Japanese Yamato-class ships, the four Iowa-class ships were the largest and most powerful battleships ever built. They may well have been a match for the Yamatos. The Iowas displaced about 48,000 tons standard and 57,500 tons fully loaded. They had an overall length of 887 feet 3 inches and a beam of 108 feet. Turret face plate armor was 18 inches. Their top speed was 33 knots. Crew size varied between 1,600 and 2,900 men. The ships were designed for 1,600 men, but the addition of many 40mm and 20mm antiaircraft guns drove up these numbers substantially. The main armament consisted of 9 16-inch 50-caliber (meaning the gun tube was 800 inches long) guns (3 in each of three turrets, 2 forward, and 1 aft). They also mounted 20 5-inch guns in dual turrets and increasing numbers of smaller antiaircraft guns.

The *Iowa* was laid down at New York Navy Yard in June 1940 and commissioned in February 1943. The *Missouri* was the last to enter service, in June 1944. All four saw service in the Pacific theater in the latter stages of World War II. The formal Japanese surrender ceremony ending World War II was held aboard the *Missouri* in Tokyo Bay. All except the *Missouri* were decommissioned during 1948–1949. They returned to service during the Korean War, when they provided highly effective shore-bombardment support to United Nations Command operations. The Iowa-class ships were then decommissioned at various times during 1955–1958.

The *New Jersey* was recommissioned to serve off Vietnam during 1968–1969, then decommissioned again. In the 1980s all four Iowa-class ships were modernized, receiving antiship and shore-attack cruise missiles and new electronics and support systems. They returned to service during 1982–1988. In 1989 the *Iowa* suffered an accidental explosion in its No. 2 turret, killing 47 sailors, and was retired from service the following year. Both the *Missouri* and the *Wisconsin* participated in the 1991 Persian Gulf War (Operation DESERT STORM), serving primarily as cruise missile launch platforms. High operating costs eventually sent them back into reserve. The *Iowa* is at Los Angeles, California, as a museum ship. The *New Jersey* and *Missouri* are museum ships at Camden, New Jersey, and Ford Island, Pearl Harbor, respectively. The *Wisconsin* is berthed at Norfolk, Virginia, also as a museum ship, although it remains in reserve status.

Further Reading

Dullin, Robert O., and William H. Garzke. *Battleships: United States Battleships in World War II.* Annapolis, MD: Naval Institute Press, 1976.

Muir, Malcolm, Jr. *The Iowa Class Battleships:* Iowa, New Jersey, Missouri, *and* Wisconsin. Poole, Dorset, UK: Blandford, 1987.

Sumrall, Robert F. *Iowa Class Battleships: Their Design, Weapons, and Equipment.* Annapolis, MD: Naval Institute Press, 1988.

Essex-Class Aircraft Carriers

The U.S. Navy Essex-class aircraft carriers, launched beginning in 1942, formed the core of the U.S. fast carrier task forces that played such an important role in the defeat of Japan during World War II. With 24 built, they also constituted the most numerous class of 20th-century heavy warships. The Essex-class ships were improved Yorktown-class carriers. Among other changes, they had enhanced underwater protection and a 3-inch armored hangar deck. Some of the ships were launched postwar.

Constructed without the restrictions imposed by interwar international naval treaties, the Essex-class ships had greater aircraft-carrying capacity and improved defensive armament. The *Essex* (CV-9), name ship of the class, was launched at the Newport News Shipbuilding Company in Virginia in July 1942 and commissioned that December. It displaced 34,881 tons full load, measured 820 feet in length and 93 feet in beam, and was capable of nearly 33 knots. Intended for 91 aircraft, during the war these ships operated as many as 103. They had a crew of 2,631. Defensive armament included 12 5-inch guns along with 32 40mm and 47 20mm cannon. Light armament varied considerably, but as the need for antiaircraft protection increased, late in the war the ships carried up to 68 40mm and 65 20mm cannon.

The Essex-class ships participated in virtually all island-hopping operations in the Pacific theater, culminating in those against the Philippines and Okinawa. They also conducted raids against the Japanese home islands. The *Franklin* sustained heavy damage on March 19, 1945. Some of the ships were broken up after the war, and others were placed in mothballs.

The introduction of an angled flight deck revolutionized carrier design, allowing simultaneous launch and recovery operations. The *Lexington, Bon Homme Richard,* and *Shangri-La* received a reconfigured flight deck to incorporate the angled landing area as well as the enclosure of the bow (hurricane bow), with improved seaworthiness. In 1952 the *Antietam* was fitted with an angled deck, but this was considered experimental. The *Shangri-La* became the first operational U.S. angled deck aircraft carrier in 1955. Thirteen of the Essex-class ships saw Cold War service, and they played important roles in the Korean War. Ten served in the Vietnam War, three of them in antisubmarine warfare and rescue roles and two as landing platform helicopter (LPH) amphibious assault ships with the U.S. Marine Corps. Of six unmodernized Essex-class carriers, three were reclassified as aircraft transports (AVTs), and the other three were LPHs. The LPH ships remained in commission with their original straight decks until about 1970. Although the remainder were stricken from the navy list in the late 1970s, the *Shangri-La* survived until the late 1980s, while the *Lexington* served until 1991 as a training ship. Four Essex-class carriers—the *Hornet, Intrepid, Lexington,* and *Yorktown*—are today preserved as museum ships.

Further Reading

Faltum, Andrew. *The Essex Class Aircraft Carriers.* Baltimore: Nautical and Aviation Publishing Company of America, 1996.

Friedman, Norman. *U.S. Aircraft Carriers: An Illustrated Design History.* Annapolis, MD: Naval Institute Press, 1983.

Kilduff, Peter. *U.S. Carriers at War.* 2nd revised ed. Annapolis, MD: Naval Institute Press, 1997.

Raven, Alan. *Essex-Class Carriers.* Annapolis, MD: Naval Institute Press, 1988.

Escort Aircraft Carriers

Aircraft proved vital in antisubmarine warfare during World War II. Fighter aircraft could deflect German bomber attacks on Allied convoys, and their speed meant that they could do battle with surfaced submarines before the latter could dive. One solution was to send fighter aircraft along with a convoy. The British equipped a number of merchantmen with a forward catapult that held a modified Hurricane fighter. After launch and intercept, the fighter would try to make landfall or else land in the water.

A more satisfactory solution was to fit a flight deck to a merchant ship hull. The German cargo passenger ship *Hannover,* taken in the West Indies in March 1940, became the first escort carrier. It underwent conversion into the flush-deck aircraft carrier *Audacity* and entered service in June 1941 carrying eight Grumman Martlet (U.S. Navy designation F4F Wildcat) fighters. Employed on convoy duty to and from Gibraltar, the *Audacity* gave effective service until it was sunk by the *U-751* off Portugal in December 1941.

Additional escort carriers soon appeared in the form of U.S.-built conversions on C-3 hulls from the Maritime Commission: the *Archer* and the three ships of the Avenger class. Originally contracted for by the Royal Navy, they were transferred to Britain under Lend-Lease and entered service in the first half of 1942. Designed to carry 15 aircraft each, the escort carriers were slow (16.5 knots) but proved invaluable.

In the U.S. Navy, escort carriers were designated CVE (Carrier Escort) but were widely known as "Jeep" carriers. During the war the United States produced 11 Bogue-class (11 others of this class were transferred to the Royal Navy under Lend-Lease as the Attacker-class) and 50 Casablanca-class CVEs. The Casablancas displaced 10,900 tons loaded and had a length of 490 feet and a beam of 65 feet 2 inches. Capable of 19 knots, they carried 28 aircraft.

Unlike their British counterparts, U.S. captains of escort carriers had complete freedom of action to carry out hunt-and-kill missions. Operating in this fashion, escort carriers proved to be one of the most significant weapons systems of the war. Teams composed of an escort carrier and a half dozen destroyers or new destroyer escorts sank 53 U-boats and captured 1. Escort carriers closed the so-called Atlantic Trench in midocean, where land-based aircraft from either side could not provide protection for or attack convoys. Escort carriers may well have been the single most important U.S. contribution to the war against the U-boats.

Further Reading

Chesneau, Roger. *Aircraft Carriers of the World, 1914 to the Present: An Illustrated Encyclopedia.* Annapolis, MD: Naval Institute Press, 1995.

Y'Blood, William T. *Hunter-Killer: U.S. Escort Carriers in the Battle of the Atlantic.* Annapolis, MD: Naval Institute Press, 1983.

Liberty Ships

Liberty ships were the U.S. Maritime Commission's mass-produced emergency cargo vessels and formed the largest single shipbuilding program of World War II. Eighteen shipyards using assembly-line methods completed 2,710 ships, beginning with the *Patrick Henry*, launched on September 27, 1941, only eight months after groundbreaking at the new Bethlehem-Fairfield yard, and ending with *Albert M. Boe*, launched in October 1945 by New England Shipbuilding.

The British *Dorington Court* (1939) was the basis for the Liberty design, adapted for welded construction and with improved crew accommodation. Liberties had a length of 441 feet 6 inches and a beam of 57 feet and displaced 7,176 tons gross and 10,865 tons deadweight. Two oil-fired boilers provided steam for a three-cylinder triple-expansion engine of 2,500 indicated horsepower that drove the ships at 11 knots.

Speedy construction and delivery was central to the Liberties' contribution to the war effort. Initially vessels required around 250 days for completion, but within a year this was reduced to less than 50 days. The Richmond Shipbuilding Corporation, a subsidiary of Henry J. Kaiser's Permanente Metals Corporation, broke all records by assembling the *Robert E. Peary* in just more than 4 days (November 8–12, 1942) and delivering the ship 3 days later. More important, American shipyards delivered 93 new ships in September 1942, totaling more than 1 million deadweight tons, of which 67 were Liberties.

Liberty ships were tough, even though classified as expendable war material. Many continued in postwar commercial service for 25 years or more. Two are preserved as tributes to the type's crucial contribution to Allied victory: the *John W. Brown* at Baltimore, Maryland, and the *Jeremiah O'Brien* at San Francisco.

Further Reading

Bunker, John. *Heroes in Dungarees: The Story of the American Merchant Marine in World War II*. Annapolis, MD: Naval Institute Press, 1995.

Cooper, Sherod. *Liberty Ship: The Voyages of the* John W. Brown, *1942–1946*. Annapolis, MD: Naval Institute Press, 1997.

Elphick, Peter. *Liberty: The Ships That Won the War*. Annapolis, MD: Naval Institute Press, 2001.

Sawyer, Leonard A., and William W. Mitchell. *The Liberty Ships: The History of the 'Emergency' Type Cargo Ships Constructed in the United States during World War II*. Newton Abbot, UK: David and Charles, 1970.

Snorkel

The snorkel is a hollow tube or tubes by which a submarine draws air from the surface in order to permit the crew to breathe and operate equipment while submerged. Snorkels can also be fitted to tanks to facilitate fording operations. The origin of the term is obscure. Although it may come from the German word meaning "ornament" or "eccentricity," it may also mean "snort." Breathing from underwater through a reed or tube dates from antiquity, and attempts were made to fit such breathing devices to the earliest submarines. In 1933 Lieutenant Commander Jan J. Wichers of the Royal Netherlands Navy patented an extensible air mast and subsequently developed a sophisticated automatic head valve to prevent water from entering it. The device was first installed on Dutch submarines in 1939.

British and German technicians made no use of the equipment themselves when they examined it (the Germans by capture in May 1940). In 1943, however, German designer Hellmuth Walter urged the adoption of the device as one means to counter the growing success of the Allied antisubmarine campaign. As a result, a modified Wichers-design snorkel was installed on German submarines beginning in September 1943.

Snorkel-equipped U-boats were able to operate in areas the Allies had considered safe from submarines. There were two principal drawbacks: the necessity for reduced speed (five to six knots) while using the snorkel to avoid breaking it and a greater radar and visual detection signature. Sound-detection gear was also deafened by the roaring of air being sucked down the tube. While snorkels were equipped with automatic valves to prevent water from being sucked into the diesels, when these valves slammed shut the engines would draw air from the submarine itself before shutting down. This was painful to the ears of the crew and sometimes even ruptured eardrums.

Nonetheless, the success of the snorkel and investigations into it after the war led other navies to install snorkel equipment in their submarines. Testing soon revealed that submarines utilizing snorkels were easily detectable by sonar. Subsequent snorkel design efforts have been directed at minimizing its drawbacks. Despite disadvantages, the snorkel is a common feature of contemporary submarines.

Further Reading

Friedman, Norman. *U.S. Submarines since 1945: An Illustrated Design History.* Annapolis, MD: Naval Institute Press, 1994.

Polmar, Norman, and Jurrien Noot. *Submarines of the Russian and Soviet Navies, 1718–1990.* Annapolis, MD: Naval Institute Press, 1991.

Rössler, Eberhard. *The U-boat.* Annapolis, MD: Naval Institute Press, 1989.

Sonar

Sonar is the system used to locate and determine the distance and direction of an object underwater through directing and measuring the running time of an electrically generated sound impulse. The word is thought to be derived from "*so*und *n*avigation *a*nd *r*anging." Sonar is similar in many ways to radar for aircraft detection and is both passive and active. Analogous to the transponder, the sonar's transducer emits and receives sonic impulses (known as pings and warbles).

The sinking of the *Titanic* from striking an iceberg in 1912 spurred interest in underwater navigation. That same year Alexander Belm in Austria described an underwater ranging device, while Lewis Richardson in England secured a patent for echo-ranging. The first working echo-ranging system was developed in 1914 by Canadian Reginald Fressenden working for the Submarine Signal Company in the United States. Fressenden's device consisted of an electromagnetic moving-coil oscillator that emitted a low sound and then switched to listening mode for an echo. Multiplying the speed with which sound traveled underwater (about 1,500 meters per second) by the time it took the signal to return determined the distance. It could detect an iceberg two miles away but could not give the direction.

During World War I, French physicist Paul Langévin and Russian scientist Constantin Chilowsky developed the first high-frequency ultrasonic echo-listening device and called it by the somewhat misleading name of "hydrophone." It employed alternating currents to vibrate quartz crystals so that sound waves pulsing through water were reflected by objects, sending an echo back to the quartz that could be detected by an electrical sensor, the actual hydrophone. The echo-listening device could detect submerged submarines up to five miles distant.

The British became aware of Langévin's work and in 1918 began their own similar experiments. Thus was born asdic, for the Admiralty's *Anti-Submarine Divisionic* (sometimes incorrectly identified as Allied Submarine Detection Investigation Committee).

By World War II, most navies deployed active sonar (the term was formally introduced by the U.S. Navy in 1931) aboard antisubmarine vessels. Such systems utilized high-frequency emissions of 14–22 kilocycles, but they were slow-operating and were only effective at short ranges (up to 2,000 yards) and at slow speeds (ideally less than 10 knots). Most navies thus relied primarily on passive hydrophones for detection and active sonar to obtain a target solution in the attack. Sonar improved greatly during the war. Technological improvements led to extended ranges and accurate depth determination.

Today, most modern ship-mounted sonars in the 2–15-kilocycle range operate in both active and passive modes, often simultaneously. In order to compensate for signal distortion through reflection or refraction of the sound waves by water layers of different temperatures or salinity, many modern devices can be towed behind the vessel at variable depths.

Sonar arrays can also be dropped in the water and towed by helicopter. The sonobuoy, dropped from maritime patrol aircraft, is another application. Sonobuoys detect enemy submarines and their position through triangulation and relay the information back to the controlling aircraft.

High-frequency sonars are also used for detecting and identifying sea mines on the ocean bottom. Such mine-hunting sonars operate between 100 kilocycles (for detection) and 300 kilocycles (for classification). Modern active homing torpedoes also use high-frequency sonars with ranges of up to two miles for target acquisition and tracking.

Further Reading

Campbell, John. *Naval Weapons of World War II*. Annapolis, MD: Naval Institute Press, 1985.

Friedman, Norman. *Naval Institute Guide to World Naval Weapons, 1994 Update*. Annapolis, MD: Naval Institute Press, 1994.

Watts, Anthony J., ed. *Jane's Underwater Warfare Systems, 1996–97*. Couldsdon, Surrey, UK: Jane's Information Group, 1996.

Leigh Light

The Leigh light was a powerful airborne searchlight developed by the British and installed on Royal Air Force Coastal Command aircraft to illuminate Axis submarines on the surface at night. It operated in conjunction with the aircraft's air-to-surface search radar, which actually located the target, to illuminate the submarine immediately prior to an attack, thus preserving surprise and maximizing the chances of success.

The minimum range of early airborne search radars was too long to allow their use to guide a night attack (the ASV Mk II was only effective between 1 and 36 miles). Dropping flares gave a submarine sufficient warning to escape before the aircraft could attack. Squadron Leader Humphrey de Verde Leigh, together with the firm of Savage & Parsons, developed a 24-inch, 22-million candlepower searchlight that could be switched on just before losing the target on radar, giving the submarine only 15–20 seconds to evade attack.

Initial testing began in March 1941, but operational aircraft equipped with the Leigh light did not enter service until mid-1942 because the Air Ministry initially preferred the Turbinlite, an existing less-powerful (and less-effective) airborne searchlight.

Leigh light–equipped aircraft over the Bay of Biscay greatly increased their contact rate but sank only two submarines during 1942, largely because U-boats began carrying radar-warning receptors. Nevertheless, the ease with which the aircraft intercepted submarines led Admiral Karl Dönitz to order his U-boats in transit to remain submerged even at night, greatly reducing their operational effectiveness. Moreover, the combination of Leigh lights and centimetric radars, which entered service in 1943, proved deadly to the U-boats, most notably during the Biscay Offensive that summer.

Further Reading

Franks, Norman L. R. *Conflict over the Bay.* London: William Kimber, 1986.
Franks, Norman L. R. *U-Boat versus Aircraft.* London: Grub Street, 1999.
King, Horace F. *Armament of British Aircraft.* London: Putnam, 1971.

Radar

Radar is the system used to detect the position, movement, and nature of distant objects. The term "radar" is an acronym for "*ra*dio *d*etection *a*nd *r*anging." Radar systems use electromagnetic waves and a directional antenna to process radio emissions reflected off distant objects. Range is calculated by measuring the time it takes for an echo to return. Radar was based on principles discovered by James Clerk Maxwell and Heinrich Hertz in the second half of the 19th century.

In the early 1920s Italian Guglielmo Marconi noted that aircraft interfered with radio communication, and by the 1930s scientists in a number of nations were working on systems to detect aircraft and ships. By 1937 the Germans developed radar for ships to allow detection of approaching aircraft, while in 1935 the British government created the Aeronautical Research Committee to develop ways to defend the nation against air attack. Although a hoped-for "death ray" failed to materialize,

U.S. soldiers man a radar array in Italy in 1944. The British took the lead in the development of radar. Advances in radar technology were of great importance to the Allies in World War II. (Library of Congress)

detection of aircraft did. Most attribute the development of British radar to committee member and physicist Sir Robert Watson-Watt, superintendent of the Radio Department of the National Physical Laboratory, and his assistant A. F. Wilkins. In 1935 they integrated transmitters and receivers, the modulators to generate microsecond pulses, and high-speed cathode-ray tubes to display the results.

All principal belligerents in World War II entered the war with some radar technology, although Japan lagged behind the others. Only the British, however, fully understood its importance and integrated radar into their defense planning, thanks in large part to the insistence of head of Fighter Command Air Chief Marshal Hugh Dowding. Britain constructed the Chain Home (CH) radar network and augmented it in 1939 with Chain Home Low (CHL) stations to detect low-flying aircraft. This was the first integrated radar defense system, and it played a key role in the 1940 Battle of Britain, providing early warning of the German bomber attacks and allowing Fighter Command to properly manage its own inferior resources against them.

In August 1940 the British government passed along much technological information to the United States, including the proximity fuze and cavity magnetron. The latter proved vital in developing centimetric radar, the lightweight radar set for aircraft and ships so invaluable in antisubmarine warfare. Advances in the United States also included high-power microwave radar systems.

Germany was slow to understand the importance of radar for defensive purposes, but Allied strategic bombing forced attention in that direction and led in 1942 to the so-called Kammhuber Line, an interlocking system of radar, aircraft, and ground controllers. Although U.S. radar identified Japanese aircraft approaching Pearl Harbor on December 7, 1941, this information was misinterpreted and thus not utilized. During the war the Japanese lagged in radar development; thus, U.S. ships had fire-control radar, while their Japanese opponents did not.

Radar was integrated into gun-direction devices and the very important proximity fuze. Improvements in radar continued after the war in missile technology. Radar was also integrated with transponders to identify friendly aircraft, the so-called IFF for "identification friend or foe." The U.S. Navy's Aegis system allows simultaneous tracking of many targets, while synthetic-aperture radar (SAR) produces high-resolution images, similar to photographs. New bistatic radar techniques have overcome much of the stealth technology designed to mask planes and ships from normal radar detection.

Further Reading

Brown, Louis. *A Radar History of World War II: Technical and Military Imperatives.* Philadelphia: Institute of Physics Press, 1999.

Buderi, Robert. *The Invention That Changed the World.* New York: Simon and Schuster, 1999.

Fisher, David. *A Race on the Edge of Time: Radar—The Decisive Weapon of World War II.* New York: McGraw-Hill, 1988.

Von Kroge, Harry. *GEMA: Birthplace of German Radar and Sonar.* Philadelphia: Institute of Physics Press, 2000.

A6M Reisen (Zero) Japanese Fighter Aircraft

The Mitsubishi A6M Reisen was the best-known Japanese fighter of World War II. An excellent original design built by Mitsubishi as a carrier aircraft, it entered service in 1940. Because the Japanese used a year designation and 1940 was the Japanese imperial year 2600, the new aircraft was officially known as the Type 0 (Reisen). The Americans first designated it the Zeke, but generally all nations referred to it as the Zero, and even the Japanese referred to them as Zero-sen.

The Zero first saw combat in China in 1940 and proved highly effective. It went through a succession of models, and more Zeros (10,449) were built during the war than any other Japanese aircraft. The A6M2 model that led the attack at Pearl Harbor had a speed of 332 miles per hour and the exceptional range of 1,930 miles. The final (1945) A6M8 model had a 1,560-horsepower engine, 60 percent more powerful than that in the A6M2, and a speed of 356 miles per hour. Most Zeros built at the end of the conflict were converted into kamikaze aircraft.

The Japanese A6M Reisen, known as the Zero. Built by Mitsubishi as a carrier aircraft, this excellent lightweight fighter joined the fleet in 1940 and remained in service through-out the war. "A" signified a carrier-based fighter, "6" stood for the sixth such model built for the navy, and "M" was for the manufacturer, Mitsubishi. Because the Japanese employed a year designation and 1940 was their imperial year 2600, it was officially known as the Type 0 (Reisen). (Bettmann/Corbis)

Although the Zero was fast and highly maneuverable, its performance came at the sacrifice of armor, structure strength, and pilot protection. The fuselage was skinned with almost paper-thin duralumin, and the plane lacked both seat armor and self-sealing gas tanks. At 6,264 pounds loaded, the A6M was almost half a ton lighter than the U.S. Navy F4F Wildcat. The Zero had the surprisingly heavy arma-ment of two 7.7mm machine guns in the upper fuselage and two wing-mounted slow-firing 20mm cannon. It could also carry 264 pounds of bombs.

Further Reading

Angelucci, Enzo. *The Rand McNally Encyclopedia of Military Aircraft, 1914–1980.* New York: Military Press, 1983.

Fredriksen, John C. *International Warbirds: An Illustrated Guide to World Military Air-craft, 1914–2000.* Santa Barbara, CA: ABC-CLIO, 2001.

Bf 109 German Fighter

The Germans possessed some exceptional aircraft during World War II. The Bf 109 (often referred to as the Me 109 for its designer Willy Messerschmitt) was a superb air-superiority fighter and one of the best all-around aircraft of the war.

Developed by Messerschmitt beginning in 1933, the Bf 109 first flew in 1935. It eclipsed its rivals at the 1937 International Flying Meet in Zurich, Switzerland, and underwent field testing in the Spanish Civil War (1936–1939). The Bf 109 entered service with the German Air Force in 1939 and served throughout World War II.

The E Model of 1939 had a top speed of 342 miles per hour and was armed with two 20mm cannon and two 7.92mm machine guns. The Bf 109 went through a variety of models; by war's end the K model had a top speed of 452 miles per hour and mounted two 15mm and one 30mm cannon. Fast and maneuverable, the Bf 109 proved more than a match for all its opponents until it encountered the British Supermarine Spitfire in the 1940 Battle of Britain. Although faster than the Spitfire, the Bf 109 could not turn as quickly.

With some 35,000 manufactured by war's end, the Bf 109 also enjoyed the distinction of having the largest production run of any fighter aircraft in history. The Bf 109 continued in service after the war in the air forces of Spain, Israel, and Czechoslovakia.

Further Reading

Angelucci, Enzo. *The Rand McNally Encyclopedia of Military Aircraft, 1914–1980*. New York: Military Press, 1983.

Fredriksen, John C. *International Warbirds: An Illustrated Guide to World Military Aircraft, 1914–2000*. Santa Barbara, CA: ABC-CLIO, 2001.

Junkers Ju 87 Stuka German Dive-Bomber

The German concept of blitzkrieg (lightning war) was based on rapid movement. Spearheaded by tanks, infantry moved in armored vehicles and trucks as mobile antitank guns provided support. Tactical airpower formed a key element. Indeed, the German Air Force remained a tactical air force. Especially important was the "flying artillery" in the form of the single-engine Junkers 87 Sturzkampfflugzeug dive-bomber, more commonly known as the Stuka.

Impressed by the accurate delivery of ordnance by U.S. Marine Corps dive-bombers in fighting in Haiti and Nicaragua, the Germans developed the Ju 87 in 1935. With its "cranked" wings and angular lines, there have been few aircraft as ugly as the Ju 87. Field tested in the Spanish Civil War (1936–1939), it officially entered service with the Luftwaffe in 1938.

The B Model of 1938 weighed 9,560 pounds and was capable of a speed of 238 miles per hour. It had a range of 490 miles, was armed with three machine guns, and could carry 1,000 pounds of bombs. It had a two-man crew (pilot and gunner, seated back-to-back in a greenhouse canopy). The D Model of 1941 had a speed of 255 miles per hour, was armed with four machine guns, and could carry 3,968 pounds of bombs.

Blitzkrieg Tactics

The Stuka was a key element in the German blitzkrieg (lightning war) tactics of World War II. Success of the blitzkrieg rested not so much in the equipment as in its employment and especially the use of combined arms teams. The problem in World War I had been the inability of reserves to close with sufficient speed in an attack once a breach had been opened in the enemy lines. Tanks were massed rather than dispersed among the infantry, as in French Army practice. The Germans could thus break through at weak points in an enemy line without benefit of preliminary bombardment.

Infantry in armored vehicles and trucks and mobile antitank guns provided support for the panzers. Tactical airpower formed a key element, especially the "flying artillery" in the Stuka. Although vulnerable to antiaircraft guns and high-performance fighters, it was also a highly mobile and accurate artillery platform. And as long as Germany controlled the skies, it could operate with relative impunity.

The blitzkrieg was a case of the sum being greater than its parts, and the well-trained and superbly led German Army was able to exploit it to its maximum potential. While it worked well in the dry, flat conditions of Poland in September 1939 and in the short distances and excellent road nets of France and the Low Countries in 1940, the blitzkrieg broke down completely amid the vast distances, poor or nonexistent roads, and other logistical challenges posed by the Soviet Union.

The Ju 87 proved to be an accurate bombing platform for the Germans in the early fighting of World War II. Fitted with a siren device that emitted a piercing sound in the dive mode, the Stukas struck fear on the ground among soldiers and civilians alike. As long as Germany controlled the skies, the Stuka could operate with relative impunity. The Ju 87, however, proved highly vulnerable to antiaircraft guns and high-performance fighters, especially when in diving, and had to be withdrawn from the Battle of Britain in the summer of 1940. It continued to render valuable service in the Mediterranean theater and on the Eastern Front, however, especially as a tank-busting aircraft. During the war Germany built a total of 5,709 Ju 87s.

Further Reading

Angelucci, Enzo. *The Rand McNally Encyclopedia of Military Aircraft, 1914–1980.* New York: Military Press, 1983.

Fredriksen, John C. *International Warbirds: An Illustrated Guide to World Military Aircraft, 1914–2000.* Santa Barbara, CA: ABC-CLIO, 2001.

Hawker Hurricane British Fighter

The British Hawker Hurricane was one of the premier aircraft of World War II and bore the brunt of the 1940 Battle of Britain, shooting down more German aircraft than the Spitfire. The Hurricane saw service throughout the war in both the European and Pacific theaters.

Designed by Stanley Camm and building on what had been learned from the Hawker Fury biplane, the Hawker Hurricane first flew in November 1935 and entered service in 1937. It was the Royal Air Force's first monoplane fighter.

The Hurricane had metal tubular structure and fabric covering, which rendered repairs easy. Its streamlined design incorporated retractable landing gear. With its Rolls-Royce Merlin II liquid-cooled in-line engine, the Mk I Hurricane was capable of a speed of 320 miles per hour. It had a maximum ceiling of 33,200 feet and a range of 460 miles. It was armed with eight .303-caliber machine guns. The Mk II had a more powerful Rolls-Royce Merlin XX engine, yielding a speed of 359 miles per hour and a ceiling of 35,600 feet. It was armed with four 20mm cannon and could also carry 1,000 pounds of bombs or rockets.

At the beginning of World War II, Hurricanes made up 60 percent of Royal Air Force Fighter Command strength. While marginally outclassed by the Messerschmitt Bf 109, the Hurricane was a strong aircraft and an excellent gun platform and was more maneuverable than the Spitfire. Later versions (Mk IID, Mk IV) were mainly built as fighter-bombers, in which guise they proved very successful. A Sea Hurricane naval version entered service in 1942. A total of 14,233 Hurricanes were built.

Further Reading

Angelucci, Enzo. *The Rand McNally Encyclopedia of Military Aircraft, 1914–1980.* New York: Military Press, 1983.

Fredriksen, John C. *International Warbirds: An Illustrated Guide to World Military Aircraft, 1914–2000.* Santa Barbara, CA: ABC-CLIO, 2001.

Supermarine Spitfire British Fighter

The Royal Air Force Supermarine Spitfire is one of the best-known aircraft of World War II. Certainly one of the top fighters of the war, it held its own against the vaunted German Messerschmitt Bf 109. The identification of the Spitfire as the leading British fighter of the 1940 Battle of Britain is false, however. The Hawker Hurricane bore the brunt of the fight, but the ability of the Mark I Spitfires to successfully engage the escorting Bf 109s enabled the more numerous Hurricanes to devastate the German bomber formations sent against Britain.

Designed by Reginald J. Mitchell, the pointed-spinner Spitfire appeared on the drawing boards in 1934 and was descended from Mitchell's Supermarine S6B that had won the 1931 Schneider Trophy. The marriage of Mitchell's aerodynamic design with Henry Royce's Merlin engine produced a superb aircraft. The Spitfire first flew in March 1936 and entered service with Fighter Command in June 1938. It went through more than 40 variants into 1947, enabling it to keep a margin of superiority over its German opponents. The Spitfire's all-metal construction provided excellent structural strength, while its Merlin engine gave it excellent speed and climbing ability. The plane itself was both very maneuverable and powerfully armed.

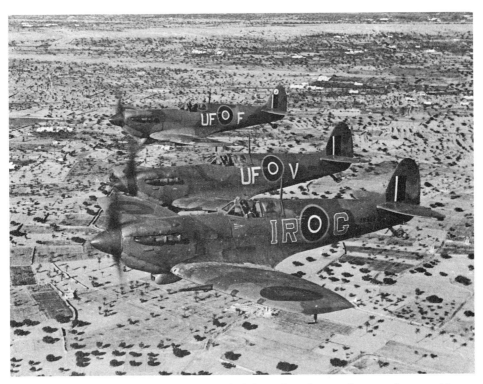

A formation of Supermarine Spitfire British fighter aircraft on an interception patrol in North Africa in 1943. The Spitfire was one of the finest fighter aircraft of the Second World War. (Library of Congress)

The Mark I was powered by a Rolls-Royce Merlin II 1,030-horsepower engine that provided a top speed of 355 miles per hour, a ceiling of 34,000 feet, and a range of 500 miles. Armament consisted of eight .303-caliber machine guns. At the beginning of the war Fighter Command had only 9 Spitfire squadrons, but that number grew to 19 by June 1940.

The Mark II entered service in late 1940. It was armed with either eight .303-caliber machine guns or two 20mm cannon and four machine guns. The Mark IV was a photoreconnaissance version. The Mark VC was the first fighter-bomber variant. It mounted a more powerful Merlin 45 1,440-horsepower engine that gave the plane a maximum speed of 374 miles per hour. The Mark IX of July 1942 was developed specifically to counter the Focke Wulf Fw 190 fighter. It had the Merlin 61 1,515-horsepower engine and a speed of 408 miles per hour. In 1943 it received the more powerful Rolls-Royce Griffon IV 1,750-horsepower in-line engine. The resulting Mark XII was more than a match for the Fw 190. In addition to cannon and machine-gun armament, the Spitfire could carry 500 pounds of bombs.

The five-bladed propeller Mark XV had the Rolls-Royce Griffon 65 2,050-horsepower engine that provided a maximum speed of 448 miles per hour, a ceiling of 44,500 feet, and a range of 460 miles. The Mark XV could successfully engage Messerschmitt Me 262 jet fighters and the V-1 buzz bomb.

The last Spitfire Mark XVI remained in service with the Royal Air Force until April 1954. Through 1947 a total of 20,351 Spitfires were built, giving it the largest production run of any British aircraft. A naval version, the Seafire, was also produced in various models, the most numerous of which had folding wings to facilitate storage on aircraft carriers. A total of 2,089 were built, including some following the war.

Further Reading

Angelucci, Enzo. *The Rand McNally Encyclopedia of Military Aircraft, 1914–1980.* New York: Military Press, 1983.

Maloney, Edward T., ed. *Supermarine Spitfire.* Fallbrook, CA: Aero Publications, 1966.

Spick, Mike. *Supermarine Spitfire.* New York: Random House, 1996.

North American P-51 Mustang U.S. Army Air Forces Fighter

The U.S. North American P-51 fighter may have been the best all-around fighter aircraft of World War II. Design of the aircraft resulted from an April 1940 British military purchasing mission. The sleek prototype flew that October, and production model NA-73 aircraft first arrived in Britain in 1941. Named the Mustang by the British, its Allison V-1710-81 1,200-horsepower engine produced a maximum speed of 390 miles per hour, a ceiling of 31,250 feet, and a range of 750 miles. Armed with four .50-caliber machine guns, it could also carry 1,000 pounds of bombs. Although the Allison engine left it underpowered, the Mustang was superior to any other U.S. fighter aircraft, and the British ordered more than 600, employing many of them in photoreconnaissance. The U.S. Army Air Forces also purchased some as the P-51A fighter and the A-36 Apache dive-bomber.

Following heavy bomber losses of up to 30 percent a month in daytime raids over Germany, the U.S. Army Air Forces began a crash program for a long-range fighter, hitherto inexplicably low on the list of military priorities. In May 1942 the P-51 was fitted with the high-performance British Rolls-Royce Merlin 61 engine, and this led in June 1943 to the P-51B, making the Mustang probably the best piston-engine fighter of the war. Its U.S.-license version of the Merlin engine, the Packard V-1650-3, produced 1,400 horsepower and a speed of 440 miles per hour. The P-51B outclassed the Messerschmitt Bf 109 in maneuverability and in speed by at least 50 miles per hour. The P-51B had a ceiling of 42,000 feet and a range of 810 miles. Mounting four .50-caliber machine guns, it could carry 2,000 pounds of bombs or rockets.

The D version, the largest production model, featured a bubble canopy for improved vision. Its Packard V-1650-7 engine delivered a speed of 437 miles per hour, a ceiling of 41,900 feet, and a range of 950 miles. Armed with six .50-caliber machine guns, it could carry 2,000 pounds of bombs. The final production P-51H model was capable of 487 miles per hour.

The British and Americans were slow to utilize drop tanks. An obvious range extender for fighter aircraft, they had been utilized by the Japanese in operations against the Philippines. With two 75-gallon drop tanks, the P-51B had a round-trip range of 1,200 miles; a further 85-gallon internal tank extended this to 1,474 miles, and even with two drop tanks the P-51B could reach 400 miles per hour and more. The Allies now had an aircraft with the range of a bomber and the speed and maneuverability of a fighter.

The P-51 and the Republic P-47 Thunderbolt, another fine fighter and rugged ground-support aircraft, arrived in the European theater at the end of 1943. With drop tanks they could protect the bombers to and from their targets, and the air war now turned dramatically. In aerial combat, Mustangs shot down 4,950 German aircraft against their own losses of 2,520. The P-51 also served with distinction in the Pacific theater, where it escorted Boeing B-29 Superfortress bombers in strikes against Japan.

The Mustang also served effectively in the Korean War as both a fighter and ground-support aircraft. A total of 15,686 Mustangs were built before the aircraft was removed from U.S. service in 1953. The P-51 saw wide foreign service with 55 other air forces and remained in service with some Latin American air forces into the 1960s. Several hundred closely related P-82 (later F-82) Twin Mustangs were also built late in World War II and served as long-range escorts and night fighters.

Further Reading

Angelucci, Enzo. *The Rand McNally Encyclopedia of Military Aircraft.* New York: Military Press, 1983.

Fredriksen, John C. *Warbirds: An Illustrated Guide to U.S. Military Aircraft, 1915–2000.* Santa Barbara, CA: ABC-CLIO, 1999.

Gruenhagen, Robert W. *Mustang: The Story of the P-51 Fighter.* Revised ed. New York: Arco, 1976.

Grumman F6F Hellcat U.S. Navy Fighter

When the United States entered World War II in December 1941, the frontline U.S. Navy carrier-based fighter, the Grumman F4F Wildcat, was easily outclassed in most performance characteristics by the Japanese Mitsubishi A6M Reisen (Zero). Recognizing its limitations, the U.S. Navy had already let a contract with Grumman in June 1941 for a replacement carrier-based aircraft. The first Prototype Hellcat flew in June 1942. It entered service in January 1943.

Fast, maneuverable, and rugged, the Hellcat soon proved itself superior to Japanese fighters, including the Zero. During Pacific theater combat, it sustained a phenomenal 19:1 kill ratio over Japanese aircraft and claimed the largest numbers of Japanese planes shot down during the war: 4,947 of 6,477.

Powered by a single 2,000-horsepower Pratt & Whitney R-2800-10 Double Wasp 18-cylinder radial air-cooled engine, the F6F-3 had a maximum speed of 376 miles per hour, a ceiling of 38,400 feet, and a range of 1,090 miles. It was armed with six .30-caliber machine guns.

The F6F-3E and F6F-3N were specially equipped night fighters, the navy's first, sporting a wing radar pod. With 7,868 built, the F6F-5 was the largest production model Hellcat. It first flew in April 1944. This variant featured extra armor protection and had an improved Pratt & Whitney R-2800-10W 2,000-horsepower engine that provided a maximum speed of 380 miles per hour. It had a ceiling of 37,300 feet and a range of 1,040 miles. Armed with six .50-caliber machine guns, it could also carry 2,000 pounds of bombs.

By the time Grumman shut down the assembly line in November 1945, a total of 12,272 F6Fs had been produced. The Royal Navy received some 3,500 F6Fs for its Fleet Air Arm. The F6F remained in service after the war until 1950. A number served with the French Air Force during the Indochina War (1946–1954), and several were used as radio-controlled explosive-filled drones against communist targets during the Korean War.

Further Reading

Angelucci, Enzo. *The Rand McNally Encyclopedia of Military Aircraft, 1914–1980.* New York: Military Press, 1983.

Campbell, J. M. *Consolidated B-24 Liberator.* Atglen, PA: Schiffer, 1993.

Fredriksen, John C. *Warbirds: An Illustrated Guide to U.S. Military Aircraft, 1915–2000.* Santa Barbara, CA: ABC-CLIO, 1999.

Ilyushin Il-2 Sturmovik Soviet Ground-Attack Aircraft

The Ilyushin Il-2 Sturmovik was the most important Soviet aircraft of World War II and perhaps the war's best ground-attack aircraft. Sergei Ilyushin developed the prototype Il-2 in 1939 specifically for ground attack. Produced by various state industries and entering service in May 1941, the low-wing, all-metal monoplane with retractable landing gear had a maximum speed of 251 miles per hour, a ceiling of 19,690 feet, and a range of 475 miles. Because the Il-2 was vulnerable to air attack when it was making its runs, in 1942 a two-seat version was introduced, with a rear gunner facing away from the pilot in the greenhouse canopy.

The Il-2 was armed with two 23mm cannon and three 7.62mm machine guns. It could carry 1,320 pounds of bombs or rockets, and the plane was heavily armored to protect its vitals of engine, crew, and fuel from enemy ground fire.

Flying low and firing rockets, the Sturmovik proved to be a highly efficient tank killer. Certainly it helped turn the tide against the Germans in the great tank battle at Kursk in July 1943. Soviet dictator Joseph Stalin said that this aircraft was "as essential to the Red Army as bread and water." The Germans called the Il-2 "Schwarzer Tod" (Black Death). The Sturmovik remained in production until 1955, with the Soviets manufacturing some 36,000 of them. Only the Polikarpov Po-2 was produced in greater numbers.

Further Reading

Angelucci, Enzo. *The Rand McNally Encyclopedia of Military Aircraft, 1914–1980.* New York: Military Press, 1983.

Fredriksen, John C. *International Warbirds: An Illustrated Guide to World Military Aircraft, 1914–2000.* Santa Barbara, CA: ABC-CLIO, 2001.

Grumman TBF/TBM Avenger U.S. Torpedo Bomber

The Grumman Aircraft Engineering Corporation TBF Avenger was not only the principal U.S. torpedo bomber but was probably the best torpedo bomber in World War II. Design work began in 1940, and the prototype flew in August 1941. The first production model TBFs were delivered to the navy beginning in January 1942. The Avenger replaced the slower misnamed Douglas TBD Devastator.

The rugged Avenger had a three-man crew (pilot, gunner, and radio operator) and featured a long canopy terminating in a large ball-shaped dorsal turret. Powered by a Wright R-2600-20 Cyclone 14-cylinder radial air-cooled 1,900-horsepower engine, the Avenger had a maximum (loaded) speed of 276 miles per hour, a ceiling of 30,100 feet, and a range of 1,215 miles. Armed with three .50-caliber machine guns (two forward firing) and one .30-caliber machine gun, it could carry up to 2,000 pounds of bombs or torpedoes in its bomb bay.

The Avenger did not get off to a good start. It first saw combat in the June 1942 Battle of Midway, when none of the six unescorted Avengers reached their target and five were shot down. The TBF went on to perform yeoman work in the war and sink large numbers of Japanese ships, including the giant Japanese battleships *Musashi* and *Yamato*. The TBF went through a number of variants, the chief one being the addition of wing-mounted rockets or drop tanks. Models included photoreconnaissance and early-warning aircraft. Many of the planes were equipped with antisubmarine radar.

Because of the great demand for the Avenger during the war, Eastern Aircraft, a division of General Motors, built nearly half of the total of 9,836 produced. Avengers built by Eastern Aircraft were known as the TBM. The British Fleet Air Arm received 958 Avengers, where the aircraft was known as the Tarpon. Another 60 went to the New Zealand Air Force.

The Avenger saw service after the war as a search and rescue aircraft, an all-weather night bomber, an electronic countermeasures aircraft, and a target tug. It remained in service with the U.S. Navy until the 1950s and with a number of foreign air forces, including those of Canada, France, Japan, and the Netherlands, until the early 1960s.

Further Reading

Angelucci, Enzo. *The Rand McNally Encyclopedia of Military Aircraft, 1914–1980.* New York: Military Press, 1983.

Fredriksen, John C. *Warbirds: An Illustrated Guide to U.S. Military Aircraft, 1915–2000.* Santa Barbara, CA: ABC-CLIO, 1999.

Tillman, Barrett, and Robert L. Lawson. *U.S. Navy Dive and Torpedo Bombers of World War II.* St. Paul, MN: MBI, 2001.

Treadwell, Terry. *Grumman TBF/TBM Avenger.* Stroud, Gloucestershire, UK: Tempus, 2001.

Avro Lancaster Heavy Bomber

The British Avro Lancaster bomber was the premier Royal Air Force strategic bomber of the war. The plane grew out of the Avro medium two-engine Manchester bomber, which was, however, grossly underpowered. With longer wingspan and four engines, the Manchester evolved into the Lancaster. The all-metal, high-wing Lancaster flew for the first time in 1941 and entered service over Germany in March 1942. Its four 1,360-horsepower Rolls-Royce Merlin XX liquid-cooled in-line engines delivered a maximum speed of 287 miles per hour, a ceiling of 24,500 feet, and a range of 1,660 miles. It had a crew of seven.

Relatively lightly defended, with 8 to 10 .303-caliber machine guns, the Lancaster sacrificed defensive firepower for bomb load. It could carry up to 22,000 pounds of bombs, as opposed to only 4,000 pounds for the Boeing B-17 (6,000 for the B-17G), and by March 1945 was dropping the "Grand Slam" 22,000-pound bomb. Within a year of entering service, the Lancaster had largely replaced the Handley Page Halifax and Short Stirling as the principal Royal Air Force bomber. The Lancaster bore the brunt of nighttime British bombing of Germany.

The United States rebuffed British suggestions that the United States halt production of the B-17 in favor of the Lancaster. A total of 7,366 Lancasters were built. The Lancaster remained in service with the Royal Air Force until 1954.

Further Reading

Fredriksen, John. *International Warbirds: An Illustrated Guide to World Military Aircraft, 1914–2000.* Santa Barbara, CA: ABC-CLIO, 2001.

Neillands, Robin. *The Bomber War: The Allied Air Offensive against Nazi Germany.* New York: Overlook, 1991.

Sweetman, Bill. *Avro Lancaster.* New York: Random House, 1988.

Tubbs, D. B. *Lancaster Bomber.* New York: Ballantine, 1972.

Wood, D. C. *The Design and Development of the Avro Lancaster.* Manchester, UK: Royal Aeronautical Society, Manchester Branch, 1991.

Boeing B-17 Flying Fortress Heavy Bomber

The Boeing B-17 heavy bomber was the principal U.S. Army Air Forces strategic bombing platform in the European theater in World War II. In the period between the two world wars, leaders of the U.S. Army Air Corps saw the long-range bomber as the best chance to carve out an offensive role; it would also justify an independent air force, the goal of many senior officers. The new Boeing B-17 "Flying Fortress" was selected for that role. The world's first modern bomber, it entered service in 1937. The easy-to-fly B-17 was a crew favorite.

An excellent bombardment platform and very rugged, the B-17 was very much in keeping with Italian airpower theorist Guilio Douhet's concept of a self-defending "battle plane." The B-17E of 1941 had a unique vertical ball turret to protect its underside as well as self-sealing gasoline tanks, while the B-17G of 1943 added a chin turret to protect the bomber from head-on attacks by German fighters. With

A Boeing B-17 Flying Fortress drops bombs on Nuremberg in 1945. The B-17 was the principal U.S. strategic bomber in the European Theater during World War II. (Library of Congress)

Inaccuracy of Strategic Bombing

The U.S. Army Air Forces was the greatest practitioner of strategic bombing in World War II, yet it was hardly the "precision bombing" that was touted. In one example, on the night of June 15–16, 1944, 75 Boeing B-29 Superfortresses flew from bases in China to attack the Yawata steelworks in northern Kyushu, Japan. Only 47 of the B-29s struck the raid's primary target. Five B-29s were lost in accidents during the operation, and 20 were destroyed by Japanese aircraft. The B-29s dropped a total of 376 500-pound bombs, but only 1 hit the target.

In the autumn of 1944 the U.S. Eighth Air Force was pummeling Germany, but only 7 percent of its bombs were falling within 1,000 feet of the aim point. Often the Germans were unable to determine the intended target of raids. It has been calculated that it would take a total of 108 B-17s crewed by 1,080 men and dropping 648 bombs to achieve a 96 percent chance of securing two hits within a 400- by 500-foot target area.

---

a crew of 10 men, the B-17G's four Wright Cyclone R-1820-97 Cyclone supercharged radial engines each delivered 1,200 horsepower and produced a maximum speed of 287 miles per hour. The B-17 had a ceiling of 35,600 feet, a range of 3,400 miles, an armament of 13 .50-caliber machine guns, and a bomb load of 6,000 pounds, considerably less than comparable British aircraft, which, however, sacrificed defensive armament. Fitted with special external racks for short-range operations, the B-17 could carry up to 17,600 pounds of bombs.

U.S. Army Air Forces leaders believed that with their heavy defensive armament, B-17s could fly unescorted over Europe. This proved unfounded, and the unescorted bombers took heavy losses. With the addition of long-range fighter aircraft as escorts, however, losses dropped substantially. B-17s also saw service in the Pacific theater.

Before the end of production in May 1945, a total of 12,726 B-17s were built (8,680 of them the G model). Just more than 200 of these were supplied to the Royal Air Force. The B-17 remained in service until the end of the war, when the Boeing B-29 "Superfortress" replaced both it and the Consolidated B-24 "Liberator" as the U.S. heavy bomber. In 2015, 13 B-17s remain in flying condition.

Further Reading

Fredriksen, John. *International Warbirds: An Illustrated Guide to World Military Aircraft, 1914–2000.* Santa Barbara, CA: ABC-CLIO, 2001.

Freeman, Roger A. *B-17 Fortress at War.* New York: Scribner, 1977.

Neillands, Robin. *The Bomber War: The Allied Air Offensive against Nazi Germany.* New York: Overlook, 1991.

Salecker, Gene E. *Fortress against the Sun: The B-17 Flying Fortress in the Pacific.* New York: Da Capo, 2001.

Consolidated B-24 Liberator Heavy Bomber

Isaac M. Laddon of Consolidated Aircraft designed the B-24 Liberator in early 1939 in response to an army requirement for an aircraft with greater range and bomb-carrying capacity than the Boeing B-17 Flying Fortress. The prototype aircraft first flew that December. The B-24 entered service with the U.S. Army Air Forces (USAAF) in 1940 and with the Royal Air Force (RAF) Coastal Command in mid-1941. It also served with the U.S. Navy.

The B-24 was a remarkable aircraft. Its high–aspect-ratio Davis high-lift wing was well in advance of its time and allowed the Liberator to carry a heavy bomb load over long ranges. The aircraft featured a blunt nose, slablike sides, twin rudders, and tricycle landing gear. Its deep fuselage had a roomy bomb bay with a unique actuation track and rollers to reduce drag. Powered by four 1,200-horsepower Pratt & Whitney R-1830-43 twin Wasp supercharged radial engines, the B-24D had a maximum speed of 303 miles per hour, a ceiling of 32,000 feet, and a range of 2,650 miles. It could carry up to 8,000 pounds of bombs and was armed with 10 .50-caliber machine guns.

USAAF B-24s saw service in the Mediterranean, European, and Pacific theaters. They carried out the August 1, 1943, raid on the Ploesti, Romania, oil refineries that, however, resulted in heavy losses to the attacking aircraft. To counter head-on German fighter attacks, the B-24G received a power nose turret with two .50-caliber machine guns. The Liberator was not always popular with its crews. It was difficult to fly and, unlike the B-17, could not sustain much punishment, especially in the wings, which could give way completely if hit in a critical location.

With its exceptionally long range, the Liberator played a key role in the Battle of the Atlantic against German submarines. Equipped with lightweight radar that enabled its crews to detect vessels through overcast, the B-24 was an effective submarine and ship killer. Its long range made it an important bombardment platform in the Pacific theater. By the end of 1944 the USAAF was operating more than 6,000 B-24s in that theater. The J Model (introduced in 1943) was powered by four 1,200-horsepower Pratt & Whitney R-1830-65 twin Wasp engines. It had a maximum speed of 300 miles per hour, a ceiling of 28,000 feet, and a range of 2,100 miles and could carry 8,800 pounds of bombs. It was armed with 10 machine guns. Crew size varied from 8 to 12 men.

Its boxy shape allowed the B-24 to be easily modified to serve in other roles, such as the C-87 transport, the F-7 photoreconnaissance aircraft, and the PB4Y patrol bomber for the navy. Until the appearance of the Boeing B-29 Superfortress in the last year of the war, B-24s and B-17s carried out all U.S. strategic bombing. According to combat records, in the Pacific theater B-24s dropped 635,000 tons of bombs and were credited with shooting down 4,189 Japanese aircraft.

During the war, Liberators were being produced not only by Consolidated but also by Ford, Douglas, and North American. By war's end, 18,188 Liberators had been built, more than any other American aircraft of World War II and also the largest production run of any bomber of the war. The Liberator remained in service until 1950.

Further Reading

Angelucci, Enzo. *The Rand McNally Encyclopedia of Military Aircraft, 1914–1980.* New York: Military Press, 1983.

Campbell, J. M. *Consolidated B-24 Liberator.* Atglen, PA: Schiffer, 1993.

Fredriksen, John C. *Warbirds: An Illustrated Guide to U.S. Military Aircraft, 1915–2000.* Santa Barbara, CA: ABC-CLIO, 1999.

Boeing B-29 Superfortress Heavy Bomber

The U.S. Boeing B-29 strategic bomber was ordered in August 1940, first flew in September 1942, and entered service in 1944. The four-engine B-29, dubbed the Superfortress, had a 10-man crew and was protected by 12 .50-caliber machine guns and a 20mm cannon in the tail. Capable of carrying 10 tons of bombs, its usual load was 4 tons because of the fuel necessary for the distance to be covered in bombing Japan.

The B-29 was a revolutionary aircraft and the most technologically advanced bomber of World War II. Unlike the Boeing B-17 "Flying Fortress" or the Consolidated B-24 "Liberator," the B-29 was fully pressurized. It also featured fully automatic gun turrets. Powered by four 2,200-horsepower turbocharged radial engines, the B-29 had a ceiling of 31,850 feet and a phenomenal range of 3,250 miles. Fast for a bomber, its maximum speed was 358 miles per hour.

The B-29 performed effectively at the close of the Pacific War, especially in the bombardment of Japan from the Marianas. B-29s carried out the firebombing of Tokyo in March 1945, the single most destructive air raid in world history, and were also used in mine-laying operations to interdict Japanese coastal shipping. The B-29 bombers *Enola Gay* and *Bockscar* dropped the atomic bombs over Hiroshima and Nagasaki, respectively. During the Korean War B-29s conducted strategic bombing of North Korea, but when a number fell prey to swift Mikoyan-Gurevich MiG-15 jet interceptors, they were withdrawn from daytime service. A number of B-29s also underwent conversion into tankers as the KB-29. A total of 3,000 B-29s were built. The bomber was entirely withdrawn from service in 1954.

Under the orders of Soviet leader Joseph Stalin, the Soviet Union produced a clone by reverse engineering from B-29s forced to land in Soviet territory in 1945. This aircraft, the Tupolev Tu-4 Bull, entered service in 1949 as the Soviet Air Force's first nuclear capable bomber.

A Boeing B-29 Superfortress, the most technologically advanced bomber of World War II. Based in the Marianas, U.S. Army Air Forces B-29s carried out the strategic bombing of the Japanese home islands during 1944-1945. (Library of Congress)

Further Reading

Birdwell, Steve. *Superfortress: The Boeing B-29.* Carrollton, TX: Squadron/Signal Publications, 1979.

Dorr, Robert F. *B-29 Superfortress Units of the Korean War.* Oxford, UK: Osprey, 2003.

Lemay, Curtis E., and Bill Yenne. *Superfortress: The Story of the B-29 and American Air Power in World War II.* New York: Berkley Publishing Group, 1989.

Pimlott, John. *B-29 Superfortress.* Secaucus, NJ: Chartwell Books, 1980.

Gliders

Gliders are unpowered aircraft. These relatively inexpensive aircraft had long been used in training. Because of prohibitions imposed on military aircraft by the Treaty of Versailles of 1919, Germany in particular embraced gliding. Soaring clubs, which developed in other countries as well, increased interest in gliding worldwide. Gliders first went to war during World War II, when they transported soldiers, supplies, and equipment into combat. Some gliders were launched by rockets, but most were towed behind transport aircraft known as tugs, to be released and land behind enemy lines, often at night, allowing the men aboard them to fight as infantry after landing.

Capture of Pegasus Bridge

Probably the most important Allied glider operation of the war came in the early morning hours of D-Day, June 6, 1944, in Operation DEADSTICK, when 181 members of the Oxfordshire and Buckinghamshire Light Infantry commanded by Major John Howard landed in six Horsa gliders to seize two key bridges in Normandy: Pegasus Bridge over the Orne River near Caen and Horsa Bridge over the Caen Canal. The operation was vital to prevent German tanks from being able to attack the eastern flank of the British landing at Sword Beach in Normandy.

Five of the gliders landed as close as 47 yards from the bridges. Within 10 minutes, the attackers had overwhelmed the German defenders and secured the two bridges. Two British soldiers died. One man drowned, while Lieutenant Den Brotheridge was killed by enemy fire, the first member of the invading Allied forces killed in the Normandy Invasion. The original Pegasus Bridge was replaced in 1994 and is now within the grounds of the Pegasus Museum located near the new bridge.

Germany was the first to develop a military glider, the DFS 230 built of plywood, steel, and fabric. A total of 1,022 were produced. DFS 230 gliders were employed in the invasion of Belgium and the Netherlands in May 1940, playing a key role in the capture of Fort Eben Emael. The Germans also used gliders in the 1941 invasion of Crete and in the Soviet Union. The Germans produced 1,528 larger German Gotha Go 242 gliders, of which 133 were adapted into powered twin-engine Go 244s.

The huge Messerschmitt Me 321 glider weighed 75,852 pounds loaded and could transport 200 troops. A total of 200 were built. Most were transformed into the six-engine Me 323 military transport.

Great Britain was the first Allied nation to deploy gliders. The Hotspur of 1940 could transport 2 crewmen and 6 soldiers. A total of 1,015 were built. In 1941 the British developed the Horsa. It could carry 2 crewmen and 25–28 passengers or two trucks. Britain manufactured some 5,000 Horsas. The British Hamilcar was the largest Allied glider, weighing 36,000 pounds loaded. It could transport 40 troops or the Tetrarch Mk.IV light tank or other cargo. A total of 412 were built.

The Soviet Union introduced the A-7 glider in 1939. It could carry a pilot and eight passengers. A total of 400 were manufactured. The Soviets utilized the A-7 glider chiefly to transport supplies to partisans working behind German lines.

The U.S. glider was the Waco, built by the Waco Aircraft Company in Troy, Ohio. Constructed of plywood, canvas, and a steel tubing skeleton, it could carry 15 troops or 3,800 pounds of cargo, including artillery pieces, a bulldozer, or a jeep. With 13,908 built, more Wacos were produced than any glider of the war.

Men and cargo were usually loaded through the wide, hinged glider nose section. Moving at an air speed of 110–150 miles per hour at several thousand feet, Douglas C-47s towed the gliders with a 300-foot rope toward a designated landing zone and then descended to release the glider at several hundred feet. En route to the release point, the glider men and the plane crew communicated with each other either by a telephone wire secured around the tow line or via two-way radios.

This was indeed hazardous duty. Sometimes gliders were released prematurely and did not reach the landing zones, and on occasion gliders collided as they approached their destination. Many gliders crashed with fatal results for the men, who often referred to them as "canvas coffins." Despite significant losses in the July 1943 Allied invasion of Sicily, gliders were employed in Operation OVER-LORD, the Allied invasion of Normandy in June 1944, and Operation MARKET-GARDEN, the Allied effort to secure a crossing of the Rhine at Arnhem in August 1944 that saw the largest airborne assault in history; 14,589 troops were landed by glider and 20,011 by parachute. Gliders were also employed in the Pacific and China-Burma-India theaters. The final U.S. glider mission of the war occurred on the island of Luzon in the Philippines in June 1945. Gliders were gradually phased out of military inventories after the war, although the Soviet Union retained them through the 1950s. The glider's role has been assumed by the troop-carrying helicopter.

Further Reading

Lowden, John L. *Silent Wings at War: Combat Gliders in World War II.* Washington, DC: Smithsonian Institution Press, 1992.

Masters, Charles J. *Glidermen of Neptune: The American D-Day Glider Attack.* Carbondale: Southern Illinois University Press, 1995.

Mrazek, James E. *Fighting Gliders of World War II.* New York: St. Martin's, 1977.

Mrazek, James E. *The Glider War.* New York: St. Martin's, 1975.

Jet and Rocket Aircraft of World War II

Compared to the piston engine, the gas turbine (or jet engine) offered unrivaled power-to-weight ratios provided that the metallurgical, mechanical, and aerodynamic design problems could be solved. While still a Royal Air Force cadet in 1928, Frank Whittle argued that the gas turbine was a practical power unit. In 1935 he formed a company, Power Jets, to develop it. In Germany, Hans-Joachim Pabst von Ohain developed a jet engine that first ran in 1937 and was flown in a Heinkel 178 test aircraft in August 1939. Whittle's prototype engine first flew in the Gloster E28/39 in May 1941.

The Germans also experimented with rocket fighters, the Messerschmitt Me 163 Komet entering service in June 1944 against U.S. bombers. The Me 163 had an incredible climb but used a highly corrosive fuel that was inclined toward instability, and many pilots were lost in landing accidents. Fewer than 50 Me 163s were operational at any one time; they had limited success, but their effect was mainly psychological.

The first operational jet fighter was the British Gloster Meteor, which entered service in July 1944. The Meteor I was distinctly underpowered and had serious limitations as a fighter, being difficult to control at speeds over Mach .67. It was armed with four 20mm cannon. All World War II jet and rocket aircraft had compressibility problems at high speeds and were generally slow to accelerate at low speed but much better than propeller-driven rivals at high speed, easily outclassing them in acceleration and zoom climb.

The best-known jet aircraft of World War II was undoubtedly the German Messerschmitt Me 262 Schwalbe (Swallow). Allied bombing, design problems, and German leader Adolf Hitler insistence that it be developed as a bomber all delayed its entrance until July 1944. It was a much better fighter than the Meteor. Its two Junkers Jumo 004 B-1 turbojet engines of 1,986 pounds thrust gave the aircraft a top speed of 540 miles per hour, faster than any other contemporary aircraft. The low swept-wing, all-metal Me 262 had a ceiling of 37,664 feet and a range of 652 miles. It was armed with four 30mm cannon and up to 24 rockets. The Me 262 bomber variant carried up to 2,207 pounds of bombs.

Of Allied fighters, only the U.S. Army Air Forces North American P-51 Mustang was a worthy opponent. In common with most jets, the Me 262 was vulnerable during landing and takeoff. Its great speed and its armament made the Me 262 the ultimate World War II bomber-killer, as only a few hits from its cannon would usually bring down a four-engine bomber. Fortunately for the Allies, the Me 262 came too late in the day to succeed. Although 1,430 were built, only about 200 of these entered squadron service by the end of the war.

The Heinkel He 162 Volksjäger (People's Fighter) jet fighter utilized nonstrategic materials and required an experienced pilot during the takeoff and landing phases. Armed with two 20mm cannon, the He 162 was prone to catastrophic structural failure if carelessly handled. A handful of He 162s became operational in April 1945.

The German Arado 234 Blitz was the world's first jet bomber. A prototype flew for the first time in June 1943, but delays in securing its engines meant that it did not enter service, and then in only very limited numbers as a reconnaissance variant, until August 1944. The first bomber version was operational in December 1944. A total of 210 were built.

The Japanese also built such aircraft. Their Yokosuka Ohka MXY 7 Oka (Cherry Blossom), built at the Yokosuka Naval Arsenal, was essentially a rocket-propelled man-guided missile, carried to the target area under a specially converted Mitsubishi G4M Betty bomber. Once the pilot was in position, the canopy was sealed shut. Employed in combat from March 1945, most Okas were shot down by Allied navy fighters, although one did sink the U.S. destroyer *Monnert L. Abele* in April.

The Bell P-59 Airacomet was the only U.S. Army Air Forces jet aircraft to see combat in the war. The twin-engine straight-wing P-59 flew for the first time in

October 1942. It had a top speed of only 400 miles per hour and offered few advantages over the piston-powered U.S. aircraft then in service. Fifty production models were initially deployed with the 412th Fighter Group in 1945. Although the P-59 proved to be a valuable testing platform, the first mass-produced U.S. jet fighter was the Lockheed P-80 Shooting Star. Utilizing the British H-1 turbojet engine, it first flew in January 1944 and exceeded 500 miles per hour on its first flight. The U.S. Army ordered 5,000 P-80s, but with the end of the war, production was scaled back to 917 aircraft. Ultimately, 1,714 were built.

Further Reading

Brown, Eric M. *Wings of the Luftwaffe.* Shrewsbury. UK: Airlife, 1993.

Ethell, Jeffrey, and Alfred Price. *World War II Fighting Jets.* Shrewsbury, UK: Airlife, 1994.

Jarrett, Philip, ed. *Aircraft of the Second World War.* London: Putnam, 1997.

Douglas C-47 Skytrain Transport Aircraft

The U.S. Douglas C-47 Skytrain is the most famous transport aircraft in history. Manufactured by the Douglas Aircraft company, it first flew in December 1935. As the DC-3 airliner, it immediately revolutionized air travel. The U.S. Army first ordered it in 1940. It entered service the next year as the C-47, but its crews knew it affectionately as the "Gooney Bird."

The low-wing, twin-engine, unarmed DC-3 was both rugged and easy to fly. It had a maximum speed of 230 miles per hour, a ceiling of 23,200 feet, and a range of 1,500 miles. It could carry five tons of cargo or 27–28 fully equipped troops and had a crew of 2–3 men.

By the end of World War II, 10,665 C-47s had been produced. A total of 568 served with the navy as the R4D. More than 9,000 C-47s were shipped to Britain, where the aircraft was known as the Dakota. An additional 2,500 were constructed under license by the Soviet Union as the Lisunov Li-2. The Japanese built 485 as the Nakajima L2D through a 1938 license.

In Allied service, the C-47 saw extensive use in every theater of the war, fulfilling a wide range of roles as a troop carrier, cargo transport, glider tug, and medical evacuation aircraft. It is perhaps best known for its role in World War II airborne operations, including the June 1944 Normandy Invasion.

The C-47 continued in service in the Cold War, most notably the Berlin Airlift of 1948–1949 and the Korean War. The four-engine C-54 largely replaced it as the prime cargo hauler, but the C-47 did see service during the Vietnam War as a gunship. Designated the AC-47 and popularly known as "Puff the Magic Dragon," its relatively low speed enabled it to loiter and provide devastating fire from door-mounted 7.62mm miniguns. It also performed in electronic reconnaissance, photographic reconnaissance, and psychological warfare roles.

Still utilized by some Latin American and Asian militaries, the DC-3 continues in civilian service in the United States.

Further Reading

Angelucci, Enzo. *The Rand McNally Encyclopedia of Military Aircraft, 1914–1980.* New York: Military Press, 1983.

Fredriksen, John C. *International Warbirds: An Illustrated Guide to World Military Aircraft, 1914–2000.* Santa Barbara, CA: ABC-CLIO, 2001.

Helicopters

Helicopters are a type of aircraft supported through the air by the aerodynamic lift created by one or more rotors, essentially rotating wings or blades, turning about a substantially vertical axis. Interest in the helicopter came about because of its highly valued ability to ascend and descend almost vertically and land in relatively small areas without benefit of lengthy landing strips.

Probably the first helicopter-like design was the "helical screw" drawn by artist-inventor Leonardo Da Vinci in the 15th century. In 1783, based on a "flying top" toy brought from China, two Frenchman named Launoy and Bienvenu built a working model of a vertical-flight machine. In the mid-19th century, British nobleman Sir George Cayley built a full-size unpowered helo-glider that flew a few feet with his coachman aboard.

These early designs had two problems: their flight was uncontrolled, and they lacked a source of power for sustained flight. With the advent of gasoline engines and shortly after the first heavier-than-air flight of Orville and Wilbur Wright, French inventor Charles Renard built a small helicopter that flew pilotless. He was followed in 1907 by Louis Breguet and Paul Cornu, who each built manned machines that lifted off the ground but suffered control problems. In 1909 before turning his inventive powers to producing large fixed-wing aircraft, Russian Igor Sikorsky initially experimented with rudimentary helicopters but was unable to solve control and stability problems.

Between 1916 and 1918, Austrian lieutenant Stefan Petroczy and Dr. Theodore von Karman designed and built two prototype vertical-lift machines for the Central Powers during World War I. The second made more than 30 successful flights before it crashed. The war ended before a third could be built. The designers of these machines sought to handle problems of control and stability by tethering the machines to cables anchored to the ground.

During the 1920s a Frenchman named Dourheret, the American father-and-son team of Emile and Henry Berliner, and George de Bothezat, a Russian under American contract, produced vertical-lift machines. All were disappointing because of stability and control problems. But in 1923 Spanish engineer Juan de la Cierva solved one instability problem caused by the retreating blade producing less lift than the advancing blade by hinging the blades for more flexibility. While Cierva's invention was a rotary-wing aircraft, it was not a true helicopter. It was an autogiro or gyroplane that depended on a propeller to provide horizontal movement, while the unpowered rotating wings provided the lift. As working rotary-wing aircraft, autogiros held the field through the late 1920s and early 1930s.

The first true helicopters appeared in the 1930s in the United States, France, and Germany. In France, Louis Breguet and René Dorand built a twin-rotor helicopter that set the speed record in 1935 and the endurance and distance record in 1936. In 1937 Heinrich Focke's helicopter set new records for time aloft, speed, distance, and altitude. Igor Sikorsky, who had immigrated to the United States in 1919, made his maiden helicopter flight in a craft of his own design in 1939.

Despite these successes, more autogiros than helicopters were used during World War II. Only Japan and the Soviet Union employed autogiros in a very limited role in support of their ground forces, while the Japanese used some in service with their navy for antisubmarine warfare and liaison. Britain deployed a few to France for observation and communications duties in 1939, but the defeat of France ended those activities.

The U.S. military program to develop helicopters began in the late 1930s and fell under the direction of the U.S. Army Air Corps. While other services, primarily the navy, looked into the possibility of helicopter use, in May 1942 the U.S. Army Air Forces took delivery of the first practical helicopter put into military service, a Sikorsky R-4.

Helicopters had no real impact in World War II. The German Army employed a small number for reconnaissance, supply, transport, and casualty evacuations, and the navy used them for shipboard reconnaissance and antisubmarine patrol. The United States and Britain employed some experimentally in antisubmarine warfare and for search and rescue operations.

By the end of the war helicopters had entered limited military service, and some had seen combat. Many commanders believed that the helicopter was too fragile and vulnerable for the battlefield and too difficult to maintain. Despite its tentative beginnings, in later wars helicopters would revolutionize military operations by providing entrance to and exit from the battlefield by means of the air nearly uninhibited by terrain.

Helicopters came into their own during the Korean War, when the U.S. Army employed them extensively for resupply in circumstances of difficult terrain, for liaison, for extraction of downed pilots, and in medical evacuation. Helicopters were used most extensively during the Vietnam War, often referred to as the "Helicopter War." There they were fitted with machine guns and rockets and used to ferry troops in airmobile operations or to attack communist positions. U.S. Army, Marine, Air Force, and Navy helicopters flew an astonishing 36.125 million sorties of all types. Perhaps the most notable helicopters of the war were the ubiquitous Bell UH-1 Iroquois (Huey), the Boeing-Vertol CH-47 Chinook, and the Bell AH-1

Cobra, the world's first true attack helicopter. During the Cold War, the United States planned to use large numbers of attack helicopters to help defeat Soviet armor in any invasion of Western Europe. The Soviet Union employed its highly effective workhorse Mil Mi-24 Hind during the Soviet-Afghan War (1979–1989). Large helicopters, such as the U.S. Sikorsky S-64 Sky Crane and Russia's Mil Mi-26 Halo, can transport all but the heaviest cargo. Among more notable recent helicopters are the U.S. Hughes (Boeing) AH-64 Apache, the Sikorsky Army UH-60 Black Hawk/Navy SH-60 Seahawk, and the Sikorsky Army CH-53E Super Stallion/Navy MH-53 Sea Dragon; the British Westland Lynx; and Russia's Mil Mi-8/Mi-17 Hip multimission helicopter. The U.S. Bell/Boeing tilt-rotor V-22 Osprey is a hybrid helicopter and airplane. It takes off and lands like a helicopter, but once it is airborne its engine nacelles can be rotated to convert it to a turboprop airplane capable of higher-speed flight. Its top speed is about 100 miles per hour as a helicopter and 315 miles per hour as an airplane. Today's helicopters fulfill a wide variety of roles over land and at sea.

Further Reading

Everett-Heath, John. *Helicopters in Combat: The First Fifty Years.* London: Arms and Armour, 1992.

Fredriksen, John C. *International Warbirds: An Illustrated Guide to World Military Aircraft, 1914–2000.* Santa Barbara, CA: ABC-CLIO, 2001.

Fredriksen, John C. *Warbirds: An Illustrated Guide to U.S. Military Aircraft, 1915–2000.* Santa Barbara, CA: ABC-CLIO, 1999.

McGowen, Stanley S. *Helicopters: An Illustrated History of Their Impact.* Santa Barbara, CA: ABC-CLIO, 2005.

Prouty, Raymond W. *Military Helicopter Design Technology.* London: Janes Defense Data, 1989.

Sikorsky R-4 Helicopter

The Sikorsky R-4 was the world's first mass-produced helicopter and the first U.S. Army helicopter to see combat service.

By the spring of 1941, Russian émigré Igor Sikorsky had his experimental VS-300 helicopter working sufficiently well for the government to award a contract to the Vought-Sikorsky Division of United Aircraft. Designated the XR-4, the prototype first flew in January 1942. Powered by a 165-horsepower Warner Super-Scarab R-500 radial engine, the two-man (pilot and observer) R-4 had a speed of 77 miles per hour, a ceiling of 8,000 feet, and a maximum range of 220 miles. During the war it served with the U.S. Army, the U.S. Navy, the U.S. Coast Guard, the Royal Air Force, and the Royal Navy Fleet Air Arm. The 52 R-4s in British service were known as the "Hoverfly" in the Royal Air Force and the "Gadfly" in the Royal Navy.

In April 1944 one of the four U.S. Air Force R-4s sent to India for experimental use rescued four men from an airplane crash site in Burma behind Japanese lines in history's first helicopter rescue operation. That same year, the R-4 was also the first helicopter to land aboard a ship, the tanker *Bunker Hill*. A total of 131 R-4s were built.

Further Reading

Fredriksen, John C. *Warbirds: An Illustrated Guide to U.S. Military Aircraft, 1915–2000.* Santa Barbara, CA: ABC-CLIO, 1999.

McGowen, Stanley S. *Helicopters: An Illustrated History of Their Impact.* Santa Barbara, CA: ABC-CLIO, 2005.

Incendiary Bombs

Employing fire against an enemy had been a technique of warfare from earliest times. Greek fire is but one example. The first incendiary devices dropped from aircraft were thermite-filled bombs used by the Germans in their zeppelin bombing campaign against London beginning in 1915. In the bombing of Guernica during the Spanish Civil War (1936–1939), the Germans experimented with a mix of high-explosive (HE) and incendiary bombs.

Incendiary devices reached a new level of destructiveness in World War II. The Allies in particular sought to take advantage of the large number of wooden structures in Germany and especially in Japan. Indeed, in the Allied strategic bombing campaign against cities, incendiary bombs proved more destructive than HE bombs, although the usual procedure was a mix of incendiary and HE. The single most destructive air raid in history was not the atomic bombing of Hiroshima or Nagasaki but the great firebomb raid on Tokyo of March 9–10, 1945. The German city of Dresden was also largely destroyed by incendiaries during February 13–15, 1945.

Concluding that daytime precision bombing was impossible and too costly to attacking aircraft, the Royal Air Force resorted to nighttime area bombing of German cities. Bomber Command soon worked out a procedure whereby the first aircraft would drop HE to create the fuel for the incendiaries. The British chiefly employed the 4-pound Magnesium IB (incendiary bomb) and the 30-pound Phosphorous IB. More HE bombs would then follow to disrupt firefighting and rescue units, concluding with yet another round of incendiaries. The British 30-pound bomb, first employed by Bomber Command in April 1943, often failed to work, however. Early British thermite bombs were filled with a mixture of iron oxide and powdered aluminum. While they produced great heat, they had the disadvantage of dissipating quickly.

The Germans developed a much more effective 2.2-pound incendiary bomb. Their B1 EZB bomb employed thermite as the igniter and a metallic magnesium

---

Tokyo Raid

By early 1945, high-altitude Boeing B29 Superfortress raids from the Mariana Islands against Japan were causing considerable destruction and forcing the dispersal of industry and the lowering of aircraft production. They were also experiencing an unacceptable 6 percent aircraft loss rate per mission. Precision bombing also proved impossible at high altitude.

Ordered to shift emphasis from industrial targets to Japanese cities, commander of XXI Bomber Group in the Marianas Major General Curtis LeMay abandoned daylight precision bombing in favor of area bombing at night. The B-29s would fly low, stripped of all armament except the tail gun to increase payloads, and would carry incendiary rather than high-explosive bombs.

On the night of March 9–10 in the single most destructive raid in the history of warfare, 334 B-29s flying at only 7,000 feet dropped 1,667 tons of incendiary bombs on Tokyo, a city largely of wooden structures. Widespread firestorms destroyed 15 square miles of central Tokyo, including 267,171 houses. Japanese sources cite 83,793 confirmed dead and 40,918 injured. More than 100,000 people were made homeless.

During the next months the B-29s hit the largest Japanese cities, one after the other; only the cultural center of Kyoto was spared. Up to 300,000 Japanese died in these attacks. B-29 losses dropped dramatically, to 1.4 percent.

---

casing as the chief incendiary material. On striking the ground, the detonator ignited the striker, which in turn ignited the thermite and set fire to the magnesium casing. The B1 burned at high temperature and could not be extinguished by water. It also had a small explosive charge in the nose to discourage firefighters. In their raid on Coventry on November 14–15, 1941, the Germans employed more than 56 tons of incendiaries.

The Japanese developed an incendiary bomb for airburst. Weighing some 550 pounds and having an overall length of 9 feet 9 inches and a diameter of 12 inches, it was fuzed to burst about 200 feet above the ground. Its HE charge scattered some 750 open-ended thermite containers in 10 layers over a radius of more than 500 feet. Should the tail fuze fail to function, a nose fuze detonated the bomb on impact.

The most deployed Allied incendiary bomb was the 4-pound thermite bomb. Almost 30 million of these were dropped on Germany and another 10 million on Japan. The bomb most employed against Japan was, however, the M60 oil bomb, with cloth ribbons rather than fins for stabilization. Weighing 6 pounds, it had a napalm filler. Clusters of 38 M60s made up a container, with the normal load for a B-29 bomber 37 containers, or 1,406 bombs. The bombs were set free from the container at 5,000 feet by a time fuze, and each exploded on ground contact. The United States also employed the M47 100-pound napalm bomb.

Incendiary devices, especially napalm, continued to be widely employed during the Korean War and the Vietnam War.

Further Reading

Boyne, Walter J. *Clash of Wings: World War II in the Air.* New York: Simon and Schuster, 1994.

Crane, Conrad C. *Bombs, Cities, and Civilians: American Airpower Strategy in World War II.* Lawrence: University Press of Kansas, 1993.

Neillands, Robin. *The Bomber War: The Allied Air Offensive against Nazi Germany.* New York: Overlook, 2001.

Wood, Tony, and Bill Gunston. *Hitler's Luftwaffe.* New York: Crescent Books, 1978.

Napalm

Although popular misconception has applied the term "napalm" to any fire-producing materials, strictly speaking it is an incendiary material made from thickened gasoline. Gasoline had been employed as an incendiary for some time, as in the case of flamethrowers in World War I. The brown, syrupy napalm mixture was far more effective than gasoline as an incendiary, for it stuck to the target area. Developed by American scientists at Harvard University early in World War II, napalm was available as a weapon in late 1942.

The name "napalm" comes from *na*phthene and *palm*itate, which when combined with gasoline create a gel-like mixture. Napalm is not only sticky but also possesses improved burning characteristics compared to gasoline and is also relatively safe to handle.

Napalm was employed both in bombs and in flamethrowers. It was initially used in the U.S. 100-pound M47 chemical weapons bomb. The United States employed the napalm bomb in its extensive firebombing campaign against Japanese cities at the close of World War II. An initial pathfinder aircraft dropped the M47 to mark the targets, while following bombers dropped 6.2-pound M69 incendiary bombs with delayed-action fuzes to allow the bombs to penetrate buildings before ignition. Napalm was also employed extensively in the Korean War and the Vietnam War. Auxiliary fuel tanks were often filled with the napalm mix and equipped with an igniter and then dropped in areas where enemy forces were thought to be located.

Improved napalm, developed after the Korean War, was known as supernapalm and napalm B. It employed benzene (21 percent), polystrene (46 percent), and gasoline (33 percent). Its great advantage was that it was less flammable, and thus less hazardous, than the original napalm. Normally, thermite is the igniter.

In the Middle East, Israel used napalm during the 1967 Six-Day War and in the 1980s in Lebanon. Egypt employed it in the 1973 Ramadan War (Yom Kippur War). Coalition forces also used napalm during the Persian Gulf War in 1991 to ignite the oil-filled fire trenches that formed part of the Iraqi barrier in southern Kuwait. The Saddam Hussein regime also subsequently employed napalm and chemical attacks

A village attacked during the Korean War by United Nations Command aircraft employing napalm. Prisoner interrogation determined that napalm was the most feared of all weapons employed by the U.S. Far East Air Force in the conflict. (National Archives)

against the Kurdish population in northern Iraq. Although the U.S. Department of Defense denied the use of napalm during the Iraq War (2003–2011), apparently incendiary weapons were employed against Iraqi troops in the course of the drive north to Baghdad, although these consisted primarily of kerosene-based jet fuel (which has a smaller concentration of benzene) rather than the traditional mixture of gasoline and benzene used for napalm.

Napalm is particularly effective against people caught in the open, who have little defense against it. Death results not only from the burning but from asphyxiation. Only those on the perimeter of the strike zone usually survive a napalm attack, although they may suffer severe burns.

Further Reading

Bjornerstedt, Rolf, et al. *Napalm and Other Incendiary Weapons and All Aspects of Their Possible Use.* New York: United Nations, 1973.

Kerr, E. Bartlett. *Flames over Tokyo: The U.S. Army Air Forces' Incendiary Campaign against Japan, 1944–1945.* New York: Donald I. Fine, 1991.

Stockholm International Peace Research Institute. *Incendiary Weapons.* Cambridge, MA: MIT Press, 1975.

Proximity Fuze

A proximity fuze is a fuze that detonates its explosive device within the optimal distance from its target, as opposed to fuzes set to explode at a specific time after firing or fuzes that point-detonate. The proximity fuze is most often employed today with field artillery shells, although it was developed originally for antiaircraft artillery. Shells armed with mechanical time fuzes were extremely difficult to set accurately because of the problems involved with determining an aircraft's altitude and position, plus whatever evasive action the aircraft pilot might take. The proximity fuze was designed to detonate when the projectile got sufficiently close to the target, regardless of the time of flight involved. Most proximity fuzes used for field artillery produce a uniform 20-meter height of burst over the target.

The British, who led the world in radar, also pioneered development of the proximity fuze, beginning in 1939. In August 1940 the British shared with the U.S. government their research into radar and the proximity fuze. The proximity fuze employed a micro radar unit mounted in the fuze body. When radar response indicated that an object was within a set range, the signal detonated the shell. Because of its size, the fuze was limited to shells of 75mm or greater size.

The Americans called it the VT fuze, standing for "variable time." The proximity fuze was a closely guarded secret, and fears that it might be compromised led to orders that initially prohibited its use except in actions over water. The proximity fuze was first successfully employed in June 1943, in 5-inch shells fired by the U.S. cruiser *Helena* to shoot down a Japanese bomber. The fuze proved of immense importance to naval units in defending against Japanese kamikaze aircraft. The British also employed the proximity fuze in antiaircraft guns against the German V-1 buzz bomb. Reportedly such fuzes were a key factor in allowing the British to shoot down 79 percent of the V-1s in the first week of the buzz bomb offensive. The proximity fuze was first used in land fighting on the continent of Europe during the desperate fighting of the Battle of the Bulge in December 1944, when it proved highly effective in producing airbursts against German troops in the open. It was first employed in the Pacific theater over land in the shelling of Iwo Jima in February 1945. Although the Germans began work on such a device, neither they nor the Japanese produced one during the war.

Further Reading
Baldwin, Ralph B. *The Deadly Fuze*. London: Jane's, 1980.
Hogg, Ivan V. *The Illustrated Encyclopedia of Artillery*. London: Hutchinson, 1987.

Panzerfaust

German antitank weapon developed during World War II, the world's first expendable antitank weapon and in effect the world's first rocket-propelled grenade. At the beginning of the war the German Army deployed antitank rifles, including the 9.92mm BzB-39 firing a tungsten-coated bullet. Improvements in armor rendered these weapons largely ineffective, however.

At the end of 1942 the Germans deployed an inexpensive, single-shot, light-weight antitank weapon utilizing a shaped charge warhead. Known as the Panzerfaust (tank fist), such weapons were easily manufactured and could be fired by one man. The Panzerfaust consisted of a very simple small-diameter disposable launcher preloaded with a three-foot-long finned projectile with an oversized warhead. The hollow tube concentrated the escaping gases away from the gunner and made the firing recoilless. Plunging the trigger ignited a small charge of propellant inside the tube, driving the projectile toward its target and exploding on impact. The warhead was a hollow or shaped charge utilizing the Munro effect, whereby the detonation of a shaped explosive charge around an open-ended cavity concentrates that blast in that direction. The resulting plasma jet penetrated the armor and killed the tank crew.

The first type was the Panzerfaust 30, firing a 6.4-pound projectile. It had a maximum effective range of only 30 meters. The Panzerfaust 60, introduced in August 1944, was the most common version. It had a practical range of 60 meters. At that distance, it took the projectile 1.5 seconds to reach its target. The Panzerfaust 100 was the final model produced in any significant quantity; it entered service at the end of 1944. Its operational range was about 100 meters. The Panzerfaust 150 entered production only in March 1945. It had a redesigned warhead and a two-stage ignition with higher velocity and greater armor penetration. Unlike its predecessors, it was designed to be reloaded. The first type Panzerfaust could penetrate 140mm of armor, while the final type could penetrate 200mm, more than sufficient to defeat the principal U.S. tank, the M4 Sherman, or any British tank. Only the most heavily armored Soviet tanks could withstand it.

Although lightweight, the Panzerfaust was a short-range weapon that required considerable courage to employ. Firing it immediately telegraphed the user's location. The Germans produced millions of these weapons in the course of the war. They were particularly effective in close-range city combat.

Further Reading

Fleischer, Wolfgang. *Panzerfaust and Other German Infantry Anti-Tank Weapons*. Atglen, PA: Schiffer, 1994.

Martin, A. R. F., and S. A. B. Hitchins. *Development of the Panzerfaust*. London: British Intelligence Objectives Sub Committee, 1945.

Bazooka

The bazooka, a U.S. antitank weapon developed during World War II, was based on the hollow or shaped charge principle. By the spring of 1942, the U.S. Army had

U.S. soldier demonstrating the M1 2.36-inch bazooka in 1943. (Library of Congress)

produced an excellent shaped-charge antitank grenade, the M10, but it lacked an effective means of delivery. Someone suggested attaching the grenade to a rocket. Rocket pioneer Robert H. Goddard had developed a tubed rocket for the army in 1918, but the end of World War I had put an end to such experiments.

Captain Leslie A. Skinner and Lieutenant David E. Uhl at Aberdeen Proving Ground had developed their own rocket and tube launcher, and in May 1943 they attached the M10s to the rocket and tested it against a tank target with success. Skinner named the new weapon the "bazooka" after a long tubular musical instrument devised by comedian Bob Burns.

U.S. Army chief of staff General George C. Marshall learned of the experiments and immediately ordered production of 5,000 bazookas—now officially designated Launcher, Rocket, Anti-Tank, M1—to be ready in 30 days. It is a considerable testimony to American manufacturing that this deadline was indeed met, with 89 minutes to spare.

The bazooka consisted of a rocket and launcher, operated by a two-man crew of gunner and loader. The launcher was a tube with a shoulder stock. The handgrip contained a trigger assembly that was an electric generator used to send a current along a wire. Each rocket had two wires extending from the nozzle at its rear; when the rocket was packed, the wires were tucked along the body and grounded with a shorting cap. The loader pulled off the shorting cap before he placed the rocket in the rear of the launcher and then individually tied off the wires against electrical posts at the back of the launch tube. When the gunner squeezed the trigger, it generated an electric current through the wires to ignite the solid fuel in the rocket.

The rocket had a diameter of 2.36 inches, and its tube launcher was 54 inches long. The rocket weighed 3.5 pounds, and tube and rocket together were 18 pounds. The 2.36-inch rocket could penetrate about 80 millimeters of armor and proved highly effective against German and Japanese tanks. The Germans used captured bazookas to produce their Raketenpanzerbüsche 54, also known as the Panzerschreck (tank terror). It in turn spurred the Americans to upgrade from a 2.36-inch to a 3.5-inch rocket.

During the Korean War, the 2.36-inch rocket proved ineffective against the North Koreans' better-armored Russian T-34 tank. The 3.5-inch M20 Super Bazooka arrived in Korea by mid-July 1950. Putting more gas at greater temperature inside a tank, it knocked out the T-34s, the chief communist advantage in the early phase of the war.

Further Reading

Gander, Terry J. *Anti-Tank Weapons.* Marlborough, UK: Crowood, 2000.

Gander, Terry J. *The Bazooka: Hand-Held Hollow-Charge Anti-Tank Weapons.* London: PRC Publishing, 1998.

Weeks, John S. *Men against Tanks: A History of Anti-Tank Warfare.* Newton Abbot, UK: David and Charles, 1975.

Katyusha Rocket

The Soviet Union's Katyusha multiple rocket launcher was developed by a design team headed by Gregory E. Langemak at the Leningrad Gas Dynamics Laboratory beginning in 1938 and was in direct response to German development in 1936 of the six-barrel Nebelwerfer rocket mortar. At first intended for aircraft, it was approved on June 21, 1941, on the eve of the German invasion of the Soviet Union. It was first employed in combat in a truck-mounted mode by the Red Army against the Germans in July 1941. The rockets were unofficially named for the title of a popular Russian wartime song, with "Katyusha" a diminutive for Ekaterina (Catherine). The Germans knew the weapon for its distinctive sound as the Stalinorgel (Stalin Organ).

The unguided Katyusha rocket appeared in a variety of sizes. The first was the BM-8 (BM for *boyevaya mashina,* meaning "combat vehicle") 82mm, but by the end of the war the Soviets were using BM-13 132mm rocket launchers. Its rocket was nearly six feet in length, weighed 92 pounds, and had a range of about three miles. Such rockets could be armed with high-explosive, incendiary, or chemical warheads. Although not an accurate weapon, the Katyusha could be extremely

Soviet Katyusha multiple rocket launchers during the Battle of Kursk in 1943. The Red Army made extensive use of the Katyushas in its operations during the Second World War. (Slava Katamidze Collection/Getty Images)

effective in saturation bombardment when large numbers of launch trucks were deployed side by side.

The launch system consisted of a series of parallel rails, with a folding frame that was raised in order to bring the rockets into firing position. The Katyusha launchers were mounted on a variety of truck beds to fire forward over the cab. Each truck deployed between 14 and 48 launchers. Trucks included the Soviet ZiS-6 and the Lend-Lease–supplied and U.S.-manufactured Studebaker US6 2.5-ton. Katyusha launchers were also mounted on T-40 and T-60 tanks and on aircraft against German tanks. They also appeared on ships and riverine vessels in a ground-support role. Fire planners were not fond of the multiple launch system, as it took up to 50 minutes to load and fired only 24 rounds, whereas a conventional howitzer could fire four to six times as many rounds in a comparable time period.

Katyushas continued to undergo refinement. During the Cold War, Soviet forces were equipped with the BM-24, 240mm Katyushas, which had a range of about six miles. Each truck mounted 12 rockets. Two racks, one of top of the other, contained 6 rockets each.

In 1963 the Soviets introduced the 122mm BM-21 launcher for the 9M22M Katyusha. The most successful Katyusha, it was exported to more than 50 countries. Even larger 220mm and 300mm Katyushas were developed. The name has, however, become a generic term applied to all small artillery rockets, even those developed by Israel and based on Katyushas captured during the 1967 Six-Day War. Their light artillery rocket has a range of some 27 miles and can be loaded with a variety of different munitions. It was employed in the 1973 Ramadan War

(Yom Kippur War). Katyushas were also employed by communist forces during the Vietnam War, by Hezbollah and Islamic Jihad militants against Israel, and by insurgents during the Iraq War (2003–2011). It has been estimated that in the fighting between Israel and Hezbollah in Lebanon during July–August 2006, Hezbollah launched as many as 4,000 Katyusha rockets against the Jewish state, with about one-quarter of them hitting densely populated civilian areas. The United States developed the tactical high-energy laser system specifically to defeat the Katyusha during flight.

The U.S. counterpart to the Katyusha is the multiple-launch rocket system M270. The tracked M270 vehicle fires 12 8.9-inch (227mm) 13-foot-long unguided rockets from two self-contained six-round pods.

Further Reading

Bellamy, Chris. *Red God of War: Soviet Artillery and Rocket Forces.* Herdon, VA: Potomac Books, 1986.

O'Malley, T. J. *Artillery: Guns and Rocket Systems.* Mechanicsburg, PA: Stackpole, 1994.

V-I Buzz Bomb

The German V-1 buzz bomb of World War II was the world's first operational cruise missile. The V-1 and the later V-2 guided missile were German leader Adolf Hitler's *Vergeltungswaffe* (vengeance) weapons directed against England, with which he hoped to turn the tide of war.

The V-1 was basically a pilotless pulse-jet aircraft. Begun as part of a secret program in 1938 to develop new aircraft propulsion systems, it utilized a pulse-jet engine designed in 1928. In June 1942 the Luftwaffe directed that it be turned into a flying bomb. The first V-1 flew in December 1942. The V-1 emerged as a 25-foot-long midwing monoplane with a 17.6-foot wingspan and a 1,870-pound warhead. It had a speed of 360 miles per hour and a range of 200 miles. Guidance was by means of a gyro-based autopilot. A small nose propeller connected to a counter determined the range. The propeller spun in flight, and when the counter reached a preset number of rotations, it cut off fuel to the engine, causing the V-1 to fall to the ground. The V-1 could be launched either by aircraft or from land, the latter by means of a steam-powered catapult. The name "buzz bomb" came from the sputtering sound of the V-1 as it flew.

Although the Germans would have preferred to wait until stockpiles could be amassed and hardened sites prepared, the Allied landing in Normandy on June 6, 1944, forced a decision, and on June 12 Hitler ordered the offensive to commence. Beginning the next day, the Germans sent V-1s against London and English coastal cities. In all, the Germans sent more than 7,900 V-1s against Britain and another 4,883 against the port of Antwerp. V-1s are believed to have killed 6,184 people and injured an additional 17,981.

The introduction of the V weapons did force the Allies to divert substantial antiaircraft assets against them, including guns, aircraft, and personnel. The V-1 moved at sufficiently low speed that intercepting pilots could on occasion use their own plane's wing tips to lift one of its wings and cause it to spin out of control. The Allies also diverted a large number of bombers to try to destroy the launch sites, which were difficult to locate. Although the V-1 was relatively ineffective, it marked the arrival of a new age in warfare.

Further Reading

Hogg, Ivan V. *German Secret Weapons of the Second World War.* London: Greenhill Books, 1999.

Kay, A. L. *German Jet Engine and Gas Turbine Development, 1930–1945.* Shrewsbury, UK: Airlife, 2002.

Pocock, Rowland. *German Guided Missiles.* New York: Arco, 1967.

V-2 Guided Missile

The V-2 for *Vergeltungswaffe* 2 (Vengeance Weapon 2) followed the V-1 buzz bomb into service against Britain. Totally different in concept from the pulse-jet V-1, the V-2 was the first operational ballistic missile. Employed against England for the first time on September 8, 1944, the V-2 had its origins in the Versailles Treaty following World War I. Because the treaty denied Germany heavy artillery and military aircraft, the German military embraced rocket technology. Key figures in early development work were chief of the Army Weapons Bureau Karl Becker and Walter Dornberger. The initial focus on solid-fuel rockets soon gave way to liquid-fuel designs, especially when scientist Werner von Braun joined the group in 1932.

The first test firing in the A liquid-fuel rocket design series occurred when an A-2 was launched from Borkum Island in the Baltic Sea in 1934. The more powerful A-3 followed, and in 1937 research moved to an expanded secret test center at Peenemünde on the Baltic. German leader Adolf Hitler had little interest in the program initially. Only with German military reverses was it accelerated, at great cost, in December 1942. An A-4, which entered service as the V-2, was launched for the first time on October 3, 1943. Production began in June 1944, and it entered service in September.

The V-2 was 46 feet long, had a launch weight of 26,665 pounds, and was powered to a maximum speed of 3,600 miles per hour by a mixture of alcohol and liquid oxygen. It carried a 2,150-pound warhead and had a maximum range of some 200 miles. A gyroscopic autopilot controlled flight by moving graphite fins located in the rocket engine's exhaust. The first V-2s used a radio-controlled fuel cutoff device to control range, but most V-2s utilized an accelerometer for that purpose.

The Germans launched more than 3,000 V-2s. Between September 8, 1945, and March 27, 1945, 1,054 fell on England, 517 hitting London. More than 2,700

Londoners died in the attacks. Nearly as many V-2s were fired against the Allied supply port of Antwerp. The Germans planned other missiles: a lighter A-9, with a range of 400 miles and radio guidance, and an A-10 two-stage intercontinental missile with a range of 2,800 miles.

The V-1 and V-2 forced the diversion of significant air defense resources, although it was impossible to intercept the V-2, which was launched almost vertically, climbed to an altitude of 60 miles, and then plunged back to Earth. The Allies also diverted substantial bomber assets in only partially successful efforts to destroy both the missiles and their mobile launch sites. Hitler hoped that the V weapons would tip the balance, but although they killed nearly 12,000 people and injured another 53,000, they came too late in the war to affect the course of events. The V-1 and V-2, however, marked a new era in weapons technology.

Further Reading

Hogg, Ivan V. *German Secret Weapons of the Second World War.* London: Greenhill Books, 1999.

Neufeld, Michael J. *The Rocket and the Reich: Peenemünde and the Coming of the Ballistic Missile Era.* New York: Free Press, 1995.

Pocock, Rowland. *German Guided Missiles.* New York: Arco, 1967.

Kamikazes

"Kamikaze" is the American term for Japanese World War II suicide aircraft. In Japanese it means "divine wind" and was the name given to the typhoon that saved Japan from an invasion by Kublai Khan's Mongol army in 1281.

Vice Admiral Onishi Takijiro first proposed suicide attacks to the First Air Fleet during the Battle of Leyte Gulf (October 23–26, 1944). The Kamikaze Special Attack Corps entered battle on October 25, when Lieutenant Seki Yukio, flying a Zero armed with a 550-pound bomb, struck and badly damaged the U.S. Navy escort carrier (CVE) *Santee.* Other CVEs were also struck, including the *St. Lô,* which suffered internal explosions before breaking apart and sinking. Impressed by these results, the Japanese expanded kamikaze operations. Other types of aircraft were adapted for suicide missions, including dive-bombers and medium bombers. Kamikazes participated in the defense of Luzon but failed to prevent the U.S. landings there.

In August 1944 the Japanese Navy had begun experiments with a specialized, piloted glide bomb. This single-seat craft, named Oka II (Cherry Blossom), carried a 2,640-pound warhead and was designed to be carried to its target by a twin-engine Betty bomber. The Americans dubbed it the Baka (Fool). A new volunteer unit, the Jinrai Butai (Corps of Divine Thunder), manned the Oka IIs, which were to operate from bases in the Philippines, Formosa (Taiwan), and Okinawa. This effort was dealt a serious blow when 50 Okas were lost in the November 29 sinking

Determination and pride show in the faces of these young Japanese kamikaze pilots in 1945. They would attempt to crash their aircraft into Allied ships. Kamikaze, meaning "divine wind," refers to a typhoon that forced Mongol invaders to quit Japan in 1281. (Library of Congress)

of the giant Japanese aircraft carrier *Shinano* by a U.S. submarine. Okas saw service in the Battle for Okinawa, but most were intercepted and shot down still attached to their mother planes.

The heaviest use of kamikazes occurred in the Battle for Okinawa in the spring of 1945. During the two months that the U.S. Navy was off Okinawa it underwent 2,482 kamikaze attacks (1,298 by the army and 1,184 navy). The U.S. Navy aircraft carrier *Franklin* was especially hard hit. Although heroic crew efforts saved the ship, 724 men were casualties, the highest total of any surviving U.S. Navy ship in any war.

Although never operational, other piloted-bomb kamikaze prototypes were in development at war's end, including the jet engine–powered Oka Model 22, the turbo-jet Kikka (Mandarine Orange Blossom), the pulse-jet Baika (Plum Blossom), and the Shinryu (Divine Dragon) glider launched by solid fuel rockets. The Japanese Army also produced the Tsurugi (Sword), similar to the navy's reciprocating engine-powered Toka (Wisteria Blossom).

During the war, 3,940 Japanese aircrew died in 2,443 army and navy aircraft involved in kamikaze missions. Although their effectiveness declined because of Allied countermeasures, kamikazes did inflict heavy losses. They also influenced the U.S. decision to employ the atomic bomb.

The largest kamikaze was in fact the battleship *Yamato*. Dispatched on a one-way mission to Okinawa, it was attacked and sunk by U.S. aircraft on April 7, 1945.

Further Reading

Inoguchi Rikihei and Tadashi Nakajima with Roger Pineau. *The Divine Wind: Japan's Kamikaze Force in World War II.* New York: Bantam Books, 1978.

Millot, Bernard. *Divine Thunder: The Life and Death of the Kamikazes.* Translated by Lowell Blair. New York: McCall, 1970.

Penicillin

Penicillin is an antibiotic agent first discovered in 1928 by Alexander Fleming in London and made available for widespread use during World War II. Discovered by happenstance as he was conducting research on staph infection, a potentially lethal malady spread by bacteria and that usually begins on the skin, Fleming observed that a mold contaminating one of his cultures had caused the bacteria to stop growing. He then transferred some of the mold to another culture, with the same result. The mold belongs to the genus *Penicillum,* which prompted Fleming to name it penicillin.

Penicillin and its related products are effective mainly against gram-positive bacteria; the drug has shown to be largely ineffective for gram-negative bacteria. Since its discovery, many variations of penicillin have been produced, widening its appeal and therapeutic qualities. Penicillin also led researchers to develop other kinds of antibiotics, including those treating gram-negative bacteria.

By the late 1930s, research at Oxford University proved that penicillin was highly effective in treating a wide variety of bacterial infections in animals, principally mice. In the spring of 1941 the first trials on humans took place, with dramatic results for patients who were desperately ill and who in all likelihood would have died without the drug. During 1942, 122 million units of penicillin were cultured and made available for clinical trials at the Mayo Clinic and at Yale University.

By the early spring of 1943, 200 patients in the United States had been given the drug, with results so impressive that U.S. surgeon general Thomas Parran Jr. ordered drug trials carried out at a military hospital. Soon the drug was widely available in hospitals, including military hospitals in the United States and overseas. By 1943 problems had been overcome, and manufacturing plants in the United States were churning out millions of doses of the drug; by war's end, 23 plants around the country were producing penicillin. Between 1943 and 1945, the U.S. military was consuming 85 percent of the nation's output of the antibiotic, which in 1943 alone accounted for 231 billion units.

There can be no doubt that penicillin revolutionized medicine in the 1940s, particularly military medicine. Indeed, many soldiers stricken with communicable diseases or infections stemming from wounds or surgery who otherwise would have died were saved by penicillin. The incidence of death from disease and/or wounds during World War II was 0.6 per 1,000; during World War I, less than 30 years prior, the death rate for soldiers was 16.5 per 1,000. Only 4 percent of soldiers who were admitted to a hospital during World War II died; during World War I, the death rate for soldiers in hospitals was double that at 8 percent.

Further Reading

Cowdrey, Albert E. *Fighting for Life: American Military Medicine in World War II.* New York: Free Press, 1994.

Wilson, David. *In Search of Penicillin.* New York: Knopf, 1976.

Enigma Machine

The Enigma was an encoding machine invented by a German, Dr. Arthur Scherbius, and demonstrated at the 1923 International Postal Congress as a commercial encoding device. The Enigma resembled a typewriter in appearance and had a series of rotors or wheels, the settings of which could be changed. Early versions of the device enabled the operator to encode a plain text in any of 150 million possible ways. An operator with a second Enigma machine set identically to the sending machine read the encoded radio message and decoded it. Settings were changed regularly according to a prearranged schedule in order to confound any interception and decoding.

As with all the major military powers, the Germans sought a secure means of military communications. They assumed that messages encoded by Enigma were unbreakable. By 1928 the

A German Enigma cipher machine, employed during World War II to encrypt communications. It somewhat resembles a typewriter in appearance. Unknown to its users, the western Allies were able to read its messages. Intelligence gleaned in this fashion considerably shortened the war. (National Cryptologic Museum/National Security Agency)

Code Breaking and the Battle of Midway

Code breaking was essential in the U.S. victory in the June 3–6, 1942, Battle of Midway, regarded by U.S. Pacific Fleet commander Admiral Chester Nimitz as the event that "made everything else possible." U.S. code breaking revealed the broad outlines of the Japanese plan.

The Japanese had repeatedly referred to the objective of their naval operation as "AF." With "AF" believed to be Midway Island, the commander there was ordered to broadcast that his water pump was out. The Japanese then relayed the message by radio that the water pump was out at "AF."

Nimitz packed Midway with bombers and set an ambush position for the three American carriers some 300 miles northeast of Midway, hoping that he might be able to catch the Japanese carriers with their planes on their decks while avoiding the same himself. Although luck certainly played a key role in the ensuing U.S. victory, which saw the destruction of four Japanese carriers for only one American carrier lost, success surely rested in the superiority of American intelligence information regarding the Japanese plan.

German military was using the Enigma machine. Japan and Italy also bought and utilized the machine. Other countries, such as the United States, purchased the Enigma but did not attempt to unlock its secrets.

The Poles, concerned about a resurgent Germany as a threat to their own security, in 1928 formed a special cryptography group at the University of Poznan. They also purchased the commercial model of Enigma, and by 1935 they had broken into the German radio codes, information that they largely shared with the British and French in 1938. Late that same year, however, the Germans added a sixth rotor, which helped to convince the Poles that the Germans were about to make an aggressive military move. The Poles modified their own machines to keep up with the German advances and continued to break into the German codes, but the defeat of their country in September 1939 came too quickly for Enigma to be of utility to them.

On the defeat of Poland, the Polish code breakers and their machines were spirited out to France and England. At Bletchley Park outside of Buckingham the British assembled a mixed group of experts to continue the work begun by the Poles. Over time Bletchley Park developed additional devices that could sort through the possible variations of an encoded text, although the Enigma's changeable settings meant that most messages could not be read in real time. Intelligence gathered from Enigma traffic was given the code name of Ultra.

The Germans continued throughout the war to make refinements to the Enigma machine. Secure in their belief that its messages could not be read, the Germans continued to rely on Enigma throughout the war. Obviously, land-line communication was even more secure, and Adolf Hitler's proscription on radio communication concerning the December 1944 Ardennes Offensive and Allied complacency led to its concealment from the Allies until the attack began. One of the great myths of the war, however, was that British prime minister Winston Churchill knew from Ultra intercepts that the Germans intended to bomb the city of Coventry but did not act to prevent it for fear of making the Germans aware of the successful code-breaking operation.

Ultra intelligence proved invaluable in the Allied military effort on a variety of fronts and undoubtedly shortened the war. Information on Ultra was not made public until 1974, when Group Captain F. W. Winterbotham published *The Ultra Secret*. Its revelations forced the rewriting of most earlier histories of the war.

Further Reading

Lewin, Ronald. *Ultra Goes to War.* New York: McGraw-Hill, 1978.

Winterbotham, F. W. *The Ultra Secret.* New York: Harper and Row, 1974.

Atomic Bomb

An atomic bomb is an explosive device employing certain radioactive isotopes (uranium 235, plutonium 239) to achieve a critical mass leading to a chain reaction in which neutrons split the nuclei of atoms. This process, known as nuclear fission, releases mass in the form of tremendous heat energy equivalent to several tons of TNT.

German scientists were in 1938 the first to achieve the fission of uranium, and physicists realized that this process might be used to create a weapon of mass destruction. A number of prominent scientists including Albert Einstein, Enrico Fermi, and Leo Szilard had left Europe to live in the United States. Szilard and Fermi convinced Einstein to send a letter to President Franklin D. Roosevelt in August 1939 in which he warned that the Germans could produce an atomic weapon. That same year Roosevelt provided modest research funding, and scientists at five U.S. universities began to conduct experiments related to nuclear energy. On December 6, 1941, Roosevelt authorized $2 billion for the Manhattan Engineering District (Manhattan Project), earmarked for the specific purpose of creating an atomic bomb. U.S. Army brigadier general Leslie Groves had charge of it, while physicist Robert Oppenheimer was its scientific leader.

In December 1942 at the University of Chicago, a team of nuclear physicists led by Fermi produced the first controlled and self-sustaining nuclear fission reaction. Project facilities were subsequently constructed in Oak Ridge, Tennessee; Hanford, Washington; and Los Alamos, New Mexico. Ultimately the project involved some 120,000 individuals, including scientists, engineers, machinists, and other skilled craftsman. Oppenheimer and his team successfully constructed and then detonated the world's first atomic bomb on July 16, 1945, at Los Alamos.

The atomic bomb cloud over the Japanese city of Hiroshima, August 6, 1945, just two minutes after the 12.5 million kiloton explosion below. (Corel)

Roosevelt's successor, President Harry S. Truman, authorized employment of the atomic bomb against Japan. The first bomb fell on Hiroshima on August 6, 1945, and a second bomb was dropped on Nagasaki three days later. The Hiroshima bomb, "Little Boy," consisted of a uranium isotope 235 core shielded by several hundred pounds of lead, encased in explosives designed to condense the uranium and initiate a fission reaction. It had an explosive force equivalent to 12.5 kilotons of TNT. "Fat Boy," the bomb dropped on Nagasaki, was a plutonium nuclear fission bomb. Its plutonium 238 isotope core consisted of two melon-shaped hemispheres surrounded by a ring of explosive charges designed to drive the sections together, achieving critical mass. The resulting chain reaction released a force equivalent to 22 kilotons of energy.

As tensions increased between the United States and the Soviet Union, the U.S. monopoly of the atomic bomb became the cornerstone of American policy designed to contain Soviet expansion. The first U.S. war plan that included the use of atomic weapons was completed in August 1947 and called for the dropping of atomic bombs on specific key governmental and other targets within the Soviet Union. The planners assumed that bombs dropped on several high-profile targets would have such a profound psychological impact that the Soviets would surrender.

By the end of 1948, the United States had produced about 100 atomic bombs. It also developed a war plan, Fleetwood, that called for a preemptive atomic attack during which the United States would deliver approximately 80 percent of its stockpile of atomic weapons in a single strike. In this Washington planned for a first-strike atomic response to any surprise Soviet attack. The assumption behind this was that employment of atomic weapons would give the United States time to mobilize and deploy its conventional forces. This emphasis on nuclear weapons led to a decision in Washington to invest only minimal sums in conventional forces.

Decision to Employ the Atomic Bomb

While the decision to employ the atomic bomb is now a controversial issue and some U.S. leaders did oppose the bomb's use, the American people did not regard it as such in August 1945. Historians point out that President Harry S. Truman employed the bomb to end the war quickly, and there is every indication that costly as the two bombs were in terms of human lives lost, their use may actually have saved Japanese lives by giving Japanese emperor Hirohito the excuse to order his armed forces to surrender. This decision prevented the certain starvation of hundreds of thousands of Japanese and the high cost in casualties of a U.S. land invasion of the Japanese home islands. Needless to say, the Japanese decision for peace also saved American lives in an invasion of Japan. One historian has estimated that the first phase of the invasion of Japan, the conquest of the island of Kyushu planned for November 1945, would have taken two months and resulted in 75,000 to 100,000 U.S. casualties. Other historians claim that Truman was in part motivated by a desire to warn the Soviet Union against additional territorial expansion and to avoid having to share the occupation of Japan with the Soviet Union.

The Soviet Union meanwhile was frantically working to develop its own atomic bomb, an effort accelerated by the activities of its spies in the United States. The Soviet Union detonated its first atomic bomb on August 29, 1949. This development shocked Washington and ultimately led to a nuclear arms race between the two Cold War superpowers. Both sides developed ever more powerful atomic weapons and finally the hydrogen bomb.

Further Reading

Holloway, David. *Stalin and the Bomb: The Soviet Union and Atomic Energy, 1939–1956.* New Haven, CT: Yale University Press, 1994.

Rhodes, Richard. *The Making of an Atomic Bomb.* New York: Simon and Schuster, 1986.

Serber, Robert. *The Los Alamos Primer: The First Lectures on How to Build an Atomic Bomb.* Los Angeles: University of California Press, 1992.

Hydrogen Bomb

A hydrogen bomb is a thermonuclear weapon that unleashes far more devastating power than an atomic bomb. Unlike an atomic bomb that relies on the fission (or splitting) of radioactive isotopes, the hydrogen bomb (H-bomb) relies on the fusion of hydrogen isotopes. Fusion occurs when neutrons collide with an unstable hydrogen isotope, causing two lighter isotopes to join together to make a heavier element. During the fusion process some of the mass of the original isotopes is released as energy, resulting in a powerful explosion. Because of the loss of mass, the end product, or element, weighs less than the total of the original isotopes.

Hydrogen bombs are referred to as thermonuclear devices because temperatures of 400 million degrees Celsius are required for the fusion process to begin. In order to produce these temperatures, a hydrogen bomb has an atomic bomb at its core. The explosion of the atomic device and the fission process in turn lead to the fusion process in hydrogen isotopes that surround the atomic core. Depending on its size, a hydrogen bomb can produce an explosion powerful enough to devastate an area of approximately 150 square miles, while the searing heat and toxic radioactive fallout from such devices can impact an area of more than 800 square miles.

The explosion of an atomic bomb by the Soviet Union in September 1949 ended the U.S. atomic monopoly and led to a nuclear arms race. Cold War tensions were then running high. Nuclear physicist Edward Teller, commissioner of U.S. Atomic Energy Commission Lewis Strauss, and other scientists formed a coalition together with military officials to urge President Harry S. Truman to initiate a program to construct a superweapon, the hydrogen bomb. This new weapon would be measured in megatons instead of kilotons and could yield an explosion equivalent to millions of tons of TNT. Despite opposition from Robert Oppenheimer and several other nuclear scientists, Truman, under siege by Republican critics as being soft on communism, authorized a hydrogen bomb program in January 1950.

The first successful test of a hydrogen bomb. Known as Operation IVY MIKE, it took place at Enewetak Atoll in the Pacific on November 1, 1952. This photo was taken 50 miles from the detonation site. The cloud ultimately pushed upward some 25 miles, deep in the stratosphere. (U.S. Air Force)

It took the combined efforts of a number of scientists as well as Stanislaw Ulam, a mathematician, to solve the theoretical and technical problems related to building a hydrogen weapon. They carried out their work at Los Alamos, New Mexico, the same facility that had helped produce the atomic bomb. The prototype hydrogen bomb was first detonated on November 1, 1952, on Enewetak (Eniwetok) Atoll in the South Pacific. The explosion virtually obliterated the island, creating a crater a mile wide and 175 feet deep.

Following the detonation of the prototype, scientists constructed a hydrogen bomb that could be dropped by aircraft. That weapon was tested successfully in 1954. The Soviet Union tested its own hydrogen bomb on August 12, 1953. The British also developed a hydrogen weapon, which they tested on May 15, 1957. The development of more powerful weapons such as the hydrogen bomb and of new methods of delivering nuclear bombs, such as ballistic missiles, were primarily a result of the Cold War conflict and the concomitant arms race.

Further Reading

Kaplan, Fred. *The Wizards of Armageddon: Strategists of the Nuclear Age.* New York: Simon and Schuster, 1983.

Rhodes, Richard. *Dark Sun: The Making of the Hydrogen Bomb.* New York: Simon and Schuster, 1996.

Neutron Bomb

The neutron bomb, also known as an enhanced radiation warhead or bomb, is a small nuclear weapon designed to produce a relatively small blast effect that minimizes collateral damage yet releases high amounts of radiation to inflict maximum personnel casualties. Neutron radiation is particularly effective against armored vehicle crews, as steel can only slightly reduce the effect. Indeed, some armor compounds employ depleted uranium that can compound the effects of radiation.

Utilizing large amounts of tritium, the neutron bomb's blast and heat effects extend over a radius of only several hundred yards, but the neutron and gamma radiation effect it produces goes much farther. The blast effects quickly dissipate but would completely disable tank crews and troops in the open in minutes, with most dying in a matter of days. Warheads of this type would also be useful in defending against a missile attack, with the radiation attacking enemy missile guidance systems. The neutron bomb can be delivered by missile or by attack aircraft.

Development of the neutron bomb is attributed to Samuel Cohen of the Lawrence Livermore laboratory beginning in 1958, although the project proceeded in fits and starts. While the United States produced the first neutron bomb, a number of other nations including Russia, China, and Israel also have the weapon. Radiation-absorbing armor has been developed to help counter its effects, including the use of special plastics.

Further Reading

Auger, Vincent A. *Dynamics of Foreign Policy Analysis: The Carter Administration and the Neutron Bomb.* Oxford, UK: Rowman and Littlefield, 1986.

Cohen, Sam. *The Truth about the Neutron Bomb: The Inventor Speaks Out.* New York: William Morrow, 1983.

AK47 Kalashnikov Assault Rifle

The Soviet AK47 assault rifle was certainly the best-known and most commonly used assault weapon of the 20th century. Simple and rugged, it and the follow-on AK74 are still considered the ideal weapons for poorly trained troops operating in adverse conditions. Designed by Mikhail Kalashnikov in 1947 (hence the "47" designation) and adopted into service in 1949, the AK47 is easy to use, handles well, is simple to strip and assemble, and is very reliable.

An insurgent weapons cache containing hundreds of AK47 assault rifles captured during the Iraq War. The AK47, developed by Russian arms designer Mikhail Kalashnikov in 1947, is the world's best known and most utilized assault rifle. (Department of Defense)

The selective-fire 7.62mm Avtomat Kalashnikova assault rifle has appeared in a wide number of variants. The original AK47 is made predominately of milled steel components and was issued with either wooden or folding metal stocks. Because the parts have considerable clearance, the weapon is not likely to jam in mud or sand, which fall away in use as the parts move. The later AKM (M for "modernized") of 1955 differs from the AK47 chiefly in the extensive use of stamped instead of milled receiver and an improved trigger/hammer unit.

The AKM has a muzzle compensator that is screwed onto the muzzle to deflect the blast of escaping propellant gases and reduce muzzle climb during firing. It also employs plastic in place of wood in the furniture. Both weapons are 34.25 inches in length and have a 16.3-inch barrel. They have a muzzle velocity of 2,410 feet per second and a cyclical rate of fire of 600 rounds per minute. Maximum effective range is about 400 yards.

The AK47 weighs 10.58 pounds, while the AKM is significantly lighter at only 8.87 pounds. From their inception both weapons employed a curved 30-round detachable magazine, although 40-round box magazines and 75-round drum magazines may also be employed. As with the U.S. M16, the AKM can be fitted with an underbarrel grenade launcher, in this case the GP-25 40mm.

Taking note of the advantages of the downsized-caliber U.S. M16 rifle that enabled an infantryman to carry more ammunition, the Soviets developed their own 5.56mm version of the AK47 and placed it in service in 1974, hence the AK74 designation. It proved even more reliable than the AK47, for the heavy bolt of the weapon worked effectively with the smaller rimmed cartridge.

Widely produced in the Soviet Union, the Soviet bloc, and the People's Republic of China during the Cold War, the AK family of weapons is still widely manufactured in many countries of the world today and not always under license. Estimates hold that more than 90 million AK-type firearms have been manufactured, making it the most widely produced infantry rifle in history.

Further Reading

Ezell, Edward Clinton, and Thomas M. Pegg. *Small Arms of the World: A Basic Manual of Small Arms.* Harrisburg, PA: Stackpole, 1983.

Rosa, Joseph G., and Robin May. *An Illustrated History of Guns and Small Arms.* London: Peerage Books, 1984.

Westwood, David. *Rifles: An Illustrated History of Their Impact.* Santa Barbara, CA: ABC-CLIO, 2005.

Recoilless Rifles

Recoilless rifles are large-caliber, direct-fire infantry weapons. In effect, they allow infantrymen to fire an artillery round–sized projectile from a bipod- or tripod-mounted weapon. Some of the smallest recoilless rifles also can be shoulder-fired, but such a procedure almost always results in unacceptable exposure to the gunner.

Recoil has long been a problem for artillery. Newton's Third Law states that "to every action there is an equal and opposite reaction." Thus, the burning gases that drive the projectile from the bore exert an equal pressure backward. Early artillery pieces without recoil mechanisms lurched backward, while large pistols and rifles still produce a sizable kick. This problem was resolved in artillery with recoil mechanisms of hydraulic buffers and springs. Such systems, however, greatly increase overall weight of the system, reducing mobility.

In the 1930s the Krupp armaments firm in Germany developed a lightweight gun for airborne and mountain troops. It featured a rocket nozzle at the breech of the gun that redirected much of the energy of the ignited propellant rearward. This eliminated much of the recoil and allowed a significant reduction in the weapon's overall weight. The negative to this was, however, the necessity of a larger shell, for to counterbalance the loss of recoil, the shell for a recoilless weapon had to have twice the powder charge of a conventional gun of equal caliber. The other negative to a recoilless weapon is its backblast, which is hazardous to anyone who might be behind the gun and immediately reveals the firing position to enemy observers.

The best-known recoilless rifles were those introduced by the United States. First developed in 1943 by the Frankfort Arsenal, the weapon was introduced into U.S. Army service in 1945 as the 57mm M18 and 75mm M20. These saw service in World War II.

A projectile fired by an M18 could penetrate one-inch armor. The M20 weighed 114 pounds and was more than seven feet in length, but its projectile was effective against four inches of armor. A 105mm M27 saw service in the Korean War, while the 90mm M67 and the 106mm M40, M40A1, and M40A2 were employed in the Vietnam War. The M40 also had a coaxially mounted .50-caliber spotting rifle.

Although primarily designed as antitank weapons, recoilless rifles proved particularly effective in knocking out enemy bunkers and machine-gun positions. During the Vietnam War, an antipersonnel round that fired thousands of small flechettes also proved especially effective.

The U.S. Marine Corps acquired 300 M50 Ontos (Greek for "Thing") light airborne tanks. The Ontos was an armored personnel carrier chassis fitted with a pyramidal-shaped hull. Six M40A1 recoilless rifles were then mounted on the hull, three on either side. The top tube had a spotting rifle, and the tubes could be fired individually or in salvo. The Ontos was deployed to Vietnam but withdrawn from service in 1970. Its chief drawback was the necessity to load the recoilless rifles from outside the vehicle.

The Soviets also developed recoilless rifles, as did other nations. The Swedish Carl Gustav 84mm M2 was a highly successful steel rifled weapon that fired a high-explosive antitank (HEAT) round and could penetrate 400mm armor. It could also fire high-explosive (HE), smoke, and illumination rounds. U.S. Army Rangers and Special Forces and armies of a dozen countries in the 1990s adopted the lightweight M3, 84mm version. Both the M2 and M3 have a 3x telescopic sight. The M3 weights 18.7 pounds and fires a wide variety of rounds, including HEAT, HE, fragmentation, illumination, and smoke. The Swedish PV-1110 Recoilless Rifle is a 90mm weapon that weighs 572 pounds and is mounted on a light vehicle. It has a 7.62mm spotting rifle above its main barrel. The French ACL-APX is an 80mm recoilless rifle that fires a projectile that then ignites a rocket motor to propel the rocket to the target. It has a maximum effective range of about 660 yards, with the projectile reaching its target in only 1.25 seconds.

The recoilless rifle differs from the rocket launcher in that it is rifled and fires a projectile from fixed ammunition. After each round, the perforated shell casing must be removed from the weapon's breech. The rocket launcher, such as the

World War II bazooka, is a smoothbore weapon that fires a self-contained rocket. The recoilless rifle consists of a steel tube with a venturi at the rear. To load the weapon, the venturi is rotated to one side, a fixed round is inserted at the breech end, and the venturi is returned to position. A firing pin striking a percussion cap in the side of the round fires the round. After each round, the breech mechanism must be opened and the empty shell casing removed, although some modern recoilless rifles have automatic extraction and ejection systems. The recoilless rifle is operated by a crew of at least two people: a gunner and a loader.

Further Reading

The Diagram Group. *Weapons: An International Encyclopedia from 5000 BC to 2000 AD.* New York: St. Martin's, 1990.

Kinard, Jeff. *Artillery: An Illustrated History of Its Impact.* Santa Barbara, CA: ABC-CLIO, 2004.

106mm Recoilless Rifle, M40A1: FM23-82. Washington, DC: U.S. Army, 1962.

Weeks, J. *Men against Tanks.* Newton Abbot, UK: David and Charles, 1975.

Armored Personnel Carriers and Infantry Fighting Vehicles

One lesson of World War II was the need for all components in a military force to be as mobile as its tanks. This led to the introduction in all armies of armored personnel carriers (APCs) for the transportation of infantry. The Soviet Union, which had benefitted tremendously toward the end of the war from substantial numbers of U.S. Lend-Lease trucks, took the lead, developing a considerable number of different APCs to transport not only men but also mounting antiaircraft weapons, rockets, and mortars.

Ultimately, the Soviet series of BTR (for *bronirovanniy transportnaya rozposnania,* meaning "armored wheeled transporter") APCs did far more than merely transport infantry to the battlefield. They evolved into the BMP (*boevaia mashina pekhoti,* meaning "combat vehicle infantry") series, the first infantry fighting vehicles in the world. Infantry could now fight from within the vehicle. Some BMPs mounted a powerful gun and carried antitank missiles, enabling them to provide effective close infantry support. They were constructed to allow infantry to fight from inside the vehicle, which is what distinguished the infantry fighting vehicle from the less capable APC.

The first Soviet post–World War II APC was the tracked BTR-50 that entered service in the mid-1950s. It was based on the PT-76 amphibious tank with the turret removed and the hull built up for the troop-carrying compartment. Weighing nearly 14 tons, it was capable of a speed of 27.3 miles per hour and could swim. It had maximum 14mm armor protection and was armed with a single 7.62mm machine gun. It had a crew of 2 and could carry 14 infantrymen in an open armored box where the turret had been located on the PT-76. The disadvantages of this arrangement are obvious. The troops were exposed to the elements and to air shell bursts and were forced to enter or leave the BTR-50 over its sides. A ramp in the rear allowed the BTR-50 to carry a 57mm antitank gun or an 85mm fieldpiece, which could be fired from it if necessary.

In the late 1950s the Soviets developed the eight-wheeled BTR-60 APC. It became the main personnel carrier of the Red Army motorized rifle divisions. Entering service in 1961 and fully amphibious, it had a crew of 2 and carried 14 fully equipped troops. It weighed 10 tons, had torsion-bar suspension, and was capable of a speed of 50 miles per hour. It had maximum 14mm armor protection. The driver and commander were in front with a hatch right behind them for a light machine gun, but the second version, the BTR-60PB had a central top turret with a 14.5mm (.57-caliber) machine gun. Subsequent versions, including the BTR-80, have full nuclear, biological, and chemical protection. Adopted by at least 18 armies, it remains in wide use.

The BMP-1 infantry combat vehicle of 1967 was a revolutionary vehicle in that it provided the infantry squad it transported with unprecedented firepower. Manned by two men, it could transport nine equipped infantry. The tracked BMP-1 had a speed of 50 miles per hour. It had a turret-mounted 73mm main gun, one 7.62mm machine gun, and an AT-3 Sagger (NATO designation) antitank missile. It was followed in 1980 by the BMP-2, armed with a 30mm automatic cannon in place of the 73mm main gun of the BMP-2. The cannon can easily penetrate most light-armored vehicles. The BMP-3 of 1990 has even greater firepower: one 100mm main gun, a 30mm automatic cannon, and one 7.62mm machine gun.

The U.S. equivalent to the BTR-60 was the U.S. M113 of 1956. Still the most widely used APC in the world, with more than 80,000 produced, it carried a total of 11 fully equipped troops. The track commander was also the infantry squad leader and the .50-caliber machine-gunner. The tracked M113 was capable of a speed of 38 miles per hour, had 45mm aluminum armor, and was armed with at minimum a .50-caliber machine gun. It saw wide service in the Vietnam War.

The U.S. equivalent to the Soviet BMP series M113 is the M2/M3 Bradley infantry fighting vehicle. Entering service in 1981, it has a crew of three men but transports only six fully equipped troops. This necessitated reducing the size of the infantry squad of eight. The Bradley has a speed of 41 miles per hour, is armed with one 25mm Bushmaster chain gun capable of single-shot or burst 100–200 rounds per minute fire, one 7.62mm (.30-caliber) machine gun, and two TOW missile launchers. The Bradley has a number of variants. One serves as a Stinger ground-to-air missile platform. It is designated the M6 Bradley Linebacker.

Further Reading

Foss, Christopher F., ed. *The Encyclopedia of Tanks and Armored Fighting Vehicles*. San Diego: Thunder Bay, 2002.

Hogg, Ivan V. *The Greenhill Armoured Fighting Vehicles Data Book*. Mechanicsburg, PA: Stackpole, 2000.

Mikoyan-Gurevich MiG-15

The Soviet Union's Mikoyan-Gurevich MiG-15 (NATO designation Fagot) is one of the most famous aircraft of its era. It first flew in December 1947 and entered service early in 1949. Artem Mikoyan and Mikhail Gurevich took advantage of captured German plans for the Focke-Wulf Ta 183 and designed the new aircraft as an interceptor able to deal with the U.S. Boeing B-29 Superfortress strategic bomber.

The swept midwing, high-tail, fuselage-engine–mounted MiG-15 was originally fitted with the RD-45 1,950 pounds thrust engine, a Soviet copy of the Rolls-Royce Nene. Later it incorporated the Klimov VK-1 turbojet 5,000 pounds thrust engine that gave a maximum speed of 668 miles per hour. The MiG-15 had a ceiling of 50,855 feet and a range of 745 miles (1,225 miles with external tanks). Its powerful armament consisted of one 37mm and two 23mm cannon and up to 1,100 pounds of bombs. The number of rounds carried (80 rounds per gun for the 23mm and 40 rounds for the 37mm) limited its effectiveness, however.

The MiG-15 came as a rude shock to U.S. pilots during the Korean War when it first appeared in the skies of North Korea on November 1, 1950. It was clearly superior to all other aircraft in the Korean War at the time. The U.S. Air Force

A Mikoyan-Gurevich MiG-15 jet interceptor. Operation MOOLAH offered $100,000 and political asylum to the first Communist pilot to defect with his MiG-15 to the United Nations Command (UNC) in Korea, which wanted the Soviet-built aircraft for assessment and evaluation. The MiG-15 shown here was flown by North Korean defector Lieutenant No Kum Sok and landed at Kimpo Airfield on September 21, 1953, after the armistice was signed. He said he was unaware of the reward. (National Archives)

immediately rushed the North American F-86 Sabre to Korea. Although the Fagot was superior to the Sabre in climb, turn ratio, and armament, superior American pilot training and tactics usually prevailed over the Soviet and Chinese pilots flying the Fagot. The MiG-15, however, wreaked havoc on other aircraft including the piston-driven B-29s, which had to be withdrawn from daytime missions in September 1951.

On September 21, 1953, a defecting North Korean pilot claimed a $100,000 reward when he flew his MiG-15 to South Korea, providing the West with its first intact Fagot for study.

Taking into account the two-seat MiG-15UTI trainer, more than 8,000 MiGs were produced in the Soviet Union, with several thousand additional aircraft built under license in Czechoslovakia (S-102 and S-103 aircraft) and Poland (Lim-1 and Lim-2). Widely exported, numerous MiG-15s served in the air forces of the People's Republic of China and the Middle East. The MiG-15 remained in frontline service through the 1960s and thereafter was the standard Eastern bloc advanced jet trainer aircraft.

Further Reading

Fredriksen, John C. *International Warbirds: An Illustrated Guide to World Military Aircraft, 1914–2000.* Santa Barbara, CA: ABC-CLIO, 2001.

Gordon, Yefim. *Mikoyan-Gurevich MiG-15: The Soviet Union's Long-Lived Korean War Fighter.* Leicester, UK: Midland, 2001.

North American F-86 Sabre Jet Fighter

The North American F-86 Sabre jet fighter was the first U.S. Air Force aircraft to incorporate German swept-wing technology. At the end of World War II, the U.S. Army Air Forces pushed for development of a second-generation jet fighter. The first design incorporated a standard wing, but in November 1945 this was modified to a wing swept back 35 degrees. The prototype first flew in October 1947, and the first production aircraft appeared in May 1948. The F-86 entered service shortly thereafter. The Sabre featured an air scoop in the nose of the fuselage, a bubble canopy forward of the wings, and swept wing and tail. The first U.S. jet to break the sound barrier, the Sabre also established a number of world speed and altitude records.

Powered by a 7,500-pound-thrust General Electric J47 turbojet engine, the single-pilot F-86 had a top speed of 692 miles per hour, a maximum ceiling of 50,000 feet, and a range of 500 miles. It was armed with six .50-caliber machine guns or four 20mm cannon and could carry 2,000 pounds of bombs. The F-86 was also the first aircraft to feature pilot ejector seats.

Rushed to Korea to deal with the Mikoyan-Gurevich MiG-15, which was more than a match for all other U.S. and United Nations aircraft in the theater, the F-86 established an enviable combat record. Although marginally inferior in some respects to the MiG-15, the Sabre usually triumphed over its Soviet swept-wing counterpart because of superior pilot training and tactics. During the Korean War, F-86 pilots received credit for shooting down 792 MiGs and 18 other aircraft. A total of 218 F-86s were lost but only 76 of these to MiGs, so the shoot-down ratio was 10:1. Since there have been fewer air combats in U.S. wars since Korea, the records of top jet aces of the Korean War still stand.

The F-86 went through a number of models. The F-86D Sabre Dog was the first U.S. Air Force aircraft to be armed entirely with missiles and the first all-weather jet interceptor, while the F-86H was developed for ground support and was capable of delivering tactical nuclear weapons.

The F-86 was widely exported and served in the air forces of 26 other nations. Australia, Canada, and Japan all established their own assembly lines to provide the aircraft. In all, 5,375 F-86 aircraft were constructed. Although the aircraft was withdrawn from U.S. service in 1960, the last of its type was produced in February 1961, in Japan. The Sabre remained in service with some second-line units into the 1970s.

Further Reading

Curtis, Duncan. *North American F-86 Sabre.* Wiltside, UK: Crowood, 2000.

Dranem, Walter, and Chris Hughes. *North American F-86 Sabrejet Day Fighters.* North Branch, MN: Specialty Press, 1997.

Fredriksen, John C. *Warbirds: An Illustrated Guide to U.S. Military Aircraft, 1915–2000.* Santa Barbara, CA: ABC-CLIO, 1999.

Boeing B-52 Stratofortress

U.S. long-range heavy bomber. Referred to by its crew of five as "Buff" (for "big ugly fat fellow"), the Boeing B-52 Stratofortress was first conceived in 1944 as a follow-on aircraft to the Boeing B-47 Stratojet. Development proceeded over the next decade. The prototype first flew in April 1952, and the B-52 entered service in February 1955. During the course of some six decades in service, 744 B-52s were built. The last model, the B-52H, was delivered to the Strategic Air Command in May 1961. The B-52H can carry up to 20 air-launched cruise missiles along with numerous conventional and nuclear bombs.

Although built for the role of Cold War–era nuclear deterrence, the B-52's conventional capabilities make the plane a vital component of current U.S. Air Force operations. With a maximum speed of 650 miles per hour and a ceiling of 50,000 feet, the B-52 has an initial combat radius of 4,480 miles. With aerial refueling, the aircraft has a virtually unlimited range limited only by crew stamina. Powered by eight 17,000-pound-thrust Pratt & Whitney TF33 turbofan jet engines, the B-52 can weigh up to 488,000 pounds at takeoff. It is armed with a single 20mm Gatling gun and is capable of carrying up to 70,000 pounds of ordnance, both conventional and nuclear.

The B-52's conventional role was first demonstrated during the Vietnam War. B-52s flying from bases in Thailand and Guam dropped millions of tons of conventional ordnance, inflicting heavy losses on communist troops and lines of communication. B-52s also flew in close support of ground troops in South Vietnam, and in Operations LINEBACKER I and LINEBACKER II, B-52s struck deep into North Vietnam.

B-52s performed highly effective service during the 1991 Persian Gulf War. Its ability to internally carry 84 500-pound bombs made the big bomber a formidable weapons delivery platform. B-52s struck Iraqi troop concentrations and fixed targets, including bunkers, airfields, and radar installations. The longest strike mission in the history of aerial warfare occurred when a B-52H took off from Barksdale Air Force Base, Louisiana, and then launched cruise missiles in Iraq during a 35-hour nonstop operation. Ultimately, B-52 bombers flew 1,741 sorties and delivered 40 percent of all aerial-delivered coalition weaponry.

Subsequently, B-52s also took part in Operation ALLIED FORCE in Yugoslavia (March–June 1999), Operation ENDURING FREEDOM in Afghanistan (2001–2014), and Operation IRAQI FREEDOM (2003–2011). There are no plans to retire the B-52, which is certainly one of the most important aircraft ever built. Eighty-five B-52s remain in active service, with nine in reserve.

Further Reading

Boyne, Walter J. *Boeing B-52: A Documentary History.* Washington, DC: Smithsonian Institution, 1984.

Dorr, Robert. *B-52 Stratofortress.* Oxford, UK: Osprey, 1995.

Lake, Jon. *B-52 Stratofortress Units in Operation Desert Storm.* Oxford, UK: Osprey, 2004.

Surface-to-Air Missiles

Although radar-controlled antiaircraft guns represented a considerable improvement over previous air defense weapons, a faster and more maneuverable projectile capable of being guided from the ground and reaching high altitudes was required to defend against new high-flying and fast strategic bombers. Surface-to-air missiles (SAMs) were designed to destroy attacking aircraft from the ground or sea. Such weapons have been employed in a number of conflicts, including the Vietnam War, the Soviet-Afghan War (1979–1989), and the Middle East wars. SAMs can be grouped in three chief categories: large permanently sited systems, vehicle-mounted systems, and man-portable air defense systems (MANPADS).

Large permanently sited systems came first, led by the U.S. Army, the branch of the military traditionally charged with air defense. Building on the German Wasserfall missile developed at the end of World War II, in February 1945 the

People's Army of Vietnam (PAVN, North Vietnam Army) personnel manning a Soviet SA-2 surface-to-air missile (SAM) launcher on the outskirts of Hanoi during the Vietnam War. Such missile systems were a key component of Democratic Republic of Vietnam (North Vietnam) air defenses. (Bettmann/Corbis)

army began development of what became the Nike Ajax missile-defense system. The world's first operational-guided SAM system, it entered service in 1954. Ultimately it was deployed in several hundred sites around the United States. The missile was 21 feet in length (34 feet 10 inches with booster) and 1 foot in diameter. It had a wingspan of 4 feet 6 inches and weighed 1,000 pounds (more than 2,455 pounds with booster). It had a range of 25–30 miles, flew at Mach 2.3 (1,679 miles per hour), and could reach up to 70,000 feet. It had three high-explosive warheads mounted in its nose, center, and aft sections.

Even while the Nike Ajax was being tested, work was begun on a new generation of missiles. Deployed beginning in 1958, the Nike Hercules had a range of about 100 miles, a top speed in excess of 3,000 miles per hour, and a maximum altitude of about 100,000 feet. It also received solid-state components in place of some vacuum tubes on the Nike Ajax. The new missile also had an optional low-kiloton nuclear warhead to improve the probability of a kill from a near miss.

Other nations, including the Soviet Union, Great Britain, and France, developed similar SAM systems. The Soviets were especially interested in air defense, given the demonstrated success of U.S. strategic bombing in World War II. U.S. reconnaissance overflights of the Soviet Union had been going on for a number of years. This fact was well known to the Kremlin, and on May 1, 1960, Soviet advances in missile technology allowed a SA-2 Guideline (NATO designation) SAM to down a high-flying U.S. Lockheed U-2 spy plane over Soviet airspace. The two-stage SA-2 carried a grooved fragmentation high-explosive 430-pound warhead (286 pounds of explosives) and could reach speeds of up to Mach 3.5, although not until it was well over 25,000 feet in altitude. Unlike predicted antiaircraft artillery fire, the SA-2's electronic guidance system could compensate for the target aircraft's evasive maneuvers. The Soviet Union shipped SA-2 missiles to the Democratic Republic of Vietnam (North Vietnam) during the Vietnam War, where they were used to down U.S. aircraft over North Vietnam and Laos.

Missiles were also developed for tactical or field use by ground units or on ships. Typical of such radar-controlled missiles are the U.S. Hawk (weighing 265 pounds and with a range of 22 miles) and the Patriot (weighing 2,200 pounds and with a range of 43 miles), the British Rapier, and the Soviet Gainful (SA-6, weighing 1,212 pounds and with a range of 37 miles). Such missiles were most often deployed on trucks and tracked transporters and were often difficult for attacking aircraft to locate.

The final category consists of the small and lightweight antiaircraft missiles capable of being transported and fired by one or two men. Normally these are heat-seeking missiles, drawn to an aircraft exhaust. As with antiaircraft guns, they have a relatively short range, are simple to operate, and can be lethal when properly employed. The U.S. Stinger and British Blowpipe proved highly effective against Soviet forces in Afghanistan, while the Soviet SA-7 Grail was employed with less success against U.S. aircraft during the Vietnam War.

Further Reading

Cullen, Tony, and Christopher F. Foss, eds. *Jane's Land-Based Air Defence, 2005–2006.* London: Jane's Information Group, 2005.

Gunston, Bill. *The Illustrated Encyclopedia of Aircraft Armament: A Major Directory of Guns, Rockets, Missiles, Bombs, Torpedoes and Mines.* Orion Books, 1988.

Werrell, Kenneth P. *Archie, Flack, AAA, and SAM: A Short Operational History of Ground-Based Air Defense.* Maxwell Air Force Base, AL: Air University Press, 1988.

Nautilus, U.S. Navy Submarine

The U.S. Navy submarine *Nautilus* (SSN 571, not to be confused with USS *Nautilus* SS-168, a World War II diesel submarine) was the world's first nuclear-powered submarine. It was built at the Electric Boat Company shipyard in Groton, Connecticut, where construction was made possible by the development of a nuclear power plant under the direction of Captain Hyman G. Rickover of the Naval Reactors Branch of the Atomic Energy Commission.

Aerial starboard quarter view of the United States Navy submarine *Nautilus* (SSN-571) moored at the Naval Shipyard, Groton, Connecticut, May 14, 1985. Commissioned in 1954, the *Nautilus* was the world's first nuclear-powered submarine and remained in service for 25 years. (Department of Defense)

In August 1949 the navy called for a nuclear-powered submarine to enter service by January 1955. Congress authorized construction in July 1951, and the keel was laid on June 14, 1952. Launched on January 21, 1954, the *Nautilus* was commissioned on September 30, the first nuclear-powered ship in the U.S. Navy. The *Nautilus* first went to sea on January 17, 1955.

The *Nautilus* had a length of 323 feet 8 inches and a beam of 27 feet 7 inches, and it displaced 3,533 tons on the surface and 4,092 tons submerged. Two Westinghouse steam turbines and one pressurized water-cooled nuclear reactor allowed the *Nautilus* to attain speeds of 22 knots on the surface and 23.3 knots submerged. It could dive to 720 feet. The *Nautilus* was equipped with six bow 533mm (21-inch) torpedo tubes and was armed with 22 torpedoes. Normal crew complement was 105 men.

The *Nautilus* shattered all previous submerged speed and distance records during its 25 years of service. On August 3, 1958, it became the first ship to reach the geographic North Pole, traveling submerged under the polar ice cap. During May 1959–August 1960 the *Nautilus* underwent a complete overhaul and received a new fuel core. It then deployed to the Mediterranean with the Sixth Fleet. Decommissioned on March 3, 1980, it had steamed nearly half a million miles. In July 1985 the *Nautilus* was moved to the Submarine Force Museum in

Groton, Connecticut, as a National Historic Landmark. It opened to the public in April 1986.

The first Soviet nuclear-powered submarine, the *K-3,* first of a class of 13 nuclear-powered submarines, was launched on August 9, 1957, and commissioned on January 7, 1958.

Further Reading

Anderson, William R. *Nautilus 90 North.* New York: New American Library, 1959.

Blair, Clay. *The Atomic Submarine and Admiral Rickover.* New York: H. Holt, 1954.

Punji Stake

The Punji stake was a simple and highly effective antipersonnel device employed by communist forces during the Vietnam War. The contemporary version of the caltrop, the punji stake was a sharpened stake, usually of bamboo, deployed as a booby trap singly or in groups and located in rice paddies or in camouflaged holes to pierce the flesh of an individual stepping or falling on them. Often they were smeared with excrement so as to create infections. Punji stakes were placed in locations in which enemy troops might travel. Similar to these were large spiked balls suspended by vines in the jungle, released to crash into and wound or kill individuals tripping them.

A Punji stake pit as employed by Communist forces in the Vietnam War. Punji stakes made from sharpened sticks of bamboo would easily wound the victim and were often coated with excrement to cause infection. (Nik Wheeler/Corbis)

Further Reading

Bunker, Robert J. "Booby Traps." In *Encyclopedia of the Vietnam War: A Political, Social and Military History,* Vol. 1, edited by Spencer C. Tucker, 75–76. Santa Barbara, CA: ABC-CLIO, 1998.

M16 Rifle

The M16 is the standard military rifle of the United States. It followed into service the 7.62mm M14 rifle. Based on the .30-caliber M1 Garand, the M14 was capable of both semiautomatic and automatic fire and featured an improved gas system. A variety of manufacturers produced some 1.4 million M14s.

In 1957 the U.S. Army extended a contract to the Armalite Division of Fairchild Aircraft Company to develop a .22-caliber rifle that would penetrate the standard helmet at 500 yards. Designed by Eugene Stoner, the new rifles did not prove reliable in testing. Colt's Patent Fire Arms Manufacturing Co. secured the rights to the new weapon and in 1962 sold the slightly modified version, now known as the AR-15, to the U.S. Air Force for testing as a base perimeter defense weapon to replace its .30-caliber M1 and M2 carbines. The air force officially adopted it as the M16 in 1964. The army tested it in Vietnam during 1965–1967.

Combat in Vietnam revealed a number of deficiencies. For one thing, the army replaced its 5.56mm (.223-caliber) cartridges Dupont IMR powder with standard ball powder used in 7.62mm NATO ammunition. This powder produced much more bore fouling, resulting in frequent jams unless the weapon was cleaned often. Yet the M16 had been billed as low maintenance, and the army did not produce cleaning supplies for it.

New powders, cleaning kits (from 1970 carried in a cavity in the buttstock), and chrome lining the barrel, chamber, and bolt in addition to proper training all corrected these problems, and the army officially adopted the modified weapon in 1967 as the 5.56mm Rifle M16A1. At the same time (ca. 1970) new 30-round magazines were introduced into service, replacing those of 20 rounds and equaling those of the Soviet and Chinese AK-47 assault rifles.

Comfortable to fire and moderately accurate up to medium combat engagement ranges (100–200 meters), the M16 is capable of automatic or semiautomatic fire. The M16A1 is 39 inches long, weighs 6.3 pounds without its box magazine, and produces a muzzle velocity of 3,250 feet per second. The M16A1 had a forward assist "bird cage" flash hider. Capable of a cyclic rate of fire of 650–750 rounds per minute, it has a maximum effective range of about 450 meters. Some M16A1s were also equipped with a 40mm M203 grenade launcher underneath the rifle barrel.

The M16A2 was modified to fire 5.56mm NATO ammunition and had a heavier barrel, modified rear sight, and spent case deflector. The M16A2 can be fired in

A marine rifleman firing his M-16 rifle at North Vietnamese troops during Vietnam War Operation PRAIRIE II on March 13, 1967. An artillery forward observer using binoculars spots targets for him. (Bettmann/Corbis)

either single-shot or three-round burst modes. The fully automatic mode is no longer issued. The M16A3 has a "flat top" upper receiver with a Picatinny rail (a bracket providing a mounting platform for accessories) and a removable carrying handle. The M-4 carbine is essentially an M-16 receiver with a short barrel and a telescoping butt stock.

The M16's lighter weight reduces soldier fatigue, and its smaller cartridge allows more ammunition to be carried, although the stopping power of the extremely light bullet has come into question. It remains the standard general-issue rifle for the U.S. armed forces. Manufactured in the United States by at least a dozen companies, M16-type rifles are also manufactured in Canada and China. Some 8 million have been produced. The M16 is in use by 15 NATO countries and more than 80 countries worldwide. However, it is not considered to be as rugged as the Soviet/Russian AK-47 and AK-74.

Further Reading

Ezell, Edward Clinton, and Thomas M. Pegg. *Small Arms of the World: A Basic Manual of Small Arms.* Harrisburg, PA: Stackpole, 1983.

Rosa, Joseph G., and Robin May. *An Illustrated History of Guns and Small Arms.* London: Peerage Books, 1984.

Westwood, David. *Rifles: An Illustrated History of Their Impact.* Santa Barbara, CA: ABC-CLIO, 2005.

M79 Grenade Launcher

The M79 grenade launcher, nicknamed "Blooper," "Thumper," and "Thump Gun," was adopted by the U.S. Army in 1961 and was widely employed during the Vietnam War. The 29-inch-long M79 resembled in both shape and device a large sawed-off, break-action shotgun. Firing a stubby 40mm grenade round, the M79 weighed 6.6 pounds loaded.

The shoulder-fired M79 had a rubber pad at the end of the stock to absorb some of the recoil. Its firing rate was 5–7 rounds per minute, and it had an effective range of about 400 meters. A flip-up ladder-type sight assisted in aiming. A well-trained infantryman could use it to place a grenade through a window-sized target at 100 meters. The M79 fired a wide variety of rounds, including high-explosive, CS riot-control gas, smoke, incendiary, and a canister round containing buckshot.

The M79 became a favorite infantry weapon in the jungles of Vietnam. Two M79 grenadiers were usually in each 10-man squad, one per fire team. The weapon was useful in ambush and counterambush operations, and the smoke round could be used to mark targets for air strikes.

The follow-on weapon to the M79 was the XM148 grenade launcher, a poorly designed weapon that was extensively redesigned and later issued as the M203. It consists of an M16 rifle with a grenade launcher mounted below the rifle's barrel. Many users consider the M-203 an awkward and cumbersome weapon, inferior to the M-79.

Further Reading

Hogg, Ivan V., ed. *Jane's Infantry Weapons, 1991–1992*. New York: Jane's Information Group, 1991.

Rosser-Owen, David. *Vietnam Weapons Handbook*. Wellingborough, Northamptonshire, UK: Patrick Stephens, 1986.

U.S. Army. *40-mm Grenade Launchers M203 and M79: FM-23-31*. Washington, DC: U.S. Government Printing Office, 1972.

M18A1 Claymore Mine

The U.S. M18A1 claymore is a directional, antipersonnel fragmentation mine. Invented by Norman A. MacLeod and named for the large Scottish broadsword, the claymore utilized the Misznay-Schardin effect, discovered by the Hungarian József Misznay (Misnay) and the German Hubert Schardin during World War II. It holds that when an explosion occurs next to metal, the blast effect is directed primarily away from that metal. The impetus for the development of the claymore came from the human-wave attacks of communist Chinese forces during the Korean War. The follow-on M18A1 claymore is essentially the same as the initial M-18 design.

The M18A1 claymore has an olive-colored plastic casing with the embossed words "Front Toward Enemy." The mine is of concave shape 8.5 inches long, 1.5 inches wide, and 3.25 inches high. It weighs 3.5 pounds and is mounted on small steel folding legs. Its charge of 1.5 pounds of composition C-4 explosive is detonated by means of a handheld clacker, a PRC 77 radio battery, that sends an electrical charge through 50 feet of wire to a No. 2 blasting cap. The resulting blast hurls 700 small steel balls in a fan-shape 60-degree horizontal projection to a maximum height of 6 feet. The steel projectiles are lethal at 50 yards and can cause casualties out to 250 yards. Although the main blast of the claymore projects in an arc forward, its detonation also produces a significant amount of back blast, which users must account for (either by ensuring that they are well clear of the back blast area or by stacking layers of sandbags behind the mine to absorb the back blast). The claymore comes in two versions, with and without a slit-type peep sight at the top. Although primarily a controlled mine, the claymore can also be used as an uncontrolled mine (so-called victim-initiated detonation) in which it is exploded by means of a trip wire, pressure release, and acoustic and vibration sensors.

The claymore is deployed by placing it so that the convex side faces toward a presumed enemy approach. The steel legs are then dug into the ground to steady the mine. Claymores were widely employed by U.S. and South Vietnamese forces during the Vietnam War. The mine was employed offensively in ambush situations but was primarily used defensively to complement minefields and for close-in protection for temporary encampments. The claymore was designed to cover the distance between effective employment ranges for hand grenades and mortars. Because the claymore is detonated up to 50 feet away, the operator's location is not immediately apparent to the enemy. The claymore subsequently appeared in similar form in the arsenals of many other nations, including the Soviet Union.

Further Reading

Croll, Mike. *The History of Land Mines.* Barnsley, UK: Leo Cooper, 1998.

Monin, L., and A. Gallimore. *The Devil's Gardens: A History of Land Mines.* London: Pimlico, 2002.

M61 Vulcan 20mm Auto Cannon

On occasion, principles developed for weapons find new application years and even decades later. In the case of the U.S. M61 Vulcan, the basic mechanical principles extend back a century. First produced in the United States in 1962, the M-61 was an electrically driven version of the Gatling gun that first appeared during the American Civil War (1861–1865). The new weapon was specifically intended to arm aircraft, where the higher speeds of jet aircraft dictated a greater volume of fire over a shorter period of time.

In 1946 the U.S. Army issued a contract to General Electric Armament Division for Project Vulcan to develop a rotating six-barrel weapon capable of firing 6,000 rounds a minute. Ground test fired in 1949, it was adapted for aircraft use. Its first employment in a production aircraft came in 1958 with the F-104 Starfighter. Problems included difficulties with the linked ammunition, leading to development of a linkless system for feeding in the ammunition.

Driven by an electric motor, the barrels each fire 1 round of 20mm ammunition per revolution. Although the firing rate is a phenomenal 100 rounds per second, as in the first Gatling gun the multiple rotating barrel system helps minimize heat buildup and barrel erosion. Rate of fire varies, depending on model and selection. It can be as high as 6,600 rounds per minute but typically is 6,000 rounds per minute (most aircraft cannot carry sufficient ammunition for one full minute of sustained firing). The Vulcan remains the standard nonmissile armament of U.S. combat aircraft. It was also deployed in an air defense role aboard U.S. Navy ships as the Mk 15 Phalanx CIWS system and the M163 Vulcan Air Defense System.

Further Reading

Berk, Joseph. *The Gatling Gun: 19th Century Machine Gun to 21st Century Vulcan.* Boulder, CO: Paladin, 1991.

Willbanks, James A. *Machine Guns: An Illustrated History of Their Impact.* Santa Barbara, CA: ABC-CLIO, 2004.

M134 (GAU-2B) Minigun

The high-rate-of-fire GAU-2B minigun (U.S. Army designation M134) is in effect a machine gun with six rotating barrels. The weapon was an outgrowth of an army contract of 1946 for such a cannon for jet aircraft that resulted in the M61 Vulcan firing a 20mm round. The army developed its own smaller and lighter version of the Vulcan for helicopter armament. First produced in 1962, it fires a 7.62mm round.

The initial weapon, the M130 was gas operated. It required no external power but utilized gas from each of the six barrels to operate the rotating mechanism. Other versions were hydraulically or pneumatically driven and electrically fired. One minigun was mounted on either side of the gunship versions of the UH-1B/C Huey helicopter as an alternate armament to the M-60C machine gun. The AH-1G Cobra, the world's first purpose-built attack helicopter, had a minigun mounted in a chin turret. The minigun also was adopted to serve as a flexible gun mounted in the doors (normally left) of both the UH-1 Huey and the HH-3 July Green Giant helicopters.

Manufactured by the Armament Division of General Electric, the GAU-2B fires the 7.62mm cartridge in a disintegrating metal-link belt. It has a selectable rate of fire of 1,000 to 4,000 rounds per minute. First employed in combat in the Vietnam War, the chief drawback was the tendency to expend all the ammunition in a very short period. In the door mount, the recoil of its firing also slid the helicopter sideways. Nonetheless, the sheer volume of fire can be devastating to any nonhardened target.

Further Reading

Berk, Joseph. *The Gatling Gun: 19th Century Machine Gun to 21st Century Vulcan.* Boulder, CO: Paladin, 1991.

Willbanks, James A. *Machine Guns: An Illustrated History of Their Impact.* Santa Barbara, CA: ABC-CLIO, 2004.

Ship-to-Ship Missiles

All major powers developed guided missiles for use against enemy ships. The only ship-launched cruise missile to have sunk a large warship is the radar-guided Soviet Styx. Nineteen feet in length and 2.5 feet in diameter with a 7.9-foot wingspan, the Styx carried a 1,000-pound high-explosive, hollow-charge warhead to a maximum range of some 48 miles.

Beginning in 1962, Egypt received several Osa-class and Komar-class missile boats from the Soviet Union. They were armed with the radar-guided Styx. On October 21, 1967, the Israeli destroyer *Eilat* approached Egypt's 12-mile territorial limit north of Port Said. Its crew did not detect two Egyptian missile boats, which fired three Styx missiles at it. All struck. Two hours after the first missile hit, the crew abandoned ship. A fourth missile struck the ship as it sank, wounding many sailors struggling in the water. Of the 190-man crew, 47 died and 90 suffered injury.

Egyptian missile boats struck again the following May, sinking the *Orit,* a small wooden fishing vessel, off El Arish. These events were a rude awakening to naval officers around the world and gave new impetus to other nations to develop antiship guided missiles. Israel, already developing its own Gabriel missile, rushed it to completion to equip its own French-built missile boats. Other nations also developed antiship missiles. These included the U.S. Harpoon, the French Exocet, and the Italian Otomat.

Perhaps the best known of antiship cruise missiles is the French Exocet. Argentina purchased these missiles from France and used them from low-flying aircraft with devastating effect against British ships, especially HMS *Sheffield,* which sank after being struck by one during the 1982 Falklands (Malvinas) War. The Exocet, which entered service in 1979, was 15.4 feet in length and had a wingspan of 3.6 feet, a range of 43 miles, and a warhead of 363 pounds. On March 17, 1987, an Iraqi Mirage aircraft fired two Exocet AM39 air-to-surface missiles at the U.S. Perry-class frigate *Stark* in the Persian Gulf. Both missiles struck and badly damaged the ship, killing 35 members of its crew.

The U.S. Harpoon AGM-84 missile, produced by Boeing (formerly McDonnell Douglas), entered service in 1977 and provides both the U.S. Air Force and the U.S. Navy with a common missile to attack surface ships. The Harpoon is a radar-guided cruise missile designed for low-level attack of ships. It can be launched from aircraft, submarines, and surface ships. Aboard submarines, it is fired from a torpedo tube in a capsule, the top of which bursts open when it reaches the surface, launching the missile. The Harpoon has its own guidance radar to locate the target.

The Harpoon has gone through upgrades, but the initial ship-launched type weighed 1,470 pounds and had a length of 15 feet, a diameter of 13.5 inches, and a wingspan of 3 feet. It was armed with a penetration high-explosive blast 488-pound warhead.

Further Reading

Hewson, Robert, ed. *Jane's Air-Launched Weapons, 2001*. London: Jane's, 2002.

Hooten, Ted. *Jane's Naval Weapons Systems, 2001–2002*. London: Jane's, 2002.

RPG-7 Rocket-Propelled Grenade Launcher

The RPG-7 (for "Ruchnoy Protivotankovyy Granatomyot," or handheld antitank grenade launcher) is a shoulder-launched, antitank grenade launcher. Designed and manufactured beginning in 1961 by the Russian firm of Bazalt, it was the successor to the RPG-2 introduced by the Soviets in 1949. Its low cost, simplicity, robust nature, ease of use, and effectiveness have made the RPG-7 the world's most widely used antitank weapon. The current Russian Federation model is the RPG-7V2.

Based on the World War II German Panzerfaust, the reloadable RPG-7 launcher is quite simple. It consists of a 40mm-diameter steel tube, 37.4 inches in length and weighing 15 pounds. The middle of the tube has a wooden heat shield. A flared breech provides blast shielding and reduces recoil. The launcher has a trigger mechanism and comes with both optical telescopic sight and open iron sights. Infrared and night sights are also available. The PG-7VL grenade consists of a booster, a sustainer motor, and a warhead.

Warheads include high-explosive antitank, thermobaric, and high-explosive fragmentation antipersonnel. They range in diameter from 40mm (1.6 inches) to 105mm (4.1 inches) and weigh between 4.85 and 9.9 pounds. The maximum range is some 1,000 yards, but effective ranges are 200 yards for the heavier antitank types and 500 yards for the lighter antipersonnel warhead. The antitank warhead can penetrate up to 500mm of armor.

The operator or assistant screws the propelling charge or booster into the end of the warhead. Once assembled, it is inserted into the launcher and aligned with the trigger, the grenade itself protruding from the launch tube. Pulling the trigger ignites a gunpowder booster charge that provides the initial propulsion for the grenade. The rocket motor ignites after 10 meters and sustains flight thereafter. The grenade is stabilized in flight by two sets of fins that deploy in flight: one large set of four fins to maintain direction and a smaller set of two fins to induce rotation.

One major drawback is that the grenade omits a cloud of blue-gray smoke on launching that gives away the location of the launcher and makes prompt reloading extremely hazardous.

More than 9 million RPG-7s have been produced. The RPG-7 is currently manufactured by nine different countries, including Airtronic USA in the United States.

Further Reading

Gander, Terry J. *Anti-Tank Weapons.* Marlborough, UK: Crowood, 2000.

Antitank Guided Missiles

Antitank guided missiles are designed to destroy enemy tanks and other armored fighting vehicles (AFVs). Such missiles vary widely in size and type from crew-served missiles to those launched from aircraft. Missiles have the great advantage of standoff capability. Earlier antitank missiles, such as bazookas, had no guidance system, and to ensure a hit, operators had to approach close to the target before firing.

First-generation guided missiles were manually directed. Once the missile had been fired, the operator guided it to the target by means of a joystick or similar device. Second-generation antitank missiles only require that the gunner keep the sight on the target. Guidance commands for the missile are transmitted by either radio or wire. The U.S. tube-launched, optically tracked, wire-guided (TOW) missile is an example of a second-generation antitank missile. Third-generation antitank missiles rely on laser painting, or marking, of the target or a nose-mounted TV camera. They are known as fire-and-forget missiles. The U.S. Javelin is such a missile.

Antitank missiles generally have a hollow-charge or shaped-charge warhead. Double warhead missiles are designed specifically to defeat special or spaced vehicle armor, while top-attack antitank missiles are designed to strike from above against the more lightly armored tops of tanks and AFVs.

Produced first by Hughes Aircraft Company and now Raytheon Systems Company, the second-generation TOW is the world's most widely distributed wire-guided antitank missile system. More than 500,000 TOWs have been manufactured, and the TOW is employed by more than 45 nations. The TOW is designed to attack tanks, AFVs, bunkers, and fortifications and to defend against amphibious landings. First entering service in 1970, the TOW underwent a number of modifications, the most recent of which is the TOW-2B of 1991. The first use of the TOW in combat came in May 1972 during the Vietnam War. It also saw wartime service with the Israeli Army against Syrian forces and in the Iran-Iraq War (1980–1988). The TOW-2B first saw combat in 2003 in the Iraq War (2003–2011).

The TOW-2B missile weighs 49.8 pounds (64 pounds with carrier) and has an explosive filler of some 6.9 pounds. The missile is 48 inches long and 5.8 inches in diameter. It has a maximum range of about 3,750 yards.

TOW missiles can be ground fired from a tripod by a crew of four or, more usually, from AFVs such as the M1/M3 Bradley. TOWs can also be fired from helicopters. The missile operates on command, line-of-sight guidance. The gunner uses a sight to locate the target, and once the missile is fired, he continues to track the target through the sight, with guidance commands transmitted along two wires that spool from the back of the missile. The TOW-2B attacks the target from the top, and its double warheads explode downward when the missile is just above the target. A bunker-buster variant is designed to defeat bunkers, field fortifications, and buildings.

The man-portable Javelin is a joint venture of Texas Instruments (now Raytheon Missile Systems) of Dallas, Texas, and Lockheed Martin Electronics and Missiles (now Missiles and Fire Control) of Orlando, Florida. The third-generation antitank Javelin missile entered service with the U.S. Army and the U.S. Marine Corps in 1996.

Designed for a two-man crew, the Javelin has a minimum range of 75 yards and a maximum range of some 2,500 yards (more than twice that of its predecessor M47 Dragon missile) and is used to attack enemy tanks and AFVs. The Javelin system consists of a missile in a disposable launch tube and a reusable command launch unit with triggering mechanism and an integrated day/night sighting device and target acquisition electronics. The missile weighs 49.5 pounds and is 5 feet 9 inches long. Fins deploy when the missile is launched. The Javelin employs a small thermal imaging TV camera and a sophisticated computer guidance system in its seeker section. To fire the missile, the gunner places a cursor over the selected target. The command launch unit then sends a lock-on-before-launch signal to the missile. The missile's infrared guidance system and onboard processing guide it after launch. The Javelin is designed for top attack and has a dual 8.5-pound warhead capable of defeating all known armor. The Javelin was successfully employed in 2003 during the Iraq War.

Further Reading

Gander, Terry J. *Anti-Tank Weapons.* Marlborough, UK: Crowood, 2000.

Flechette Ammunition

Flechette is French for "dart" (literally "little arrow"). Flechettes are small darts with pointed tip and tail fins for stabilization during flight. Small dart weapons were employed in the ancient world, and during World War I they were dropped from aircraft against enemy troops in the open. Similarly, U.S. aircraft dropped 1.75-inch-long flechettes during the Korean War and the Vietnam War. Propelled by gravity alone, the falling flechettes struck at subsonic speeds with the force of a .50-caliber bullet.

Experiments with a flechette rifle cartridge proved unsuccessful, but larger-bore flechette weapons have been used with great tactical effect.

The so-called beehive rounds for the 105mm howitzer and the 90mm and 106mm recoilless rifles were used extensively during the Vietnam War by U.S. forces in defensive positions against attacking communist infantry. The name "beehive" comes from the distinctive noise of the many flechettes moving through the air at supersonic speeds. Each 105mm antipersonnel round contains approximately 8,500 flechettes, which spread over a wide area on firing. The M50A1 Ontos, employed by the U.S. Marine Corps in Vietnam, was a light tank chassis mounting six 106mm recoilless rifles that fired high-explosive, high-explosive antitank, and beehive rounds.

Human rights groups have protested Israeli Army use of flechette tank rounds as too injurious to civilians, but the Israeli Supreme Court ruled in favor of their use.

Further Reading

Foss, Christopher F. *Jane's Armour and Artillery, 1998–1999.* London: Jane's Information Group, 1998.

Lockheed U-2 Dragon Lady Reconnaissance Aircraft

The Lockheed U-2 is undoubtedly history's most famous spy aircraft. The detonation by the Soviet Union of a hydrogen bomb in 1953 led the Central Intelligence Agency and the U.S. Air Force to call for a new high-flying reconnaissance aircraft that would be able to conduct overflights of the Soviet Union and monitor its weapons and missile programs. Brilliant aircraft designer Clarence "Kelly" Johnson of the Lockheed Corporation directed the program that began in 1954. The prototype single-crewman U-2 first flew in 1955 and entered service in 1956.

The exceedingly light U-2 was modeled after a glider with a long wingspan in relation to fuselage (the first model had a wingspan of 80 feet 2 inches and a length of 49 feet 7 inches). Its Pratt & Whitney J57 turbojet engine delivered 11,200 pounds thrust for a maximum speed of 500 miles per hour and a range of 2,600 miles. Its chief advantage was its ability to fly at very high altitudes, up to 70,000 feet, beyond the range of Soviet fighters and surface-to-air missiles.

Between 1956 and 1960, U-2s made repeated overflights of the Soviet Union, which the Kremlin also kept secret because of the inability to down the plane. On May 1, 1960, however, a U-2 piloted by Francis Gary Powers was shot down over the Soviet Union by three missiles detonated underneath it.

U-2s have taken a prominent role in many U.S. operations since, including the October 1962 Cuban Missile Crisis, when another was shot down. Much of its secret surveillance work was subsequently assigned to the Lockheed SR-71 Blackbird and to satellites.

The U-2 underwent considerable modification. In 1981, now designated the TR-1, it received enhanced electronic surveillance capabilities. The plane now exists in two variants: the U-2R and the U-2S. The U-2R has a wingspan of 104 feet 10 inches and a length of 63 feet 1 inch. Its J75 turbojet engine provides

The U.S. Lockheed U-2 aircraft. Capable of altitudes of 70,000 feet, the U-2 first took to the air in 1955 and is undoubtedly the world's most famous reconnaissance aircraft. (U.S. Air Force)

18,500 pounds thrust for a maximum speed of 510 miles per hour. Reportedly, its maximum ceiling is 90,000 feet and its range is more than 3,000 miles. The S version has a General Electric F118-GE0191 engine that delivers 18,500 pounds thrust. Because the engine is lighter and more fuel efficient, the aircraft can fly both higher and more than 1,200 miles farther without refueling.

U-2s took part in the Persian Gulf crisis in 1990–1991, in support of 1990s North Atlantic Treaty Organization operations in Bosnia and Kosovo, and in U.S. operations in Afghanistan beginning in 2001 and in the Iraq War of 2003–2011. Although production halted in 1989, some 32 U-2 aircraft remain in service. The U-2 outlasted its Mach 3 Lockheed SR-71 Blackbird replacement (retired in 1998) and is one of a very few aircraft to have remained in the U.S. Air Force inventory for more than 50 years.

Further Reading

Jenkins, Dennis R. *Lockheed U-2 Dragon Lady*. North Branch, MN: Specialty Press, 1998.

Pedlow, Gregory W., and Donald Welzenbach. *The CIA and the U-2 Program, 1954–1974*. Washington, DC: Central Intelligence Agency, 1998.

Peebles, Curtis. *Twilight Warriors: Covert Air Operations against the USSR*. Annapolis, MD: Naval Institute Press, 2005.

McDonnell Douglas F-4 Phantom II

Known as the "Rhino" and "Double Ugly," the McDonnell (later McDonnell Douglas) F-4 Phantom first flew in May 1958. It entered service with the U.S. Navy as the Phantom II in 1960. The aircraft was designed as an all-weather

The two-seat, rugged and highly versatile McDonnell Douglas F-4 Phantom II entered service with the U.S. Air Force in 1961 and provided highly effective service in a wide variety of roles. It continues in service with some foreign air forces today. (Juan DeLeon/Southcreek)

fleet-protection missile-equipped interceptor. It had a two-man crew of a pilot and a weapons system operator.

The Phantom underwent a series of upgrades during its long service life. Its two 17,900-pound-thrust (with afterburner) J79-GE-17 turbojet engines delivered a maximum speed of 1,485 miles per hour. It had a ceiling of 71,000 feet and a range of 1,841 miles. The F-4 mounted one 20mm cannon carried in an external pod and could carry 16,000 pounds of bombs, rockets, or missiles.

The Phantom proved so successful that the U.S. Air Force began flying the F-4C model in 1963. It was also flown by the U.S. Marine Corps, primarily in a ground-support role. The F-4 became the premier fighter-bomber during the Vietnam War after 1965, providing air cover for and later replacing less capable F-100s and F-105s. F-4s registered the first air-to-air kills against North Vietnamese MiGs for both the U.S. Navy and the U.S. Air Force in June and July 1965, respectively. Rugged and versatile, the workhorse Phantom served in many roles, including but not limited to fleet defense, air superiority, close air support, interception, air-defense suppression (so-called Wild Weasel missions to search out and destroy North Vietnamese antiaircraft defense systems), long-range strike, and reconnaissance.

Production halted in 1979, but a total of 5,195 F-4s were produced (the last 138 by Mitsubishi Aircraft Company in Japan), making it the largest-run production of Western fighter aircraft of the Cold War. Of 5,057 built in the United States, 2,874 went to the U.S. Air Force, and 1,264 went to the U.S. Navy and the U.S. Marine Corps. The United States exported some 919 F-4s to 11 allied countries. While retired from first-line U.S. service in 1996, the Phantom continued to be flown thereafter by some reserve and National Guard units, and it remained in service abroad.

Further Reading

Angelucci, Enzo. *The American Combat Aircraft and Helicopters of the Vietnam War.* Illustrations by Pierluigi Pinto. New York: Orion Books, 1986.

Fredriksen, John C. *Warbirds: An Illustrated Guide to U.S. Military Aircraft, 1915–2000.* Santa Barbara, CA: ABC-CLIO, 1999.

Wagner, Ray. *American Combat Planes.* 3rd enlarged ed. Garden City, NY: Doubleday, 1982.

Republic F-105 Thunderchief

In 1951 Republic Aircraft began work designing a supersonic fighter-bomber that could deliver nuclear weapons and that would replace the U.S. Air Force F-84 Thunderstreak. Republic received an air force contract in 1952, and the prototype aircraft first flew in October 1955. The sweptback wings of the final design were relatively small for the aircraft. This ensured a smoother ride at lower altitudes but sacrificed some agility. It also necessitated a longer takeoff. The Republic Aircraft F-105 Thunderchief, popularly known as the "Thud," went through a difficult development period, in part caused by shifting air force requirements. Any damage to its reputation from this was rectified by its role in the Vietnam War. The F-105 entered service in 1959.

The F-105B was the first production model. The definitive model F-105D first flew in June 1959. Earlier aircraft were brought up to its specifications during 1962–1964. The F-105D was powered by a Pratt & Whitney J57-P-19W engine that provided 16,100 pounds thrust (24,500 pounds with afterburner) and a maximum speed of 1,390 miles per hour. Maximum ceiling was 45,000 feet, and range was 1,500 miles (2,390 with external tanks). The F-105D's nose was slightly lengthened to store the AN/ASG-9 Thunderstick system featuring a multimode radar that added low-level terrain-following and weapons-delivery capabilities. The aircraft was armed with a single General Electric M61 six-barrel 20mm Vulcan Gatling gun, firing from the left side of the nose. The F-105D could carry a very heavy load of ordnance aloft: 8,000 pounds of munitions in its bomb bay and another 4,000 pounds of stores on five external pylons, one on the aircraft centerline and two under each wing. The F-105F of 1963 incorporated a second crewman to improve its fighter-bomber capability.

A U.S. Air Force Republic F-105 Thunderchief refuels at a flying gas station while en route to Vietnam on a bombing mission in January 1966. The F-105 fighter-bomber bore the brunt of Operation ROLLING THUNDER, the bombing of North Vietnam during the Vietnam War. A total of 385 F-105s were lost in the war to all causes. (National Archives)

The multirole F-105 has been described both as the world's best fighter aircraft of the early 1960s and the largest engine single-seat combat aircraft. During the Vietnam War, F-105s flew three-quarters of the aerial missions against the Democratic Republic of Vietnam (North Vietnam) and provided excellent service in both fighter-bomber and Wild Weasel electronic countermeasures roles. During the war, 385 Thunderchiefs were lost in action either to combat or mechanical failure. Flak and surface-to-air missiles claimed 312, while North Vietnamese MiGs shot down another 22 (although Thunderchiefs downed 27.5 MiGs in return). A total of 833 Thunderchiefs were manufactured. F-105s in service were transferred to reserve units in 1980 and retired altogether in 1984.

Further Reading

Fredriksen, John C. *Warbirds: An Illustrated Guide to U.S. Military Aircraft, 1915–2000.* Santa Barbara, CA: ABC-CLIO, 1999.

Green, William, and Gordon Swanborough. *The Complete Book of Fighters.* London: Salamander Books, 1994.

Rendall, Ivan. *Rolling Thunder.* New York: Free Press, 1997.

Bell UH-1 Iroquois Helicopter

The Bell UH-1 Iroquois, popularly known as the "Huey," is the largest production-run helicopter in history and probably the best known. With more than 15,000 built in the United States and under foreign license in Italy and Japan, the Huey is the largest production aircraft since World War II next to the Soviet-era Antonov AN-2 biplane transport.

In 1955 the U.S. Army awarded Bell a contract for a medical evacuation (medevac) helicopter. Designated by Bell as Model 204, the first prototype flew in October 1956. The army ordered 183 of the now-designated HU-1A. "HU" stood for "helicopter utility," giving rise to its name of Huey. The first delivery occurred in June 1959, and production was completed in 1961.

The rounded nose, wide-bodied, and twin-bladed rotor HU-1A was the first U.S. Army turbine-powered helicopter, easily identified by its "whomp whomp" sound in flight. The Huey could carry the pilot, copilot, and two stretchers across the cabin and a medical attendant or six passengers. Deployed to Vietnam, a number of the Hueys were fitted with a single Browning M-60 .30-caliber machine gun on a fixed mount to each side door and twin forward-firing packs of 70mm (2.75-inch) unguided rockets, with 8 rockets per pack for a total of 16.

The Huey underwent numerous modifications. In September 1962 "HU" became "UH," and the follow-on UH-1B had an improved turboshaft engine and a redesigned wider-span rotor blade. A stretched fuselage allowed transport of three stretchers, two sitting casualties, and a medical attendant; seven passengers; or 3,000 pounds of cargo. Powered by a 1,400-horsepower Lycoming T-53 turboshaft engine, it had a maximum speed of 127 miles per hour, a ceiling of 12,700 feet, and a range of 777 miles. Armament consisted of four 7.62mm machine guns (two each on an outrigger outboard of each door) and the two rocket packs. The pilot aimed the machine guns by means of a cockpit-mounted sight and a hydraulic activation system.

Troops in Vietnam knew the transport Hueys as "Slicks" for their lack of externally mounted, fixed armament, while the medevac helicopters were known as "Dustoffs." Slicks usually carried door-mounted M-60 7.62mm machine guns to provide covering fire to troops. Gunship-version UH-1Bs lacked sufficient power to keep up with the transport Hueys, so Bell came up with the more powerfully engined UH-1C, introduced in September 1965. The AH-1 HueyCobra (more often simply called the Cobra) gunship was based on the UH-1C design and employed its engine, rotors, and some other systems.

The Huey was one of the signature weapons of the Vietnam War, dubbed by many "the first helicopter war." By 1973 some 2,500 Hueys had been lost in Vietnam, about half of them to combat. Despite these losses, the Hueys proved both rugged and reliable. Although replaced in U.S. service by the UH-60 Black Hawk, the Huey remains in service with the military establishments of some 35 nations.

Further Reading

Fredriksen, John C. *Warbirds: An Illustrated Guide to U.S. Military Aircraft, 1915–2000.* Santa Barbara, CA: ABC-CLIO, 1999.

McGowen, Stanley S. *Helicopters: An Illustrated History of Their Impact.* Santa Barbara, CA: ABC-CLIO, 2005.

Mesko, Jim. *Airmobile: The Helicopter War in Vietnam.* Carrollton, TX: Squadron Signal Publications, 1984.

Bell AH-1 Cobra and AH-1W SuperCobra Attack Helicopters

The U.S. Army Bell AH-1 Cobra was the world's first purpose-designed attack helicopter gunship. It served effectively during the Vietnam War and in a number of subsequent conflicts.

The Vietnam War demonstrated the need for a helicopter that could escort lightly armed troop-carrying helicopters and also serve in a ground-attack role. In 1965 the army initiated a design competition for such an aircraft, which Bell won. The new helicopter utilized a number of systems that had proven highly successful in the Bell UH-1 Huey. Instead of the wide body of the latter, however, the AH-1 Cobra was both thin and streamlined. It also featured both a chin turret and short winglets for improved lift and to serve as weapons platforms. Its long canopy provided excellent visibility for the two-man tandem-seated (one behind the other) crew. Tests proved so successful that the Cobra was ordered into production in April 1966. It entered service the next year, when it also arrived in Vietnam and proved to be an immediate success in both escort and ground-attack roles. Bell built 1,116 AH-1s for the army between 1967 and 1975.

The twin-blade Cobra was powered by one 1,800-horsepower Lycoming T55 turboshaft engine that provided a maximum speed of 141 miles per hour, a ceiling of 12,200 feet, and a range of 315 miles. Armament varied. Earlier versions mounted 7.62mm miniguns; later versions had the three-barreled 20mm Gatling gun and eight TOW and Hellfire antitank missiles on the winglets.

Cobras helped break up the North Vietnamese invasion of South Vietnam in the 1972 Spring or Easter Offensive, in the process knocking out large numbers of communist tanks. They also performed well in the Persian Gulf War in 1991. The Israeli Air Force employed its Cobras to destroy dozens of Syrian tanks and armored vehicles in Operation PEACE FOR GALILEE in 1982. The Cobra has now been entirely replaced in U.S. Army service by the Hughes (McDonnell Douglas/ Boeing) AH-64 Apache.

In 1969 a new, more powerful version of the Cobra entered service, developed for the U.S. Marine Corps. The AH-1J SuperCobra/SeaCobra was powered with two 1,600-horsepower General Electric T700 turboshaft engines that provided nearly twice the horsepower of its predecessor and half again the speed as well as an increased margin of safety for a craft that would be operating over water much of the time. It had a maximum speed of 218 miles per hour, a ceiling of 17,500 feet, and a maximum range of 395 miles. It had the same armament capacities as its predecessor. Iran purchased several hundred SuperCobras.

In 1975 the AH-IT KingCobra was introduced. It featured a larger airframe capable of carrying more fuel for increased range, a longer tail boom, and an improved rotor. In 1983 the AH-1W SuperCobra appeared, with a more powerful General Electric T700 GE-401 engine and more sophisticated electronic systems as well as enhanced night-fighting capabilities. It is armed with a three-barreled 20mm cannon (750 rounds) and missiles, which could include the Sidewinder (antiair) and Sidearm (antiradar). The SuperCobra performed effectively for U.S. marines in Grenada and in the Persian Gulf War and the Iraq War. The U.S. Marine Corps prefers it to the Apache because of its smaller footprint aboard ship and because it is easier to maintain. The SuperCobra is primarily employed against enemy armor. Constant upgrades ensure that the SuperCobra will remain in service for some years to come. SuperCobras are also operated by a number of other nations.

Further Reading

Fredriksen, John C. *Warbirds: An Illustrated Guide to U.S. Military Aircraft, 1915–2000.* Santa Barbara, CA: ABC-CLIO, 1999.

McGowen, Stanley S. *Helicopters: An Illustrated History of Their Impact.* Santa Barbara, CA: ABC-CLIO, 2005.

Mil Mi-24 Hind Helicopter

Designed by Mikhail Mil in the Soviet Union, the Mil Mi-24 Hind is based on Mil's earlier Mi-8 transport helicopter design and propulsion system. Development of the Hind (NATO designation) was in large part prompted by the appearance of the world's first dedicated helicopter gunship, the U.S. Bell AH-1 Cobra, which was introduced in 1967 and proved its effectiveness in the Vietnam War. Entering service in 1973, the Mi-24 was the Soviet Union's first helicopter gunship. It is also the world's largest and most heavily armed helicopter gunship and has been described as a "flying tank." Its U.S. counterparts are the Cobra and the Hughes AH-64 Apache, but unlike these and other Western attack helicopters, the Hind is an assault transport that can carry up to eight fully equipped troops.

The Hind features a five-blade main rotor and a three-blade tail rotor. Flown by a crew of two men, it is powered by two 2,190-horsepower Kilmov TV3–117 turbine engines and has a cruising speed of 208 miles per hour, a ceiling of 14,750 feet, and a range of 456 miles. Its short, stubby wings located at the midsection of the fuselage provide added lift. Each has three weapons stations that can mount a variety of systems. The most usual configuration is a chin-turret–mounted 23mm

Gatling gun and antitank rockets on the winglets. In addition, troops aboard can fire their weapons through the cabin windows.

The MI-24's armored cockpit and titanium rotor head can withstand 20mm cannon fire. The Hind is also equipped with an overpressurization system to allow it to operate in a nuclear-biological-chemical warfare environment. Because of its large size and weight the Mi-24 is not easily maneuverable, and for that reason tactical doctrine calls for it to be employed in pairs, often approaching a targeted area from different directions.

In addition to acting as a gunship and an assault transport, the Mi-24 serves in air support, antitank, armed escort, and air-to-air combat roles. The Mi-24 was a signature weapon of the Soviet invasion of Afghanistan (1979–1989). At first it enjoyed great success in operating against the lightly armed Afghan guerrillas, but then it sustained substantial losses from U.S.-supplied Stinger antiaircraft missiles.

Some 2,300 Mi-24s have been built. Still regarded as a highly effective antitank platform, it serves with the Russian Air Force and was widely exported within the communist bloc and to Third World nations. The M-24 is flown by the air forces of some 59 nations.

Further Reading

Fredriksen, John C. *International Warbirds: An Illustrated Guide to World Military Aircraft, 1914–2000.* Santa Barbara, CA: ABC-CLIO, 2001.

McGowen Stanley S. *Helicopters: An Illustrated History of Their Impact.* Santa Barbara, CA: ABC-CLIO, 2005.

FIM-92 Stinger

The FIM-92 Stinger is a man-portable shoulder-fired ground-to-air missile. All such systems are known as MANPADS, for "*man-*portable *a*ir *d*efense *s*ystems." Developed by the U.S. Army, the Stinger is issued to all branches of the U.S. military as its primary short-range air defense weapon. Manufactured by Raytheon, a division of General Dynamics, it was conceived in 1967 as an improved Redeye. The army renamed it the Stinger. Produced beginning in 1978, it entered service in 1981, replacing the Redeye that had been introduced in the 1960s.

As with its predecessor, the Stinger is a fire-and-forget weapon that utilized a passive infrared heat seeker to locate its target. As such, it is similar to the British Blowpipe and the Soviet Grail (SA-7). The Stinger represented a considerable improvement over the Redeye in enhanced range and maneuverability, better countermeasures immunity, and an IFF (identification friend or foe) system to preclude shooting down friendly aircraft. Improved models of the Stinger also appeared. The C model has a reprogrammable microprocessor (RMP) to allow for upgrades. The RMP Block I was introduced in 1995, and the RMP Block II was introduced in 2004. These increased the range and effectiveness of the missile.

Two members of the 3rd Low Altitude Air Defense Battalion, U.S. Marine Corps acquire an aircraft target with an FIM-92 Stinger missile weapon system during a training exercise at Tinian in the Northern Mariana Islands in September 2014. (Department of Defense/Lance Cpl. Tyler Ngiraswei)

The Stinger is packaged within its launch tube. A separate reusable battery coolant unit must be inserted in the hand guard prior to firing. This releases argon gas into the system, allowing it to operate. The launch tube is 5 feet long by 5.5 inches in diameter. The Stinger 92C missile itself is 5 feet long and 2.75 inches in diameter (fin span is 3.6 inches). The complete system weighs 34.7 pounds, with the rocket weighing 22.3 pounds. Powered by a solid-fuel two-stage motor, the missile flies at Mach 2.2+ speeds. It has a range of 15,700 feet (26,000 feet for the Block II). The warhead weighs 6.6 pounds and is of blast-fragmentation type. Set off by impact, it also has a self-destruct timer.

Stinger launch teams usually consist of two gunners and two missile launchers. The gunners can either assist one another or fire independently. The missile can also be launched from a variety of platforms, including vehicles such as the Avenger and the Bradley Stinger fighting vehicle as well as helicopters.

The first recorded kill of an aircraft by a Stinger came during the 1982 Falklands War between Britain and Argentina when on May 21, 1982, one downed an Argentine Pucara ground-attack aircraft. The Stinger and its adversary, the Mil Mi-24 Hind helicopter, were the signature weapons of the Soviet-Afghan War (1979–1989). Provided to the Afghan mujahideen fighting the Soviets, the Stinger was decisive in defeating Soviet airpower in the conflict. Stingers have been credited with

270 aircraft kills. Supplied to 29 other nations, the Stinger is also built in Germany by EADS. Reportedly, some 70,000 Stingers have been produced.

Further Reading

Chant, Christopher. *World Encyclopedia of Modern Air Weapons.* New York: HarperCollins, 1989.

Cullen, Tony, and Christopher F. Foss, eds. *Jane's Land-Based Air Defence, 2005–2006.* London: Jane's Information Group, 2005.

Gunston, Bill. *The Illustrated Encyclopedia of Aircraft Armament: A Major Directory of Guns, Rockets, Missiles, Bombs, Torpedoes and Mines.* New York: Orion Books, 1988.

AIM-9 Sidewinder Missile

Among missiles developed after World War II were those carried aloft by aircraft specifically to shoot down other aircraft. Air-to-air missiles (AAM) are guided, directed to the target usually by radar or infrared sensing. Although these are the two principal types, there are also laser guidance and optical tracking systems. AAM warheads are detonated either by impact or proximity fuzing.

Radar guidance is usually employed at long or medium ranges, where the heat source may be too faint for the infrared system to track. Infrared systems home in on the heat emitted by the aircraft exhaust, and the missile flies into the target aircraft's engine. As a defensive measure, aircraft will often drop flares in an effort to confuse the missile's guidance system. Infrared tends to be less expensive than other systems, can be used in all conditions, and allows the pilot firing it to leave the area and take evasive action.

AAMs are long and thin cylinders in shape in order to minimize drag at high speed. From front to rear, AAMs usually consist of the seeking system, avionics that control the missile, the warhead, the explosive charge, and the rocket motor, which is usually a dual-thrust solid-fuel type. There are many different types of AAMs. Among the best known are the Soviet AA-1 Alkali (NATO designation) and AA-2 Atoll, the French-made Magic, the Israeli Python, and the U.S. AIM-7 Sparrow and AIM-9 Sidewinder.

The Sidewinder is an infrared-guided missile with a roll-stabilizing rear wing/ rolleron assembly. It is known for its exceptional reliability and maneuverability. Named for the snake that seeks out its prey by detecting body heat, the Sidewinder is the most widely used Western AAM. Originally developed for the U.S. Navy and designed by William McLean at the Naval Ordnance Test Station beginning in 1952, it built on German research at the end of World War II on an infrared-guided missile, the Enzian. A prototype Sidewinder was successfully test fired in September 1953, and the missile was declared operational in 1956.

A number of firms, chief among them Aerojet and Raytheon, manufacture components for the Sidewinder, which has gone through many improvements. The

AIM-9X Sidewinder is 9 feet 5 inches long and 5 inches in diameter with a fin span of 2 feet .75 inches. Its launch weight is 190 pounds, and it travels at Mach 2.5 speed. It is capable of locking on a target that is behind it. The warhead also detonates in the case of a near miss. Most earlier models are armed with a 22-pound warhead, although the X model has an annular blast fragmentation warhead consisting of a case of spirally wound spring steel filled with 8 pounds of tritonol.

A reduced smoke propellant makes it difficult for the pilot of the targeted aircraft to spot and avoid the missile. The AIM-9X also had smaller wings and fins. The Sidewinder also has the advantage of being relatively inexpensive, at $84,000 a copy.

The Sidewinder was first employed in combat by Republic of China (ROC) aircraft battling People's Republic of China MiG fighters over the Taiwan Straits. The Soviet K-13/R-3S missile (NATO designation AA-2 Atoll) was copied from one of the first ROC Sidewinders that struck a MiG-15 without exploding. The MiG was able to return to base with the missile lodged in its airframe. Soviet and Chinese scientists used the knowledge gained from studying the Sidewinder to develop the Atoll, which was in production for nearly 30 years. Sidewinders were also employed by U.S. aircraft during the Vietnam War. While in combat between Israel and the Arab states, the missile's greater speed and agility gave the Israeli Air Force a decided edge against aircraft belonging to Egypt and Syria that employed Soviet AAMs. Through 2006, more than 110,000 Sidewinders had been produced for the United States and 27 other nations, with some 270 aircraft destroyed by them.

Further Reading

Aloni, Shlomo. *Arab-Israeli Air Wars, 1947–1982.* London: Osprey, 2001.

Shannon, Chris. *Air-to-Air Missile Directory.* London: Centurion, 2005.

Satellites

Earth-orbiting space satellites have had immense military repercussions. On October 4, 1957, a new era opened when the Soviet Union launched *Sputnik I,* the first man-made object to orbit Earth. *Sputnik I* weighed about 183 pounds and was able to transmit radio messages back to Earth. A month later, the Soviets launched into orbit *Sputnik II.* Considerably heavier at 1,120 pounds, it carried cameras. Although the United States initially trailed the Soviet Union in what became known as the space race, it soon caught up with and surpassed its rival.

The first military communications satellite was the U.S. SCORE (Signal Communications by Orbital Relay Equipment). Boosted into space by an Atlas rocket in December 1958, it lasted in orbit only 13 days. A bewildering number of different types of Earth-orbiting satellites with enhanced longevity followed, each with greater capabilities than its predecessor.

Geostationary orbits allowed a few satellites to achieve global coverage. Satellites fulfilled a variety of missions. Equipped with cameras of ever higher resolution, they supplemented manned photoreconnaissance aircraft and rendered unnecessary reconnaissance aircraft overflights of another nation's airspace. Today's sophisticated intelligence satellites can identify even small objects and transmit this information continuously to ground reception stations. Some satellites have infrared capability to see through cloud cover. Satellites have made possible for the first time the accurate mapping of Earth's surface and the pinpointing of its resources. They also provide accurate meteorological data, always of intense interest to battlefield and air commanders.

Networks of satellites also make possible rapid military communication. Beginning in 1994, the United States placed in geostationary orbit the first satellites of the Military Strategic Tactical and Relay (Milstar) satellite program. Other nations followed suit. The Global Positioning System (GPS) allowed an individual to determine his or her location anywhere on Earth to a matter of several feet.

As satellites grew in military utility, antisatellite weaponry was developed in order to defeat them if need be. The first such appeared as early as 1959 in the SAINT (satellite interceptor) project. By 1964 the United States had its first antisatellite system, utilizing Thor and Nike Zeus rockets.

Further Reading

Bull, Stephen. *Encyclopedia of Military Technology and Innovation.* Westport, CT: Greenwood, 2004.

Chetty, P. R. K. *Space Technology and Its Applications.* New York: McGraw-Hill, 1988.

Dutton, L. *Military Space.* London: Brassey's, 1990.

Intercontinental Ballistic Missiles

Intercontinental ballistic missiles (ICBMs) are long-range, rocket-propelled guided missiles capable of carrying one or more conventional or nuclear warheads. They may be either land- or sea-based; the Skybolt was even an air-launched ICBM. Land-based ICBMs deployed by the United States and the Soviet Union during the Cold War, along with manned bomber and submarine-launched ballistic missiles, made up the strategic nuclear triad of these two superpowers. The People's Republic of China later also developed ICBMs.

ICBMs offered quick delivery of nuclear weapons over long distances. Throughout the Cold War, the accuracy, reliability, and flexibility of ICBM systems continuously improved. At the peak of the Cold War in 1984, the United States maintained 1,054 ICBMs deployed in underground silos, while the Soviet Union possessed 1,398 ICBMs deployed in silos and in rail- and road-mobile systems.

Development of the ICBM began shortly after the end of World War II. ICBMs are normally defined as long-range missiles that can attack targets located great distances from their launch sites. In 1966 the Air University Aerospace Glossary defined ICBMs as those missiles with a range of 5,000 miles or more. Other sources have defined the ICBM as a missile with a range of 1,500 to 2,000 miles.

Initial missile programs, especially in the United States, focused more on "air-breathing," jet-powered cruise missiles than ballistic systems. By the late 1940s, however, both the United States and the Soviet Union had determined that ballistic missiles were better for long-range attack missions, since flight times, survivability, and accuracy were much better than they were for slower aerodynamic vehicles. By 1953, the development of smaller, lighter thermonuclear weapons made it possible to construct long-range missiles capable of delivering nuclear payloads. The earliest systems were complicated liquid-fueled missiles that employed liquid oxygen and kerosene or storable hypergolic chemicals (fuel and oxidizer that ignited and burned when mixed without a separate igniter) as propellants. The first versions were deployed on unhardened aboveground launchers that required anywhere from 15 minutes to several hours of preparation to launch. They were guided by ground-based radio guidance systems that limited the number of missiles that could be launched at a single time. The first U.S. operational ICBM system, the Atlas D, was a 75-foot-long missile weighing over 250,000 pounds. It was housed in either aboveground gantries or ground-level concrete structures known as "coffins," with three missiles and one guidance system at each complex. The first American ICBM attained nuclear alert (ready) status in October 1959.

Inertial guidance systems replaced the radio systems early in the life of ICBMs, with only the Atlas D and the Titan I deployed with radio guidance. The inertial system was more accurate and reliable than radio guidance and allowed missiles to be based individually, providing a higher survivability scenario during a nuclear exchange. The early U.S. liquid-fueled cryogenic missiles were expensive to maintain, had low reliability, and were not exceptionally accurate. These systems, the Atlas and Titan I, carried single four-megaton nuclear warheads. The United States was quick to replace these missiles with the solid-fueled Minuteman missile, and by 1965 all Atlas and Titan I missiles were removed from service, to be replaced by the Minuteman and the hypergolic-fueled Titan II.

These new systems were easier to maintain and required far fewer missile combat crew members and maintenance personnel to keep them on alert. They were also much more survivable, with hardened underground silos scattered over wide areas, and were accurate to a few hundred feet of the target. The United States maintained a force of 54 Titan II missiles, each with a nine-megaton warhead, on alert from the early 1960s to the mid-1980s. The Minuteman, which was developed in three versions (I, II, and III), first came on alert in 1962.

By 1967, 1,000 Minuteman missiles were on alert at six U.S. bases. The Minuteman I and Minuteman II had single warheads of about 1.1 megatons, while the

Minuteman III featured a multiple independently targeted reentry vehicle system equipped with up to three warheads of either 170 or 340 kilotons of yield. The entire force of Minuteman and Titan II missiles could be launched in a matter of minutes after the decision to execute was made. In the late 1980s, 50 Minuteman missiles at F. E. Warren Air Force Base, Wyoming, were replaced by 50 Peacekeeper missiles, a larger system that could carry up to 10 300-kiloton warheads capable of hitting 10 different targets.

The Soviets developed more varieties of missiles than did the Americans, early on relying on both cryogenic and hypergolic storable propellant systems. As with the Americans, the Soviets quickly realized that the cryogenic systems were slow to launch and hard to maintain, but unlike the United States, the Soviet Union concentrated on ICBM designs in the 1960s through the 1980s that featured storable liquid-fueled systems, with missiles deployed in both underground silos and mobile launchers. The first Soviet ICBM, the SS-7 or R-16, employed storable propellants and was first put on alert on November 1, 1961.

The Soviets were slower to adopt solid-fueled ICBMs but replaced their second- and third-generation liquid-fueled missiles with systems similar to the Minuteman and Peacekeeper systems. Soviet warheads were generally in the 1-megaton range, but two Soviet ICBMs (the SS-9 and SS-18) carried enormous 25-megaton warheads. In 1984 at the peak of the Cold War, the Soviets had 1,398 ICBMs deployed, including 520 SS-11s, 60 SS-13s, 150 SS-17s, 308 SS-18s, and 360 SS-19s.

China tested its first missile in 1960 but did not complete development and testing of an ICBM until 1980. China's first ICBM was liquid-fueled. China did not develop a solid-fueled ICBM until the early 1990s. Compared to the United States and the Soviet Union, China has maintained a very small ICBM force, with most of the emphasis on countering the threat posed by the Soviet Union rather than from the United States.

Strategic arms limitation and reduction agreements between the United States and Russia resulted in a significant reduction in the number of ICBMs. The United States reduced its force to only 500 Minuteman III missiles, which will eventually have only one warhead apiece. All Minuteman II missiles were removed and silos were destroyed at three bases between 1994 and 1998, and Peacekeeper missiles were removed between 2002 and 2007. At the end of 2002 the Russians maintained a force of 709 ICBMs, a mix of SS-18, SS-19, SS-24, SS-25, and SS-27 liquid- and solid-fueled missiles in silos or mobile launchers.

Further Reading

Gibson, James N. *Nuclear Weapons of the United States: An Illustrated History.* Atglen, PA: Schiffer, 1996.

Levi, Barbara G., et al., eds. *The Future of Land Based Ballistic Missiles.* New York: American Institute of Physics, 1989.

Neufeld, Jacob. *The Development of Ballistic Missiles in the United States Air Force, 1945–1960.* Washington, DC: Office of Air Force History, 1989.

MX Missile System

The U.S. MX (Mobile Experimental) intercontinental ballistic missile (ICBM) was the centerpiece of the U.S. arms buildup of the late 1970s and 1980s. Formally known as the LGM-118A Peacekeeper, the MX was a four-stage rocket. The largest ICBM ever in the U.S. arsenal, it had a length of 71 feet and a diameter of 7 feet 8 inches and weighed at launch some 198,000 pounds. The first three stages were of solid propellant, while the fourth stage was liquid propelled. The MX had a range of greater than 6,000 miles and a speed at burnout of up to 15,000 miles per hour. It carried 10 Avco MJ 21 multiple independently targeted reentry vehicles (its predecessor Minuteman III had only three less powerful warheads) and was believed to be more accurate than any other ICBM. The MX missiles were ultimately placed in canisters in former Minuteman silos to protect them against damage and give them a cold-launch capability. At launch, the Peacemaker was ejected by pressurized gas some 50 feet in the air before first-stage ignition occurred. It was the first ICBM to employ such technology.

Development of the Peacemaker began in 1971 with the search for a successor to the Minuteman, sparked by a perceived growing threat from Moscow in the form of more accurate Soviet missiles. The Strategic Air Command sought a missile with greater range, increased accuracy, and variable yield warheads that could take advantage of multiple independently targeted reentry vehicle technology and counter the new monster Soviet SS-18 missile capable of launching 10 warheads at separate targets. Many experts held that deployment of such a missile with a first-strike capability would be destabilizing, and this along with funding issues and basing questions impeded development.

Concerned about vulnerability to a Soviet first strike, in 1976 Congress passed legislation blocking funding for any ICBM situated in a fixed silo. The U.S. Air Force then presented a variety of different plans. Finally, in 1976 the Jimmy Carter administration adopted the shell game plan in which

Test flight of an LGM-118A Peacekeeper Intercontinental Ballistic Missile at Vandenberg Air Force Base, California, November 13, 1985. (Courtesy U.S. Department of Defense)

200 MX missiles would each be shuttled around among 23 different silos. The logic behind this plan was that the Soviets would have to employ 23 warheads to ensure that they had destroyed one MX or 4,600 warheads to hit them all. When Ronald Reagan became president, he scrapped the Carter mobile plan in favor of placing the MX missiles in existing Minuteman silos. In 1983 Congress and the Reagan administration reached a compromise. While the MX missiles would be placed in silos, the United States would also build 500 single-warhead ICBMs, dubbed the Midgetman. The Midgetman was never built, however.

The U.S. Air Force successfully carried out the first test of the Peacemaker missile in June 1983. Following additional tests, it went into production in February 1984. The first 50 missiles were deployed in the Minuteman silos at F. E. Warren Air Force Base, Wyoming. The 50th missile was delivered in December 1988.

Additional deployments were halted in July 1985 when Congress cut the total number of MX missiles to only 50 until the Reagan administration could produce a more survivable basing plan. The Reagan administration proposed a rail garrison concept with 2 missiles on each of 25 special trains to be deployed onto the national rail net in periods of international tension. This plan was never implemented, and all 50 missiles were based at F. E. Warren Air Force Base. Following the Strategic Arms Reduction Treaty II (START II), the United States agreed to eliminate its multiple reentry vehicle ICBMs. The last of the MX missiles went off alert status in September 2005.

Further Reading

Gold, David, and Christopher Paine. *Misguided Expenditures: An Analysis of the Proposed MX Missile System.* New York: Council on Economic Priorities, 1981.

Graham, Thomas, Jr., and Damien J. La Vera. *Cornerstones of Security: Arms Control Treaties in the Nuclear Era.* Seattle: University of Washington Press, 2003.

Cruise Missiles

One of the most dangerous weapons of modern warfare, cruise missiles essentially are unmanned aircraft that cruise until they dive or crash into their targets. Cruise missiles trace their roots to the World War II German V-1 buzz bomb. The only real differences between today's cruise missile and the V-1 are the propulsion and guidance systems, range, accuracy, and warhead. The V-1's pulse-jet engine and simple gyro-timing guidance system have given way to highly efficient turbofans and a variety of guidance system tailored to the missile's specific mission or target. Today's cruise missiles can fly a terrain-hugging deceptive flight route to a target 1,000 miles distant and have a 70 percent probability of a direct hit (99 percent chance of hitting within 10 yards of it).

Following World War II, both the United States and the Soviet Union exploited German V-1 technology in order to develop their own cruise missiles. By 1950, both countries had working prototypes of turbojet-powered "flying bombs" under development. The best known of the American models were the U.S. Navy's Regulus and the U.S. Air Force's Hound Dog. As with the V-1, these cruise missiles were seen as area attack weapons. Only the American missiles carried nuclear instead of conventional warheads. The Regulus had a range of 600 miles and was to be submarine-launched, while the similarly ranged Hound Dog was air-launched from Boeing B-47 Stratojet and Boeing B-52 Stratofortress strategic bombers. Neither missile was particularly accurate, and both left service by the mid-1966s.

With more accurate and powerful submarine-launched ballistic missiles entering service, the major Western naval powers suspended their cruise missile programs. Aircraft carriers obviated the need for surface ships to have a long-range strike capability. However, the Soviet Union lacked aircraft carriers and therefore pushed ahead with a cruise missile intended to attack ships. This was the SS-1, which entered service in 1958. It was followed two years later by the SS-2. These missiles differed from their American counterparts primarily in having a radar-based terminal guidance system.

France was the only nation to see value in developing its own antiship missiles, but the program enjoyed only a low priority. All that changed in 1967 when the Egyptian Navy sank the Israeli destroyer *Eilat* with an SS-N-2. All navies then embraced antiship cruise missiles as the poor man's naval strike weapon. Moreover, they recognized the value of such weapons in situations where increasingly expensive aircraft carriers were not available. Antiship cruise missiles, such as the French *Exocet* and the American *Harpoon* and *Tomahawk,* were the first to enter service, but their relative light weight and expense when compared to carrier aviation led some to examine their use in the land-attack role. Meanwhile, the Soviets developed their own family of long-range antiship cruise missiles, notably the SSN-3, SS-N-12, SS-N-19, and SS-N-22.

By the early 1980s, advances in microminiaturization, avionics, and navigation systems brought land-attack cruise missiles back into vogue, for both conventional and nuclear missions. The American land-attack Tomahawk initially had a terrain contour matching guidance system that enabled it to navigate overland by matching its onboard radar's picture of the terrain below against a computer-developed map of its flight route to the target. By the late 1990s, this system and missile accuracy was replaced by a module that guided the missile by the Global Positioning System (GPS), making the missile accurate to within a few yards. Finally, a digital scene matching area (DSMA) correlation feature was added to ensure that the missile would select the right target as it entered the target area by matching a digital image of the target scene (radar, optical, or infrared or a combination of these) against an onboard image data base. DSMA is particularly useful against mobile targets. By the end of the Cold War, treaties and other considerations had driven all nuclear-armed cruise missiles from service. Conventionally armed cruise missiles were now so accurate that Western political and military leaders had come to see them as politically safe precision weapons that could be employed in an infinite variety of situations.

The present U.S. air-launched AGM-86 and the submarine- or ship-launched BGM-109 Tomahawk are quite similar in size and capability. The AGM-86 is 20 feet 7 inches long, weighs 3,150 pounds, flies at 550 miles per hour, and has a range of some 1,500 miles. The Tomahawk is only slightly smaller and has a range of 700 miles.

Cruise missiles are a relatively inexpensive, expendable alternative to expensive aircraft and ballistic missiles. They have become the weapon of choice for retaliatory strikes and the initial military operations conducted during a war. The newest cruise missiles incorporate stealth technologies to make them more difficult to detect and engage. Others rely on supersonic dash speeds to defeat air defenses. Cruise missiles are employed to take out key enemy command centers, air defense sites, and airfields before manned aircraft are committed to the fight. In peacetime, they are used for situations where a rapid, precise attack is required and the political-military leadership does not wish to risk pilot losses. The twenty-first century has seen a proliferation of cruise missiles, and in combination with unmanned aerial vehicles, cruise missiles have become an increasingly prominent element of modern warfare.

Further Reading

Frieden, David R. *Principles of Naval Weapons Systems.* Annapolis, MD: U.S. Naval Institute, 1985.

Hewson, Robert, ed. *Jane's Air-Launched Weapons, 2001.* London: Jane's, 2002.

Hooten, Ted. *Jane's Naval Weapons Systems, 2001–2002.* London: Jane's, 2002.

Polaris Missile

The Polaris was the U.S. Navy submarine-launched ballistic missile (SLBM) carried in nuclear-powered submarines. The SLBM system constituted the initial seaborne leg of what became America's nuclear triad and was part of its nuclear deterrence strategy. This strategy called for the United States to have a survivable nuclear retaliation capability, known as second strike, in order to deter a potential Soviet first strike. Bombers and land-based intercontinental ballistic missiles in hardened silos provided the other legs of the triad, each with its particular advantages and disadvantages. The submarine-based element offered stealth, denying the Soviets knowledge of the number and locations of the embarked missile systems. It was a sound enough strategy, but the Polaris leg was almost scratched.

Navy leaders of the 1950s favored cruise missiles over ballistic missiles. They were cheaper and were easier to install on ships and submarines, and the technology was already well understood. However, ballistic missiles offered more range, greater accuracy, and faster response times, and perhaps more important, there was no known defense against ballistic missiles at the time. By 1956, the U.S. Navy began to examine the challenges of installing a missile system aboard ships and submarines. The initial proposal to install Jupiter missiles was rejected because of the dangers of storing the missiles' liquid-oxygen oxidizer component in an enclosed hull for any significant period of time. Solid rocket fuel was the chosen option, and the primary contractor, Lockheed, concentrated on developing new and more powerful solid rocket fuels for the project.

Lockheed Missile and Space Division engineers lower a Polaris missile into a fiberglass sleeve aboard the ballistic missile submarine *George Washington* at Port Canaveral, Florida, in 1960. (Naval Historical Center)

The first test flight took place in September 1959, and the Polaris A-1 Missile entered service aboard the U.S. Navy submarine *George Washington* in November 1960. The first improved model, the A-2 Polaris, became operational in 1961. It replaced the Regulus cruise missile.

The Polaris was the first missile to be fired from a submerged submarine and the first to use a cold-launch system. That is, a missile's rocket engine did not ignite until after it left the launch tube. A compressed-air slug lifted the missile out of the tube and above the ocean's surface. The rocket engine ignited after the missile broke the ocean's surface. This avoided the challenge, expense, and danger of containing a rocket-ignition system within the submarine's hull. This procedure proved reliable in service and has been the standard method for all submarine-launched missiles developed during and after the Cold War.

The Polaris A-1 was 28 feet 6 inches long and 4 feet 6 inches wide. It weighed 28,800 pounds and was powered by a two-stage solid propellant rocket engine. Each stage used four nozzles with thrust-vectoring for flight control. It had a range of 1,200 nautical miles and could deliver a single 600-kiloton nuclear warhead within 3,000 feet of the target. The A-2, deployed beginning in June 1962, had a slightly longer first stage and a lighter second stage, giving an improved range of 1,500 nautical miles. The still lighter A-3 had three reentry vehicles, each with a 200-kiloton warhead. An improved navigation system enabled accuracy to about 2,000 feet. The A-3 became operational in September 1964.

To save money, the navy chose to modify an attack submarine design to carry the missiles. Research and development experience with early nuclear-powered submarines had demonstrated that they had the power to support the missile system and the underwater endurance to prevent the Soviets from detecting the launch platform. Hull testing with the *Albacore* had also indicated the best hull form. Navy engineers took the design for the new class of attack submarines with an *Albacore* hull and simply plugged in a missile compartment to hold 16 Polaris missiles. Thus was born the George Washington class of nuclear-powered ballistic missile submarines. Close coordination between the missile and submarine design teams precluded any major problems with construction. The lead submarine unit was completed in time to join the missile test program in late 1959.

The Polaris remained the cornerstone of the U.S. Navy's ballistic missile system throughout the 1960s and early 1970s. The first Poseidon SLBMs joined the fleet in 1974, but the last Polaris A-3 was not withdrawn from service until October 1981. Between 1959 and 1968, Lockheed produced some 1,150 Polaris missiles, with more than half of them the A-3.

Further Reading

Gibson, James N. *Nuclear Weapons of the United States: An Illustrated History*. Atglen, PA: Schiffer, 1996.

Spinardi, Graham, et al. *From Polaris to Trident: The Development of U.S. Fleet Ballistic Missile Technology*. Cambridge: Cambridge University Press, 1994.

Precision-Guided Munitions

Precision guided munitions (PGMs), sometimes referred to as smart bombs, are air-dropped, air-fired, or surface-fired munitions that are guided to their targets, as opposed to iron or dumb bombs, which have no guidance systems. Obviously, accurate delivery of a munition is of paramount importance in war, both to maximize damage to the target and to minimize civilian casualties.

The United States experimented with guided bombs during World War I with only limited results. During World War II, the Germans developed two steerable radio-controlled glide bombs. The first of these was the free-fall FX-1200. It weighed 3,460 pounds, had a 771-pound warhead, and had small wings (5 feet 3 inches). The Germans employed FX-1200s on September 9, 1943, to sink the Italian battleship *Roma* and severely damage the battleship *Italia*. The Hs-293 was a guided and winged bomb fitted with a rocket motor. It weighed about 2,140 pounds, of which 1,124 pounds were in the warhead. It employed a wire-guided system for control and had a useful range of almost 10 nautical miles.

Near the end of the war, the United States developed the AZON (*az*imuth *on*ly) bomb. Officially designated the VB-1 (vertical bomb), it was a 1,000-pound bomb with a radio-controlled tail fin. A bright flare located on the tail of the bomb enabled the pilot to observe and control the bomb once it had been released from a modified consolidated B-24 Liberator bomber.

Work on smart bombs continued after World War II, and in the 1960s the United States developed the electro-optical bomb. These had television cameras that transmitted a view of the target back to the controlling aircraft, where the operator transmitted radio signals to manipulate the fins on the bomb to control it. These proved immensely useful to the United States in the Vietnam War during Operation ROLLING THUNDER, the bombing of North Vietnam, in circumstances where there was considerable opposition in the United States to the bombing campaign and concerns over civilian casualties. The Walleye TV camera–guided bomb and the BOLT-117, the world's first laser-guided bomb (LGB), were both employed in the bombing of difficult-to-strike point targets, such as bridges. Enhanced Walleyes continue in use more than 40 years later.

During the 1991 Persian Gulf War, coalition forces made much of the use of PGMs, showing footage at press briefings of their apparent pinpoint accuracy. The public drew the incorrect conclusion that most bombs dropped by coalition forces were of this type and that civilian casualties were but few. Yet only some 9 percent of all bombs dropped in the war were of the smart variety. By the Iraq War (2003–2011), however, 70 percent of the bombs were of the smart variety, and only 30 percent of aerial munitions were of the dumb variety. North Atlantic Treaty Organization aircraft also employed large number of LGBs with great effectiveness during the 1999 Kosovo War.

Of PGMs, perhaps the best known are the Paveway LGBs developed by Texas Instruments. All laser-guided weapons depend on the target being illuminated or painted by a laser target designator. This may be done by special forces on the ground or by a laser from the attacking aircraft itself.

Thanks to PGMs, the change in bombing effectiveness has been dramatic indeed. World War II saw the first so-called precision bombing, but despite claims to the contrary, it was essentially area bombing. By the time of the Persian Gulf War, however, two crewmen in a single aircraft could drop two LGBs with a 90 percent or better chance of success, barring an outright munitions failure.

Further Reading

Hallion, Richard P. *Precision Guided Munitions and the New Era of Warfare.* Air Power Studies Center Working Paper No. 53. Fairbairn, Australia: Air Powers Studies Center, Fairbairn RAAF Base, 1995.

334 | Cluster Bomb/Munition

McFarland, Stephen L. *America's Pursuit of Precision Bombing, 1910–1945.* Washington, DC: Smithsonian Institution Press, 1995.

Richardson, M., et al. *Surveillance and Target Acquisition Systems.* London: Brassey's, 1997.

Cluster Bomb/Munition

Cluster bombs or cluster munitions are bombs or shells containing many smaller munitions, commonly referred to as submunitions or bomblets. Although there are specialized cluster munitions for very specific uses, most are employed against enemy personnel or armor. Cluster munitions can be delivered by bombs, artillery shells, mortars, or rockets.

Although the principle was exploited in World War I mortars, cluster munitions were first used in significant numbers during World War II. Probably the first cluster bomb was the German Spreng Dickwändig 2 kg (SD-2), commonly known as the Butterfly Bomb. The Japanese also developed a 550-pound incendiary bomb for airburst that was fuzed to burst open about 200 feet off the ground and scatter 750 thermite containers over a 500-foot radius. The Americans dropped M60 napalm-filled bombs on Japan. Weighing 6 pounds each with a cloth ribbon for stabilization, they were loaded 38 to a container. Boeing B-29 bombers carried several dozen containers in a normal bomb load. The containers were on time fuzes, set to break apart at about 5,000 feet and scatter the M60s, which then exploded on ground contact.

The major military powers continued research on cluster munitions after World War II. In the United States, such artillery-fired weapons came to be known as improved conventional munitions. The Soviets employed large numbers of cluster munitions in the Soviet-Afghan War (1979–1989), many of them disguised as innocent-looking items that would explode if moved. Most advanced cluster munitions, such as the Israeli M85, contain timed self-destruct mechanisms designed to minimize their danger to civilians or others after the immediate need for the munitions has passed.

In air-dropped cluster bombs, the dispenser or bomb is usually of streamlined shape with fins for stabilization. It may contain as many as 2,000 submunitions, which often have small parachutes or cloth streamers to stabilize their descent, resulting in optimal dispersion patterns. Other submunitions are simply round antipersonnel explosive devices that explode when any pressure is placed on them. Such submunitions might be as small as 1.7 inches in diameter.

Dual-purpose improved conventional munitions (DPICMs) are effective against both personnel and armor. Some DPICM submunitions have shaped charge warheads, and some carry explosively formed penetrators. Specialized antirunway submunitions are designed to penetrate the surface of a runway before exploding, while mine-laying cluster bombs scatter numerous smaller mines for later detonation. During the NATO intervention in Kosovo in 1999, the United States employed the CBU-94/B, a cluster bomb with bomblets containing aluminum-coated conductive fibers designed to produce short circuits in high-voltage power lines. These knocked out some 70 percent of the Serbian power supply. Although they have not been used in warfare, both the United States and Soviet Union, and undoubtedly other powers, have developed special cluster munitions for the dispersal of chemical weapons.

Among the most commonly employed cluster munitions is the U.S MK-20 Rockeye cluster bomb, developed by ISC Technologies. A free-fall, unguided (dumb) bomb, the 500-pound Rockeye is designed to act against tanks and armored vehicles. It consists of a clamshell dispenser, a mechanical MK-339 timed fuze, and 247 dual-purpose armor-piercing shaped-charge bomblets, each weighing 1.32 pounds with a .4-pound shaped-charge warhead of high explosive that can penetrate some 7.5 inches of armor. First fielded in 1968, it was extensively employed during the Persian Gulf War in 1991. Typically, the Rockeye spreads its bomblets over an area of some 1,700 square feet.

The nondiscriminatory nature of cluster munitions, which are designed to scatter over a wide area, and the small size of their submunitions have meant that many civilians, especially children, have fallen prey to them. This in turn has led to widespread appeals that they be banned from warfare. In June 2006, Belgium was the first country to issue a ban on the use, transportation, export, stockpiling, and production of cluster munitions. As of September 2014, the 2010 Convention on Cluster Munitions had been signed by 109 nations. The major military powers of the United States, Russia, China, and Israel are not among them.

Further Reading

Bailey, Jonathan B. A. *Field Artillery and Firepower.* Annapolis, MD: Naval Institute Press, 2004.

Hogg, Ivan V. *Artillery 2000.* London: Arms and Armour, 1990.

Lennox, Duncan, ed. *Jane's Air-Launched Weapons.* Alexandria, VA: Jane's Information Group-Sentinel House, 1999.

M48 and M60 U.S. Main Battle Tanks

The Korean War caught the U.S. Army in the midst of development of a new medium tank. The T42 design was not ready, but its turret and new gun were. As a stopgap measure, these were adapted to the M46 hull, in effect the World War II M26 Pershing with a new engine and other upgrades. This became the M47 Patton, which entered service in 1952. It proved to be a successful design. The well-contoured turret had a prominent bustle for radio equipment.

The Patton was among the first tanks to mount a gun equipped with a blast deflector and bore evacuator fume extractor. It also had an optical range finder in the turret roof, and some later production vehicles had an early ballistic computer. The M47 had a five-man crew. It weighed nearly 102,000 pounds, had an 810-horsepower engine, and was capable of a speed of 37 miles per hour. It was armed with a 90mm gun and three machine guns and had maximum 100mm armor protection. Patton variants had a long service life in the U.S. Army and abroad.

As with the M47, its follow-on design, the M48 Patton II main battle tank (MBT), was rushed into service as a consequence of the Korean War and Soviet pressure in Berlin. The M48, however, was a brand new design with new hull, turret, tracks, suspension, and transmission. The M48 went through a large number of modifications to become one of the most important of post–World War II tanks. Compared to the M47, the M48 had a more rounded cast turret and a wider and lower cast hull. It weighed approximately 114,000 pounds, had a 750-horsepower engine, and was capable of a speed of 30 miles per hour. Design work began at the end of 1950, and the tank entered service in July 1952.

The M48 was the first U.S. medium tank to do away with the hull-mounted machine gun. This change dispensed with the assistant driver/machine-gunner and reduced the crew size to four men. The M48 was easily identified by a large infrared/white light 1 million–candle power searchlight for effective night operation, usually mounted atop the mantlet. The first variants of the M48 had the 90mm gun; the M48A5 version, however, mounted the British-designed 105mm gun and substituted a diesel engine. It was very similar to the follow-on M60 tank.

The M48 saw considerable service during the Vietnam War with both the U.S. Army and the U.S. Marines Corps but rarely against communist armor. In Middle Eastern fighting with the Israeli Army, however, the M48 achieved an enviable record against its Soviet-built opponents. Many other nations received the M48. During the 1982 Israeli invasion of Lebanon, some Israeli M48s were the first tanks fitted with explosive reactive armor.

The M60 was essentially a refinement of the M48 begun in the late 1950s; later a number of M48s were rebuilt as M48A5s, essentially M60s. The two were virtually indistinguishable. The M60 entered service in 1960.

A competition for the main gun of the M60 resulted in the selection of the new British L7A1 105mm (4.1-inch) gun (known in U.S. service as the M68). The M60 also had a new fire-control system. It also mounted two machine guns, a 7.62mm machine gun coaxial with the main gun, and a .50-caliber machine gun in the commander's hatch. The new tank weighed nearly 116,000 pounds and had a four-man crew. Its 750-horsepower engine produced a maximum speed of 30 miles per hour.

M60 variants included the M60A1, with a new turret; the M60A2, with a new turret with the 152mm gun/launcher developed for the M551 Sheridan; and the M60A3, which returned to the 105mm gun but with a thermal barrel jacket, a new fire-control computer with laser range finder, an infrared searchlight, and night vision equipment. Most M60A1s were later modified to M60A3s. Other design improvements have been added but with no change in model number.

Although it did not see service in Vietnam, the M60 remained the principal U.S. MBT for 20 years, until the introduction of the M1 Abrams. The M60 saw combat in the Arab-Israeli Wars and in the 1991 Persian Gulf War, serving with the U.S. Marine Corps and the Saudi Arabian Army. M60s remain in service in the armies of a number of nations around the world. Israel alone received some 1,350 M60s. Upgrades by General Dynamics Land Systems have converted M60s of a number of nations to the M60-2000. This upgrade incorporates many of the advantages of the M1 Abrams but at far less cost. Conversion kits include the M1 turret and the 120mm (4.72-inch) smoothbore gun, a new diesel power plant, and an M1 transmission system.

Further Reading

Foss, Christopher F., ed. *The Encyclopedia of Tanks and Armored Fighting Vehicles.* San Diego: Thunder Bay, 2002.

Tucker, Spencer C. *Tanks: An Illustrated History of Their Impact.* Santa Barbara, CA: ABC-CLIO, 2004.

T-54/T-55 Soviet Main Battle Tank

Despite many who believed that atomic weapons had rendered conventional weapons obsolete, tanks continued to see wide service in the world's armies after World War II. The Soviet Union saw them as an essential element of forces that would engage and defeat an enemy on the great plains of Central and Eastern Europe.

The day of the heavy tank also came to an end in the 1950s. Technological advances allowed the functions usually fulfilled by heavy tanks to be performed by the lighter, more maneuverable, and less expensive main battle tanks (MBTs). The new, most powerful tanks on the battlefield, the MBTs in essence combined the capabilities and roles of the old World War II medium and heavy tanks. During the Cold War, systems were developed to provide some protection for tank crews against the new threats of nuclear, biological, and chemical (NBC) attack. In addition, new sights, night vision equipment, improved fire-control systems, and more powerful guns and projectiles came into widespread use. All these served to increase the tanks' lethality and battlefield survivability.

The IS-3 tank, introduced in 1945, remained the principal Soviet heavy tank in the period immediately after World War II. Weighing 102,500 pounds with 230mm armor and a 122mm main gun, it was certainly the most formidable tank in the world at the time. The first postwar Soviet MBT, introduced in 1948, was the T-54, itself a refinement of the T-44, the short-lived redesign of the T-34/85 at the end of World War II.

The T-54 had improved mechanical capability, especially in its torsion bar suspension and transmission. It also had improved tracks. The T-54 had a longer hull than the T-44 as well as a larger and better-shaped turret. The original turret design tended to deflect rounds downward into the turret slip ring and was replaced by a more hemispherical frying pan shape with internal mantlet. The T-54 weighed 79,300 pounds and had a crew of four. Its 520-horsepower diesel engine produced a maximum road speed of 30 miles per hour. It had maximum 203mm armor protection and mounted a 100mm main gun and three machine guns.

In the mid-1950s the T-54's main gun received a bore evacuator mounted near the muzzle and was also improved for elevation stability. The T-54B of 1957–1958 introduced a stabilized gun for both elevation and traverse. It also had infrared driving lights and snorkel equipment, enabling it to cross rivers submerged.

The T-55 appeared beginning in 1958. The chief difference with it and the T-54 was the T-55's more powerful 580-horsepower diesel engine. The T-55 also had a slightly modified turret, an improved 100mm main gun, better transmission, a revolving turret floor (meaning that the crew did not have to shift position as the turret rotated), and increased ammunition storage. In 1963 the T-55 received an NBC system. The bow machine gun was also then eliminated. In the late 1980s the T-55s received new supercharged engines, improved fire-control and laser range-finding systems, and appliqué and explosive armor.

The T-54/T-55 had a very long service life. Production continued until 1981, with a phenomenal 95,000 tanks manufactured, making it the most widely produced tank in history. Both the Chinese and Romanians produced variants under license. Even at the end of the Cold War the T-54/T-55 comprised some 38 percent of Soviet tank strength and as much as 86 percent of non-Soviet Warsaw Pact armor. Reliable and relatively inexpensive, the T-54/T-55 was exported to more than 35 nations, including Arab states. Although obsolescent, these tanks remain in service today. Egypt upgraded its T-55s with U.S. engines, guns, and fire-control systems. Israel captured a number of T-54/T-55s from Egypt and Syria and upgraded them with General Motors engines and 105mm M68 guns.

The T-54/T-55s have had a mixed combat record. While sufficient to crush the Hungarian Revolution of 1956, they were not successful against Western-supplied Israeli armor in the 1967 Six-Day War, even though the Israelis for the most part had only upgraded World War II tanks. The T-54/T-55 continued as the mainstay of both Egyptian and Syrian armor in the 1973 Yom Kippur War and inflicted some losses on Israeli tanks in situations where the Israelis were vastly outnumbered. The T-55 served in Africa, Asia, Afghanistan, and Iraq. Coalition armor easily outclassed the Iraqi T-55s in the 1991 Persian Gulf War.

Further Reading

Foss, Christopher F., ed. *The Encyclopedia of Tanks and Armored Fighting Vehicles.* San Diego: Thunder Bay, 2002.

Tucker, Spencer C. *Tanks: An Illustrated History of Their Impact.* Santa Barbara, CA: ABC-CLIO, 2004.

M1A1 and M1A2 Abrams Main Battle Tank

The M1A1 and M1A2 Abrams is the most powerful U.S. tank and one of the top main battle tanks (MBTs) in the world. Designed to replace the M60, which had entered service in 1960, it began as a project by the Federal Republic of Germany and the United States for an MBT able to engage and defeat the vast number of tanks the Soviet Union and its satellites might field in an invasion of Central Europe. Designated the MBT-70, the new tank was to center on the Shillelagh gun/missile launcher and a 1500-horsepower engine, neither of which, however, worked out as planned.

Collapse of the MBT-70 project and cancellation of the follow-on XM803 program led to a brand-new program, begun from ground up in 1972. That same year the army came up with a concept of what it wanted in the new MBT, and two companies—Chrysler Defense and the Detroit Diesel division of General Motors—built prototypes of what was then designated the XM1 MBT. Both were tested in early 1976, and that November the army declared Chrysler the winner. Following manufacture of a number of test vehicles, the first production model M1 tank came off the assembly line in February 1980. The new tank was named for General Creighton Abrams, armor tank battalion commander in World War II, commander of allied forces in Vietnam, and then army chief of staff.

The M1 was a revolutionary design and a sharp departure from previous U.S. tanks, with their rounded surfaces and relatively high profile. The M1 was more angular and had flat-plate composite Chobham-type armor, with appliqué armor boxes that can be opened and the armor changed according to the threat. It was also considerably lower (8 feet) than the M60 (10 feet 9 inches).

From the start, the army's intention was to arm the M1 with the 105mm gun. As a result of a program aimed at securing a common main armament for U.S., British, and German tanks, the army made the decision, after initial M1 production had begun, to arm the M1 with a German-designed Rheinmetall 120mm smoothbore gun. But that gun was still under development when the tank was ready, and so the army decided to continue with the 105mm M68 gun utilized in the M60. The 120mm M256 gun, essentially the German-designed gun with a U.S. breech, was available in 1984, and the first M1A1 with this new armament came off the production line in August 1985. The M1A1HA introduced a new steel-encased depleted uranium armor, designated HA (heavy armor), which is virtually impenetrable but also dramatically increased the tank's weight to nearly 146,000 pounds. A total of 3,273 M1s were produced for the U.S. Army. Prior to the 1991 Persian Gulf War,

U.S. Marines fire the main gun of their M1A1 Abrams tank in the western desert of Najaf Province, Iraq, during a training exercise in January 2005. (Department of Defense/ Gunnery Sgt. Robert K. Blankenship)

upgrades were carried out in Saudi Arabia on all in-theater M1A1 tanks to bring them to M1A1HA status.

A total of 4,796 M1A1s were produced for the U.S. Army. The U.S. Marine Corps received 221, along with 403 M1s transferred from the army, to replace its more than 700 M60A1s. Kuwait also purchased 218 Abrams tanks, and Saudi Arabia bought 315. Egypt also arranged to produce 551 of them under a coproduction arrangement where they were built in Egypt by the Halwan Tank Plant. In 2006–2007 the Australian Army took delivery of 59 M1A1s.

During the 1991 Persian Gulf War the M1A1 Abrams and British Challenger proved their great superiority over their Soviet-built opposites, especially in night fighting. Of some 600 M1A1 Abrams that saw combat, none were penetrated by an enemy round; 3 were struck by depleted uranium shells fired from other M1s, but none of the 3 were permanently disabled, and there were no crew fatalities. This reflected the survivability features built into the tank, including armored bulkheads to deflect blasts outward. Conversely, the M1A1's 120mm gun proved lethal to Iraqi MBTs. It could engage the Iraqi armor at some 3,000 yards, twice the Iraqi effective range, and its superior fire-control system could deliver a first-round hit while on the move, and the depleted uranium penetrators could almost guarantee a kill.

The M1A2 was first produced in 1986. Most changes are internal. These include a thermal viewer for the tank commander, a new land-navigation system, and the Inter-Vehicular Information System. The latter is a datalink compatible with other advanced armored fighting vehicles and helicopters. Although only 77 M1A2s were delivered new, more than 500 M1A1s were upgraded to M1A2s. The M1A2 weighs some 139,000 pounds and mounts a 120mm gun and three machine guns (two 7.62mm): one for the loader, the other mounted coaxially to the right of the main gun, and one .50 caliber for the tank commander. A six-barrel smoke grenade discharger is located on either side of the turret, and the tank can also lay a smoke screen by an engine-operated system.

Although the Abrams achieved an enviable combat record against Soviet-manufactured T-72 tanks during the invasion of Iraq at the beginning of the Iraq War (2003–2011), it did not fare as well against insurgent attacks, many of these with improvised explosive devices. By December 2006, more than 530 Abrams tanks had been shipped back to the United States for repair. Some M1s received the Tank Urban Survival Kit, which added protection to the rear and sides to improve the tank's survivability in a hostile urban environment.

Production of the M1A2 was completed in 1996 but can be reopened if necessary. The M1A2 is also in service with Kuwait and Saudi Arabia.

Further Reading

Foss, Christopher F., ed. *The Encyclopedia of Tanks and Armored Fighting Vehicles.* San Diego: Thunder Bay, 2002.

Tucker, Spencer C. *Tanks: An Illustrated History of Their Impact.* Santa Barbara, CA: ABC-CLIO, 2004.

Merkava Israeli Main Battle Tank

The vagaries of overseas suppliers were a constant concern to the Israeli defense establishment and government, and in the 1970s Israel began development of its own tank. Known as the Merkava, it entered service in 1978. The Merkava built on lessons learned by the Israel Defense Forces in its long experience in tank warfare to that point, with the primary concerns being firepower and armor protection.

The Merkava underwent continued upgrades, with the Mk 2 appearing in 1983, the Mk 3 in 1990, and the Mk 4, entirely on Israeli manufacture, in 2002. One of the world's most powerful tanks, the Merkava also affords perhaps the best crew protection. Its engine is mounted in front, and the turret is mounted slightly to the rear of the vehicle and has a distinctly pointed front. The turret also has a large bustle at the rear. The hull is of cast and welded armor and incorporates rear doors that allow access to the fighting compartment for resupply of ammunition or even transportation of a limited number of infantry if fewer main gun ammunition rounds are carried.

The Merkava I weighs some 132,000 pounds and has a crew of four and a 900-horsepower engine that can move the tank at a maximum road speed of 34 miles per hour. The Mk 1 mounts a 105mm gun, three machine guns, and a 60mm mortar in the turret roof; the Mk 2 has the same armament but improved armor and a new fire-control system. These two models were superseded by the Mk 3, introduced in 1990. A major improvement over its predecessors, it incorporates widespread upgrades in armament, armor, and other systems. The Mk 3 mounts a 120mm smoothbore gun in place of the 105mm gun on the Mk 1 and Mk 2. Its 900-horsepower engine has been upgraded to 1,200 horsepower. The tank weighs approximately 134,000 pounds and sports a new transmission, suspension system, and armor. It also has threat warning systems and an improved fire-control system. Its nuclear-biological-chemical protection package completely seals the tank and allows the crew to work in ordinary clothing. The Merkava Mks 1–3 rely on some foreign-built components.

Further Reading

Foss, Christopher F., ed. *The Encyclopedia of Tanks and Armored Fighting Vehicles.* San Diego: Thunder Bay, 2002.

Tucker, Spencer C. *Tanks: An Illustrated History of Their Impact.* Santa Barbara, CA: ABC-CLIO, 2004.

Sikorsky UH-60 Black Hawk Helicopter

Sikorsky entered the U.S. Army's 1972 Utility Tactical Transport Aircraft System competition with its S-70 and won a protracted fly-off in 1976. The S-70 entered service with the army as the UH-60 Black Hawk in 1978, replacing the Bell UH-1 Iroquois.

Two General Electric T700-GE-700 1,620-horsepower turbo shaft engines turn the UIH-60's composite titanium and fiberglass 53-foot 8-inch four-bladed main rotor and a four-bladed tail rotor. The UH-60 has a long, low profile shape in order to enable it to be transported (with some disassembly) by a C-130 Hercules transport. It also features a Stability Control Augmentation System, transmissions and gearboxes that have a 30-minute dry-run capability, and rotors and drive shafts designed to sustain multiple hits by up to 23mm cannon fire and remain operational.

The UH-60 has a maximum speed of 159 miles per hour, a ceiling of 19,000 feet, and a combat radius of 368 miles. It has a 4-man crew: 2 pilots and 2 crew chiefs. Manned by crew chiefs/gunners, it can carry two 7.62mm machine guns, two 7.62mm miniguns, or two 12.7mm (.50-caliber) GAU-19 Gatling guns. It has two hard points on each of two stub wings that allow it to carry combinations of rockets and missiles. The UH-60 can carry 11 troops with equipment or 6 stretchers and can lift 2,640 pounds of cargo internally or 9,000 pounds externally by a sling. It can also transport a M119 105mm howitzer, 30 rounds of ammunition, and a 4-man crew.

As a utility helicopter, the Black Hawk performs a great number of different missions, including troop and equipment transport, electronic countermeasures, and aeromedical evacuation. The UH-60 *Marine One* transports the president of the

United States. Modified versions have served with the U.S. Army, the U.S. Air Force, the U.S. Navy (SH-60B Seahawk), and the U.S. Coast Guard (HH-60J Jayhawk medium-range rescue). The UH-60 also serves in the military establishments of some two dozen other nations. Black Hawks have had a distinguished record in service with U.S. forces from the U.S. invasion of Grenada in 1983 to the present with both regular and Special Operations units. Some 4,000 UH-60s have been built.

Further Reading

Bishop, Chris. *Sikorsky UH-60 Black Hawk.* Oxford, UK: Osprey, 2008.

Leoni, Ray D. *Black Hawk: The Story of a World Class Helicopter.* Reston, VA: American Institute of Aeronautics and Astronautics, 2007.

McGowen, Stanley S. *Helicopters: An Illustrated History of Their Impact.* Santa Barbara, CA: ABC-CLIO, 2005.

Hughes (McDonnell Douglas/Boeing) AH-64 Apache Helicopter

The AH-64 Apache helicopter was the world's first dedicated attack helicopter and, in its D model, the most advanced. Credit for the aircraft is confusing. Hughes Aircraft won the design competition but sold its helicopter business to McDonnell Douglas in 1984, which in 1997 was acquired by Boeing. The Apache grew out of Cold War concerns in the United States over the large number of Warsaw Pact tanks. It was to have standoff capability, to be able to strike and destroy targets from ranges where it could be safe from most enemy antiaircraft fire. Hughes Aircraft and Bell submitted designs, and the army selected that from Hughes. The AH-64 Apache replaced the Bell AH-1 Cobra (official designation HueyCobra), and was designed to attack and destroy targets in all weather conditions. The Apache entered service in 1985.

Designed to fight and survive in a hostile environment, the Apache can withstand 20mm cannon fire. Heavily automated, it includes target acquisition and designation sighting equipment as well as an infrared laser range finder. An integrated helmet and display system allows the pilot to aim weapons merely by looking at the target. Powered by two 1,536-horsepower General Electric T700 turbo shaft engines, the AH-64 has a maximum speed of 232 miles per hour, a ceiling of 21,000 feet, and a maximum combat range of 380 miles. Armament consists of one 30mm automatic Boeing M230 chain gun under the fuselage (with storage for 1,200 rounds) and 16 Lockheed Martin/Boeing AGM-14D Longbow Hellfire antitank missiles (eight under each winglet) or 76 70mm (2.75-inch) unguided rockets (formerly known as Hydra and now designated the Advanced Precision Kill Weapon System, or APKWS).

The Apache first saw combat in the U.S. invasion of Panama in 1989 and then performed brilliantly in the 1991 Persian Gulf War, when Apaches destroyed Iraqi

A Hughes (Boeing) AH-64 Apache. The world's first attack helicopter, it was designed to fight and survive in a hostile environment. It has night vision equipment and is able to stand off and engage targets at a distance. The Apache distinguished itself in the 1991 Persian Gulf War. (Lockheed Martin)

radar sites and several hundred tanks for no losses of their own. The more capable AH-64D Apache Longbow entered service in 1997. It features the Longbow milli-meter wave fire-control radar and the Longbow Hellfire missile. The AH-64D saw service in the Afghanistan War (2001–) and in the Iraq War (2003–2011). In these conflicts, however, the Apache was shown to be vulnerable to infantry ground fire at short ranges. In 2003 it was also deployed to South Korea.

Older AH-64A helicopters have been upgraded to the AH-64D standard and are now receiving a new targeting and night-vision system, known as Arrowhead. All (more than 700 in 2006) U.S. Army Apaches were to be equipped with the Arrow-head system by 2011. Apaches have been exported to a number of other nations. The United Kingdom version is built by the Augusta Westland consortium and is known as the AH Mk.1. It features a folding blade assembly to facilitate carrier operations.

Further Reading

Fredriksen, John C. *Warbirds: An Illustrated Guide to U.S. Military Aircraft, 1915–2000.* Santa Barbara, CA: ABC-CLIO, 1999.

McGowen, Stanley S. *Helicopters: An Illustrated History of Their Impact.* Santa Barbara, CA: ABC-CLIO, 2005.

Hawker-Siddeley/McDonnell Douglas Sea Harrier

The Hawker-Siddley Harrier is one of the most remarkable aircraft in aviation history and a major triumph for British military aviation. The Harrier is the first vertical short takeoff and landing (VSTOL) combat airplane in history. Developed as a land plane, the naval version Sea Harrier proved successful as a carrier aircraft.

Work on the Harrier began in 1957 as a collaborative venture between Hawker Siddeley and designers at the Bristol Engine Company, which had begun work on a turbofan engine, the exhaust from which could be vectored downward. The prototype aircraft first flew in October 1960. The project was conceived as a North Atlantic Treaty Organization (NATO) joint venture to fill close support and reconnaissance roles.

During the next two years, six prototype aircraft underwent extensive testing. Following modifications, another nine aircraft were produced. The first of this new aircraft, the Kestrel, flew in March 1964. The nine Kestrels were formed into a squadron to undergo joint testing by British, American, and West German pilots beginning in October 1964. West Germany subsequently withdrew from the project, but six of the aircraft were sent to the United States for further testing, where they attracted the interest of the U.S. Marine Corps.

With the collapse of the project as a NATO venture, the British decided to continue development of the aircraft on their own. The first preseries aircraft, dubbed the Harrier, flew in August 1966. Resembling the Kestrel in outward appearance, the Harrier incorporated enhanced avionics and equipment. The first production model flew in December 1967, and the aircraft entered service with the Royal Air Force in April 1969. Subsequently the Harrier received more powerful Pegasus Mk-102 and then Mk-103 engines.

In 1969 the U.S. Marine Corps ordered 12 Harrier aircraft, with a designation of AV-8A. Subsequently the United States ordered 110 of the aircraft, including 8 of the two-seat trainer version. McDonnell Douglas later acquired the U.S. rights.

In 1975 the Royal Navy adopted a navalized Harrier for carrier service. Known as the Sea Harrier, it entered service in 1978. Hawker Siddeley was merged into British Aerospace (BAe) in 1977, and the BAe Sea Harrier was designed to operate from a new series of commando carriers. A new Sea Harrier, the FA.2, entered service in 1982. It could carry both Sidewinder and Sea Eagle missiles. Sea Harriers were retired from Royal Navy service in March 2006.

McDonnell Douglas subsequently entered into an agreement with British Aerospace (Hawker-Siddeley merged into BAe in 1977) for an enhanced AV-8B to be produced for both countries. Entering service in 1991, the McDonnell Douglas AV-8B featured an enlarged wing of new composite construction. This larger wing allowed more fuel and greater armaments to be carried. The engine was identical to the AV-8A. In the U.S. Marine Corps the AV-8B replaced both the AV-8A and the Douglas A-4M Skyhawk light attack aircraft. McDonnell Douglas also sold some

AV-8B aircraft to Spain (where it was known as the Matador) and to Italy and India for naval use.

The single-seater AV-8B was powered by a Rolls-Royce Pegasus F402-RR-406 turbofan engine capable of 23,800 pounds of thrust, producing a maximum speed of 629 miles per hour, a ceiling of 50,000 feet, and a range of 685 miles with three-hour combat patrol endurance time. The plane featured a bicycle-type configuration undercarriage. The AV-8B was armed with a fuselage-mounted GAU-23U 25mm gun system (left pod) and 300 rounds of ammunition (right pod). Its standard air-to-ground armaments load was six 500-pound bombs, while the standard air-to-air load was four AIM-9L/M Sidewinder missiles. Seven armaments stations made it possible to carry up to 13,200 pounds of ordnance.

The great advantage of the VSTOL Harrier was that it could operate from very small areas, even a woodland-cleared field. The plane had the ability to hover in the air like a helicopter, and among novel ideas tested were the Skyhook, a crane that could launch the plane from either a ship or even a submarine and then retrieve it afterward without the necessity of a flight deck.

Sea Harriers proved their worth during the Falklands War of 1982, when they shot down 21 Argentine aircraft for no combat losses of their own (2 succumbed to ground fire and 4 to accidents). Harriers also saw extensive duty in the Balkans and in the Persian Gulf War in 1991, when they were the most forward-deployed tactical strike aircraft in the theater. Both land- and sea-based Harriers also provided highly effective service with British and U.S. forces in the 2003–2011 Iraq War. The vast majority of them were flown from carriers.

Further Reading

Angelucci, Enzo. *The Rand McNally Encyclopedia of Military Aircraft, 1914–1980.* New York: Military Press, 1983.

Barybrook, Roy. *British Aerospace Harrier and Sea Harrier.* London: Osprey, 1984.

Davies, Peter E., and Anthony M. Thornborough. *The Harrier Story.* Annapolis, MD: Naval Institute Press, 1996.

Nordeen, Lon O. *Harrier II: Validating V/STOL.* Annapolis, MD: Naval Institute Press, 2006.

Night-Vision Devices

Traditionally during hours of darkness, armies have not operated at all or have conducted only limited operations. If armies made recourse to fires, flares, and other illumination devices, these allowed the enemy to see as well. This has now changed dramatically, thanks to night-vision devices (NVDs).

The two basic night-observation systems that do not use white light illumination are active and passive. The active systems came first, during World War II, and were still around in some forms through the Vietnam War. Active systems had two basic components: an infrared light source to illuminate the target with light not visible to the human eye and a scope that could see the infrared. The early infrared scopes for rifles looked very much like the later starlight scopes except with an infrared spotlight about six to eight inches in diameter mounted above it.

The U.S. M-48 tank and some early models of the M-60 tank had a huge spotlight mounted above the main gun. The spotlight had both infrared and white light modes. The tanks also had onboard infrared scopes. These systems were classified as active because they had to project their own light. The problem with active systems was that they were easily detectable if the enemy was equipped with infrared sights. These systems have all now been replaced by the passive systems, which only magnify ambient light. Since they project no light themselves, they are not detectable by the enemy.

During World War II, the Germans developed the cascade image tube. Contacted by the U.S. military after the war, the Radio Corporation of America (RCA) developed a greatly improved cascade image tube. The new system, known as image intensification, had major problems, however. The image was projected upside down, and the large size of the device was also a problem. By the mid-1960s most of these problems had been overcome, and the first passive NVDs were issued to U.S. troops. NVDs first were employed in combat in the Vietnam War and played an increasingly important role in both the Persian Gulf War (1991) and the early fighting of the Iraq War (2003–2011). Especially in the latter conflict, NVDs allowed the U.S. Army to "own the night."

NVDs are of two types: image intensifiers and thermal infrared detectors. Image-intensifying devices magnify light and then display the image electronically. They must have some light available to function but can magnify it from 2,000 to 5,000 times, in effect allowing soldiers to turn the battlefield from night into day. Thermal forward-looking infrared detectors, sometimes known as sensors, detect differences in temperature between objects and their environment.

Among such systems, the best known is probably the U.S. Army

A U.S. Army pilot positions his night vision goggles on his flight helmet in preparation for a night helicopter training mission at Alamagordo, New Mexico, in April 1997. (Department of Defense/Spc. Gary A. Bryant)

Starlight Scope. It entered service in 1964 and could either be handheld or fitted to such weapons as the M16 rifle. Later models included a control allowing a uniform level of illumination and flash protection to prevent damage from very bright light and permit the user to see the rounds from the weapon strike the target. Initially the Starlight Scope was only effective to about 300 yards, but later versions provided significantly greater range.

Subsequent image enhancers are far more effective and lighter. Night-vision goggles, which first appeared in 1977, are one such development. Issued to individual soldiers, night-vision goggles are electro-optical systems that magnify existing light. The light source to be amplified may come from the moon or stars or the glow on the horizon from a distant city. Users do not look through the goggles; rather, the users see a greatly amplified electronic image on a phosphor screen, much as a TV screen. That screen is colored green because the human eye is able to differentiate more shades of green than any other phosphor color. Range is 100–400 feet.

Such systems and lasers have largely replaced infrared systems on the battlefield. Larger image intensifiers may also be mounted in vehicles. Research on NVDs now centers on expanding the field of vision (currently only about 40 degrees with NVDs, whereas a normal field of vision is 120 degrees), higher sensitivity, and increased resolution.

Further Reading

Richardson, M., et al. *Surveillance and Target Acquisition Systems.* London: Brassey's, 1997.

Aegis

The U.S. Navy weapons system Aegis, officially the Weapons System Mk 7, employs the SPY-1 phased-array radar to detect, classify, and track surface and aerial targets as well as to control a warship's missiles. Begun in the late 1960s to provide surface combatants with a means of countering the growing Soviet air threat to U.S. Navy carrier task forces, Aegis narrowly escaped the budget ax in the tight fiscal climate of the mid-1970s.

Developed by the Naval Ordnance Systems Command under the project direction of Captain Wayne E. Meyer and pushed forward by chief of surface warfare Vice Admiral James H. Doyle Jr., Aegis went to sea first in the Ticonderoga-class missile cruisers, the lead ship commissioning in 1983. By certain estimates, one of these capable warships doubled the effectiveness of the air defenses of a carrier task force.

During the 1990s, destroyers of the new Arleigh Burke class also received Aegis. Over time, the system has proved amenable to upgrading. By the end of the 1980s, Aegis could track simultaneously several hundred separate targets and control a dozen missiles in the air at once. The guidance system of Aegis substantially extended the range of antiaircraft missiles by plotting more efficient trajectories. The Tomahawk long-range attack missile was integrated into Aegis in 1987. The system proved itself in the 1991 Persian Gulf War when the missile cruiser *Bunker Hill* (CG-52) assumed tactical control of 26 warships and over 300 aircraft; the Aegis cruiser directed thousands of strikes, intercepts, tanker missions, and reconnaissance flights without significant problem.

Further Reading

Friedman, Norman. *World Naval Weapons Systems, 1997–1998.* Annapolis, MD: Naval Institute Press, 1997.

Muir, Malcolm, Jr. *Black Shoes and Blue Water: Surface Warfare in the United States Navy, 1945–1975.* Washington, DC: Naval Historical Center, 1996.

Mk 15 Phalanx

The Phalanx is a U.S. ship-mounted close-in weapons system (CIWS, pronounced "sea-whiz"). The Phalanx is designed to defend against incoming antiship missiles and aircraft at close range. Manufactured by the Hughes Missile Systems Company (purchased from the General Dynamics Pomona Division in 1992), now the Raytheon Systems Company, the Phalanx point-defense system consists of two 20mm gun mounts. It automatically identifies and engages incoming missiles and high-speed low-flying aircraft. Each mount includes an M-61A1 20mm Vulcan Gatling-type rotating six-barrel cannon controlled by search and tracking radars. The Phalanx was designed to be the final defense against enemy missiles and aircraft that had succeeded in penetrating other defenses.

The Phalanx system underwent operational testing and evaluation aboard the destroyer USS *Bigelow* in 1977 and more than met specifications. Production began the next year, and the Phalanx was first deployed aboard the aircraft carrier USS *Coral Sea* in 1980. The updated Phalanx was first deployed in 1988 aboard the battleship USS *Wisconsin*.

The first model was capable of firing some 3,000 rounds per minute. The addition of a pneumatic gun drive increased this to 4,500 rounds per minute. Firing can be continuous or in bursts of 60 or 100 rounds. The ammunition drum initially held 989 rounds, but this was subsequently increased to 1,550 rounds. The 20mm subcaliber sabot projectile has a 15mm tungsten or depleted uranium penetrator, which is enclosed in a discarding plastic sabot and lightweight metal pusher.

A variety of upgrades have been made to the Phalanx system. These include new computer systems, improved fire control, better forward-looking infrared radar, and integrated multiweapon operations capabilities.

Since entering service, the Phalanx system has been the primary point-defense weapon of virtually every class of U.S. Navy ship. It is also deployed on the ships of more than 20 allied navies. The U.S. Army utilizes a land-based version of the Phalanx system. It, however, employs high-explosive incendiary tracer self-destruct ammunition.

Further Reading

Hooten, Ted. *Jane's Naval Weapons Systems, 2001–2002*. London: Jane's, 2002.

Hovercraft

Hovercraft are vehicles capable of travel on a cushion of pressurized air generated by powerful ducted fans. The concept was first under development as early as 1875 in the Netherlands, but it was not brought to fruition until British engineer Sir Christopher Cockerell's 1950 design of a working hovercraft eventually yielded the first Saunders-Roe prototype hovercraft, the SR.N1, in 1959. Commercial interest in a hovercraft capable of traversing the English Channel led in 1968 to the production of several variants of the successful model SR.N4, the last two of which plied the route until October 2000. These car-and-passenger ferries displaced 165 to 200 tons and could carry a mix of up to 278 persons and 36 cars. Four Proteus gas turbines powered the four topside propulsion propellers and the four cushion-generating centrifugal fans, the exhaust of which was contained under the hull by a neoprene skirt. Though capable of reaching a speed of 100 knots, usual service cruising speed was 55–70 knots. Further commercial applications can be found in Europe and Russia.

The United Kingdom, the Soviet Union, and the United States all anticipated the applications for amphibious warfare of hovercraft, particularly their ability to skim over water and land. The Soviet Union was the largest developer of hovercraft, and the world's largest by far is the 1988 Soviet Pomornik-class at 550 tons, while the most numerous is the U.S. Navy's 184-ton LCAC (Landing Craft Air Cushion), with more than 90 in service since 1984. An innovative 1990s British design is the lightweight composite ABS M10 medium-lift hovercraft, the economical twin-diesel power plant of which also greatly simplifies engine upkeep over the usual gas turbine installation. Other nations with hovercraft include China and Iran.

Hovercraft excel at quickly moving vehicles and matériel ashore in amphibious landings, but the vulnerability of their exposed propulsion and cushioning components to defensive fire better suits them to operations after a landing area has been secured. Hovercraft can be useful in minesweeping operations. However, hovercraft are expensive to produce and difficult to service. U.S. hovercraft have seen service in the Persian Gulf and in Somalia.

Further Reading

Jane's Amphibious Warfare Capabilities. Coulson, Surrey, UK, and Alexandria, VA: Jane's Information Group, 2000.

Jane's High-Speed Maritime Transportation, 2000–2001. Coulson, Surrey, UK, and Alexandria, VA: Jane's Information Group, 2000.

Nimitz-Class U.S. Navy Aircraft Carriers

In 1955 the U.S. Navy commissioned the first of its four Forrestal-class aircraft carriers. The first supercarriers, these ships incorporated many features intended for the canceled aircraft carrier *United States.* The Forrestal-class ships had an overall length of 1,086 feet, a displacement of 75,900 tons (full load, which made them 25 percent heavier than the World War II Nimitz class), and a maximum speed of 33 knots. The Forrestals were the first aircraft carriers designed specifically for jet aircraft and the first to have angled flight decks (making possible simultaneous launch and recovery) and steam catapults. They were also the first since the Lexington class to have enclosed bows. The last joined the fleet in 1959. These ships provided excellent service during the Vietnam War and the Persian Gulf War. All were decommissioned during 1993–1998.

Four follow-on aircraft carriers, identified as the improved Forrestal class, were commissioned during 1961–1968. But the next aircraft carriers, the Nimitz-class ships, were of an entirely different design and were the largest and most powerful warships ever constructed. Nuclear-powered derivatives of the aircraft carrier *John F. Kennedy* (CVA-67) of 1975, the first ships of the class were approved during the Vietnam War. Displacing over 91,000 tons at full load, the *Nimitz* measures 1,088 feet in overall length and 257 feet in flight deck width. The relatively compact two-reactor power plant allows great storage space for ammunition and aircraft fuel while producing 280,000 shaft horsepower for a speed of more than 30 knots. It joined the fleet in 1975.

Survivability features include advanced torpedo protection, intricate subdivision (23 watertight transverse bulkheads and over 2,000 compartments), and Kevlar armor. The ship's pumps can correct a 15-degree list in only 20 minutes. The U.S. Navy claims that the *Nimitz* could withstand at least three times the punishment survived by Essex-class carriers such as the *Franklin* and *Bunker Hill* late in World War II. Defensive weaponry consists of the ship's fighters, Sea Sparrow antiaircraft missiles, and the Phalanx close-in weapons system.

For striking power, the *Nimitz* relies on its air group of 90 aircraft. Four elevators and four steam catapults help speed flight operations. In addition to the *Nimitz,* there are nine other ships in the class: the *Dwight D. Eisenhower, Carl Vinson, Theodore Roosevelt, Abraham Lincoln, George Washington, John C. Stennis, Harry S. Truman, Ronald Reagan,* and *George H. W. Bush* (the last in the class, it was commissioned in 2009). Thus, Nimitz-class carriers have been built for over 30 years, setting a record for the construction of modern capital ships to one basic design.

Further Reading

Chesneau, Roger. *Aircraft Carriers of the World, 1914 to the Present: An Illustrated Encyclopedia.* Annapolis, MD: Naval Institute Press, 1995.

Friedman, Norman. *U.S. Aircraft Carriers: An Illustrated Design History.* Annapolis, MD: Naval Institute Press, 1983.

Polmar, Norman. *Ships and Aircraft of the U.S. Fleet.* 17th ed. Annapolis, MD: Naval Institute Press, 2000.

Ohio-Class U.S. Navy Submarines

There are 18 U.S. Navy Ohio-class submarines. Fourteen of them are ballistic missile submarines (SSBN), and four are cruise missile submarines (SSGN). Designed for extended patrol duties (currently of some 70–90 days each but limited only by the food supply carried), the Ohio-class submarines were initially planned as a class of 24, but 6 were cancelled. They were constructed during 1976–1997 and first entered commission in 1981. The 14 Trident missile-armed SSBNs carry some 50 percent of the entire thermonuclear deterrent of the U.S. armed forces.

As the new dreadnoughts, with the exception of the *Henry W. Jackson,* the submarines of the Ohio class are all named for states, an honor hitherto reserved for battleships. The largest U.S. Navy submarines ever, the Ohio-class submarines are 560 feet in length with a beam of 42 feet. Propelled by an S8G PWR nuclear reactor, they have two geared turbines. Each also has a reserve Fairbanks Morse auxiliary diesel engine. The submarines displace 16,499 tons surfaced and 18,450 tons submerged. They have official speeds of 12 knots surfaced and 20 knots submerged, although submerged speeds of 25 knots have been reported. The submarines have crews of 15 officers and 140 enlisted personnel.

Each submarine has four 21-inch torpedo tubes for the Mark 48 torpedo, and each carries 24 Trident missiles. While two classes of Russian submarines are larger (the Typhoon class is twice the Ohio class in displacement, and the Borei class is some 25 percent greater), these both carry fewer missiles (20 for the Typhoon class and 16–20 for the Borei class).

With the end of the Cold War, beginning in 2002 four of the Ohio-class (*Ohio, Florida, Georgia,* and *Michigan*) were converted to carry Tomahawk cruise missiles. Designated SSGNs, each of these submarines has been fitted with 22 vertical launch tubes for Tomahawk missiles, and each of these submarines may carry 154 Tomahawk cruise missiles with either conventional or nuclear warheads. They can also launch Harpoon missiles through their torpedo tubes and can carry other payloads to include unmanned aerial vehicles or those for countermine warfare.

The navy plans to retain the Ohio class in service through 2029.

Further Reading

Fontenoy, Paul E. *Submarines: An Illustrated History of Their Impact.* Santa Barbara, CA: ABC-CLIO, 2007.

Hutchinson, Robert. *Jane's Submarines: War beneath the Waves from 1776 to the Present Day.* New York: HarperCollins, 2001.

Laser

The term "laser" is an acronym for "*l*ight *a*mplification by *s*timulated *e*mission of *r*adiation." While most light sources emit photons in all directions, lasers amplify light and concentrate photon emission in a coherent narrow beam. Typically, laser light is nearly monochromatic.

Building on theories developed by Albert Einstein in 1916, Theodore H. Maiman at Hughes Research Laboratories in Malibu, California, demonstrated the first laser in 1960. The first major industry application of laser technology appeared in the form of the supermarket scanner in 1974. Today many different types of lasers perform a wide variety of functions, from consumer electronics to medicine, industry, science, and war. Laser types include gas, chemical, excimer, solid state, semiconductor, and dye.

Most military lasers are employed in target illumination and acquisition, such as in tanks. Lasers are integral to target acquisition in many so-called smart bombs and cruise missiles. Research work is ongoing to develop smaller solid-state laser weapon systems that might be mounted on a vehicle or carried in an aircraft. Scientists at the Lawrence Livermore National Laboratory in Livermore, California, have developed a laser that can penetrate one inch of steel. Such lasers, known as SSHCL (for solid-state heat-capacity laser), might be used to destroy enemy shells and missiles as well as to attack targets hundreds of miles distant.

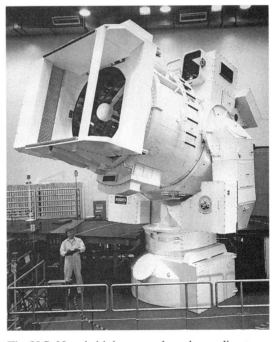

The U.S. Navy's high-energy laser beam director built by Hughes Aircraft Company for use in high-energy laser research and development. The experimental pointing and tracking system was designed to track targets in flight and direct a high-powered laser beam to selected aimpoints. (U.S. Department of Defense)

Further Reading

Richardson, M., et al. *Surveillance and Target Acquisition Systems.* London: Brassey's, 1997.

Svelto, Orazio, ed. *Principles of Lasers*. Translated by David C. Hanna. New York: Springer, 2004.

Stealth Technology

In contemporary usage, stealth technology refers to efforts to obscure or completely mask aircraft, ships, missiles, and other military equipment from radar or infrared detection. Masking weapons from an enemy is as old as warfare itself. The development of radar in the mid-1930s provided the means to detect aircraft and ships at great distances, but early on Sir Robert Watson-Watt, one of its pioneers, noted that radar reflectivity might be reduced in bomber aircraft. Radar operators also observed that some types of aircraft were easier to detect than others.

During World War II, British and American bombers dropped aluminum strips known as chaff (or window) that produced a multitude of indecipherable reflections on German radar screens. By the close of the war, the Germans were actively working on stealth aircraft that used materials in their construction to absorb rather than reflect radar waves. The Germans also experimented with shielding metal snorkel devices on submarines with rubber to inhibit airborne radar detection. Stealth technology, however, reached a new level of sophistication late in the Cold War in a U.S. Air Force project begun in 1977 that culminated in the Lockheed F-117A Nighthawk stealth fighter, which entered service in 1982.

Basically, stealth technology relies on two principles. The first is to modify the shape of the ship or plane so that the contoured surfaces so easily detected by radar are replaced by flat surfaces and sharp angles that reflect radar signals away from the receiving radar antenna. The second important principle of stealth technology is to construct the plane or ship with critical surfaces made of nonmetallic materials that absorb radar or infrared waves. Special exterior paint can augment this effect. Stealth design principles also emphasize positioning engines and propulsion plants in positions that mask infrared signatures and reduce the wakes of ships and aircraft.

The first stealth ship was the Swedish Visby corvette. Other examples of stealth ships are the French La Fayette–class frigates as well as the British Type 45 destroyer and the U.S. Navy DD(X) destroyer designs. Stealth ships employ sharply reduced numbers of right angles. They also utilize an outer layer of carbon fiber that absorbs radar waves. A tumble-home design also reduces the radar cross section.

Stealth technology cannot render a plane or ship entirely invisible but can dramatically reduce the radar signature. Reportedly in the F-117A and in the B-2 Spirit stealth bomber, this is so small as to resemble a small bird or even a bumblebee.

Although the new U.S. stealth technology made its first appearance in warfare during the 1989 invasion of Panama, it was especially important, and most identified with, the 1991 Persian Gulf War when F-117As flew undetected over Baghdad to drop laser-guided bombs. During that war Nighthawks flew 1,271 sorties

A Northrop Grumman B-2 Spirit bomber (top) and a T-38 Talon fighter (bottom) on display at Andrews Air Force Base in Maryland. The B-2 bomber was the world's first stealth bomber. At a cost of $2.1 billion each, it is also easily the most expensive aircraft ever produced. (Department of Defense)

without a loss. Again, in the Iraq War (2003–2011) the United States employed stealth aircraft to attack such high-value targets as command and control centers. To counter the new stealth technologies, nations are developing passive radar arrays and low-frequency radars able to detect the new planes and ships. Nonetheless, development of stealth technologies continues.

Further Reading

Richardson, Doug. *Stealth Warplanes: Deception, Evasion, and Concealment in the Air.* Osceola, WI: Motorbooks International, 2001.

Sweetman, Bill. *Stealth Aircraft: Secrets of Future Airpower.* Osceola, WI: Motorbooks International, 1986.

Northrop Grumman B-2 Spirit

The Northrop Grumman B-2 Spirit is the world's first stealth bomber. With the advent of new radar-evading technologies, in 1981 the U.S. Air Force initiated Project Senior to design a strategic bomber capable of penetrating Soviet airspace without being detected by radar. Congressional approval was secured in 1987 for the procurement of 132 such aircraft, but with the end of the Cold War and mounting costs, the number was reduced to 21.

Building on technologies for the Lockheed Martin F-117A Nighthawk stealth fighter, Northrop Grumman proceeded with the new aircraft. The prototype XB-2 was publically revealed in rollout in November 1988, and its first test flight was in July 1989. The B-2 first became operational in 1993, with the entire fleet achieving that status in December 2003. In appearance the B-2 greatly resembles the radical design XB-35 Flying Wing developed by Northrop in 1946. Lacking any vertical stabilizer, the B-2's sharply swept 33-degree wing terminates in a double "W" outline.

The above-wing mounted engines stop short of the trailing edge in order to re-duce infrared detection. The B-2s also have an exhaust temperature control system to minimize thermal signature. The plane is built of radar-absorbing composite materials, and its surfaces have a special radar-absorbent coating. These and its design leave only the smallest radar signature.

The B-2 has a two-man crew, seated side by side, of aircraft commander and mission commander, compared to four men for the North American/Rockwell B-1B Lancer and five in the Boeing B-52 Stratofortress. The B-2 has a wingspan of 172 feet and a length of 69 feet. Four 17,300-pound-thrust General Electric F-118 turbofan engines produce a maximum speed of some 600 miles per hour. The B-2 has a ceiling of 50,000 feet and a range of more than 6,000 miles (10,000 miles with one refueling), which means that it can fly anywhere in the world with one in-flight refueling. It can carry, in twin bays underneath the wing, eight nuclear weapons, eight cruise missiles, or 40,000 pounds of conventional bombs or mines.

Unlike the B-1B, which was designed for high-speed, low-altitude penetration of an enemy airspace, the relatively slow B-2 Spirit was developed specifically for multirole, high-altitude, subsonic missions. At a cost of $2.1 billion (1997 dollars) apiece, the B-2s are easily the most expensive aircraft ever built. The B-2 is ex-pected to remain in service for decades to come and, along with the B-1 and B-52, provide the United States with great flexibility in strategic bombing missions.

Further Reading

Goodall, James. *America's Stealth Fighters and Bombers.* Osceola, WI: Motorbooks In-ternational, 1992.

Holder, Bill. *Northrop Grumman B-2 Spirit: An Illustrated History.* Atglen, PA: Schiffer, 1998.

Miller, Jay. *Northrop B-2 Spirit.* Leicester, UK: Midland, 1995.

Global Positioning System

The establishment of satellites in space for the first time in history made pos-sible accurate navigation on Earth. In the 1970s the U.S. Navy and the U.S. Air Force launched the Navstar Global Positioning System (GPS). GPS has many ci-vilian users, but the system was designed for and is operated by the U.S. military.

Controlled by the Department of Defense from a central station at Falcon Air Force Base in Colorado Springs, Colorado, GPS employs a network of 24 satellites that orbit Earth in a 12-hour period. At any given time, from five to eight of these satellites are accessible to a GPS receiver from any point on Earth. The Soviet Union undertook the launching of satellites for a similar system, known as Glonass, beginning in 1982.

Satellites in the system send radio signals from space. GPS receivers then process these signals to compute position, velocity, and time. GPS can provide a fix anywhere on Earth's surface and is accurate to within 12 feet. The military implications of GPS are enormous, including the rescue of downed air crews; the coordination of the movements of larger units even to individual soldiers, vehicles, and ships; artillery fire direction control; the control of tactical and strategic air strikes; the targeting of precision-guided munitions; and the processing of intelligence collected by space-based platforms.

Further Reading

Bull, Stephen. *Encyclopedia of Military Technology and Innovation.* Westport, CT: Greenwood, 2004.

Chetty, P. R. K. *Space Technology and Its Applications.* New York: McGraw-Hill, 1988.

Dutton, L. *Military Space.* London: Brassey's, 1990.

Unmanned Aerial Vehicles

Unmanned aerial vehicles (UAVs), commonly called drones and also known as remotely piloted aircraft, came into being after World War I. Although the term "unmanned aerial vehicle" could apply to anything from cruise missiles to kites, generally speaking the term is used to reference reusable heavier-than-air craft. UAVs were initially unsophisticated radio-controlled model aircraft developed to train antiaircraft gunners. Interest in such craft increased sharply during the Cold War with advances in avionics, computer technology, and photographic equipment. UAVs also have the great advantages of being much less expensive than manned aircraft and not risking the life of a pilot. In civilian service UAVs perform myriad functions. In the military they do far more than reconnaissance missions, including the delivery of munitions.

The United States employed some UAVs during the Vietnam War in a reconnaissance role. Israel and the United States have led in their development. As early as 1982, the Israeli Aircraft Industries was involved in UAVs. The Israel Defense Forces employed them for the first time in Operation PEACE FOR GALILEE, its 1982 invasion of Lebanon. The United States purchased the IAF Pioneer UAV in 1985 and employed it in both the 1991 Persian Gulf War and the 2003–2011 Iraq War. The Pioneer has an endurance time of 5.5 hours, a ceiling of 12,000 feet, and a payload of 75 pounds.

A U.S. Air Force General Atomics MQ-9 Reaper (originally the MQ-9B Predator) unmanned aerial vehicle (UAV) landing at Joint Base Balad, Iraq, on November 10, 2008. (Department of Defense)

Among the most sophisticated of current UAVs is the RQ-1/MQ-1/MQ-9 Predator. A long-endurance, medium-altitude UAV, it is a midwing monoplane with a slender fuselage, a high aspect ratio wing, and inverted-V tails. It requires line of sight with its ground control station. The Predator can fulfill a variety of missions from reconnaissance to ground attack. Developed by General Atomics Aeronautical Systems for the U.S. Air Force, the Predator first flew in 1994 and entered production in 1995.

The Predator is 27 feet in length and has a wingspan of 48 feet 7 inches. Fitted with video cameras, the RQ-1 Predator can provide real-time intelligence information from over the battlefield. The upgraded MQ-1 Predator incorporates many improvements. Powered by a Rotax 914F turbocharged four-cylinder 115-horsepower engine and pusher propeller, its maximum takeoff weight is 2,250 pounds. Its normal cruising speed is 81–103 miles per hour (maximum speed is 135 miles per hour) with a ceiling of 25,000 feet and an effective range of 675 miles. Endurance time is 24 hours. Surveillance and reconnaissance payload is 450 pounds. Its radar system provides all-weather surveillance capability. It can carry an assortment of munitions, including two AGM-114 Hellfire missiles. The Predator is also fitted with an emergency recovery parachute.

Predators provided intelligence data, including bomb-damage assessment, during the 1999 NATO Kosovo air campaign. In 2001 they were deployed as part of Operation ENDURING FREEDOM in the Afghanistan War (2001–), and in November 2002 an MQ-1 Predator in Yemen fired a Hellfire to destroy a car carrying suspected terrorists. Predators have also carried out similar ground-attack missions in Pakistan, Somalia, Libya, and Iraq.

The 14,500-pound (takeoff weight) U.S. Northrop Grumman high-altitude RQ-4 Global Hawk, which resembles in appearance and mission the U-2 reconnaissance aircraft, has a payload of 1,900 pounds and a maximum endurance time of 42 hours and can survey as many as 40,000 square miles of territory a day.

Virtually all major military powers now employ drones. Most military analysts predict that their use will only increase and that they will take on a larger number of roles, perhaps excluding only for the immediate future air-to-air combat.

Further Reading

U.S. Office of the Secretary of Defense. *Unmanned Reconnaissance Systems Roundup, 2005–2006.* Washington, DC: U.S. Government Printing Office, 2005.

Panzerhaubitze 2000 German Self-Propelled Howitzer

The German Panzerhaubitze (armored howitzer) 2000 155mm self-propelled tracked howitzer, or PzH 2000, is recognized as the world's most advanced tube artillery piece. Developed by the German firms of Krauss-Maffel Wegmann and Rheinmetall, it evolved from an international program that was canceled because of funding and design problems. Germany then proceeded alone. The prototype PzH 2000 was completed in 1993. Plans to purchase 1,254 of the self-propelled howitzers were reduced to only 185. The PzH 2000 entered service with the German Army in 1998.

The PzH 2000 is 38 feet 5 inches in length, 11 feet 10 inches in width, and 10 feet 2 inches in height. Its combat weight is 55.8 tons. It has a fully enclosed 14.5mm armored welded steel turret. Powered by the MTU 8811 Ka-500 engine, it has a road speed of 41 miles per hour, an off-road speed of 29 miles per hour, and an operational range of 261 miles.

The PzH 2000 has a crew of five: commander, driver, gunner, and two loaders. Its Rheinmetall 155mm main gun (with 60 rounds of ammunition) with automatic ammunition feed can fire 3 rounds in 9 seconds and 10 rounds in 56 seconds. Maximum range is 18.6 miles for high-explosive rounds and 24.9 miles for rocket-assisted rounds. Its ability to provide accurate fire to such ranges had been a major selling point. Secondary armament consists of a top-mounted Rhinemetall MG3 7.62mm machine gun.

The PzH 2000 is in the service of half a dozen nations. It first saw action in August 2000 in Afghanistan with the Dutch Army, firing against Taliban targets in Kandahar Province.

Further Reading

Bailey, Jonathan B. A. *Field Artillery and Firepower.* 2nd ed. Annapolis, MD: Naval Institute Press, 2003.

Zabecki, David T. "Great Guns! Benchmark Artillery Pieces That Shaped Military History." *MHQ* (August 2014): 76–84.

Thermobaric Bomb

The thermobaric bomb is an antipersonnel bomb used to penetrate and destroy deeply buried targets. The U.S. BLU-118/B thermobaric bomb was rushed through development and testing following the September 11, 2001, terrorist attacks on New York and Washington, D.C. Developed in a span of only several months and first exploded at the Nevada Test Site on December 14, 2001, the bomb utilizes principles of heat and pressure discovered in investigations into deadly cave mine explosions.

The BLU-118/B warhead is encased in a 98.5-inch-long, 2,000-pound bunker-busting bomb. Carried to the target area by an F-15E Strike Eagle or a B-1 or B-52 bomber, it is then guided to the target, penetrating through the concrete at the cave entrance. A fuze munition unit creates a small initial explosion, causing a fine aerosol mist. A second larger explosion then ignites this mix, creating an intense fireball and propelling it through the cave complex at supersonic speed. Heat and pressure are immense. Temperatures of as high at 3,000 degrees Celsius—more than double that of a conventional explosion—traveling at 10,000 feet per second suck in all the air from the complex and cause catastrophic damage to the internal organs of individuals present.

The principle is not new. The United States had employed a somewhat similar fuel-air bomb at the end of the Vietnam War, while the Russians had employed thermobaric rocket-launched weapons in fighting for Chechnya and Dagestan in 1999–2000. Following its successful testing, the BLU-118/B was first employed in early 2002 by U.S. forces in Operation ENDURING FREEDOM against cave complexes in the Gardez region of Afghanistan where Al Qaeda and Taliban fighters were believed to be located.

Further Reading

Meyer, Rudolph, Joseph Khler, and Axel Homburg. *Explosives.* 6th ed. Hoboken, NJ: Wiley-VCH, 2007.

Improvised Explosive Devices

Improvised explosive devices (IEDs) have been employed in warfare almost since the introduction of gunpowder, although the term has only come into use since the Iraq War (2003–2011). They remain the weapon of choice for insurgent/resistance groups that lack the numerical strength and firepower to conduct conventional operations against an opponent. IEDs are the contemporary name for both booby traps and other command-detonated explosive charges employed in World War II and the Vietnam War. In more recent times IEDs have been employed against civilian targets by Basque separatists, the Irish Republican Army, and the Taliban in Afghanistan.

Attempt to Assassinate Napoleon I

One of the more spectacular uses of an IED that almost changed history occurred in an attempt to assassinate Napoleon Bonaparte on Christmas Eve 1800. Seeking to take advantage of the first consul's well-known punctuality, monarchist conspirators filled a water cart with explosives designed to detonate as Bonaparte traveled in his carriage to the opera for the first performance of Haydn's oratorio *The Creation*.

The ensuing blast killed 22 bystanders and wounded another 57. Among the dead was a little girl who had been paid to hold the horses of the water cart. The emperor escaped injury thanks to the accident of the coachman in his carriage being drunk and driving too fast. Bonaparte's wife Josephine, traveling in the second carriage, also escaped injury thanks to it being delayed because of her tarrying to arrange her cashmere shawl.

Increasingly, IEDs were the chief weapon used by insurgents during the Iraq War from 2003 to attack U.S. forces and Iraqi police and army personnel and to carry out sectarian violence. The simplest type of IED was a hand grenade, a rigged artillery shell, or a bomb triggered by a trip wire or simple movement. It might be as simple as a grenade with its pin pulled and handle held down by the weight of a corpse. When the corpse was raised, the grenade exploded. Obtaining the material for such weapons was made easy for the insurgents in the Iraq War by the failure of U.S. and coalition forces in the heady days of the March 2003 drive on Baghdad to recognize a potential insurgent threat and secure the extensive Iraqi Army ammunition dumps. Thousands of tons of bombs and artillery shells simply disappeared.

Soon insurgents were employing these weapons against U.S. troops. By 2004, the insurgents employed more effective wireless detonators in the form of garage door openers and two-way radios. U.S. forces responded with radio-jamming devices known as Warlocks and by employing heavier armor on vehicles. By 2006, assisted by outside powers such as Iran, the insurgents introduced much more sophisticated IEDs triggered by infrared motion sensors as well as more powerful explosives and even shaped charges in order to attack armored vehicles. U.S. forces attempted to counter these by better intelligence and technological innovation, such as remote-controlled vehicles and the Buffalo 23-ton anti-IED vehicle with a 30-foot robotic arm. In spite of U.S. efforts, IEDs exacted a growing toll. By 2005, IEDs were responsible for 62 percent of U.S. combat deaths and 72 percent of the wounded. Estimated U.S. spending on research and development to defeat IEDs jumped from $150 million in 2004 to $3.3 billion in 2006.

Placed in any imaginable location such as in donkey carts, paint cans, and trash bags, IEDs appeared on the roadsides, in markets, and even in schoolyards. They also took the form of cars packed with explosives, which would be driven into a crowded area and detonated by their suicide-bomber drivers. The insurgents began employing IEDs in pairs, with the second device exploding after responders had arrived to take care of injured personnel from the first blast. Suicide belts and vests might also be considered IEDs.

IEDs were used to create the maximum harm at the least cost to the insurgents in order to influence public opinion and affect morale. Shia and Sunni groups have used IEDs extensively against each other in the sectarian violence that has swept Iraq. Casualty totals are one way to judge the effectiveness of a military operation, and growing casualties from IEDs in the 1980s and 1990s induced the Israeli Army to withdraw from southern Lebanon.

Further Reading

Crippen, James B. *Improvised Explosive Devices (IED).* New York: CRC Press, 2007.

DeForest, M. J. *Principles of Improvised Explosive Devices.* Boulder, CO: Paladin, 1984.

Tucker, Stephen. *Terrorist Explosive Sourcebook: Countering Terrorist Use of Improvised Explosive Devices.* Boulder, CO: Paladin, 1994.

Bibliography

Aloni, Shlomo. *Arab-Israeli Air Wars, 1947–1982.* London: Osprey, 2001.

Anderson, Roger Charles. *Oared Fighting Ships.* London: Percival Marshall, 1962.

Anderson, William R. *Nautilus 90 North.* New York: New American Library, 1959.

Angelucci, Enzo. *The American Combat Aircraft and Helicopters of the Vietnam War.* Illustrations by Pierluigi Pinto. New York: Orion Books, 1986.

Angelucci, Enzo. *The Rand McNally Encyclopedia of Military Aircraft, 1914–1980.* New York: Military Press, 1983.

Ashdown, Charles H. *European Arms and Armor.* New York: Barnes and Noble, 1995.

Auger, Vincent A. *Dynamics of Foreign Policy Analysis: The Carter Administration and the Neutron Bomb.* Oxford, UK: Rowman and Littlefield, 1986.

Bailey, Jonathan B. A. *Field Artillery and Firepower.* 2nd ed. Annapolis, MD: Naval Institute Press, 2003.

Baker, A. D., III. *Allied Landing Craft of World War Two.* Annapolis, MD: Naval Institute Press, 1985.

Baker, David. *The Rocket: The History and Development of Rocket & Missile Technology.* New York: Crown, 1978.

Baldwin, Ralph B. *The Deadly Fuze.* London: Jane's, 1980.

Ball, Robert W. D. *Mauser Military Rifles.* Iola, WI: Krause, 1996.

Bamford, Paul. *Fighting Ships and Prisons.* Minneapolis: University of Minnesota Press, 1973.

Barnaby, W. *The Plague Makers.* London: Vision, 1999.

Barybrook, Roy. *British Aerospace Harrier and Sea Harrier.* London: Osprey, 1984.

Baxter, James Phinney. *The Introduction of the Ironclad Warship.* New York: Archon, 1968.

Bean, Tim, and William Fowler. *Russian Tanks of World War II: Stalin's Armored Might.* St. Paul, MN: MBI, 2002.

Beauchamp, Ken. *History of Telegraphy.* London: IEE, 2001.

Bellamy, Chris. *Red God of War: Soviet Artillery and Rocket Forces.* Herdon, VA: Potomac Books, 1986.

Bennett, Frank M. *The* Monitor *and the Navy under Steam.* Boston: Scribner, 1900.

Berk, Joseph. *The Gatling Gun: 19th Century Machine Gun to 21st Century Vulcan.* Boulder, CO: Paladin, 1991.

Berndt, Thomas. *Standard Catalog of U.S. Military Vehicles, 1940–1965.* Iola, WI: Krause, 1993.

Birdwell, Steve. *Superfortress: The Boeing B-29.* Carrollton, TX: Squadron/Signal Publications, 1979.

Bishop, Chris. *Sikorsky UH-60 Black Hawk.* Oxford, UK: Osprey, 2008.

Bishop, Denis, and W. J. K. Davies. *Railways and War before 1918.* London: Blandford, 1972.

Bjornerstedt, Rolf, et al. *Napalm and Other Incendiary Weapons and All Aspects of Their Possible Use.* New York: United Nations, 1973.

Blackmore, D. *Arms & Armour of the English Civil War.* London: Royal Armouries, 1990.

Blackmore, H. L. "The Percussion System." In *Pollard's History of Firearms,* edited by Claude Blair, 161–187. New York: Macmillan, 1986.

Blair, Claude, ed. *Pollard's History of Firearms.* New York: Macmillan, 1983.

Blair, Clay. *The Atomic Submarine and Admiral Rickover.* New York: H. Holt, 1954.

Boyd, Carl, and Akihiko Yoshida. *The Japanese Submarine Force and World War II.* Annapolis, MD: Naval Institute Press, 1995.

Boyne, Walter J. *Boeing B-52: A Documentary History.* Washington, DC: Smithsonian Institution, 1984.

Boyne, Walter J. *Clash of Wings: World War II in the Air.* New York: Simon and Schuster, 1994.

Bradbury, Jim. *The Medieval Archer.* New York: Barnes and Noble, 2000.

Brodie, Bernard. *Sea Power in the Machine Age.* Princeton, NJ: Princeton University Press, 1941.

Brown, D. K. *Before the Ironclad: Development of Ship Design Propulsion and Armament in the Royal Navy, 1815–60.* Annapolis, MD: Naval Institute Press, 1990.

Brown, David K. *The Eclipse of the Big Gun: The Warship, 1906–45.* Annapolis, MD: Naval Institute Press, 1992.

Brown, Eric M. *Wings of the Luftwaffe.* Shrewsbury. UK: Airlife, 1993.

Brown, G. I. *The Big Bang.* Stroud, Gloucestershire, UK: Sutton, 2005.

Brown, Louis. *A Radar History of World War II: Technical and Military Imperatives.* Philadelphia: Institute of Physics Press, 1999.

Brown, M. L. *Firearms in Colonial America: The Impact on History and Technology, 1492–1792.* Washington, DC: Smithsonian Institution Press, 1980.

Brown, Stephen R. *A Most Damnable Invention: Dynamite, Nitrates, and the Making of the Modern World.* New York: St. Martin's, 2005.

Bruce, R. *German Automatic Weapons of World War II.* Crowood, UK: Marlborough, 1996.

Buderi, Robert. *The Invention That Changed the World.* New York: Simon and Schuster, 1999.

Bulkley, Robert J., Jr. *At Close Quarters: PT Boats in the United States Navy.* Washington, DC: Naval Historical Division, 1962.

Bull, Gerald V., and C. H. Murphy. *Paris Kanonen: The Paris Guns (Wilhelmgeschütze) and Project HARP.* Herford, Germany: Verlag E. S. Mittler and Sohn, 1988.

Bull, Stephen. *Encyclopedia of Military Technology and Innovation.* Westport, CT: Greenwood, 2004.

Bull, Stephen. *Military Technology and Innovation.* Westport, CT: Greenwood, 2004.

Bull, Stephen. *Trench: A History of Trench Warfare on the Western Front.* London: Osprey, 2010.

Bunker, John. *Heroes in Dungarees: The Story of the American Merchant Marine in World War II.* Annapolis, MD: Naval Institute Press, 1995.

Bunker, Robert J. "Booby Traps." In *Encyclopedia of the Vietnam War: A Political, Social and Military History,* Vol. 1, edited by Spencer C. Tucker, 75–76. Santa Barbara, CA: ABC-CLIO, 1998.

Burns, Russell W. *Communications: An International History of the Formative Years.* London: Institute of Electrical Engineers, 2004.

Bykofsky, J., and H. Larson. *The U.S. Army in World War II: Transportation Corps Operations Overseas.* Washington, DC: Center of Military History, 1957.

Campbell, J. M. *Consolidated B-24 Liberator.* Atglen, PA: Schiffer, 1993.

Campbell, John. *Naval Weapons of World War II.* Annapolis, MD: Naval Institute Press, 1985.

Caruana, Adrian B. *The History of English Sea Ordnance,* Vols. 1 and 2. Ashley Lodge, Rotherfield, East Sussex, UK: Jean Boudriot Publications, 1994, 1997.

Chamberlain, Peter, and Chris Ellis. *British and American Tanks of World War Two: The Complete Illustrated History of British, American and Commonwealth Tanks, Gun Motor Carriages and Special Purpose Vehicles, 1939–1945.* London: Cassell, 2000.

Chamberlain, Peter. *Tanks of World War I: British and German.* New York: Arco, 1969.

Chamberlain, Peter, and Hilary Doyle. *Encyclopedia of German Tanks of World War II.* Revised ed. London: Arms and Armour, 2001.

Chamberlain, Peter, H. L. Doyle, and Thomas L. Jentz. *Encyclopedia of German Tanks of World War Two: A Complete Illustrated Directory of German Battle Tanks, Armoured Cars, Self-Propelled Guns and Semi-tracked Vehicles, 1933–1945.* New York: Arco, 1978.

Chamberlain, Peter, and Terry Gander. *Anti-Aircraft Guns of World War II.* New York: Arco, 1976.

Chandler, Charles deForest, and Frank P. Lahm. *How Our Army Grew Wings.* New York: Ronald, 1943.

Chant, Christopher. *World Encyclopedia of Modern Air Weapons.* New York: HarperCollins, 1989.

Chesneau, Roger. *Aircraft Carriers of the World, 1914 to the Present: An Illustrated Encyclopedia.* Annapolis, MD: Naval Institute Press, 1995.

Chetty, P. R. K. *Space Technology and Its Applications.* New York: McGraw-Hill, 1988.

Cipolla, Carlo M. *Guns, Sails, and Empires.* New York: Pantheon Books, 1965.

Cocroft, Wayne. *Dangerous Energy: The Archaeology of Gunpowder.* London: English Heritage Publications, 2000.

Coe, Michael D., et al. *Swords and Hilt Weapons.* New York: Barnes and Noble, 1996.

Cohen, Sam. *The Truth about the Neutron Bomb: The Inventor Speaks Out.* New York: William Morrow, 1983.

Colby, C. B. *Military Vehicles: Gun Carriers, Mechanical Mules, Ducks and Super Ducks.* New York: Coward McCann, 1956.

Connolly, Peter. *Greece and Rome at War.* Englewood Cliffs, NJ: Prentice Hall, 1981.

Cook, Melvin A. *The Science of High Explosives.* New York: Reinhold, 1958.

Cook, Tim. *No Place to Run: The Canadian Corps and Gas Warfare in the First World War.* Vancouver: University of British Columbia Press, 1999.

Cooper, Sherod. *Liberty Ship: The Voyages of the* John W. Brown, *1942–1946.* Annapolis, MD: Naval Institute Press, 1997.

Corbett, Julian S. *Fighting Instructions, 1530–1816.* London: Naval Records Society, 1905.

Cotterell, Arthur. *Chariot: From Chariot to Tank, the Astounding Rise and Fall of the World's First War Machine.* Woodstock, NY: Overlook, 2004.

Cowdrey, Albert E. *Fighting for Life: American Military Medicine in World War II.* New York: Free Press, 1994.

Cowie, J. S. *Mines, Minelayers and Minelaying.* Oxford: Oxford University Press, 1949.

Crane, Conrad C. *Bombs, Cities, and Civilians: American Airpower Strategy in World War II.* Lawrence: University Press of Kansas, 1993.

Crippen, James B. *Improvised Explosive Devices (IED).* New York: CRC Press, 2007.

Croll, Mike. *The History of Land Mines.* Barnsley, UK: Leo Cooper, 1998.

Cross, Wilbur. *Zeppelins of World War I.* New York: Paragon House, 1991.

Crow, Duncan, ed. *AFV's of World War I.* Windsor, UK: Profile Publications, 1970.

Cullen, Tony, and Christopher F. Foss, eds. *Jane's Land-Based Air Defence, 2005–2006.* London: Jane's Information Group, 2005.

Curtis, Duncan. *North American F-86 Sabre.* Wiltside, UK: Crowood, 2000.

Curtis, Howard M. *2,500 Years of European Helmets: 800 B.C.–1700 A.D.* North Hollywood, CA: Beinfield Publishing, 1978.

Dahlgren, John A. *Shells and Shell Guns.* Philadelphia: King and Baird, 1856.

Davenant, Charles. *An Essay upon Ways and Means of Supplying the War.* London: Printed for Jacob Tonson, 1695.

Davies, Peter E., and Anthony M. Thornborough. *The Harrier Story.* Annapolis, MD: Naval Institute Press, 1996.

Dean, Bashford. *Helmets and Body Armor in Modern Warfare.* New Haven, CT: Yale University Press, 1920.

DeForest, M. J. *Principles of Improvised Explosive Devices.* Boulder, CO: Paladin, 1984.

De Syon, Guillaume. *Zeppelin! Germany and the Airship, 1900–1939.* Baltimore: Johns Hopkins University Press, 2001.

The Diagram Group. *Weapons: An International Encyclopedia from 5000 BC to 2000 AD.* New York: St. Martin's, 1990.

Dorr, Robert. *B-52 Stratofortress.* Oxford, UK: Osprey, 1995.

Dorr, Robert F. *B-29 Superfortress Units of the Korean War.* Oxford, UK: Osprey, 2003.

Downey, Fairfax. *Cannonade: Great Artillery Actions of History; The Famous Cannons and the Master Gunners.* New York: Doubleday, 1966.

Doyle, David. *Standard Catalog of U.S. Military Vehicles.* 2nd revised ed. Iola, WI: Krause, 2003.

Dranem, Walter, and Chris Hughes. *North American F-86 Sabrejet Day Fighters.* North Branch, MN: Specialty Press, 1997.

Duff, Scott A. *The M1 Garand, World War II: History of Development and Production, 1900 through 2 September 1945.* Export, PA: Scott A. Duff, 1996.

Dullin, Robert O., and William H. Garzke. *Battleships: United States Battleships in World War II.* Annapolis, MD: Naval Institute Press, 1976.

Dunstan, J. *Self Propelled Howitzers.* London: Arms and Armour, 1988.

Dunstan, S. *Flak Jackets.* London: Osprey, 1984.

Dutton, L. *Military Space.* London: Brassey's, 1990.

Ege, Lennart A. T. *Balloons and Airships, 1783–1973.* Edited by Kenneth Munson. New York: Macmillan, 1981.

Ellis, John. *Eye-Deep in Hell: Trench Warfare in World War I.* New York: Pantheon Books, 1977.

Elphick, Peter. *Liberty: The Ships That Won the War.* Annapolis, MD: Naval Institute Press, 2001.

Ethell, Jeffrey, and Alfred Price. *World War II Fighting Jets.* Shrewsbury, UK: Airlife, 1994.

Everett-Heath, John. *Helicopters in Combat: The First Fifty Years.* London: Arms and Armour, 1992.

Ezell, Edward Clinton, and Thomas M. Pegg. *Small Arms of the World: A Basic Manual of Small Arms.* Harrisburg, PA: Stackpole, 1983.

Fagan, M. D., ed. *A History of Engineering and Science in the Bell System: National Service in War and Peace (1925–1975).* New York: Bell Telephone Laboratories, 1980.

Faltum, Andrew. *The Essex Class Aircraft Carriers.* Baltimore: Nautical and Aviation Publishing Company of America, 1996.

Fisher, David. *A Race on the Edge of Time: Radar—The Decisive Weapon of World War II.* New York: McGraw-Hill, 1988.

Fleischer, Wolfgang. *Panzerfaust and Other German Infantry Anti-Tank Weapons.* Atglen, PA: Schiffer, 1994.

Fontenoy, Paul E. *Submarines: An Illustrated History of Their Impact.* Santa Barbara, CA: ABC-CLIO, 2007.

Fordham, Stanley. *High Explosives and Propellents.* Oxford, UK: Pergamon, 1980.

Foss, Christopher F. *Jane's Armour and Artillery, 1998–1999.* London: Jane's Information Group, 1998.

Foss, Christopher F., ed. *The Encyclopedia of Tanks and Armored Fighting Vehicles.* San Diego: Thunder Bay, 2002.

Foulkes, C., and E. C. Hopkinson. *Sword, Lance and Bayonet.* London: Arms and Armour, 1967.

Franks, Norman L. R. *Conflict over the Bay.* London: William Kimber, 1986.

Franks, Norman L. R. *U-Boat versus Aircraft.* London: Grub Street, 1999.

Fredriksen, John C. *International Warbirds: An Illustrated Guide to World Military Aircraft, 1914–2000*. Santa Barbara, CA: ABC-CLIO, 2001.

Fredriksen, John C. *Warbirds: An Illustrated Guide to U.S. Military Aircraft, 1915–2000*. Santa Barbara, CA: ABC-CLIO, 1999.

Freeman, Roger A. *B-17 Fortress at War*. New York: Scribner, 1977.

Frieden, David R. *Principles of Naval Weapons Systems*. Annapolis, MD: U.S. Naval Institute, 1985.

Friedman, Norman. *British Carrier Aviation: The Evolution of the Ships and Their Aircraft*. Annapolis, MD: Naval Institute Press, 1988.

Friedman, Norman. *Naval Institute Guide to World Naval Weapons, 1994 Update*. Annapolis, MD: Naval Institute Press, 1994.

Friedman, Norman. *U.S. Aircraft Carriers: An Illustrated Design History*. Annapolis, MD: Naval Institute Press, 1983.

Friedman, Norman. *U.S. Destroyers: An Illustrated Design History*. Annapolis, MD: Naval Institute Press, 1982.

Friedman, Norman. *U.S. Submarines since 1945: An Illustrated Design History*. Annapolis, MD: Naval Institute Press, 1994.

Friedman, Norman. *World Naval Weapons Systems*. Annapolis, MD: Naval Institute Press, 1991.

Friedman, Norman. *World Naval Weapons Systems, 1997–1998*. Annapolis, MD: Naval Institute Press, 1997.

Galuppini, Gino. *Warships of the World: An Illustrated Encyclopedia*. New York: Military Press, 1989.

Gander, Terry J. *Anti-Tank Weapons*. Marlborough, UK: Crowood, 2000.

Gander, Terry J. *The Bazooka: Hand-Held Hollow-Charge Anti-Tank Weapons*. London: PRC Publishing, 1998.

Gander, Terry J. *Browning M2 Heavy Machine Gun*. London: PRC Publishing, 1999.

Gander, Terry J. *The Browning Automatic Rifle*. London: PRC Publishing, 1999.

Gardiner, Robert. *Frigates of the Napoleonic Wars*. Annapolis, MD: Naval Institute Press, 2000.

Gardiner, Robert, ed. *Conway's All the World's Fighting Ships, 1860–1905*. Annapolis, MD: Naval Institute Press, 1979.

George, James L. *History of Warships: From Ancient Times to the Twenty-First Century*. Annapolis, MD: Naval Institute Press, 1998.

Gibbon, Edward. *The History of the Decline and Fall of the Roman Empire,* Vol. 6. Edited by J. B. Bury. London: Methuen, 1912.

Gibbons, Tony, ed. *The Encyclopedia of Ships*. London: Amber Books, 2001.

Gibson, James N. *Nuclear Weapons of the United States: An Illustrated History.* Atglen, PA: Schiffer, 1996.

Gold, David, and Christopher Paine. *Misguided Expenditures: An Analysis of the Proposed MX Missile System.* New York: Council on Economic Priorities, 1981.

Goldsmith, Duff L., and R. Blake Stevens. *The Devil's Paintbrush: Sir Hiram Maxim's Gun.* 2nd ed. Toronto: Collector Grade Publications, 1993.

Gonen, Rivka. *Weapons of the Ancient World.* London: Cassell, 1975.

Goodall, James. *America's Stealth Fighters and Bombers.* Osceola, WI: Motorbooks International, 1992.

Gordon, Yefim. *Mikoyan-Gurevich MiG-15: The Soviet Union's Long-Lived Korean War Fighter.* Leicester, UK: Midland, 2001.

Götz, Hans Dieter. *German Military Rifles and Machine Pistols, 1871–1945.* Translated by Edward Force. West Chester, PA: Shiffer, 1990.

Graham, Thomas, Jr., and Damien J. La Vera. *Cornerstones of Security: Arms Control Treaties in the Nuclear Era.* Seattle: University of Washington Press, 2003.

Granesay, S. V. *Arms and Armour.* London: Hamlyn, 1964.

Gray, Edwyn. *The Devil's Device: Robert Whitehead and the History of the Torpedo.* Revised and updated ed. Annapolis, MD: Naval Institute Press, 1991.

Gray, Peter, and Owen Thetford. *German Aircraft of the First World War.* London: Putnam, 1992.

Grbasic, Zvonimir, and Velimir Vuksic. *The History of Cavalry.* New York: Facts on File, 1989.

Green, Michael. *Military Trucks.* New York: Grolier Publications, 1997.

Green, William, and Gordon Swanborough. *The Complete Book of Fighters.* London: Salamander Books, 1994.

Griffith, Paddy. *Fortifications of the Western Front, 1914–18.* Illustrated by Peter Dennis. Oxford, UK: Osprey, 2014.

Grosz, Peter M. *Windsock Datafile 91, Fokker E.I/II.* Berkhamsted, UK: Albatros Productions, 2002.

Gruenhagen, Robert W. *Mustang: The Story of the P-51 Fighter.* Revised ed. New York: Arco, 1976.

Guilmartin, John Francis, Jr. *Gunpowder and Galleys: Changing Technology and Mediterranean Warfare at Sea in the Sixteenth Century.* New York: Cambridge University Press, 1974.

Guilmartin, John Francis, Jr. *Naval Warfare under Oars: 4th to 16th Centuries.* Annapolis, MD: Naval Institute Press, 1940.

Gunston, Bill. *The Illustrated Encyclopedia of Aircraft Armament: A Major Directory of Guns, Rockets, Missiles, Bombs, Torpedoes and Mines.* New York: Orion Books, 1988.

Haber, L. F. *The Poisonous Cloud: Chemical Warfare in the First World War.* Oxford: Oxford University Press, 1986.

Hall, Bert S. *Weapons and Warfare in Renaissance Europe: Gunpowder, Technology, and Tactics.* Baltimore: Johns Hopkins University Press, 1997.

Hallion, Richard P. *Precision Guided Munitions and the New Era of Warfare.* Air Power Studies Center Working Paper No. 53. Fairbairn, Australia: Air Powers Studies Center, Fairbairn RAAF Base, 1995.

Hallion, Richard P. *Rise of the Fighter Aircraft, 1914–1918.* Annapolis, MD: Nautical and Aviation Publishing Company of America, 1984.

Hamilton, C. I. *Anglo-French Naval Rivalry, 1846–1870.* Oxford: Oxford University Press, 1993.

Harding, David, ed. *Weapons: An International Encyclopedia from 5000 B.C. to 2000 A.D.* New York: St. Martin's, 1990.

Hardy, Robert. *Longbow: A Social and Military History.* Cambridge, UK: Patrick Stephens, 1978.

Harris, Sheldon. *Factories of Death.* London: Routledge, 1994.

Hartcup, Guy. *Camouflage: A History of Concealment and Deception in War.* New York: Encore Editions, 1980.

Hartcup, Guy. *Code Name Mulberry: The Planning, Building and Operation of the Normandy Harbours.* New York: Hippocrene Books, 1977.

Hartmann, Gregory K., with Scott C. Truver. *Weapons That Wait: Mine Warfare in the U.S. Navy.* Annapolis, MD: Naval Institute Press, 1991.

Haselgrove, Michael J. *Helmets of the First World War: Germany, Britain, and Their Allies.* Atglen, PA: Schiffer, 2000.

Hawkey, Arthur. *Black Night off Finisterre: The Tragic Tale of an Early British Ironclad.* Annapolis, MD: Naval Institute Press, 1999.

Haws, Duncan, and Alex A. Hurst. *The Maritime History of the World,* Vol. 1. Brighton, UK: Teredo Books, 1985.

Hazlett, James C., Edwin Olmstead, and M. Hume Parks. *Field Artillery Weapons of the Civil War.* Cranbury, NJ: Associated University Presses, 1983.

Herlihy, David V. *Bicycle: The History.* New Haven, CT: Yale University Press, 2004.

Hewson, Robert, ed. *Jane's Air-Launched Weapons, 2001.* London: Jane's, 2002.

Hezlet, Sir Arthur. *Electronics and Sea Power.* New York: Stein and Day, 1975.

Hill, Tracie L., R. Blake Stevens, and Rick Cartledge. *Thompson, the American Legend: The First Submachine Gun.* Coburg, Ontario: Collector Grade Publications, 1996.

Hobbs, David. *Aircraft Carriers of the Royal and Commonwealth Navies: The Complete Illustrated Encyclopedia from World War I to the Present.* London: Greenhill Books, 1996.

Hodges, P. *Royal Navy Warship Camouflage.* London: Almark, 1973.

Hogg, I. V. *Mortars.* Marlborough, UK: Crowood, 2001.

Hogg, I. V., and J. Weeks. *Browning M2 Heavy Machine Gun.* London: PRC Publishing, 1999.

Hogg, I. V., and J. Weeks. *Military Small Arms of the Twentieth Century.* New York: Hippocrene, 1994.

Hogg, Ivan. *Military Small Arms Data Book.* Philadelphia: Stackpole, 1999.

Hogg, Ivan, and John Batchelor. *Naval Gun.* Poole, Dorset, UK: Blandford, 1978.

Hogg, Ivan V. *Anti-Aircraft: A History of Air Defense.* London: MacDonald and Jane's, 1978.

Hogg, Ivan V. *Artillery 2000.* London: Arms and Armour, 1990.

Hogg, Ivan V. *German Secret Weapons of the Second World War.* London: Greenhill Books, 1999.

Hogg, Ivan V. *The Greenhill Armoured Fighting Vehicles Data Book.* Mechanicsburg, PA: Stackpole, 2000.

Hogg, Ivan V. *The Guns, 1914–1918.* New York: Ballantine, 1971.

Hogg, Ivan V. *A History of Artillery.* Astronaut House, Feltham, Middlesex, UK: Hamlyn Publishing Group, 1974.

Hogg, Ivan V. *The Illustrated Encyclopedia of Ammunition.* London: New Burlington, 1985.

Hogg, Ivan V. *Infantry Weapons of World War II.* London: Bison, 1977.

Hogg, Ivan V. *Jane's Dictionary of Military Small Arms Ammunition.* London: Jane's, 1985.

Hogg, Ivan V., ed. *Jane's Infantry Weapons, 1991–1992.* New York: Jane's Information Group, 1991.

Holder, Bill. *Northrop Grumman B-2 Spirit: An Illustrated History.* Atglen, PA: Schiffer, 1998.

Holloway, David. *Stalin and the Bomb: The Soviet Union and Atomic Energy, 1939–1956.* New Haven, CT: Yale University Press, 1994.

Hooten, Ted. *Jane's Naval Weapons Systems, 2001–2002.* London: Jane's, 2002.

Hough, Richard. *Fighting Ships.* New York: Putnam, 1969.

Howard, Frank. *Sailing Ships of War, 1400–1860.* London: Conway Maritime, 1979.

Howard, Michael. *The Franco-Prussian War.* New York: Routledge, 2001.

Hoyden, G. A. *The History and Development of Small Arms Ammunition.* Tacoma, WA: Armory, 1981.

Huff, Rolland. *The Sten Submachine Gun.* El Dorado, AR: Desert Publications, 1991.

Hughes, Gordon, and Barry Jenkins. *A Primer of Military Knives: European & American Combat, Trench & Utility Knives.* Brighton, UK: Military Press, 1973.

Hughes, M., and C. Mann. *The Panther Tank.* Staplehurt, UK: Spellmount, 2000.

Hughes, M., and C. Mann. *The T-34 Tank.* Staplehurt, UK: Spellmount, 1999.

Hunnicutt, R. P. *Armoured Car: A History of American Wheeled Combat Vehicles.* Novato, CA: Presidio, 2002.

Hutchinson, Robert. *Jane's Submarines: War beneath the Waves from 1776 to the Present Day.* New York: HarperCollins, 2001.

Inoguchi Rikihei and Tadashi Nakajima with Roger Pineau. *The Divine Wind: Japan's Kamikaze Force in World War II.* New York: Bantam Books, 1978.

Jane's Amphibious Warfare Capabilities. Coulson, Surrey, UK, and Alexandria, VA: Jane's Information Group, 2000.

Jane's High-Speed Maritime Transportation, 2000–2001. Coulson, Surrey, UK, and Alexandria, VA: Jane's Information Group, 2000.

Jane's Infantry Weapons, 2000–2001. Coulson, Surrey, UK: Jane's Information Group, 2000.

Jarrett, Philip, ed. *Aircraft of the Second World War.* London: Putnam, 1997.

Jenkins, Dennis R. *Lockheed U-2 Dragon Lady.* North Branch, MN: Specialty Press, 1998.

Jenkins, E. H. *A History of the French Navy: From Its Beginnings to the Present Day.* Annapolis, MD: Naval Institute Press, 1973.

Jobé, Joseph, ed. *Guns: An Illustrated History of Artillery.* New York: Crescent Books, 1971.

Kaplan, Fred. *The Wizards of Armageddon: Strategists of the Nuclear Age.* New York: Simon and Schuster, 1983.

Kay, A. L. *German Jet Engine and Gas Turbine Development, 1930–1945.* Shrewsbury, UK: Airlife, 2002.

Kelly, Jack. *Gunpowder: Alchemy, Bombards, and Pyrotechnics: The History of the Explosive That Changed the World.* New York: Basic Books, 2004.

Kemp, Peter, ed. *The Oxford Companion to Ships and the Sea.* Oxford: Oxford University Press, 1988.

Kennett, Lee. *The First Air War, 1914–1918.* New York: Free Press, 1991.

Kerr, E. Bartlett. *Flames over Tokyo: The U.S. Army Air Forces' Incendiary Campaign against Japan, 1944–1945.* New York: Donald I. Fine, 1991.

Kiesling, Paul. *Bayonets of the World.* Kedichem, Lingedijk, Netherlands: Military Collectors Service, 1973.

Kihlberg, Bengt, ed. *The Lore of Ships.* New York: Crescent Books, 1986.

Kilduff, Peter. *U.S. Carriers at War.* 2nd revised ed. Annapolis, MD: Naval Institute Press, 1997.

Kinard, Jeff. *Artillery: An Illustrated History of Its Impact.* Santa Barbara, CA: ABC-CLIO, 2007.

Kinard, Jeff. *Pistols: An Illustrated History of Their Impact.* Santa Barbara, CA: ABC-CLIO, 2003.

King, Horace F. *Armament of British Aircraft.* London: Putnam, 1971.

Knight, Bob, Harry Smith, and Barry Barnett. *PLUTO: World War II's Best-Kept Secret.* Bexley, UK: Bexley Council, 1998.

Lake, Jon. *B-52 Stratofortress Units in Operation Desert Storm.* Oxford, UK: Osprey, 2004.

Lambert, Andrew. *The Last Sailing Battlefleet: Maintaining Naval Mastery, 1815–1850.* London: Conway Maritime, 1991.

Lambert, Andrew. Warrior: *The First and Last Ironclad.* London: Conway Maritime, 1987.

Lambert, Andrew D., ed. *Steam, Steel, and Shellfire: The Steam Warship, 1815–1905.* London: Conway Maritime, 1992.

Landström, Björn. *The Ship: An Illustrated History.* Garden City, NY: Doubleday, 1961.

Langer, William L. *Gas and Flame in World War I.* New York: Knopf, 1965.

Lavery, Brian. *Nelson's Navy: The Ships, Men and Organisation, 1793–1815.* Annapolis, MD: Naval Institute Press, 1989.

Lavery, Brian. *The Ship of the Line: Design, Construction, and Fittings.* 2 vols. London: Conway Maritime, 1983.

Lavery, Brian, ed. *The Line of Battle: The Sailing Warship, 1650–1840.* London: Conway Maritime, 1992.

Lavine, A. Lincoln. *Circuits of Victory.* Garden City, NY: Country Life, 1921.

Lazenby, J. F. *The First Punic War: A Military History.* Stanford, CA: Stanford University Press, 1996.

Ledebur, Gerhard Freiherr von. *Die Seemine.* Munich: J. Lehmanns Verlag, 1977.

Lemay, Curtis E., and Bill Yenne. *Superfortress: The Story of the B-29 and American Air Power in World War II.* New York: Berkley Publishing Group, 1989.

Lenk, Torsten. *The Flintlock: Its Origin and Development.* New York: Bramhall House, 1965.

Lennox, Duncan, ed. *Jane's Air-Launched Weapons.* Alexandria, VA: Jane's Information Group-Sentinel House, 1999.

Leoni, Ray D. *Black Hawk: The Story of a World Class Helicopter.* Reston, VA: American Institute of Aeronautics and Astronautics, 2007.

Levert, Lee J. *Fundamentals of Naval Warfare.* New York: Macmillan, 1947.

Levi, Barbara G., et al., eds. *The Future of Land Based Ballistic Missiles.* New York: American Institute of Physics, 1989.

Lewin, Ronald. *Ultra Goes to War.* New York: McGraw-Hill, 1978.

Lowden, John L. *Silent Wings at War: Combat Gliders in World War II.* Washington, DC: Smithsonian Institution Press, 1992.

Macksey, Kenneth, and John H. Batchelor. *Tank: A History of the Armoured Fighting Vehicle.* New York: Scribner, 1970.

Maloney, Edward T., ed. *Supermarine Spitfire.* Fallbrook, CA: Aero Publications, 1966.

Manceron, Claude. *The French Revolution,* Vol. 3, *Their Gracious Pleasure, 1782–1785.* Translated by Nancy Amphoux. New York: Knopf, 1980.

March, Edgar J. *British Destroyers: A History of Development, 1893–1953.* London: Seeley Service, 1966.

Margiotta, Franklin D., ed. *Brassey's Encyclopedia of Land Forces and Warfare.* Washington, DC: Brassey's, 1996.

Marsden, E. W. *Greek and Roman Artillery, Historical Development.* Oxford, UK: Sandpiper, 1999.

Martin, A. R. F., and S. A. B. Hitchins. *Development of the Panzerfaust.* London: British Intelligence Objectives Sub Committee, 1945.

Massie, Robert K. *Dreadnought: Britain, Germany, and the Coming of the Great War.* New York: Random House, 1991.

Masters, Charles J. *Glidermen of Neptune: The American D-Day Glider Attack.* Carbondale: Southern Illinois University Press, 1995.

Mayor, Adrienne. *Greek Fire, Poison Arrows, and Scorpion Bombs: Biological and Chemical Warfare in the Ancient World.* New York: Overlook Duckworth, 2003.

McCallum, Henry D., and Frances T. McCallum. *The Wire That Frenched the West.* Norman: University of Oklahoma Press, 1965.

McFarland, Marvin W., ed. *The Papers of Wilbur and Orville Wright.* New York: McGraw-Hill, 1953.

McFarland, Stephen L. *America's Pursuit of Precision Bombing, 1910–1945.* Washington, DC: Smithsonian Institution Press, 1995.

McGonagle, Seamus. *The Bicycle in Life, Love, War and Literature.* New York: A. S. Barnes, 1968.

McGowen, Stanley S. *Helicopters: An Illustrated History of Their Impact.* Santa Barbara, CA: ABC-CLIO, 2005.

Mesko, Jim. *Airmobile: The Helicopter War in Vietnam.* Carrollton, TX: Squadron Signal Publications, 1984.

Messimer, Dwight R. *Find and Destroy: Antisubmarine Warfare in World War I.* Annapolis, MD: Naval Institute Press, 2001.

Meyer, Rudolph, Joseph Khler, and Axel Homburg. *Explosives.* 6th ed. Hoboken, NJ: Wiley-VCH, 2007.

Miller, David, and John Jordan. *Modern Submarine Warfare.* London: Salamander Books, 1987.

Miller, Edward N. *U.S.S.* Monitor: *The Ship That Launched a Modern Navy.* Annapolis, MD: Leeward Publications, 1978.

Miller, Henry W. *The Paris Gun.* New York: Jonathan Cape and Harrison Smith, 1930.

Miller, Jay. *Northrop B-2 Spirit.* Leicester, UK: Midland, 1995.

Miller, Nathan. *Sea of Glory: The Continental Navy Fights for Independence, 1775–1783.* New York: David McKay, 1974.

Millot, Bernard. *Divine Thunder: The Life and Death of the Kamikazes.* Translated by Lowell Blair. New York: McCall, 1970.

Monin, L., and A. Gallimore. *The Devil's Gardens: A History of Land Mines.* London: Pimlico, 2002.

Moore, Rufus J. "Operation PLUTO." *United States Naval Institute Proceedings* 80(6) (1954): 647–653.

Moore, William. *Gas Attack: Chemical Warfare, 1915 to the Present Day.* London: Leo Cooper, 1987.

Morrison, John S., John F. Coats, and N. Boris Rankov. *The Athenian Trireme: The History and Reconstruction of an Ancient Greek Warship.* 2nd ed. Cambridge: Cambridge University Press, 2000.

Mountcastle, John W. *Flame On! U.S. Incendiary Weapons, 1918–1945.* Shippensburg, PA: White Mane, 1999.

Mrazek, James E. *Fighting Gliders of World War II.* New York: St. Martin's, 1977.

Mrazek, James E. *The Glider War.* New York: St. Martin's, 1975.

Muir, Malcolm, Jr. *Black Shoes and Blue Water: Surface Warfare in the United States Navy, 1945–1975.* Washington, DC: Naval Historical Center, 1996.

Muir, Malcolm, Jr. *The Iowa Class Battleships:* Iowa, New Jersey, Missouri, *and* Wisconsin. Poole, Dorset, UK: Blandford, 1987.

Munson, Kenneth. *Bombers: Patrol and Reconnaissance Aircraft, 1914–19.* New York: Macmillan, 1968.

Munson, Kenneth. *Fighters, Attack and Training Aircraft, 1914–19.* Poole, UK: Blandford, 1976.

Myatt, F. *Illustrated Encyclopedia of Pistols and Revolvers.* London: Salamander Books, 1980.

Myrvang, Folke. *MG34-MG42: German Universal Machineguns.* Cobourg, Ont.: Collector Grade Publications, 2002.

Neillands, Robin. *The Bomber War: The Allied Air Offensive against Nazi Germany.* New York: Overlook, 1991.

Nelson, Curtis L. *Hunters in the Shallows: A History of the PT Boat.* Washington, DC: Brassey's, 1998.

Neufeld, Jacob. *The Development of Ballistic Missiles in the United States Air Force, 1945–1960.* Washington, DC: Office of Air Force History, 1989.

Neufeld, Michael J. *The Rocket and the Reich: Peenemünde and the Coming of the Ballistic Missile Era.* New York: Free Press, 1995.

Nicolle, David. *Medieval Siege Weapons,* Vol. 1, *Western Europe, AD 585–1385.* Illustrated by Sam Thompson. London: Osprey, 2002.

Nordeen, Lon O. *Harrier II: Validating V/STOL.* Annapolis, MD: Naval Institute Press, 2006.

Norris, John. *German 88 mm Flak 18/36/37 and Pak 43 1936–45.* London: Osprey, 2002.

Norris, John. *Infantry Mortars of World War II.* London: Osprey, 2002.

Oakeshott, R. Ewartt. *The Sword in the Age of Chivalry.* New York: Praeger, 1965.

Oldham, P. *Pillboxes of the Western Front.* London: Leo Cooper, 1995.

Olmstead, Edwin, Wayne Stark, and Spencer C. Tucker. *The Big Guns: Civil War Siege, Seacoast, and Naval Cannon.* Alexandria Bay, NY: Museum Restoration Service, 1997.

O'Malley, T. J. *Artillery: Guns and Rocket Systems.* Mechanicsburg, PA: Stackpole, 1994.

O'Malley, T. J. *Military Transport: Trucks and Transporters.* London: Greenhill Books, 1995.

106mm Recoilless Rifle, M40A1: FM23-82. Washington, DC: U.S. Army, 1962.

Osborne, Eric W. *Cruisers and Battle Cruisers: An Illustrated History of Their Impact.* Santa Barbara, CA: ABC-CLIO, 2004.

Padfield, Peter. *Guns at Sea.* New York: St. Martin's, 1974.

Palazzo, Albert. *Seeking Victory on the Western Front: The British Army and Chemical Warfare in World War I.* Lincoln: University of Nebraska Press, 2000.

Parkes, Oscar. *British Battleships* Warrior *(1860) to* Vanguard *(1950): A History of Design, Construction, and Armament.* London: Seeley Service, 1970.

Partington, James Riddick. *A History of Greek Fire and Gunpowder.* Baltimore: Johns Hopkins University Press, 1998.

Pawle, Gerald. *The Secret War.* London: G. G. Harrap, 1956.

Payne-Gallway, Ralph. *The Book of the Crossbow.* New York: Dover, 1995.

Payne-Gallwey, Ralph. *Crossbow: Medieval and Modern, Military and Sporting; Its Construction, History and Management.* New York: Bramhall House, 1958.

Pedlow, Gregory W., and Donald Welzenbach. *The CIA and the U-2 Program, 1954–1974.* Washington, DC: Central Intelligence Agency, 1998.

Peebles, Curtis. *Twilight Warriors: Covert Air Operations against the USSR.* Annapolis, MD: Naval Institute Press, 2005.

Perlmutter, Tom. *War Machines, Sea.* London: Octopus Books, 1965.

Perret, Geoffrey. *There's a War to Be Won: The United States Army in World War II.* New York: Random House, 1991.

Peterson, Harold L. *Arms and Armor in Colonial America, 1526–1783.* New York: Bramhall House, 1956.

Peterson, Harold L. *Round Shot and Rammers.* Harrisburg, PA: Stackpole, 1969.

Pimlott, John. *B-29 Superfortress.* Secaucus, NJ: Chartwell Books, 1980.

Pocock, Rowland. *German Guided Missiles.* New York: Arco, 1967.

Polmar, Norman. *Ships and Aircraft of the U.S. Fleet.* 17th ed. Annapolis, MD: Naval Institute Press, 2000.

Polmar, Norman, and Jurrien Noot. *Submarines of the Russian and Soviet Navies, 1718–1990.* Annapolis, MD: Naval Institute Press, 1991.

Popham, Hugh. *A Damned Cunning Fellow: The Eventful Life of Rear-Admiral Sir Home Popham, KCB, KCH, KM, FRS, 1762–1820.* Tywardreath, Cornwall, UK: Old Ferry Press, 1991.

Preston, Anthony. *Destroyers.* Englewood Cliffs, NJ: Prentice Hall, 1977.

Prouty, Raymond W. *Military Helicopter Design Technology.* London: Janes Defense Data, 1989.

Raven, Alan. *Essex-Class Carriers.* Annapolis, MD: Naval Institute Press, 1988.

Rendall, Ivan. *Rolling Thunder.* New York: Free Press, 1997.

Reynosa, Mark A. *Post World War II M-1 Helmets: An Illustrated Study.* Atglen, PA: Schiffer, 1999.

Rhodes, Richard. *Dark Sun: The Making of the Hydrogen Bomb.* New York: Simon and Schuster, 1996.

Rhodes, Richard. *The Making of an Atomic Bomb.* New York: Simon and Schuster, 1986.

Richardson, Doug. *Stealth Warplanes: Deception, Evasion, and Concealment in the Air.* Osceola, WI: Motorbooks International, 2001.

Richardson, M., et al. *Surveillance and Target Acquisition Systems.* London: Brassey's, 1997.

Richter, Donald. *Chemical Soldiers: British Gas Warfare in World War I.* Lawrence: University Press of Kansas, 1992.

Rihll, Tracey. *The Catapult: A History.* Yardley, PA: Westholme, 2007.

Rimell, Raymond L. *Zeppelin! A Battle for Air Supremacy in World War I.* London: Conway Maritime, 1984.

Ripley, Warren. *Artillery and Ammunition of the Civil War.* New York: Van Nostrand Reinhold, 1970.

Roberts, John. *The Battleship Dreadnought.* Annapolis, MD: Naval Institute Press, 1992.

Robertson, Frederick L. *The Evolution of Naval Armament.* London: Harold T. Storey, 1968.

Robinson, J. Russell. *Oriental Armour.* New York: Waler, 1967.

Rodger, N. A. M. *The Safeguard of the Sea: A Naval History of Britain,* Vol. 1, *660–1649.* London: HarperCollins, 1997.

Rogers, H. C. B. *A History of Artillery.* Secaucus, NJ: Citadel Press, 1975.

Roland, Alex. *Underwater Warfare in the Age of Sail.* Bloomington: Indiana University Press, 1978.

Rolt, L. T. C. *The Aeronauts: A History of Ballooning, 1783–1903.* New York: Messner, 1958.

Ropp, Theodore. *The Development of a Modern Navy: French Naval Policy, 1871–1904.* Edited by Stephen S. Roberts. Annapolis, MD: Naval Institute Press, 1987.

Rosa, Joseph G., and Robin May. *An Illustrated History of Guns and Small Arms.* London: Peerage Books, 1984.

Rosser-Owen, David. *Vietnam Weapons Handbook.* Wellingborough, Northamptonshire, UK: Patrick Stephens, 1986.

Rössler, Eberhard. *The U-boat.* Annapolis, MD: Naval Institute Press, 1989.

Routledge, N. W. *History of the Royal Regiment of Artillery: Anti-Aircraft Artillery, 1914–55.* London: Brassey's, 1994.

Ruhe, Benjamin, and Eric Darnell. *Boomerang: How to Throw, Catch, and Make It.* New York: Workman Publishing, 1985.

Runis, Edwin. *Weapons: A Pictorial History.* New York: World Publishing, 1954.

Ryan, J. W. *Guns, Mortars and Rockets.* London: Brassey's, 1982.

Salecker, Gene E. *Fortress against the Sun: The B-17 Flying Fortress in the Pacific.* New York: Da Capo, 2001.

Saunders, Anthony. *Dominating the Enemy: War in the Trenches 1914–1918.* Phoenix Mill, UK: Sutton, 2000.

Sawyer, Leonard A., and William W. Mitchell. *The Liberty Ships: The History of the 'Emergency' Type Cargo Ships Constructed in the United States during World War II.* Newton Abbot, UK: David and Charles, 1970.

Scheips, Paul J., ed. *Military Signal Communication,* 2 vols. New York: Arno, 1980.

Searle, Adrian. *PLUTO: Pipe-Line under the Ocean.* Isle of Wight, UK: Shanklin Chine, 1995.

Seelinger, Matthew J. "M2/M101 105 mm Howitzer." *On Point: The Journal of Army History* 2(4) (Spring 2006): 6–7.

Sellier, K. G., and B. P. Kneubuehl. *Wound Ballistics.* Amsterdam: Elsevier, 1894.

Serber, Robert. *The Los Alamos Primer: The First Lectures on How to Build an Atomic Bomb.* Los Angeles: University of California Press, 1992.

Shannon, Chris. *Air-to-Air Missile Directory.* London: Centurion, 2005.

Simpson, Andy, ed. *Hot Blood and Cold Steel: Life and Death in the Trenches of the First World War.* London: Tom Donovan, 1993.

Skennerton, Ian. *.303 Lewis Machine Gun.* N.p.: Arms and Armour Militaria Press, Australia, 2001.

Skulski, Janusz. *The Battleship* Yamato. Annapolis, MD: Naval Institute Press, 1988.

Sloan, C. E. E. *Mine Warfare on Land.* London: Brassey's, 1986.

Smith, Peter. *Hard Lying: The Birth of the Destroyer, 1893–1913.* Annapolis, MD: Naval Institute Press, 1971.

Smith, W. H. B. *A Basic Manual of Military Small Arms.* Harrisburg, PA: Military Service Publishing, 1945.

Smith, W. H. B. *Mauser Military Rifles and Pistols.* Harrisburg, PA: Military Service Publishing, 1946.

Smith, W. H. B. *Small Arms of the World.* 9th ed. Harrisburg, PA: Stackpole, 1969.

Snyder, Thomas S., ed. *Air Force Communications Command, 1938–1991: An Illustrated History.* Scott Air Force Base, IL: Office of History, 1991.

Spick, Mike. *Supermarine Spitfire.* New York: Random House, 1996.

Spinardi, Graham, et al. *From Polaris to Trident: The Development of U.S. Fleet Ballistic Missile Technology.* Cambridge: Cambridge University Press, 1994.

Spurr, Russell. *A Glorious Way to Die: The Kamikaze Mission of the Battleship* Yamato. New York: Newmarket, 1981.

Stanley, R. M. *To Fool a Glass Eye: Camouflage versus Photoreconnaissance in World War II.* Shrewsbury, UK: Airlife, 1998.

Starkey, Armstrong. *European and Native American Warfare, 1675–1815.* Norman: University of Oklahoma Press, 1998.

Stephens, F. J. *Bayonets.* London: Arms and Armour, 1968.

Stephens, Frederick J. *Fighting Knives.* London: Arms and Armour, 1980.

Stockholm International Peace Research Institute. *Incendiary Weapons.* Cambridge, MA: MIT Press, 1975.

Stone, G. C. *A Glossary of the Construction, Decoration and Use of Arms and Armor.* New York: Southworth, 1934.

Sumrall, Robert F. *Iowa Class Battleships: Their Design, Weapons, and Equipment.* Annapolis, MD: Naval Institute Press, 1988.

Svelto, Orazio, ed. *Principles of Lasers.* Translated by David C. Hanna. New York: Springer, 2004.

Sweetman, Bill. *Avro Lancaster.* New York: Random House, 1988.

Sweetman, Bill. *Stealth Aircraft: Secrets of Future Airpower.* Osceola, WI: Motorbooks International, 1986.

Taylorson, A. *The Revolver.* 3 vols. London: Arms and Armour, 1966–1970.

Temple, Robert. *The Genius of China: 3000 Years of Science, Discovery, and Invention.* New York: Simon and Schuster, 1986.

Terry, T. W., et al. *Fighting Vehicles.* London: Brassey's, 1991.

Thiel, J. H. *A History of Roman Sea-Power before the Second Punic War.* Amsterdam: North-Holland Publishing, 1954.

Thompson, Jim. *The Complete M1 Garand.* New York: Paladin, 1998.

Tillman, Barrett, and Robert L. Lawson. *U.S. Navy Dive and Torpedo Bombers of World War II.* St. Paul, MN: MBI, 2001.

Treadwell, Terry. *Grumman TBF/TBM Avenger.* Stroud, Gloucestershire, UK: Tempus, 2001.

Trench Fortifications, 1914–1918: A Reference Manual. Uckfield, East Sussex, UK: Naval and Military Press, 2014.

Truby, J. David. *The Lewis Gun.* 2nd ed. Boulder, CO: Palladin, 1978.

Tubbs, D. B. *Lancaster Bomber.* New York: Ballantine, 1972.

Tucker, Jonathan B. *War of Nerves: Chemical Warfare from World War I to Al-Qaeda.* New York: Pantheon Books, 2006.

Tucker, Spencer C. *Arming the Fleet: U.S. Naval Ordnance in the Muzzle-Loading Era.* Annapolis, MD: Naval Institute Press, 1989.

Tucker, Spencer C. "The Carronade." *Nautical Research Journal* 42(1) (March 1997): 15–23.

Tucker, Spencer C. *Handbook of 19th Century Naval History.* Stroud, UK: Sutton, 2000.

Tucker, Spencer C. "The Navy Discovers Shore Bombardment." *Naval History* 8(5) (October 1994): 30–35.

Tucker, Spencer C. *Tanks: An Illustrated History of Their Impact.* Santa Barbara, CA: ABC-CLIO, 2004.

Tucker, Stephen. *Terrorist Explosive Sourcebook: Countering Terrorist Use of Improvised Explosive Devices.* Boulder, CO: Paladin, 1994.

Tunis, Edwin. *Weapons: A Pictorial History.* New York: World Publishing, 1954.

Turnbull, Stephen R. *Fighting Ships of the Far East (2): Japan and Korea, 612–1639.* Buffalo, MN: Osprey, 2003.

Tylden, Geoffrey. *Horses and Saddlery: An Account of the Animals Used by the British and Commonwealth Armies from the Seventeenth Century to the Present Day, with a Description of Their Equipment.* London: J. A. Allen, 1965.

U.S. Army. *Browning Automatic Rifle: Caliber .30 M1918A2.* Washington, DC: U.S. Government Printing Office, 1951.

U.S. Army. *FM 23–65: Browning Machine Gun Cal. 50 HB, -2.* Washington, DC: U.S. Government Printing Office, 1944.

U.S. Army. *40-mm Grenade Launchers M203 and M79: FM-23-31.* Washington, DC: U.S. Government Printing Office, 1972.

U.S. Department of the Army. *Hand and Rifle Grenades: FM 23-30.* Washington, DC: U.S. Government Printing Office: 1949.

U.S. Office of the Secretary of Defense. *Unmanned Reconnaissance Systems Roundup, 2005–2006.* Washington, DC: U.S. Government Printing Office, 2005.

U.S. War Department. *Handbook on German Military Forces.* 1945; reprint, Baton Rouge: Louisiana State University Press, 1995.

Von Kroge, Harry. *GEMA: Birthplace of German Radar and Sonar.* Philadelphia: Institute of Physics Press, 2000.

Vuksic, Velimir, and Zvonimir Grbasic. *Cavalry: The History of a Fighting Elite, 650 B.C.–A.D. 1914.* Herndon, VA: Cassell, 1993.

Wagner, E. *European Weapons and Warfare, 1618–1648.* London: Octopus, 1979.

Wagner, Ray. *American Combat Planes.* 3rd enlarged ed. Garden City, NY: Doubleday, 1982.

Wahl, Paul, and Don Toppel. *The Gatling Gun.* New York: Arco, 1965.

Wallinga, H. T. *The Boarding-Bridge of the Romans.* Groningen: J. B. Wolters, 1956.

Ware, Chris. *The Bomb Vessel: Shore Bombardment Ships of the Age of Sail.* Annapolis, MD: Naval Institute Press, 1994.

Watts, Anthony J., ed. *Jane's Underwater Warfare Systems, 1996–97.* Couldsdon, Surrey, UK: Jane's Information Group, 1996.

Wawro, Geoffrey. *The Franco-Prussian War: The German Conquest of France in 1870–1871.* New York: Cambridge University Press, 2003.

Webb, Alf. *Archaeology of Archery.* Tolworth, UK: Glade, 1991.

Wedlake, G. E. C. *SOS: The Story of Radio Communication.* North Pomfret, VT: David and Charles, 1973.

Weeks, John S. *Men against Tanks: A History of Anti-Tank Warfare.* Newton Abbot, UK: David and Charles, 1975.

Werner, Muller. *The 88 mm Flak in the First and Second World Wars.* West Chester, PA: Schiffer, 1998.

Werrell, Kenneth P. *Archie, Flack, AAA, and SAM: A Short Operational History of Ground-Based Air Defense.* Maxwell Air Force Base, AL: Air University Press, 1988.

Westermann, Edward B. *Flak: German Anti-Aircraft Defenses, 1914–1945.* Lawrence: University Press of Kansas, 2001.

Westwood, David. *Rifles: An Illustrated History of Their Impact.* Santa Barbara, CA: ABC-CLIO, 2005.

Westwood, John N. *Railways at War.* San Diego: Howell-North Books, 1981.

Whitley, M. J. *Destroyers of World War Two: An International Encyclopedia.* Annapolis, MD: Naval Institute Press, 1988.

Wilkinson-Latham, R. J. *British Military Bayonets from 1700 to 1945.* London: Hutchinson, 1967.

Willbanks, James A. *Machine Guns: An Illustrated History of Their Impact.* Santa Barbara, CA: ABC-CLIO, 2004.

Williams, Peter, and David Wallace. *Unit 731.* New York: Free Press, 1989.

Wills, H. *Pillboxes.* London: Leo Cooper, 1985.

Wilson, David. *In Search of Penicillin.* New York: Knopf, 1976.

Wilson, Geoffrey. *The Old Telegraphs.* London: Phillimore, 1976.

Winterbotham, F. W. *The Ultra Secret.* New York: Harper and Row, 1974.

Wood, D. C. *The Design and Development of the Avro Lancaster.* Manchester, UK: Royal Aeronautical Society, Manchester Branch, 1991.

Wood, Tony, and Bill Gunston. *Hitler's Luftwaffe.* New York: Crescent Books, 1978.

Woodman, Harry. *Early Aircraft Armament.* London: Arms and Armour, 1989.

Woods, David L., ed. *Signaling and Communicating at Sea.* 2 vols. New York: Arno, 1980.

Wrigley, Walter, and John Hovorka. *Fire Control Principles.* New York: McGraw-Hill, 1959.

Y'Blood, William T. *Hunter-Killer: U.S. Escort Carriers in the Battle of the Atlantic.* Annapolis, MD: Naval Institute Press, 1983.

Yoshida, Mitsuru, *Requiem for the Battleship* Yamato. Annapolis, MD: Naval Institute Press, 1965.

Zabecki, David T. "Artillery Types." In *The Encyclopedia of World War II: A Political, Social, and Military History,* edited by Spencer C. Tucker, 136–41. Santa Barbara, CA: ABC-CLIO, 2005.

Zabecki, David T. "Great Guns! Benchmark Artillery Pieces That Shaped Military History." *MHQ* (August 2014): 76–84.

Zabecki, David T. *Steel Wind: Colonel Georg Bruchmüller and the Birth of Modern Artillery.* Westport, CT: Praeger, 1994.

Zabecki, David T., ed. *World War II in Europe: An Encyclopedia,* Vol. 2. New York: Garland, 1999.

Index

Please note the **boldface** locators indicated a complete discussion of the topic.

About the Author

Spencer C. Tucker, PhD, held the John Biggs Chair of Military History at his alma mater, the Virginia Military Institute in Lexington, for 6 years until his retirement from teaching in 2003. Before that, he was professor of history for 30 years at Texas Christian University, Fort Worth. He has also been a Fulbright scholar and, as a U.S. Army captain, an intelligence analyst in the Pentagon. Currently the senior fellow of military history at ABC-CLIO, he has written or edited 52 books, including the award-winning *American Civil War: The Definitive Encyclopedia and Document Collection; Battles That Changed History: An Encyclopedia of World Conflict;* and *World War I: The Definitive Encyclopedia and Document Collection,* all published by ABC-CLIO.